An International Redistribution of Wealth and Power
(Pergamon Policy Studies-21)

Pergamon Titles of Related Interest

Carman   Obstacles to Mineral Development: A Pragmatic View

Francisco/Laird/Laird   The Political Economy of Collectivized Agriculture: A Comparative Study of Communist and Non-Communist Systems

Golany   Arid Zone Settlement Planning: The Israeli Experience

Goodman/Love   Management of Development Projects: An International Case Study Approach

Laszlo/Baker/Eisenberg/Raman   The Objectives of the New International Economic Order

Lozoya/Estevez/Green et al.   Alternative Views of the New International Economic Order: A Survey and Analysis of Major Economic Research Reports

Morris   Measuring the Condition of the World's Poor: The Physical Quality of Life Index

Stepanek   Bangladesh—Equitable Growth?

PERGAMON
POLICY
STUDIES

An International Redistribution of Wealth and Power

A Study of the Charter of Economic Rights and Duties of States

Robert F. Meagher

Pergamon Press
NEW YORK • OXFORD • TORONTO • FRANKFURT • PARIS

Pergamon Press Offices:

U.S.A.	Pergamon Press Inc., Maxwell House, Fairview Park, Elmsford, New York 10523, U.S.A.
U.K.	Pergamon Press Ltd., Headington Hill Hall, Oxford OX3 0BW, England
CANADA	Pergamon of Canada, Ltd., 150 Consumers Road, Willowdale, Ontario M2J, 1P9, Canada
AUSTRALIA	Pergamon Press (Aust) Pty. Ltd., P O Box 544, Potts Point, NSW 2011, Australia
FRANCE	Pergamon Press SARL, 24 rue des Ecoles, 75240 Paris, Cedex 05, France
FEDERAL REPUBLIC OF GERMANY	Pergamon Press GmbH, 6242 Kronberg/Taunus, Pferdstrasse 1, Federal Republic of Germany

Library of Congress Cataloging in Publication Data

Meagher, Robert F
    An international redistribution of wealth and power.

    (Pergamon policy studies)
    "The Charter of economic rights and duties of
States": p.
    Includes bibliographical references and index.
    1. United Nations. General Assembly. Charter of
economic rights and duties of States. 2. International
economic relations. I. United Nations. General
Assembly. Charter of economic rights and duties of
States. 1979. II. Title.
K3823.M3   341.7'5   78-27906
ISBN 0-08-022478-4

Printed in the United States of America

This book is dedicated to:

Donna Marie Dowsett, without whose
support, wisdom, encouragement,
editorial advice, and assistance there
would have been no book at all

and

the memory of Wolfgang G. Friedmann,
a great scholar, a great humanist, and
a great friend.

Contents

List of Tables

Preface

The perspective on international economic relations which I bring to this book goes back to the year I spent in India as a Fulbright Scholar at the Bombay School of Economics. Subsequently, research in foreign aid and a law career took me to virtually all of the developing countries of Asia and Africa including the Middle East.

It is now more than twenty-five years since I first visited India. The developing countries have consolidated their political independence but remain in a vulnerable position externally. They operate in an international economic order which they have played no part in establishing and which accords them little decision making power. As their political consciousness of the gap between the rich and the poor states has increased, their efforts to make new international rules and to influence, if not control, the most important international institutions have also intensified.

In 1973-74, the developing countries used the oil embargo to launch a coordinated movement to try to obtain legal status for certain economic rights and duties favoring developing countries. The principal outcome of this effort was the Charter of Economic Rights and Duties of States, approved in December 1974 by 120 member states of the United Nations. The industrial powers, most of which were strongly opposed to certain provisions of the Charter, nonetheless agreed to 85 percent of its provisions.

The major differences between developing countries and the industrialized world are reflected in the word-by-word negotiations of the separate articles of the Charter. Private foreign investment and trade in commodities are the most prominent areas of debate. With little capital of their own and a shortage of skilled labor, the developing countries have relied on private foreign investment to promote their economic development. They increasingly doubt the wisdom of a development strategy dependent upon foreign direct investment and therefore look for alternative channels for the transfer of capital, technology and management. With respect to trade in commodities, they seek to limit price fluctuations of their exports and to raise prices through international commodity stocks funded by a Common Fund. In this as in other areas, the developing countries seek to obtain a commitment by the developed countries to pursue on the international level interventionist policies long practiced within individual developed countries.

The international versus the nation-state solution to problems brings us into an area of great concern to lawyers: jurisdiction. Who is responsible to whom? Even if the developing countries succeeded in expanding the body of international law and establishing international responsibility for development matters, the problem of implementation of international policies within particular states would remain. Federal governments recognize the difficulty of drawing lines of authority and have tended to resolve the problem by centralizing decision-making in key areas. There has also been a tendency to centralize authority over critical international economic and social problems.

The principal issues, then, are the distribution of decision making power in international organizations, private foreign investment, trade in commodities, and jurisdiction over international economic conflicts. Chapter 1 of this volume explains the role of the 1973 Arab oil boycott in providing the developing countries with the leverage to force the developed countries to consider seriously Third World proposals in these areas. Chapter 2 demonstrates that the institutional and conceptual framework which permits the developing countries to win a hearing for their proposals has its origin in the structures established as part of the League of Nations. Created by the Treaty of Versailles primarily as a collective security organization, the League of Nations Council established specialized organizations which fostered a habit of technical cooperation among countries on issues which formerly had been the exclusive preserve of nation-states, including trade policy, reconstruction, disaster relief, nutrition, and housing.

The four central chapters of the book describe in depth the articles of the Charter, their negotiation, and the origin and recent evolution of the issues they embody. The time period covered is from the end of World War I through the completion of the Conference on International Economic Cooperation in June 1977.

Acknowledgments

Initial work on this book began during my sabbatical year 1975-76. I would like to thank both Tufts University and the Rockefeller Foundation, each of which provided a part of the funding for my work. In addition, the Rockefeller Foundation invited me to spend a month at their research center at Bellagio, Italy, in the Villa Serbelloni, to prepare part of the manuscript.

My base during the sabbatical year was at the Overseas Development Council in Washington, D.C. I am grateful for having spent a year as a Visiting Fellow in this concerned and effective institution. Through the ODC and its imaginative staff I had willing listeners to my many ideas as well as providers of hard data on all development issues. Jim Grant, its President, kept me up to date on what was going on in the "real world" as he attended conference after conference in all corners of the globe. Although all the staff was helpful, I would like to single out for special thanks John Sewell, Jim Howe, Guy Erb, Valeriana Kallab, Denis Goulet, Martin McLaughlin, James Boyle, Paul Watson, and Michael O'Hara.

Four research assistants did excellent work in collecting and analyzing the many documents and publications underlying this study. Dale Andrew contributed strongly to Chapter 3, Elsie Garfield to Chapter 2, Karla Hoff to Chapter 4 and Appendix A, and Jerry Gumpel to Chapter 6. In addition to their research, each was invaluable in assisting in the editing of various chapters. Karla Hoff worked long hours on the final editing of Chapters 1, 2, 4, 5, 6, and 7.

Friends and colleagues, both at the Fletcher School and elsewhere, read the manuscript and made valuable comments. Special thanks to James Hyde, Robert L. West, Benjamin J. Cohen, Alfred Rubin, Peter Bloch, Barbara Crane, Jonathan Silverstone, Harold O. Martin, and Richard Feen. A.A. Fatouros and Martin Murphy provided me with extremely detailed comments for which I am very grateful.

Much of my data was collected abroad from participants in the negotiations as well as members of various governments and international organizations. I would like to thank each of the following for their generosity in helping me: John Freeland, Emile van Lennep, Stephen Schwebel, Heinz W. Dittmann, Colin F. Teese, Isi Foighel, Sergio Gonzalez-Galvez, Manuel Armendariz, Donald Mills, Hortencio Brillantes, Erskine Childers, Leila Doss, Dan Caulfield, I.S. Chadha, Ralph Zacklin, Eric Suy, Miodrag Sukijasovic, M.R. de Stercke, Manuel Perrez-Guerrero, Jean Sommerhausen, R.K. Hazari, Sandra Fuentes-Berain, Ted Tanen, William Milam, C. Fred Bergsten, Theodore Moran, James Baker, Charles Wessner, Diana Boernstein, John Dawson, Alexander Borg Olivier, John Curry, Blain Sloan, and Henri Guda.

I would also like to thank Zygmunt Nagorski for arranging a dinner meeting at the Council on Foreign Relations where I had an opportunity to discuss my ideas with a select and informed audience.

Barbara Fennessy managed, through snow storms and constant interruptions, to complete the typing on the manuscript without once complaining about my scrawling penmanship and the frequent changes in the text.

Needless to say, thoughts expressed in this book represent my personal views on a series of complex events. I alone am responsible for these views.

Glossary

ACP	African, Caribbean and Pacific States
AIOEC	Association of Iron Ore Exporters
APEF	Association of Iron Ore Exporting Countries
CERDS	Charter of Economic Rights and Duties of States
CIEC	Conference on International Economic Cooperation
CIPEC	Intergovernmental Council of Copper Exporting Countries
CMEA	Council on Mutual Economic Assistance
COMECON	Council on Mutual Economic Assistance
DAC	Development Assistance Committee (OECD)
ECA	Economic Commission for Africa
ECAFE	Economic Commission for Asia and the Far East (now known as Economic Commission for Asia and the Pacific)
ECAP	Economic Commission for Asia and the Pacific
ECE	Economic Commission for Europe
ECLA	Economic Commission for Latin America
ECOSOC	Economic and Social Council of the United Nations
ECWA	Economic Commission for West Asia
EDF	European Development Fund (EEC)
EEC	European Economic Community
EPTA	Expanded Program of Technical Assistance (UN)
FAO	Food and Agriculture Organization
FIDES	International Fund for Economic and Social Development (France)

GATT	General Agreement on Trade and Tariffs
GSP	General System of Preferences
Group of 8	Developed Country Negotiating Group at CIEC
Group of 19	Developing Country Negotiating Group at CIEC
IBA	International Bauxite Association
IBRD	International Bank for Reconstruction and Development (World Bank)
ICP	Integrated Commodity Program
IDA	International Development Association
IEA	International Energy Agency
IFAD	International Fund for Agricultural Development
IFC	International Finance Corporation
ILO	International Labor Organization
IMF	International Monetary Fund
IMIT	International Minerals Investment Trust
IRB	International Resources Bank
ICO	International Coffee Organization
ITO	International Trade Organization
LDC	Less Developed Country
MFN	Most Favored Nation clause (GATT)
MNC	Multinational Corporation
MNE	Multinational Enterprise
MTN	Multilateral Trade Negotiations (the GATT Tokyo Round)
NIEO	New International Economic Order
OAPEC	Organization of Arab Petroleum Exporting Countries
OAS	Organization of American States
ODA	Official Development Assistance
OECD	Organization of Economic Cooperation and Development
OEEC	Organization of European Economic Cooperation
OOF	Other Official Flows
OPEC	Organization of Petroleum Exporting Countries
OPIC	Overseas Private Investment Corporation (U.S.)
SCSE	Conference on Security and Cooperation in Europe

STABEX	Commodity Stabilization Program of the EEC (Lomé Convention)
TNC	Transnational Corporation
UNCTAD	United Nations Conference on Trade and Development
UNESCO	United Nations Educational, Scientific, and Cultural Organization
UNIDO	United Nations Industrial Development Organization
WHO	World Health Organization

...the greatest of evils and the

worst of crimes is poverty...

George Bernard Shaw
Preface to Major Barbara

1
1974—The Year of The Third World

The year 1974 was the highpoint of developing country (1) ambitions to restructure international economic relations. At the Sixth Special Session of the United Nations General Assembly in April, a Declaration on the Establishment of a New International Economic Order (2) and a Program of Action (3) set forth developing country demands for a restructuring of international economic relations. In December of the same year, the Twenty-ninth General Assembly approved overwhelmingly the Charter of Economic Rights and Duties of States, (4) setting forth the rights and duties of states under a proposed new international economic order.

The euphoria of the developing countries about the prospects for changing world economic relations stemmed from the oil embargo of the Organization of Arab Petroleum Exporting Countries (OAPEC) (5) in October 1973, and from the dramatic rise of oil prices following actions of the Organization of Petroleum Exporting Countries (OPEC). (6) The embargo suggested to the developing countries that control of raw materials markets might bring a major realignment of world power. This assumption and the hopes generated by the Sixth Special Session and the Charter of Economic Rights and Duties of States would prove to be overly optimistic.

THE OIL CRISIS, 1973

The convergence of several important economic and political factors led to the "oil crisis" of 1973. (7) These factors included the rising bargaining power of the oil exporting countries vis à vis the international companies, particularly in regard to pricing policy; the short supply of oil as a result of the rapidly increasing demand by developed countries; and the political tensions stemming from the 1973 Arab-Israeli war. To express its condemnation of the developed country stance in the war, OAPEC imposed an oil boycott first on the U.S. and subsequently on Western Europe and Japan. Simultaneously, the OPEC countries acted to increase the price of oil without

1

agreement of the oil companies. In the period October 1973 to January 1974, the price of oil rose by 400 percent. (8)

These actions resulted in new-found international importance for the OPEC countries and in a changed perception by the West of Third World demands regarding the international economic order. The OPEC countries had demonstrated that they had the power to disrupt developed country markets, and that they would use this power as a lever to bargain for a more equitable international economic order.

The crisis represented the first effective exercise of market power by a group of developing country exporters of primary products. It had a demonstration effect on other developing countries, while it produced a fear among industrial countries that such power might be exercised by associations of exporters of other primary products.

Reaction to the oil crisis took three forms. On January 9, 1974, the United States called for the convening of a conference of the foreign ministers of the eight major oil consuming nations to discuss world energy problems. (9) The U.S. advised OPEC members that they would subsequently be invited to meet with the consumer nations. (10) Meanwhile, U.S. Secretary of State Kissinger warned other oil consuming states against entering into bilateral arrangements with OPEC countries (e.g., making their own contracts and arranging their own internal oil market). (11)

France, with its greater dependence on oil imports, sought an approach believed to be more conciliatory towards OPEC and developing country concerns. First, it affirmed the right of each nation to deal with the oil situation bilaterally. Second, it proposed that Third World countries should be included in the consultations which should take place within the framework of the United Nations. On January 18, 1974, the French Foreign Minister requested United Nations Secretary General Waldheim to convene a world energy conference to determine principles of cooperation between energy producers and consumers. (12)

Meanwhile Algeria strongly criticized United States efforts, which it characterized as attempts to control European policies. In February, Algerian President Boumedienne, acting as President in office of the Group of Non-Aligned Countries, (13) formally requested the United Nations Secretary General to convene a Special Session of the General Assembly to consider the problems of raw materials and development. (14) By February 15, the requisite majority of United Nations members had agreed to hold a Special Session. (15)

THE SIXTH SPECIAL SESSION

Three important conferences took place prior to the opening of the Special Session on April 9, 1974. The Washington Conference of oil-consuming states convened in February to examine "the international energy situation" and to develop "a course of action to meet this challenge." (16) The oil-consuming states considered conservation, diversification of energy supplies, and international energy research and development programs to be the key components of any program of action. The Washington Conference established a coordinating body and endorsed the forthcoming United Nations Special Session, with the reluctant assent of the United States. (17) Misgivings arose in the United States from a belief that the convening of a Special Session on energy and raw materials represented a Third World effort to sidestep the issue of the oil crisis.   The United States wanted to consolidate consumer nation strength before entering into discussions on energy issues in a representative international forum.

A meeting of the coordinating bureau of the Group of Non-Aligned Countries provided the forum for development of a Third World strategy for the Special Session. (18) The optimistic atmosphere of the meeting is evident in Algerian Minister of Foreign Affairs Bouteflika's statement that "We know now that they [the LDCs] do not need to depend on the charity of others but have the means to take their destinies and their resources into their own hands." (19) OPEC's actions were seen as a model for other raw material producer associations. The 17-page communique issued by the meeting called for the complete restructuring of international economic relations. (20) It raised the issues of commodity prices, access to markets, transfer of technology, monetary reform, and the role of multinational corporations. All of these issues had been discussed before in international forums and in particular in the Third United Nations Conference on Trade and Development (UNCTAD III) held in Santiago, Chile, in 1972. In the present circumstances, the Non-Aligned Countries made an impressive show of Third World unity, despite the concern of oil-importing developing countries with the devastating impact of oil prices on their balance of payments.

The OPEC countries met separately to work out their strategy for the Special Session. At their meeting in Geneva, on April 7, 1974, they agreed to establish a special fund to aid developing countries most seriously affected by the oil crisis. (21)   This action diverted some of the criticism directed at OPEC because of the adverse effect of the price rise on other developing countries.

The Sixth Special Session convened in New York on April 9, two days after the OPEC meeting.   The opening plenary speaker, Algerian President Boumedienne, reflected the mood of the developing countries at the Special Session.

> In the eyes of the vast majority of humanity it is an (economic) order that is as unjust and as outdated as the colonial order to which it owes its origin and its substance. Inasmuch as it is maintained and consolidated and therefore thrives by virtue of a process which continually impoverishes the poor and enriches the rich, this economic order constitutes the major obstacle standing in the way of any hope of development and progress for all the countries of the Third World. (22)

Thus, he argued, it was not merely a question of raw materials but, rather, a whole complex of international economic relations which was at the heart of developing country concerns. President Boumedienne proposed a five-point program for restructuring the international economic order, which included:

(1) control of natural resources through nationalization by the developing countries, which would then set their own prices;

(2) integrated development of agriculture and industry based on local processing of raw materials;

(3) full mobilization of assistance from the wealthy developed countries in accordance with developing country priorities;

(4) lightened financial burden on developing countries and, in particular, the cancellation or refinancing of $80 billion in external debts; and

(5) establishment of a special program for the least developed of the developing countries.

In a direct appeal to the developed countries, President Boumedienne pointed out that increasing world interdependence required cooperation and a redefinition of developed/developing country relations:

> For the developed countries, the question is whether they have understood that their future cannot be dissociated from that of the peoples of the Third World.... In particular, since they presently control the levers of economic power, they must accept, as a requirement for the maintenance of peace and as a tribute to progress, that the developing countries regain and assume the rightful share they deserve in the leadership and management of world economic activities. (23)

The delegates to the Sixth Special Session reached agreement on a draft Declaration on the Establishment of a New International Economic Order and a Program of Action. Both were presented to the General Assembly (24)

The draft Declaration was based largely on working papers submitted by the Group of 77, (25) which in turn were derived from the Economic Declaration and Action Programme for Economic Cooperation of the Non-Aligned Nations. (26) It declares 20 principles for the establishment of a new international economic order based on "equity, sovereign equality, interdependence, common interest, and cooperation among all states, irrespective of their economic and social systems..." The more controversial principles include the right of every state to full and permanent sovereignty over its natural resources and economic activities, including the right to nationalize with "appropriate" compensation set by national tribunals rather than under international law; the right to restitution and compensation for the exploitation and depletion of resources by foreigners; the right to regulate the activities of multinational corporations; the right to prevent the deterioration of terms of trade between the exports and imports of developing countries by linking export prices to import prices; preferential treatment of developing countries in order to promote their development; better access to technology; the right to form producers' associations; and an increased role for the United Nations in the establishment of a new international economic order. (27)

The purpose of the Program of Action was to implement the Declaration on the Establishment of a New International Economic Order. The Program addressed all the major issues under discussion in the UNCTAD working group on the proposed Charter of Economic Rights and Duties of States: trade in primary commodities, the international monetary system, industrialization, transfer of technology, regulation of transnational corporations, promotion of cooperation among developing countries, permanent sovereignty over natural resources, and the proposed Charter. In addition, the Program of Action made proposals on the establishment of a Special Fund to channel bilateral and multilateral assistance to those developing countries most seriously affected by escalating oil prices. (28)

If little of substance was new in the developing country demands, the tone in which they voiced them represented a dramatic change from that of earlier years. Their long-suppressed frustration had bubbled to the surface and burst. This produced an understandable defensive reaction on the part of the developed countries, particularly the United States. None of the developed countries was prepared to respond in depth to the detailed attack which cut so deeply into the established way of doing things. This was even more true because the Special Session was a hastily called meeting and no comprehensive agenda had been prepared in advance.

During the Sixth Special Session the Group of 77 negotiated separately with the Western Europeans, the Eastern Europeans, and the Chinese. Only the United States refused to meet with the Group of 77. Four days after the draft Declaration and Programme reached the floor of the General Assembly for debate, the United States submitted an alternative to the Group of 77's proposal for a special program. (29) The U.S. proposal dealt with only one of the ten sections of the draft Program of Action, that of the Special Fund. It amounted to an offer to set a target of $4 billion for additional aid to the poorest developing countries, contingent upon the modification of the Declaration or the abandonment of the Program of Action. The U.S. proposal was all but ignored, and the United States subsequently withdrew it from consideration.

A series of parliamentary maneuvers by the Group of 77 resulted in the adoption of the draft Declaration and Program, in slightly modified form, as a "consensus document." (30) However, they did not preclude statements of exception by individual industrial countries to both parts of the documentation. At the concluding meeting of the Special Session in May 1, 1974, U.S. Ambassador Scali remarked that "...the document which will be printed as the written product of this special General Assembly does not, in fact, whatever it is called, represent a consensus in the accepted meaning of the term." (31) He specifically stated his government's reservations about those provisions relating to permanent sovereignty over natural resources, producer associations, price indexation, and compensation for damage to resources and people.

Armed with the Declaration on the Establishment of a New International Economic Order and the Programme of Action on the Establishment of a New International Economic Order, the developing countries left New York for meetings in Mexico City and Lima. Their next step was to analyze the results of the Sixth Special Session in order to develop a strategy for the Twenty-Ninth General Assembly, where the proposed Charter of Economic Rights and Duties of States was to be discussed.

THE TWENTY-NINTH GENERAL ASSEMBLY

Establishment of a 40-nation working group of developed and developing countries to draft such a Charter had been initiated through a resolution of the UNCTAD III meeting in 1972. (32)   The working group had met three times in Geneva prior to the Mexico City meeting which convened shortly after the Sixth Special Session concluded its work. (33)   The Program of Action envisioned the Charter as "an effective instrument towards the establishment of a new system of international economic relations based on equity, sovereign equality, and interdependence of the interests of developed and developing countries." (34)   The principles expressed in the Charter were not newly conceived because of the oil crisis or the Sixth Special Session, but represented demands the Latin American countries had made as early as 1950 in the Economic Commission for Latin America (ECLA). (35)

On December 6, 1974, the Second Committee of the United Nations General Assembly voted overwhelmingly to adopt the Charter (115-6-10). (36) It was subsequently approved by the full General Assembly on December 12, with the support of the Third World, Eastern Europe, and the Soviet Union (120-6-10).   The six negative votes and ten abstentions were all by developed countries. (37)

Tempers were frayed and confrontation between the developed and developing worlds had reached a peak when the vote on the Charter was finally taken.   The exasperation of the former in the face of the confrontational stance of the developing countries is captured in the following excerpts from a speech by Ambassador Scali.   He delivered the speech after the adoption of the Charter by the Second Committee.

Last year the United States Delegation sought to call attention to a trend...to adopt one sided, unrealistic, resolutions that cannot be implemented.

...This trend has not only continued but accelerated...

...The most meaningful test of whether the Assembly has succeeded in this task bridging the differences among member states is not whether a majority can be mobilized behind any single draft resolution, but whether those states whose cooperation is vital to implement a decision will support it in fact...

The function of all parliaments is to provide expression to the majority will.   Yet, when the rule of the majority becomes the tyranny of the majority, the minority will cease to respect or obey it, and the parliament will cease to function.   Every majority must recognize that its authority does not extend beyond the point where the minority becomes so outraged that it is no longer willing to maintain the covenant which binds them. (38) (Emphasis added)

Ambassador Scali pointed out that the United States was the principal financial supporter of the United Nations.   Moreover, the 16 countries which withheld their support from the Charter supplied 95 percent of the UN budget. Noting that the developing countries' voting power was no substitute for Western financial power, he seemed to suggest that the United States might reduce its financial support for the organization.

It is ironic that the country which had unilaterally dominated United Nations policy from its inception until the early 1960s should decry a "tyranny of the majority." The outcome of the Twenty-Ninth Session showed that most of the Western industrial states were not prepared to accept either a new configuration of power in the United Nations or a new international economic order.

The issues embodied in the Charter were not newly conceived because of the oil crisis or the Sixth Special Session, which simply represented the latest stages in a gradual but steady movement towards a more equitable and increasingly interdependent international economic order. The spirit and content of the Charter reflect long-term, and probably irreversible, trends towards greater international decision making. Nevertheless, the struggle between national sovereignty and international decision making is by no means over, as the strong opposition to certain provisions of the Charter and events following its passage in 1974 would show.

2 The Background to The New International Economic Order

Although the call for a New International Economic Order (NIEO) emanated from the Sixth Special Session of the General Assembly, held in April 1974, the foundations for it preceded the energy crisis. Third World demands for equity of participation and distribution of wealth do not represent a radical departure from Western concepts of equity, but rather an attempt to extend them to the international level. Evaluation of the prospects for the Third World's achievement of substantial concessions from the industrial countries requires that the NIEO be put in the context of the evolutionary process by which the world community has accepted increasing responsibility for the welfare of its individual members. This process has led to a growing role for international organizations in influencing national policy and formulating and implementing international policy.

The precedents for increased international intervention in social and economic matters may be traced back to the turn of the twentieth century. The years 1916 to 1945 were characterized by extensive efforts to foster international cooperation through the League of Nations and its Auxiliary Agencies. Many international agreements were achieved, although few were implemented. In the post-World War II period, most of the principles agreed on in the inter-war years were finally carried out, with the purpose of reconstructing the war-devastated economies and of increasing the resilience of the world economic and social order.

WORLD WAR I - WORLD WAR II (1916-1940)

Long before most Third World countries achieved political independence, Western Europe and the United States had experimented with cooperative international social and economic measures. Prior to World War I, the Hague Peace Conferences of 1899 and 1907 established the precedent of consultation among the nations of the world on general problems of mutual concern.

Cooperation of a more concrete and practical nature existed in the form of the General Postal Union (1874), (1) the International Telegraph Union (1865), (2) and similar functional public international organizations. Various non-governmental international societies also existed prior to World War I. (3)

During World War I, the Inter-Allied Maritime Transport Council demonstrated that when confronted with the exigencies of wartime emergencies, countries were both willing and able to organize international production and distribution systems in food, raw materials, and munitions. Given the pressing need for tonnage during the war, the Council created a system of interallied shipping control to allocate tonnage available. The council involved the personal integration of the national administrations of the allied states, rather than any formal delegation of executive power. Economic cooperation on this scale proved to be strictly a wartime phenomenon. In 1919 the Inter-Allied Maritime Transport Council was superseded by a Supreme Economic Council, which tried unsuccessfully to cope with the problems of European reconstruction. (4)

At the end of World War I, all of the major allied nations espoused the establishment of some form of world organization to promote and preserve peace. (5) The Covenant of the League of Nations was drafted by the allied powers as part of the Treaty of Versailles. The original membership of the League comprised 42 countries, either signatories of the Treaty or neutral parties. The only allied country which failed to join the League was the United States, which had initially been one of the League's most ardent promoters. (6)

The League Assembly functioned as a forum for discussion of issues of international concern and was made up of delegations from all member countries. Although it did not have legislative powers, it approved draft treaties and model conventions which could then be enacted into the municipal law of each national government.

The dual purpose of the League was to preserve peace and security and to promote international cooperation through the collective action of its members. International cooperation was not originally understood to mean economic cooperation, and the Covenant provided few specific references to economic matters. (7) Nevertheless, the League has a history of increasing activity in this area, beginning with its involvement in the reconstruction of Europe after World War I. The League established many Auxiliary Agencies, including the Economic and Financial Organization, the Health Organization, the Communications and Transit Organization, the Mandates Commission, and numerous others concerned with specific issues (e.g., Committee on Traffic in Opium and Dangerous Drugs, the Organization for Refugees, etc.). The scope and importance of these Auxiliary Agencies was not initially foreseen.

A provisional Economic and Financial Organization was created in 1920. It was an outgrowth of the 1920 Financial Conference of Brussels. The Organization was divided into an Economic Committee and a Finance Committee of ten members each. The Committee members were appointed by member governments as individual experts rather than as national representatives and had no authority to make decisions binding upon their governments.

The Finance Committee lacked the resources to play a direct role in

European reconstruction, but in a few cases it provided assistance to countries in making reconstruction plans and obtaining private reconstruction loans. A key feature of these operations was the granting of extensive control over international domestic economic and financial policies to an international agency in return for financial assistance. (8)   The Finance Committee unsuccessfully solicited support for an International Credits Scheme which would have involved the creation of a new type of security (guaranteed by the League) to be sold in the private capital markets, the proceeds to be used to finance reconstruction programs.

The International Labor Organization (ILO) (9) provides a unique example of international cooperation during the first half of this century.   It was created by the Treaty of Versailles to formulate and oversee international standards regarding employment policy (both public and private sector), labor conditions, and related issues.   While it existed as part of the League of Nations system and was financed by the League, it maintained organizational and legal autonomy. Its tripartite structure provided for representatives of the government, employers, and workers from each member country; each member was entitled to a total of four representatives (2 government, 1 employer, 1 worker).   The General Conference had a mandate to meet annually, and the Governing Body (much like the Council of the League) functioned in a directive, coordinating capacity.

The unique aspect of the ILO stems from the special legal nature of its recommendations and conventions. For the first time, sovereign member states of an international organization were subjected, by law, to the exercise of moral suasion so that they would enact the organization's recommendations, irrespective of whether the individual member states had voted in favor of the policies.

During the Versailles Peace Conference there was fundamental disagreement between Italy and the United States over the legal power which ILO Conventions should have.

> . . .the Italian school was eager for the Conference to possess direct legislative power so that a Convention which obtained a two-thirds majority in the Conference would be immediately binding on all states, and even those who had voted against it would be under an obligation to implement the Convention within one year. On the other hand, the United States. . .was anxious to restrict the element of legal obligation to a minimum. (10) (emphasis added)

In other words, Italy argued that the Conventions enacted by the General Conference should have the "force of international law" and thus be legally binding, even on those states which had not voted for them. But the United States did not wish to yield its national sovereignty in this matter. The compromise agreement which was finally embodied in the ILO Constitution was the following:

> The solution agreed upon was that a Convention, when adopted, would give rise to certain legal obligations even for those states who had voted against its adoption. However, there would be no legal obligation to implement the Convention in municipal law unless a state had formally ratified a particular Convention. (11)

All ILO members were obligated to submit an annual report to the International Labor Office on their law and practices concerning ILO Conventions and Recommendations and, furthermore, to account for actions taken to meet the requirements of the Conventions and Recommendations. (12)

Another forum for international economic cooperation was world economic conferences, convened largely through the efforts of the League of Nations.

The first World Economic Conference, held in May 1927, was to mark the highpoint of efforts during the 1916-1945 period to reach international agreement on principles governing economic relations among states. Experts from 50 countries, chosen by their governments but serving as private individuals, unanimously adopted a Final Report of the Conference, which provided a survey of world economic conditions and argued that in order to raise the level of world prosperity and trade, obstacles to international trade (e.g., tariffs, quotas and other non-tariff barriers, and exchange controls) should be eliminated. The effect of the Conference recommendations on members' policy was twofold. First, a number of bilateral treaties committing the signatories to the reduction of tariff barriers were concluded. Second, a Conference on Import and Export Prohibitions, specifically concerned with the elimination of trade barriers, was held in October 1927. Unlike the earlier Conference in May, this was an official meeting aimed at the drafting of a formal treaty. By July 1928, 29 states had signed the Convention for the Abolition of Import and Export Prohibitions, obliging them to abolish existing prohibitions and restrictions on exports and imports and to refrain from imposing new ones. However, the Convention failed to receive a sufficient number of signatories for ratification. (13)

By 1919, the cooperative spirit in international economic relations had deteriorated, and the attempts made to implement the objectives of the 1927 Convention met with no success. The 1929 Assembly meeting of the League accepted in principle a British proposal for a two-year "truce" on tariff increases; but a draft agreement on the tariff truce, submitted for consideration to an international economic conference in March 1930, was not approved. Indeed, the United States and other non-European nations refused even to attend the conference. Disintegration of cooperation and agreement accelerated further during the Depression period (1929-1939). Italy, Japan, and Germany rejected international initiatives on economic matters, and all efforts to eliminate protection of national economic interests through trade restrictions and exchange controls thereby fell apart. (14)

Throughout the Depression period, there were repeated attempts to stem the tide of protectionism. At the ILO Conference of April 1932, there was a formal request for a World Economic Conference, which the Council of the League agreed in July to sponsor and direct. The crucial issue facing the Economic Conference, which convened in London (June 1933), was stabilization of the international monetary system, which was considered a prerequisite to consideration of trade matters. (15) Unfortunately, the United States, in a decisive and rather abrupt shift of policy, announced its unwillingness to cooperate in this area. (16) Hence, the only constructive outcome of the Conference concerned such functional issues as approval of the International Wheat Agreement between producers and consumers to ensure a steady market and level of supply commensurate with demand.

What role could the League play under such conditions? F.P. Walters, in his authoritative account, A History of the League of Nations, described its course of action as follows:

> It was useless to renew the attempt to create a world-wide cooperation in economic policy by means of specific plans which could be effective only when accepted and applied by a large number of governments. The economic and financial institutions of the League did not indeed abandon their convictions or change their aim: but they were forced to turn to new methods. Henceforth, their activities were concerned more with the individual than with the State. They began to work in close conjunction with the Health Organization, the International Labour Office, and the International Institute of Agriculture in Rome. The result was a series of practical studies and specialized conferences on such questions as housing, rural hygiene and rural conditions in general, standards of living, and nutrition. Simultaneously they organized the scientific study of the underlying causes of the economic and financial troubles of the world. (17)

As Walters notes, the focus of the League in the economic and social realms shifted from inter-governmental agreements to information-gathering and smaller-scale conferences.

With the expansion of the League's economic and social activities, it became increasingly evident that a structural change within the League was necessary. In 1938, the League Council appointed the Australian representative, S.M. Bruce, to direct a commission to study "appropriate measures of organization" to ensure the continued development and expansion of the League's ability to handle economic and social questions. By 1939, economic and social activities had come to account for some 60 percent of the League's total budget.

The Bruce Commission issued its report August 22, 1939, (18) 12 days before the declaration of World War II. The Report stressed the importance of international action to promote "economic and social welfare." To this end it called for an "interchange of experience and the coordination of action between national authorities" in order to solve problems of common concern. (19) It argued that the tendency towards a "closer knit" world and the convergence of economic structures meant that governments around the world faced similar problems. Economic and social cooperation was urgent, it said, to ensure world prosperity and world peace.

The Bruce Commission recommended that the League Council be replaced by a Central Committee for Economic and Social Questions, created under separate constitutional authority. It would consist of 24 government representatives and 18 technical experts. It would coordinate, supervise, and finance the various committees undertaking economic and social functions. Non-League nations could participate provided they contributed financial support. This would permit greater involvement and responsibility than previously possible for nonmembers. The Bruce Commission recommendations were approved by the League's Assembly in December 1939, and an Organization Committee was charged with implementing them. Although

World War II made the whole subject irrelevant for the duration, the Report did have a significant impact on post-War international organization, for with slight modification the Commission's recommendations later became the basis for the Economic and Social Council (ECOSOC) of the United Nations.

In 1940, the Economic, Financial and Transit Departments of the League Secretariat were transferred from Europe to Princeton, New Jersey, for the duration of the war. They made a major contribution to post-war economic cooperation in the form of the Princeton Mission reports. The reports were based on economic information gathered throughout the war years and made recommendations for post-war reconstruction. (20)

The evolution of international cooperation on economic and social questions under the League's auspices from 1916 to 1940 left an important legacy which guided the formulation of post-World War II policy in these areas. Although many of these early efforts at international cooperation through consultation and adoption of legal agreements were unsuccessful, they clearly indicated that the countries of the world were beginning to seek international solutions to their common problems. Moreover, the League established the important precedent of collecting and disseminating information regarding national economies and international economic activity and policy.

The general principles governing the economic relations between states which emerged at the various League-sponsored conferences re-emerged and were incorporated into the Bretton Woods Agreements and General Agreement on Trade and Tariffs (GATT). These principles included: (1) the most-favored-nation concept of extending equal treatment to all nations in granting reductions of barriers to trade; (2) agreement that competitive increases of trade barriers should be controlled if not eliminated; and (3) agreement concerning the necessity of returning to fixed exchange rates. Evaluation of the Depression experience reinforced the belief that these were the appropriate principles to guide international economic relations.

WORLD WAR II TRANSITION PERIOD (1941-50)

During and after World War II, it was widely accepted that economic and social, as well as military, cooperation should be explicitly provided for. This period was characterized by intensive planning and institution-building for economic cooperation. The Great Powers took the lead in formulating the plans. The structure and purposes of the economic institutions which they created focused on the reconstruction of Western Europe and the expansion of trade.

The Latin American nations tried, in various international forums, to draw attention to the problems of poor countries, but with limited effect. Within the United Nations system they succeeded with the support of the United States in bringing about the establishment of the United Nations Expanded Program of Technical Assistance (1950), and the regional economic commissions for Latin America (1948) and Asia and the Far East (1947). Most of the issues currently raised by the developing countries in support of their appeals for a "new international economic order" were voiced originally during the years 1941-50, if not earlier. The plans made in this period for new approaches to international cooperation revealed that the lines of cleavage that had been drawn in the 1930s among the industrial countries, and between them and the underdeveloped countries, were enduring.

The United Nations

Like the League of Nations, the United Nations was established for the primary purpose of maintaining peace and security. It was largely the creation of the United States, the United Kingdom, and the Soviet Union. In the Moscow Declaration on General Security (1943), the United Kingdom, Soviet Union, and United States declared that they:

> . . .recognized the necessity of establishing. . .a general international organization, based upon the sovereign equality of all peaceloving states, and open to membership of all such states, large and small, for the maintenance of international peace and security. (21)

Following this Declaration, planning began within the respective national agencies regarding the nature and scope of future postwar international cooperation.

The three countries agreed at Yalta to invite all nations who had declared war on the "common enemy" to attend a United Nations Conference on International Organization in San Francisco. Fifty nations attended the 1945 conference, including among the Third World states 20 Latin American countries plus Egypt, Ethiopia, India, Iran, Iraq, Lebanon, the Philippines Commonwealth, Saudi Arabia, Syria, and Turkey. Egypt and most of the Asian states attending had only recently become independent. The 50 countries signed the Charter of the United Nations on the last day of the Conference, June 26, 1945, and it was ratified shortly thereafter.

Two opposing principles coexist in the structure of the United Nations. The General Assembly, the United Nations' "supreme advisory body," operates on the principle of sovereign equality of "peaceloving states"; each member is entitled to a delegation and one vote, regardless of its population, land area, or economic strength. On the other hand, the Security Council is based on the principle of the special role of the Great Powers. It originally had 11, later increased to 15 members. The permanent members are the United States, United Kingdom, Soviet Union, China, and France; the nonpermanent members are elected by the General Assembly for two-year terms. Unanimity among the five permanent members is required for the approval of substantive matters and decisions are binding on all United Nations members.

During the San Francisco Conference, the Latin Americans, in particular, sharply criticized the form of Security Council representation (22) and tried unsuccessfully to increase the number of nonpermanent members as well as to narrow the range of decisions which would be affected by the veto prerogative. The structure of the Security Council and the fact that the

Great Powers finance most of the operating costs of the United Nations means that effective power in the organization rests with a very small number of countries. (23)

Although the primary function of the United Nations is to maintain peace and security, its founders also envisioned a role for it in providing "higher standards of living, full employment, and conditions of economic and social progress and development" (Article 55 of the Charter). The role of the Economic and Social Council (ECOSOC) as a principal organ of the United Nations was an important subject of negotiations at the San Francisco Conference. ECOSOC was created in accordance with the recommendations of the Bruce Commission to oversee all United Nations' activities in the economic and social areas (Chapter X) and to coordinate the activities of the Specialized Agencies (Article 63). It is under the supervisory authority of the General Assembly, and its members are elected by the General Assembly for three-year terms. The Specialized Agencies whose activities it coordinates each has a separate constitution, staff, budget, and organizational structure. Some of the more important Specialized Agencies are: the Food and Agriculture Organization (FAO, established 1945); World Health Organization (WHO, 1946); International Labor Organization (ILO, 1916); and the United Nations Educational, Scientific and Cultural Organization (UNESCO, 1945). Finally, the Charter authorizes ECOSOC to establish commissions to carry out its work; by the end of 1951, eight functional and three regional commissions had been established, including the Economic Commission of Europe (1947), the Economic Commission of Asia and the Far East (1947) and the Economic Commission of Latin America (1948).

Post-War International Economic Institutions

Unlike the situation which prevailed during World War I, when postwar economic concerns were essentially neglected, plans for future international economic cooperation were already well underway during World War II. (24) Within the United States Treasury and State Departments, extensive plans for postwar international economic institutions were being developed. The situation is described by Robert Oliver:

. . .At the conclusion of the war, the world [would] be faced by three problems among others: the maintenance of monetary systems and foreign-exchange markets; the restoration of foreign trade; and the relief, reconstruction and recovery of national economies.

The task of solving these problems [could] only be handled through international action.

The establishment of appropriate international agencies [could] not wait upon the conclusion of the war. (25)

The general principles underlying the United States' approach to the postwar economic order were embodied in the Atlantic Charter (August 1941):

The Atlantic Charter declared that the United States and the United Kingdom would endeavor, with due regard to their existing obligations, to further the enjoyment by all states of access on equal terms to the trade and raw materials of the world; that they desired to bring about the fullest collaboration among nations in obtaining for all improved labor standards, economic development and social security; and that they hoped to establish a peace that would enable all men to live out their lives in freedom from fear and want. (26) (Emphasis added)

It is evident that international economic cooperation was considered necessary and desirable. In particular, the United States and other Western powers perceived the need for two organizations: a Fund, to stabilize foreign-exchange rates; and a Bank, to provide capital.

Henry Dexter White, head of the Division of Monetary Research of the United States Treasury Department, drafted a comprehensive plan which became the basis for the International Monetary Fund (IMF) and the International Bank for Reconstruction and Development (IBRD or World Bank). (27) Consultation with the British on these matters had begun in 1942. In 1943 the United States made public a revised form of the White plan, and the British proposed John Maynard Keynes' International Clearing Union plan as an alternative to White's plan for a Fund. The Bretton Woods Conference (July 1944) culminated in the drafting of Articles of Agreements for the IMF and IBRD.

International Monetary Fund (IMF)

Both the White and Keynes plans dealt with exchange stability, orderly arrangements for currency convertability, and avoidance of competitive exchange rate devaluations. The key differences between them concerned the scope and nature of international intervention in national economic policy. The Keynes plan was modeled on a central bank arrangement. It entailed substantial international liquidity through the creation of an international reserve asset and the demonetization of gold; the right of a member to draw on up to one-fourth of its quota in order to meet balance-of-payments difficulties; the freedom to adjust exchange rates; the payment of interest by both surplus and deficit countries (i.e., both bearing the cost of balance-of-payments adjustments). (28)   The White plan, by comparison, called for less liquidity; fixed exchange rates with currency values pegged to gold rather than to an international reserve asset; and greater emphasis on the deficit country's responsibility for adjusting internal policies to alleviate balance-of-payments disequilibria. (29)

The final Articles of Agreement of the IMF had the following features:

(a) Par values for exchange rates which are fixed with a one percent permissible variation; these are adjustable in situations of "fundamental disequilibrium."   IMF permission is needed for more than a 10 percent cumulative adjustment. Members are expected to maintain exchange values through central bank activities.

(b) Exchange controls are prohibited except as a transitional measure to adjust to peacetime conditions.

(c) A gold-exchange system is maintained. The dollar is pegged to gold and all other currencies are pegged to the dollar. The United States is required to convert dollars into gold at a fixed price.

(d) Members have "drawing rights" on the fund of reserves. They can draw on these in proportion to their quota in order to meet short-term balance of payments disequilibria (i.e., 3-5 years). Access to these funds, however, is contingent on an internal adjustment policy.

(e) Voting is weighted according to the size of a member's contribution (which in turn is based on the size and prosperity of one's economy).

International Bank for Reconstruction and Development (IBRD)

The Bretton Woods Conference also drew up the Articles of Agreement for an international lending agency, the IBRD. The establishment of such an agency was motivated by concern that an adequate volume of capital to finance reconstruction would not be forthcoming, and, therefore, a source of long-term low interest loans for productive purposes was a necessary feature of the postwar international economic order. (30) Membership in the IBRD is contingent upon membership in the IMF. Subscriptions to the initial $10 billion capital stock was determined on the basis of national income and other economic factors (similar to the IMF), although a member's right to receive loans is not tied to its subscription amount. (31) Like the IMF, voting in the IBRD is weighted in relation to subscriptions.

Article I of the IBRD's Articles of Agreement states that the purposes of the Bank are:

(a)   To assist in reconstruction and development of members "by facilitating the investment of capital for productive purposes, including the restoration of economies destroyed or disrupted by war, the reconversion of productive facilities to peacetime needs and the encouragement of the development of productive facilities and resources in less developed countries."

(b)   To promote private foreign investment through guarantees, participations, and to supplement investment through Bank capital when it is unavailable on reasonable terms.

(c)   To promote long-range balanced growth of international trade and maintenance of equilibrium in balance of payments through investment in productive resources.

At the Bretton Woods Conference, the Latin American nations insisted that the stated objectives of the Bank include an explicit commitment to development as well as to reconstruction. They were responsible for the word "development" being incorporated into the title of the Bank, and for equal emphasis being placed on development and reconstruction in the Articles of Agreement. They were not successful, however, in their attempt to ensure that one-half of the IBRD's resources would be designated for development purposes. (32)

(Proposed) International Trade Organization (ITO)

Besides drafting the Articles of Agreement of the IBRD and IMF, the Bretton Woods Conference called for an international agreement on principles to guide international trade. At the time of the Conference, consultations were underway between the United Kingdom and United States regarding implementation of the 1942 Mutual Aid Agreement, which provided, in Article VII, for reduction and eventual elimination of tariffs and other trade barriers. A United States/United Kingdom draft charter (1945) served as the basis for discussions at the United Nations Conference on Trade and Employment held in Havana, Cuba, November 21, 1947 to March 24, 1948.

The Havana Conference was organized by the Preparatory Committee for an International Trade Organization (ITO), appointed by ECOSOC in 1946. The 53 governments which attended reached agreement on the Havana Charter for an International Organization (March 24, 1948). The signatories pledged themselves "to promote national and international action designed to attain the following objectives":

(a)   to contribute to an expanding and growing world economy by encouraging increasing income and production, consumption, and exchange of goods;

(b) to foster and assist industrial and general economic development;

(c) to further the enjoyment by all countries, on equal terms, of access to the markets, products, and productive facilities which are needed for their economic prosperity and development;

(d)   to promote, on a reciprocal and mutually advantageous basis, the reduction of tariffs and other barriers to trade and the elimination of discriminatory treatment in commerce; and

(e)   to facilitate, through consultation and cooperation, the solution of problems relating to international trade. (33)

The Havana Charter also included measures addressing employment policy, economic development and reconstruction, commercial policy (including tariffs, taxation, non-tariff barriers, state trading), restrictive business practices, commodity agreements, and the establishment of the ITO.

Although the United Kingdom and United States had given little consideration to the trade problems of poor countries in their preparation of a draft charter, in the final stages of consultation before the Havana Conference and at the Conference itself, Australia, India, Brazil, and Chile pressed for inclusion of a special section on economic development. Accordingly, Chapter III of the Havana Charter is devoted to LDC concerns, and it provides inter alia for exceptions to generally agreed principles in the interests of development: allowance of quantitative restrictions on imports when this is necessary for development purposes (Article 13); rights of members over foreign investment (Article 12); certain rights of exception to the most-favored-nation (non-discriminatory) measures (Article 15); approval of regional preference agreements (Article 15); and special treatment of primary commodities (Article 27).

The Havana Charter was never ratified and the ITO never came into existence. The United States Congress did not seriously consider it until 1950, by which time the political climate for approval had passed. (34) Nevertheless, most of the key commercial principles were put into effect through an interim agreement which had been negotiated prior to the Havana Conference, the General Agreement on Trade and Tariffs.

General Agreement on Trade and Tariffs (GATT)

The failure of the Western powers to ratify the Havana Charter resulted in GATT's emergence as the chief international instrument for implementing international trade norms, a role which it continues to perform.

The GATT was originally conceived as a three-year interim agreement which would serve as an instrument for tariff negotiations on a product-by-product basis. The GATT was signed on October 10, 1947, by the representatives of 23 countries, and by the next year all 23 had become contracting parties. (35) It was much more limited in scope than the Havana Charter. In particular, it did not cover economic development and investment, nor did it provide for exceptions to generally agreed principles in the interest of poor countries. It also lacked the enforcement powers and legally binding character of the Havana Charter, since it did not require the total incorporation of its principles into municipal law, and it was financially dependent on the United Nations.

The GATT formalized the following two fundamental principles of commercial policy:

(a) <u>Non-discrimination</u>. The most-favored-nation principle guaranteed that all GATT members would extend similar treatment to all other members regarding access to their markets. "Any advantage, favour, privilege or immunity granted by any Member to any product originating in or destined for any other country shall be accorded immediately and unconditionally to the like product originating in or destined for all other Member countries" (cf., Article 16 of the Havana Charter). The only exceptions permitted were in cases of preferences which had been in force when the member signed GATT, and in cases of customs unions, free trade associations, and underdeveloped countries in certain circumstances.

(b) <u>Reciprocity</u>. Tariff concessions were to involve a fair exchange of benefits and costs incurred.

Although GATT permits tariff protection, it prohibits all other forms of protectionism, except in situations of severe balance of payments disequilibrium or threats to a country's development plan.

United Nations Expanded Program of Technical Assistance (EPTA)

Established in 1950, EPTA was the first long-term international technical assistance program devoted exclusively to the needs of poor countries. It provided for the coordination of ongoing United Nations technical assistance activities through a Technical Assistance Board, made up of the executive heads of the United Nations and Specialized Agencies. (36) It also provided for a special account for technical assistance, supplied by Country and World Bank contributions. (37) The contributions were then transferred from EPTA to the Specialized Agencies as Executing Agencies for the purpose of carrying out technical assistance. Technical assistance activities which were not the special responsibility of any of the Specialized Agencies were undertaken by the United Nations.

The creation of EPTA was in response to the growing demands of developing countries, in particular the Latin American countries in ECOSOC and the General Assembly. (38) They argued that, while economic surveys and other forms of technical assistance were essential, they were inadequate. The establishment of EPTA led to a dramatic shift in Specialized Agency activities away from research and standard-setting and towards field operations. (39)

Post-War Bilateral Economic Programs

United States

Although it was generally expected that the new, postwar, international institutions would play the decisive role in reconstruction, the efforts of the United Nations' system were for the most part overshadowed by United States' bilateral assistance. (40) The United Nations Relief and Rehabilitation Administration (a pre-United Nations agency, 1943) and other special United States grants and loans provided relief assistance to the war-damaged areas during 1945-47. In June 1947, the United States offered to provide large-scale capital assistance for a European Recovery Program (the Marshall Plan), to be designed by the Europeans and to entail coordinated planning of postwar reconstruction. The scope of the commitment ($12.5 billion disbursed over a four-year period) was unprecedented. (41)

In accordance with the United States' proposal, 16 European nations formed the Organization of European Economic Cooperation (OEEC), which designed a plan to meet three major economic problems: (a) low productivity, reflecting the war-wrought destruction of productive capacity; (b) lack of resources to purchase necessary imports ("dollar shortage"); and (c) inflation. The European Recovery Program was approved by the United States Congress under the Foreign Assistance Act of 1948. The Marshall Plan, as the four-year program was called, was largely responsible for the reconstruction of Europe. Moreover, it led the way in 1957 for expanded economic cooperation within Europe under the auspices of the OEEC (subsequently renamed the OECD) and the European Economic Community (EEC). (42)

While massive aid was provided to Europe and some parts of Asia, the United States' program provided relatively little aid to the Third World. President Truman's Point Four Program committed the United States to a bilateral technical assistance program "for making the benefits of our scientific advances and industrial progress available for the improvement and growth of underdeveloped areas." Essentially, this entailed technical assistance to Latin America and the dependencies and recently independent former colonies of the European participants in the Marshall Plan. In 1950, the United States committed $25 million to the Point Four Program.

United Kingdom and France

Following World War II, an important change occurred in the orientation of British and French colonial policy, as both countries assumed direct financial responsibility for the economic development of their colonies. The British and French substantially modified their long-standing position that colonial economic development should be self-supporting, and agreed to transfer significant amounts of aid from the home country budget to the colonies. (43) The British Colonial Development and Welfare Act of 1940, as amended in 1945, provided for grants from the annual Colonial Office budget to support development efforts in the colonies. Assistance was contingent upon the preparation of ten-year development plans. (44) The French instituted a similar policy in 1946. Under the Ten-Year Plan for the French Union, financial assistance for economic development in the colonies was to be provided in grant form from the Investment Fund for Economic and Social Development (FIDES) and in loan form from the Caisse Centrale de Cooperation Economique.

DECOLONIZATION AND THE SEARCH FOR ECONOMIC INDEPENDENCE (1951-73)

The 1951-73 period and, in particular, the years after 1960, were characterized by the emergence of a large number of new nations and a difficult adjustment on the part of the developed countries, as the implementation of their professed democratic principles led to a diminution of their political power within international organizations.

Preoccupied with reconstruction and security problems immediately following World War II, the developed countries began only in the early 1950s to face the issue of economic development in the Third World. Security and development were closely linked. Aid programs became a feature of the Cold War, with the Soviet Union and United States waging a battle for the allegiance of the newly independent, or soon to become independent, countries of Asia and Africa. Meanwhile, France and the United Kingdom continued to focus on their respective colonies and former colonies. In the late 1950s the now reconstructed Germany and Japan joined the ranks of the aid donors.

The struggle for political independence in the 1950s and early 1960s left very little time for most Asian and African states to worry about economic development. It was principally the Latin American countries, who had achieved political independence a century earlier, that focused on economic issues. Under the leadership of Raul Prebisch, the United Nations Economic Commission for Latin America (ECLA) systematically developed a framework for analysis of the nature of economic development in the primary commodity exporting countries. The Afro-Asians and the Latin Americans did not formally join forces until December 1962, when they voted together in the

United Nations to pass a resolution to convene a special conference on trade and development. It was at this Conference in 1964 (UNCTAD I) that the Group of 77 was formed as the spokesman for the LDCs. In the 1960s, the UN Conference on Trade and Development emerged as the institutional and ideological center for the Group of 77.

As the developed countries slowly came to realize that they had lost control of the General Assembly to the developing countries, they began to shift discussions of their mutual economic interests from the institutional framework of the United Nations to that of the OECD. The United States seemed to minimize the importance of the trend until the early 1960s, perhaps believing that its economic power, which had served it well in the past, would continue to do so.

Economic Commission for Latin America (ECLA)

The United Nations Economic Commission for Latin America (ECLA) was established in 1948, following the formation of two similar regional commissions for Europe and for Asia and the Far East. From its inception, ECLA was concerned primarily with economic development. Although it also dealt with some short-term war-related economic problems, including the postwar inflation and the contraction of European demand for Latin American exports, it considered them to be only symptoms of more fundamental structural problems stemming from underdevelopment. (45) In 1951, ECLA submitted for ECOSOC approval an amendment of its terms of reference to place explicit emphasis on its role in promoting economic development:

[ECLA shall] give special attention in its activities to the problems of economic development and assist in the formulation and development of coordinated policies as a basis for practical action in promoting the economic development of the region. (46)

To this end, in its early years, ECLA focused on researching and analyzing basic economic data (regional, national and sectoral), with the technical assistance of other United Nations agencies. It instituted an annual Economic Survey of Latin America and undertook numerous, more specific, studies (e.g., on the need for technical assistance, prospects for trade expansion, economic and legal status of foreign investment in Latin America). The training of Latin American economists and the elaboration of economic theory relevant to the Latin American experience were also given much attention and importance. (47)

Under the leadership of its Executive Secretary, Raul Prebisch, (48) ECLA contributed significantly to the development of that analysis which currently underlies Third World arguments for a "new international economic order." A salient aspect of the analysis was the examination of the influence and effect of the existing international order, in particular in commercial relations, on the economic development of Latin American nations. The Report of the Fourth Session of ECLA and The Economic Development of Latin America and Its Principal Problems (49) contain a clear formulation of ECLA's diagnosis of the problems of underdevelopment in Latin America. The themes developed in these documents would continually re-emerge in later ECLA and UNCTAD documents over the following 25 years. The most important of these are summarized below:

(a)   Developing countries should be safeguarded against world economic fluctuations which affect their capacity to import ant export, and generally result in persistent balance-of-payments disequilibrium.

(b)   In order to reduce the magnitude of the external disequilibrium and to increase the resilience of the internal economies, developing countries must diversify their exports and develop their domestic productive capacity, in particular in the basic necessities of life. (50)

(c)   Economic growth requires a change in the composition of imports towards capital goods and away from simple consumer items.   The link between external fluctuations and economic development is their effect on the capacity to import capital goods essential to development of increased productive capacity.   Prebisch describes the position of the developing countries in terms of their function as the primary-producing "periphery" of the international economic order. (51) The "periphery" will remain in a dependent underdeveloped status until the external economic environment is made more stable and the internal economic environment more flexible and autonomous.

(d)   Technical progress, which tends to raise productivity levels in manufacturing more rapidly than in the production of primary commodities, should result, over time, in lower prices of manufactured goods relative to primary goods.   However, for the period 1870-1947, the purchasing power of the primary commodity exporting countries had declined as a result of several factors:

(i)   the price of industrial goods did not fall with increased productivity, but instead wage rates went up;

(ii)   price and income elasticities of demand for primary products were less favorable than those for manufactures.

The result has been a long-term deterioration in terms of trade of developing countries. (52)

(e)   The lack of an adequate and stable flow of foreign capital to supplement domestic investment resources is a crucial bottleneck to development.

(f)   Regional integration of markets for the development of industrial capacity can play an important role because of the demand stimulus of larger markets.

(g)   Planning and setting priorities for the use of scarce resources is an essential aspect of the development process.

The simultaneous emergence of a well-developed diagnosis of underdevelopment, the leadership of Raul Prebisch, the training of a cadre of ECLA economists, and the development of strong intraregional ties permitted ECLA to assume the role of spokesman for Third World economic concerns in the 1950s and early 1960s. (53)

Decolonization

The Latin Americans were the only independent, articulate group of developing countries which could have been described as a "bloc" in the early postwar period. In 1945, Egypt, Ethiopia, Liberia, and South Africa were the only independent African states; although Egypt had been nominally independent since 1929, the British still played a pervasive role. Large areas of western Asia remained under World War I mandate; and, with the exception of Thailand, all of south and southeast Asia was under colonial rule. In northeast Asia, Korea had just gained independence from Japan, and Hong Kong remained a British colony. China was in the midst of a civil war. Consequently, the dominant issue among these countries during the 1950s was their own political struggle for independence. British colonies in Asia were among the first to receive independence: by 1950, these included India, Pakistan, Ceylon (Sri Lanka), and Burma. The Philippines, Laos, and Indonesia also achieved independence during this period. By 1955, this configuration was little changed; only Libya had been added to the list of independent nations.

Strong anticolonial sentiments were manifested at the first meeting of the Afro-Asian states at the Bandung Conference (April 18-24, 1955). The Conference was not held under the auspices of the United Nations system but was supported and planned by Indonesia, India, Burma, Pakistan, and Ceylon. Twenty-nine countries attended. (54) The stated purposes of the Conference were quite general: (55) to "promote goodwill and cooperation among nations of Asia and Africa"; to consider social, economic, and cultural problems and relations; and to examine the position of these nations in the world. In fact, the Conference was primarily concerned with the political situation in Asia, and in particular with the failure of major powers to consult Afro-Asian countries on issues relevant to them. The Final Communique called for an end to colonialism, an evil "in all its manifestations," (56) and for the representation of Afro-Asian countries on the Security Council.

Decolonization accelerated in 1960 with the independence of the French African states. Following the entry of 18 new members into the United Nations in 1960-61, voting power in the General Assembly shifted in favor of the Third World. This had a profound effect on the conduct of international relations in that organization, and led to a number of Amendments of the United Nations Charter. After several earlier unsuccessful attempts, the General Assembly voted in 1963 to amend the Charter to enlarge LDC representation on the Security Council and ECOSOC. (57) In 1965, the Security Council was expanded from 11 to 15 members, with decisions to be made by nine votes including those of the five permanent members. ECOSOC was expanded from 18 to 27 members, of which developing countries would number 17. Voting was by simple majority.

Another indication of the growing impact of Third World concerns on the international climate was President John Kennedy's speech to the General Assembly in December 1961. In that speech he suggested that the 1960s be instituted as the United Nations Development Decade. (58) His gesture was heartily endorsed by the developing countries. The stated priorities of the Development Decade included a five percent target rate of economic growth.

The Non-Aligned Conferences

Outside of the United Nations, the Afro-Asian states began to meet as a group of non-aligned nations in 1961. Until the inclusion of Argentina and Peru at the Algiers Conference in 1973, the non-aligned nations included countries only from Africa, Asia, and the Middle East, with Latin Americans participating only in an observer capacity. The Belgrade Conference of Non-Aligned States was convened at the initiative of Presidents Tito, Nasser, and Nehru in September 1961, and was attended by 25 Afro-Asian countries and three observers from Latin America. (59) They were brought together by their intense dislike of colonialism and their desire to remain uncommitted to either of the two Cold War blocs. As with the Bandung Conference, the nations gathered in Belgrade were concerned principally with political issues: the end of colonialism in Algeria, the Portuguese colonies, and South Africa; disarmament; and reform of the United Nations (i.e., expansion of ECOSOC and the Security Council). However, the Conference also formulated some economic goals. It urged the convening of an international economic conference and actions to close the "ever-widening gap in the standard of living between the few economically advanced countries and the many economically less developed countries." It also called for the creation of a special United Nations capital fund, while it criticized trade practices which adversely affected non-aligned countries.

Since the Belgrade Conference, the non-aligned nations have continued to meet as a loosely defined group, (60) which has argued for a "moral spirit of peaceful co-existence" in international relations. As the heated political issues surrounding decolonization were resolved, its role as political advocate has declined, while its preoccupation with economic matters has grown. The tone and content of the non-aligned conferences changed markedly at the Algiers Conference in September 1973. The parameters of the discussion shifted from colonial oppression to confrontation between rich and poor nations - economic oppressor (developed countries) and economically oppressed (LDCs). The Conference declared that detente did not mean that the struggle against imperialism, neocolonialism, direct colonialism, and apartheid had ended. In its Economic Declaration and Action Program for Economic Cooperation, it blamed the failure of the International Development Strategy on the lack of political will by the developed countries and on the inadequacy of the growth target relative to the real needs of the developing countries. It set forth the plight of the LDCs in dramatic terms:

The developing world, which accounts for 70 percent of mankind, subsists on only 30 percent of world income.

TABLE 2.1   Roster of the United Nations by Year of Entry (1)
(Total 146 Members as of April 1976)

1945

Argentina
Australia
Belgium
Bolivia
Brazil
Byelorussian Soviet
  Socialist Republic
Canada
Chile
China
Colombia
Costa Rica
Cuba
Czechoslovakia
Denmark
Dominican Republic
Ecuador
Egypt (2)
El Salvador
Ethiopia
France
Greece
Guatemala
Haiti
Honduras
Iran
Iraq
Lebanon
Liberia
Luxembourg
Mexico
Netherlands
New Zealand
Nicaragua
Norway
Panama
Paraguay
Peru
Poland
Saudi Arabia
South Africa
Syrian Arab Republic (2)
Turkey
Ukranian Soviet
  Socialist Republic
Union of Soviet
  Socialist Republics
United Kingdom
United States
Uruguay
Venezuela
Yugoslavia

1946

Afghanistan
Iceland
Philippines (1946)
Sweden
Thailand

1947

India (1947)
Pakistan (1947)
Yemen

1948

Burma (1948)

1949

Israel

1950

Indonesia (3) (1945)

1955

Albania
Austria
Bulgaria
Democratic Kampuchea
            (1955)
Finland
Hungary
Ireland
Italy
Jordan
Lao People's Democratic
    Republic (1949)
Libyan Arab Republic
            (1952)
Nepal
Portugal
Romania
Spain
Sri Lanka (1948)

1956

Japan
Morocco (1956)
Sudan (1956)
Tunisia (1956)

1957

Ghana (1957)
Malaysia (4)

1958

Guinea (1958)

1960

Benin (1960)
Central African
  Republic (1960)
Chad (1960)
Congo (1960)
Cyprus (1960)
Gabon (1960)
Ivory Coast (1960)
Madagascar (1960)
Mali (1960)
Niger (1960)
Nigeria (1960)
Senegal (1960)
Somalia (1960)
Togo (1960)
United Republic of
  Cameroon (1960)
Upper Volta (1960)
Zaire (1960)

1961

Mauritania (1960)
Mongolia
Sierra Leone (1961)
United Republic of
  Tanzania (5)

Table 2.1 - Continued

1962

Algeria (1962)
Burundi (1962)
Jamaica (1962)
Rwanda (1962)
Trinidad and Tobago (1962)
Uganda (1962)

1963

Kenya (1963)
Kuwait (1961)

1964

Malawi (1964)
Malta (1964)
Zambia (1964)

1965

Gambia (1965)
Maldives (1965)
Singapore (4)

1966

Barbados (1966)
Botswana (1966)
Guyana (1966)
Lesotho (1966)

1967

Democratic Yemen (1967)

1968

Equatorial Guinea (1968)
Mauritius (1968)
Swaziland (1968)

1970

Fiji

1971

Bahrain (1971)
Bhutan (1971)
Oman (1971)
Qatar (1971)
United Arab Emirates (1971)

1973

Bahamas (1973)
Germany, Democratic Republic of
Germany, Federal Republic of

1974

Bangladesh
Grenada (1974)
Guinea-Bisseau (1974)

1975

Cape Verde (1975)
Comoros (1975)
Mozambique (1975)
Papua New Guinea (1975)
São Tomé and Principe (1975)
Surinam (1975)

1976

Angola (1976)
Seychelles (1976)

1   Year of independence in parenthesis for those countries becoming independent after World War II.

2   Egypt and Syria, both of which became members on 24 October 1945, joined together following a plebiscite in those countries on 21 February 1958 to form the United Arab Republic. On 13 October 1961 the Syrian Arab Republic, having resumed its status as an independent state, also resumed its separate United Nations membership, and the United Arab Republic continued as a member. The latter reverted to the name of Egypt on 2 September 1971.

3   In a letter dated 20 January 1965, Indonesia informed the Secretary General that it had decided "at this stage and under the present circumstances" to withdraw from the United Nations. In a telegram dated 19 September 1966, Indonesia notified the Secretary General of its intention to resume membership. On 28 September 1966, the General Assembly took note of the decision of the Government of Indonesia and the President invited the Indonesian representatives to take their seats in the Assembly.

4   On 16 September 1963, Sabah (North Borneo), Sarawak and Singapore joined the Federation of Malaya, which became a United Nations member on 17 September 1957, to form Malaysia. On 9 August 1965, Singapore became independent and on 21 September 1965 it became a member of the United Nations.

5   Tanganyika was a United Nations member from 14 December 1961 and Zanzibar from 16 December 1963. Following the establishment, on 26 April 1964, of the United Republic of Tanganyika and Zanzibar, it continued as a single member in the United Nations, changing its name on 1 November 1964 to Tanzania.

Sources: United Nations, Yearbook, 1973
           UN Monthly Chronicle, April 1976
           New York Times Index, 1977

Of the 2,600 million inhabitants of the developing world, 800 million are illiterate, almost 1,000 million are suffering from malnutrition or hunger, and 900 million have a daily income of less than 30 U.S. cents.

In the light of all these considerations, estimates up to 1980 are extremely pessimistic. Assuming that the targets set for the Second Development Decade can be achieved, and this is by no means certain, gross national income per capita in the developing countries would increase by only 85 U.S. dollars as against 1,200 U.S. dollars in the industrialized states. By the end of the present decade, average annual per capita income will be 3,600 U.S. dollars in the developed countries, but only 265 U.S. dollars in the developing countries. (61)

In order to solve the problems of the poor countries, it was argued that "a new type of international relations" was necessary. The elements of the new order came under the following headings: trade and monetary relations; food; sovereignty over natural resources, including the right to nationalize property under national law; regulation of transnational corporations; transfer of technology; cooperation among developing countries, and between them and developed countries; the environment; a charter of economic rights and duties of states; special measures for the least developed countries, including land-locked countries; and the preservation and development of national cultures. Virtually all of these points later found their way into the resolutions passed at the Sixth Special Session of the United Nations General Assembly.

Although the non-aligned nations shifted their focus to economic issues, they lacked the organizational structure to lobby effectively for changes in international economic policies. In fact, the non-aligned group rejected proposals for the creation of a permanent secretariat at both Lusaka (1970) and Algiers (1973). Consequently, as UNCTAD's efforts progressed during the 1960s and early 1970s, the Group of 77 assumed an increasingly important role in Third World negotiating activities. It received a strong input from the non-aligned nations. The non-aligned group provided both leadership and support for the activities of the larger bloc of developing countries.

United Nations Conference on Trade and Development (UNCTAD)

In the early 1960s, ECLA demands for reform of the international economic system gained an audience among those United Nations' members and regional groupings which had previously concentrated their energies on the struggle for independence. The ECLA diagnosis and prescription for the problems of underdevelopment were adopted to a large extent by the countries of Asia and Africa. Like the ECLA, the developing country members of the United Nations argued that trade expansion was an important means of accelerating their economic development, but that the prevailing trade patterns favored developed countries. They proposed the imbalance should be righted principally through a reduction of barriers to LDC exports and stabilization of the prices of primary product exports. They also proposed the establishment of a new institution to promote the developing countries' interest in trade.

The 1962 Cairo Conference on the Problems of Developing Countries, attended by delegates from 36 states and Raul Prebisch as representative of the U.N. Secretary-General, gave impetus to the movement among developing countries to hold a trade conference. In the face of developed countries' arguments that GATT and ECOSOC were adequate institutions to oversee international trade, the developing countries used their superior voting strength to win General Assembly approval in December 1962 for the convening of a trade conference. (62) Raul Prebisch was appointed Secretary General of the Conference in early 1963. In November 1963, developing countries presented to the General Assembly a Joint Declaration of 75 Developing Countries on UNCTAD, (63) proclaiming LDC guidelines and expectations for the upcoming conference. In particular, it called for the establishment of a permanent international trade organization to implement conference decisions. (64)

UNCTAD I

UNCTAD I, attended by 120 nations, met in Geneva from March 23 to June 16, 1964. (65)   The themes of UNCTAD I were set forth by the Declaration of 75 and were more fully developed in Secretary General Raul Prebisch's report to the Conference, entitled Towards A New Trade Policy for Development. (66) This report examines the structural characteristics of the international economic order which perpetuate and reinforce the economic inequality among nations.   It states that the key principles of GATT - reciprocity and non-discrimination - are beneficial to the economically advantaged but hurt the less developed who lack equal bargaining power. The economic differences between the industrial and the less developed countries render the principle of contractual equality of negotiating parties, upon which GATT is based, invalid:

> [GATT] seems to be inspired by a conception of policy which implies that expansion of trade to the mutual advantage of all merely requires the removal of the obstacles which impede the free play of these forces in the world economy. These rules and principles are also based on an abstract notion of economic homogeneity which conceals the great structural differences between industrial centres and peripheral countries with all their important implications. Hence, GATT has not served the developing countries as it has the developed ones. In short, GATT has not helped to create the new order which must meet the needs of development, nor has it been able to fulfill the impossible task of restoring the old order. (67)

Furthermore, the report claims that tariff reductions in the GATT are made predominantly in favor of products of interest to industrial countries, whereas GATT condones the protectionist policies of these same countries against the exports of the developing countries. In these ways, the liberal trade notions of GATT are implemented at the discretion, and in the interest, of the developed world. (68)

Assuming the United Nations Development Decade's target rate of growth of five percent would be achieved, Prebisch predicted that a "trade gap" would develop between the demand for essential imports and the demand for

LDC primary goods exports. The disequilibrium reflected a structural characteristic of both the international economy and the trade policies of industrial countries. Through differences in wage-setting practices between primary and manufactured goods industries, the prices of manufactures rose with increased productivity while those of primary goods decreased. Thus, the terms of trade of primary product exporting countries tended to deteriorate. Moreover, the relative income inelasticity of the demand for primary products meant that developing countries did not share proportionately in the expansion of world trade. For these two reasons their capacity to purchase imports decreased over time. (69) The trade policies of industrial countries aggravated the difficulties of developing countries in expanding their exports. In order to protect domestic producers, industrial countries limited the access of developing countries to markets for certain primary commodities and processed raw materials and manufactures.

Prebisch advocated several measures to remedy the ills of the international economic system. To foster the development of infant industries, he urged tariff preferences, non-reciprocity in trade concessions, and regional industrialization. To alleviate the presumed deterioration in the terms of trade, he called for international commodity agreements and compensatory payments. He also advocated the creation of an international trade organization to examine and implement such policies.

Prebisch acknowledged that international and national policy were interdependent. The primary responsibility for development rested with each developing country. However, its task might be made impossible by the structure of the international economy and the ways in which that structure impinged on a national development program.

There are both internal and external factors to be attacked simultaneously. To emphasize the former and exclude the latter, or vice versa, would be an aimless exercise and only divert our attention from the real solutions. (70)

The arguments and analysis which emerged at UNCTAD I were certainly not new; many harked back to the Havana Charter and to Prebisch's earlier work in ECLA in the 1950s, as he notes in the conclusion of his report to the Conference:

Such are the issues for which this Conference must seek international solutions in support of internal endeavor. They are solutions which must be embodied in a new policy, not necessarily in response to new ideas -for the ideas presented here are not fundamentally new. (71)

The major accomplishments of UNCTAD I were threefold: it established a permanent institution devoted to the trade and other development problems of LDCs, it marked the agreement of the Latin American and the Afro-Asian nations on a common front to promote their economic objectives, and it established generally agreed principles for analyzing the situation of the developing countries in the international economy.

UNCTAD was established as a permanent organ of the General Assembly in spite of the opposition of the developed countries. The fact that UNCTAD was made directly responsible to the General Assembly, rather than to ECOSOC (in which the developing countries did not yet have a voting majority), proved to be advantageous. The developing countries viewed UNCTAD as a means of circumventing developed country control of the various international financial institutions, a control which was ensured through weighted voting.

A major confrontation took place at Geneva over the method of voting to be employed by UNCTAD. The developed countries sought a dual voting structure, which would have required a majority of the 12 major trading powers as well as a normal majority of the whole, to approve resolutions. The compromise solution finally agreed on called for a simple majority vote, with provision for formal conciliation procedures in the event of serious disagreement by a smaller number of members. The compromise solution also provided for a somewhat larger representation of the industrialized nations on the 55-member Trade and Development Board than would have been warranted by their numbers alone. (72)

The developing countries emerged from the Geneva Conference as the Group of 77. Their unity of purpose and intention to function as a negotiating bloc was made quite clear in the Joint Declaration of the 77 Developing Countries, (73) issued at the close of the Conference. UNCTAD became the institutional forum of the LDCs; it was their agency, rather than a remnant of postwar planning, and they hoped that it would become the coordinator and overseer of all United Nations activities in the development field. In other words, it would function more like an LDC-controlled ECOSOC than a GATT. The delegates at Geneva agreed that the UNCTAD organization would include three principal structures: a Conference of all members which would meet at least once every three years, a Trade and Development Board which would serve as a standing committee elected by the Conference, and a Secretariat. (74)

The Final Act of UNCTAD I, adopted June 15, 1964, contains 15 General Principles and 13 Special Principles to guide the work of the new trade and development organization. (75)   Principle Four states that "economic development and social progress should be the common concern of the whole international community" and that:

> . . .all countries pledge themselves to pursue internal and external economic policies designed to accelerate economic growth throughout the world. . .in order to narrow the gap between the standard of living in developing countries and that in developed countries. (76)

Principle Five commits the developed countries to assist the developing countries in this effort. (77) The remaining Principles call for greater access to developed country markets through elimination of trade barriers and granting of preferences, stabilization of primary product prices, maintenance of the terms of trade between primary exports and manufactured imports, and increased financial flows (both international and bilateral) to the developing countries to meet the UN target of one percent of national income. (78)

Once the UNCTAD Secretariat was established and Prebisch appointed as Secretary-General (February 1965), the Trade and Development Board began to exercise its policy making functions. It established four standing committees for Commodities, Manufactures, Shipping, and Invisibles and Financing Related to Trade. The Board also took over supervision of the Interim Co-ordinating Committee on International Commodity Agreements. (79) In these years, the Interim Co-ordinating Committee worked on data collection and the issues of international commodity agreements, supplementary and compensatory finance, and transfer of technology.

The interim between UNCTAD I and II saw several important changes in policy outlook - if not actual practice- in international economic relations. In February 1965 Part IV was added to GATT, and it became effective in June 1966. (80) Part IV called for high priority to be placed on developing country concerns with improved market access, primary product price stabilization, and cooperation with developed countries for the purpose of trade promotion and development. Also, GATT and UNCTAD jointly sponsored the International Trade Center as a data collection and technical assistance center. The Kennedy Round of trade negotiations (1963-67) under GATT legitimated nonreciprocity and concessions for developing countries, but left them dissatisfied because they correctly assessed that their gains from the Kennedy Round had been much less than those of the developed countries. In the Charter of Algiers, issued shortly before UNCTAD II, the Group of 77 called for the immediate implementation of tariff cuts beneficial to LDCs, and for the inclusion of all LDCs under the agreement - rather than only the GATT members. (81) Other important agreements reached prior to UNCTAD II included the Yaoundé Convention of June 1964 (the trade agreement between the EEC and its 18 associated African states) (82) and the 1967 IMF decision to create Special Drawing Rights as an additional source of international liquidity. (83)

UNCTAD II

The objective of the Group of 77 in UNCTAD II (New Delhi, February 1-March 29, 1968), was to negotiate concrete policies and mechanisms for implementing the recommendations of UNCTAD I. LDC efforts were directed towards bridging "...the gap between the intent expressed in the Final Act adopted in Geneva in 1964 and its fulfillment." (84) The Group of 77, now swollen to 88 members, met at the ministerial level in Algiers in October 1967 to formulate the Third World position. The position was fundamentally the same as that in Prebisch's report to UNCTAD II, entitled Towards a Global Strategy of Development. (85) It was notable for the absence of an explicit recognition of the benefits of the existing international economic system. Among the "long term trends in the structure of world trade which operate to the relative disadvantage of the majority of developing countries," (86) it singled out the adverse movement of the terms of trade, inadequate financial assistance on reasonable terms, and the declining share of developing country exports in total world trade.

No global strategy of world development emerged from UNCTAD II.

There was some examination of ways of improving the institutional structure of UNCTAD to make it more effective, but most substantive issues remained unresolved. The following comment, which Prebisch made during the course of UNCTAD II, reflects the Third World's impatience at UNCTAD's limited ability to effect changes in international economic relations:

> We have to recognize that UNCTAD has as yet not been an effective institutional machinery consistent with its purposes. Will UNCTAD continue to be a mechanism absorbing aspirations and producing frustrations? Or will it become an effective organ of the United Nations which not only acts as a forum for debate, but as a practical instrument of action? (87)

The most tangible agreement reached at UNCTAD II concerned a generalized system of preferences (GSP). The GSP would provide for generalized lowering of tariffs on the import by developed countries of bilaterally agreed semi-manufactures and manufactures from developing countries for a fixed period of time. Preferences had been strongly opposed by the United States until 1967, when President Johnson indicated a willingness to consult on the matter. (88) LDCs had called for such a scheme in the 1967 Charter of Algiers. At an OECD meeting prior to UNCTAD II, the developed countries agreed to negotiate a GSP for manufactures and semi-manufactures. (89) Resolution 21, adopted unanimously by UNCTAD II, (90) supported the GSP principle and established a Special Committee on Preferences to work out an implementation scheme. However, the developing countries were dissatisfied; the GSP would not, for the most part, cover processed agricultural products which are the most important source of LDC export revenues, and the numerous safeguard measures virtually excluded those manufactured products in which developing countries have a comparative advantage, namely textiles, leather goods, and shoes. (91) By 1970, the EEC and the other major developed countries, with the exception of the United States, each devised GSPs which were implemented separately. (92)

UNCTAD III

The tone of UNCTAD III (Santiago, Chile, April 13- May 21, 1972) was set by the monetary crisis of 1971. It had been precipitated by President Nixon's declaration of the inconvertibility of the dollar and his imposition of a temporary 10 percent surcharge on imports. These actions initiated intense discussions within the Group of 10 on the reform of the international monetary system. (93)

The Declaration of Lima in November 1971, (94) expressing the views of the Group of 77 (now including 96 members), reflects the Group's disappointment at being rudely reminded that the developing countries were still considered very marginal to great power political and economic interests:

> The hopes which we had entertained when the Charter of Algiers was adopted in 1967 have been frustrated. Once again, therefore, we confront the conscience of world opinion with facts, figures, agreements, and

programs. We trust that the understanding of the Statesmen of the developed world will become more responsive and will generate the necessary political will to lend vigour to international cooperation. (95)

. . .

It is entirely unacceptable that vital decisions about the future of the international monetary system which are of concern to the entire world community are sought to be taken by a limited group of countries outside the framework of the IMF. (96)

LDCs demanded full and equal participation in international monetary reform. They soundly criticized the developed countries for attempting to solve their balance of payments problems at the expense of the economic well-being of the rest of the world. They considered the surcharge to be particularly detrimental as they were more dependent on export revenues for economic stability than were the developed countries. They did not want to institute floating exchange rates. They called for the establishment of a compensation mechanism to deal with reserve losses in the crisis situation, as well as for a link between SDR creation and development finance. (97)

The Group of 77 stated its belief that UNCTAD must become more action-oriented. (98) To this end it recommended some institutional changes such as the enlargement of the membership on the Trade and Development Board and the UNCTAD Committees.

UNCTAD III's assessment of the world economic situation and its recommendations for remedying that situation were largely a continuation of the themes expressed in UNCTAD I and II. UNCTAD III advocated vigorous action on commodity prices and access to developed country markets, the extension of the GSP scheme, greater attention to the needs of the least developed and land-locked LDCs, increased external finance, the reduction of trade barriers, and technology transfer on a more equitable basis. (99) The newest addition to the list of UNCTAD undertakings was a resolution which established a working group to draft a Charter of Economic Rights and Duties of States. (100) The Charter was intended to be an internationally endorsed code of principles to guide the international economic order.

During the decade following 1964, UNCTAD served the needs and interests of the LDCs in several important respects. It was an institutional forum for dialogue among Third World nations and between these nations and the developed countries. The work of UNCTAD's Committees provided the factual basis for proposals concerning the gap between development goals and the actual status of LDCs in the international economy. UNCTAD successfully altered the framework of discussion of development issues and engaged the developed countries in a dialogue from which they could not easily retreat. UNCTAD represented the culmination of LDC organizational efforts to change the nature and structure of international economic relations, and it brought recognition and legitimacy to their concerns. However, it was constrained by the absence of political will on the part of the developed countries to undertake the proposed reforms. The Group of 77 lacked the bargaining power to force change on the economically more powerful nations of the world, despite their voting majority in many of the international organizations concerned with economic cooperation. Their efforts to engage the developed countries in the negotiation of a Charter of Economic Rights and Duties of States, discussed in the following chapter, represented the next tactic employed by the Third World to alter the rules governing the conduct of international economic relations in their favor.

3 An Overview of the Charter of Economic Rights and Duties of States

The Charter of Economic Rights and Duties of States embodies the past achievements, current activities, and future hopes of the Third World. Originally conceived as a binding agreement which would govern international economic relations, it evolved into a document having only the force of a United Nations resolution. (1)   Nevertheless, this in no way diminishes the fact that 120 countries, representing over 70 percent of the world's population, voted in favor of the Charter, and, for this reason alone, it is worth reviewing to gain insight into the kind of world these nations aspire to build.

BACKGROUND

In 1971 President Luis Echeverria of Mexico decided that the cause of the Third World would be aided if the economic rights and duties of states were codified in the form of a charter to be approved by all nations.   Basic documents were prepared by the Mexican Ministry of External Affairs, and after discussions with Chile and Brazil, the three countries arrived at a general consensus.   The documentation was subsequently approved by the Latin American Group prior to the planning session of UNCTAD III held in Santiago, Chile, in 1972. (2)

President Echeverria's idea captured the imaginations of other LDC delegates to the UNCTAD III Conference.   "Let us remove economic cooperation from the realm of good will and crystallize it in the field of international law," he proposed.   "A just order and a stable world are not possible, as long as obligations and rights which protect the weak states are not created."   He then listed the following ten principles which should "form the basis of a Charter of Economic Rights and Duties of States." (3)

37

- the freedom to dispose of natural resources
- the right of every nation to adopt the economic structure it considers most suitable and to treat private property as the public interest required
- renunciation of the use of economic pressures
- subjection of foreign capital to domestic laws
- prohibition of interference by the supranational corporations in the internal affairs of states
- abolition of trade practices that discriminate against the exports of non-industrial nations
- economic advantages proportionate to the levels of development
- treaties guaranteeing stable and fair prices for commodities
- transfer of technology
- greater economic resources for long-term untied foreign aid

UNCTAD III took up President Echeverria's suggestion of translating the principles governing international economic relations into a legal instrument by adopting Resolution 45 (III) (by 90 votes in favor, none against, and 19 abstentions), (4) which noted the urgent necessity for "generally accepted norms to govern international economic relations, systematically," and called upon a Working Group to prepare a charter for submission in its final version to the Twenty-Eighth Session of the General Assembly - an extremely short time to deal with such a complex series of issues. The Working Group was instructed to use the general and special principles adopted at UNCTAD I, (5) the proposals made at UNCTAD III, (6) the documents of the Second Development Decade, (7) and the principles in the Charter of Algiers (8) and the Declaration of Lima. (9) That is, almost all of the demands that LDCs had made previously in other forums were to serve as bases for the Charter. The implicit goal of these demands might generally be described as a more equitable distribution of world power and resources, to be achieved by replacing the special position of great powers. This was to be done by international decision making within the United Nations General Assembly, where LDCs control more than two-thirds of the votes. It was hoped that this would be accomplished with the acquiescence of the industrialized developed countries.

Lest the Group of 77 had not already sensed it, by the time the last 10 of the 19 abstaining countries explained their "difficulties" with Resolution 45(III), it was clear that the Working Group would face serious obstacles in elaborating a legal instrument acceptable to all nations. The reservations voiced centered around the fact that Resolution 45(III) had been adopted very quickly and that the Economic and Social Council (ECOSOC) of the United Nations would have been a more appropriate forum for such a charter to have been drafted. (10) The United States did not bother to elaborate on the reasons for its opposition, stating only that it had "serious reservations about a number of features of the resolution." (11) Given the intent or implicit goal of Resolution 45(III) as characterized above, it is understandable that most industrialized countries were not eager to begin a process of voluntarily diminishing their relative power at the international level.

First Session of the Working Group (February 1973)

The Group of 40, (12) as the Working Group became known, first met in Geneva from February 12 to 23, 1973. Two of the Working Group's initial decisions represented major departures from normal United Nations' procedures. First, it was decided that UNCTAD members not among the 40 could participate in the discussions, as could intergovernmental organizations (IGOs). This decision provoked the ire of some developed countries who felt that it complicated already difficult negotiations by adding still more participants. Eighteen other UNCTAD members and two IGOs attended the First Session. The second decision, that summary records would not be kept, was publicly regretted by Chile, Ivory Coast and Jamaica. (13) The consequence of that decision was to prevent the clarification of ambiguous text by subsequent reference to the records.

Jorge Castañeda, Mexico's Ambassador to the United Nations in Geneva and a noted legal expert, was elected Chairman of the Working Group. In an opening statement he laid down the quesions that he believed the Working Group needed to address, including the necessity to formulate a juridical instrument of rights and duties which would be neither a simple repetition of past programs of action nor a restatement of the International Development Strategy. (14) It should not be simply a codification of existing law, but should contribute to the progressive development of international law. Finally, it should be universal, that is, acceptable to or "at least tolerated by" the principal groups of states. (15) The Working Group would find that Ambassador Castañeda's lofty goals were unattainable: in particular, the hope that the Charter would be tolerated by most groups of states was not realized, for among the 16 nations which would eventually abstain or vote against the Charter resides most of the world's economic strength.

In addition to the 36 nations (of 58 present) which commented on the various questions raised in Mexico's opening statement to the Working Group, three observers spoke. The Group of 77 generally wanted a legally binding instrument that would be more than an expression of intent and that would go beyond existing international legal norms. However, the developed countries disagreed. France, Canada, and the Netherlands argued that codifying existing customary international law would, in fact, contribute to the development of international law. The United States and United Kingdom, more interested in maintaining the status quo, wanted to adhere closely to accepted international law and thought that provisions which had not previously been codified should not be included in the Charter.

After lengthy discussions on the general and specific provisions which the member governments wanted incorporated into the Charter, (16) a sub-group of 18 members produced a draft outline based on working papers submitted by some of the LDCs and the Eastern European socialist countries. (17) This was taken note of by the Working Group, which was unable to examine it in detail, and was transmitted to all member governments of UNCTAD for comment before the Second Session of the Working Group met.

The draft outline (18) proposed the structure of the Charter: an introductory preamble and five chapters. The preamble incorporated the following broad principles: reaffirmation of the fundamental purposes of the United Nations Charter, creation of improved and equitable economic conditions, the establishment and maintenance of a just and rational world economic and social order, and collective economic security. It was substantially enlarged in the course of the next three sessions of the Working Group. Chapter I (entitled "Fundamentals of International Economic and Social Relations") included seven more specific principles drawn from the United Nations Charter or other instruments accepted by large parts of the international community: non-intervention, cooperation in accordance with the United Nations Charter, international social justice, self-determination, peaceful coexistence, legal equality of all states, and respect for national sovereignty of states. In the final version of the Charter, this section has been modified and expanded to include 15 such principles. In Chapter II ("Economic Rights and Duties"), the heart of the draft outline and of the Charter itself, the general principles of Chapter I were applied to such specific issues as private investment, trade and commodity arrangements, foreign aid, international organizations and East/West relations. Chapter III ("Common Responsibilities towards the International Community") dealt with the seabed and the environment. Chapter IV ("Implementation") covered implementation machinery and the reporting and settling of differences; and Chapter V ("Final Provisions") concerned adherence to the Charter. Six developed countries proposed the deletion of Chapters IV and V, fearing that such provisions would lend the Charter the nature of a treaty. (19) In the final Charter, Chapters IV and V were combined and dispute settlement was dropped.

The hopes voiced by the LDCs contrasted sharply with the reservations and doubts expressed about the draft outline by the developed countries, reflecting the fact that the rich and the poor were yet a long way from reaching a working consensus on the nature and content of the Charter. Some rich countries were to accept the idea of a formulation of the principles of the future world economic order and would seriously negotiate over details. Others, including the socialist states, felt relatively unaffected. However, a core group of the United Kingdom, the Federal Republic of Germany, and the United States continued to oppose the process itself and thereby precluded the possibility of an internationally agreed, legally binding instrument.

Second Session of the Working Group (July 1973)

The Second Session of the Working Group met in the Palais des Nations, Geneva, in July 1973. (20) The comments and suggestions of 31 governments on the draft outline were circulated to the Working Group (21) as was a reference paper prepared by the UNCTAD Secretariat (22) comprising excerpts from United Nations and other international documents relevant to each provision. On the opening day, the Philippines distributed a complete draft of a proposed Charter. (23) The Working Group divided into two sub-groups: one to consider the preamble and Chapter I, and the other to work on Chapters II through V. (24)

By the next to last day of the Second Session, it was obvious that the Working Group would have nothing which could be considered a consensus vocument ready for adoption.   Chairman Castañeda had introduced an informal working paper (25) utilized by the Working Group in synthesizing significantly different alternatives side by side - on the more controversial articles, there were still up to eight different wordings. For this reason, the Philippines' delegate proposed that the Trade and Development Board request the General Assembly to approve two more sessions of the Working Group. (26) The proposal was adopted and sent to the Trade and Development Board at its Thirteenth Session, (27) and the Twenty-Eighth General Assembly extended the Working Group for two more sessions and requested a final report by the Twenty-Ninth General Assembly. (28)

Third Session of the Working Group (February 1974)

Under the extending resolution, the Working Group met for a third time in Geneva in February 1974, again dividing into two sub-groups. (29)

Sub-group I reached substantial agreement on the preamble. In Chapter I, eleven fundamentals of international economic relations were agreed upon, but disputes on "peaceful coexistence" and "international cooperation for development" continued unresolved. (30)

Sub-group II, on the other hand, produced only four agreed texts on relatively well established international principles, including: the right of states to choose their economic, political, social, and cultural systems without outside interference; the responsibility of states to cooperate in the economic, social, cultural, scientific, and technological fields; the strengthening of economic cooperation and expansion of mutual trade among developing countries to enhance the effective mobilization of their own resources; and the need for special attention to be directed towards the least developed of the LDCs, land-locked and island developing countries. (31) The remaining fourteen texts were specified as needing "further considera-tion." (32) Included in this second, more controversial category were most-favored-nation (MFN) treatment, international division of labor, the right to participate in the international decision making process, obligations of regional organizations, transfer of technology, liberalization of international trade, transnational corporations, disarmament, preferences for developing countries, foreign aid, permanent sovereignty over natural resources, and foreign investment. Even a cursory review of this list of items makes it apparent that fundamental international relationships were being discussed, and that, if consensus were to be achieved, it would either take long negotiations or the result would be ambiguously drafted provisions.

The struggle within the sub-groups on some of the issues is illustrated by the fact that there were eight alternative texts on permanent sovereignty over natural resources and seven on foreign investment. They reflected not only the divergent viewpoints of the poor and the rich countries, but also ideological conflicts between market economy and centrally planned economy nations. Nevertheless, the principal battle was one of North/South (rich vs. poor), rather than East/West (centrally planned vs. market economies). (33) As the Third Session drew to a close, one delegation noted officially that progress had been disappointing. (34) Informal consultations were continued in intersessional meetings before the Fourth and final Session, which was to meet in Mexico City at the invitation of the Mexican Government. (35)

Fourth Session of the Working Group (June 1974)

The last Working Group session was held from June 10 to 28, 1974, in a highly charged atmosphere due to the events of the preceding eight months. In response to a sudden Algerian request in February, a Sixth Special Session of the United Nations General Assembly had been convened in May 1974 to discuss raw materials and development. (36) The importance of this act becomes clear when viewed in the context of the OAPEC oil embargo of 1973-74, which had resulted in a quadrupling of oil prices. To LDC raw material exporters, this newly found "commodity power" was an opening wedge marking the beginning of a realignment of North/South economic relations. The industrialized countries were essentially unprepared for the Sixth Special Session; they had difficulty in quickly defining an integrated, comprehensive policy on raw materials. They felt piqued about a situation which was obviously not their "show," and their approach was understandably negative. Conversely, the Group of 77 had worked out a mutually acceptable Declaration and a Programme of Action on the Establishment of a New International Economic Order, (37) two resolutions which were adopted by a "consensus," a description to which a number of countries took exception. (38)

The Fourth Session of the Working Group met in Mexico City, during the month following the Sixth Special Session confrontation, with the task of framing in a Charter many of the same controversial points found in the Declaration and Programme of Action. Four small negotiating teams worked on specific paragraphs, while others were dealt with in informal consultations. Most interest and attention was focused on the group concerned with Article 2 (permanent sovereignty, nationalization, compensation, and jurisdiction in cases of disputes), because it was commonly believed that consensus on Article 2 was the key to agreement on the Charter. At the beginning of the last week, the four teams were replaced by a contact group of twelve members, including representatives of the UNCTAD regional groups. (39) Language was tentatively agreed upon for five of the outstanding paragraphs, but lack of progress was the more notable feature of this Fourth Working Group Session.

The Mexicans had been particularly optimistic about the likelihood of an agreement on a final draft Charter. However, the sting of the recent Sixth Special Session of the General Assembly still smarted among some of the developed countries, who responded even more rigidly than before on some key issues. The United States, for example, had never been enthusiastic about a Charter, and for the entire three weeks that delegation's negotiating instructions were to avoid compromise on fundamental principles, especially in relation to Article 2. Incited by this attitude, key LDC delegates refused, in turn, to compromise by raising the level of generality of the language on the most important issues, which would have introduced sufficient ambiguity to allow all parties to interpret the provisions as they might wish.

Chairman Castañeda, in his closing speech to the Fourth Session, accused certain "interests of a clear neocolonial physiognomy, who refuse to recognize the evidence of a change in the contemporary world" of sabotaging the Charter. Mexico and the Group of 77 rejected the possibility of arriving at a "document of universal validity," as President Echeverria had proposed two years earlier in 1972, if that meant yielding on basic principles such as permanent sovereignty over natural resources. "We are not interested in a limp Charter or half a law. We are firm in maintaining our fundamental principles, and if the superpowers did not agree to cooperate with us, then the Charter will, in every way, be a permanent conviction in the fight for the liberation of the people of the Third World." (40)

Fourteenth Session of the Trade and Development Board (September 1974)

Although the Working Group's mandate had expired a second time, it was agreed that informal meetings would continue during the Fourteenth Session of the Trade and Development Board in Geneva in September 1974. (41) In fact, there was already agreement on 26 articles, or about eighty percent of the Charter. Besides Article 2 on private foreign investment, the remaining controversial provisions related to application of most-favored-nation treatment to Eastern European states, producer associations, indexation of raw material prices against the prices of manufactures, and colonialism and apartheid.

However, little progress was made during the Trade and Development Board Session, with agreement on only four minor paragraphs. (42) The developed nations asked for more time, expressing confidence that an agreement could eventually be reached, and stating that it was important to proceed "slowly and judiciously." (43) The Board recommended further informal consultations prior to consideration of the Charter by the forthcoming Twenty-Ninth General Assembly in New York. (44) From October 8 to 18, just one month before the Charter was turned over to the General Assembly's Second Committee (Economic and Financial), two groups of contact delegates met, one to work on Article 2 and the other on trade questions.

Second Committee of the Twenty-Ninth General Assembly
(November 1974)

On the opening of the Twenty-Ninth General Assembly, the draft Charter passed from the Trade and Development Board to the Second Committee of the General Assembly, responsible for economic and financial questions. On November 25, Mexico officially introduced the Group of 77's draft Charter. (45) In those cases where the informal consultations of September and October had failed to produce texts acceptable to the different parties, the Group of 77 language was inserted. Various combinations of 14 developed nations proposed 18 amendments to the Charter, (46) including, inter alia, revisions on all parts of Article 2 and total deletion of the articles on cartels, disarmament, colonialism and apartheid, generalized preferential treatment for LDCs, and indexation. In a final effort to reconcile outstanding issues, Mexico acted on behalf of the Group of 77 in proposing eight amendments to its draft Charter to accommodate developed country concerns, (47) but only three of these were accepted by the OECD countries, who, in turn, withdrew their corresponding amendments. (48) On December 6, France introduced an amendment on behalf of the EEC which would have postponed sending the Charter to the plenary of the General Assembly until the Seventh Special Session in September 1975, (49) pleading for another year of negotiations, "with a view to submitting a completed and generally accepted draft Charter to the special session..." The move to postpone was defeated.

Separate votes were taken on each of the developed countries' proposed amendments, although their sponsors mustered at most 22 votes in favor of any one amendment. (50)   The Charter was then voted on article by article, (51) and a final vote on the whole draft Charter found 115 in favor, 6 against, and 10 abstentions. (52) Those voting against (United States, United Kingdom, Federal Republic of Germany, Belgium, Denmark, and Luxembourg) and those abstaining (Austria, Canada, France, Ireland, Israel, Italy, Japan, Netherlands, Norway, and Spain) represented the non-communist industrialized countries. Australia, New Zealand, and Sweden, all voting in favor, were the only major exceptions.

Plenary of the Twenty-Ninth General Assembly (December 1974)

On December 12, 1974, the General Assembly plenary took up the Charter. Resolution 3281, containing prefatory remarks and the Charter of Economic Rights and Duties of States, was adopted by a vote of 120 to 6, with 10 abstentions. (53) The preface to the Resolution, accepting the report of the Second Committee, gives support to the UNCTAD goal "to establish generally accepted norms to govern international economic relations systematically" and recognizes that "it is not feasible to establish a just order and a stable world as long as a charter to protect the rights of all countries and in particular the developing states is not formulated..." The Charter was acknowledged as "the first step in the codification and development of the matter..."   The Resolution also stresses that the establishment of a new system of international economic relations will be based on "equity, sovereign equality, and interdependence of interests of developed and developing countries."

Reflection on the language of Resolution 3281 provides some insight into how fundamental the discussion on the Charter really was. There is no doubt that in the minds of some countries, the Charter's call for "equity" implied a redistribution of existing world power and wealth. The terms "sovereign equality" and "interdependence" suggest that countries need one another, but that, somehow, the nature of their relationship should be based on consensus rather than imposition. These three ambiguous and abstract terms convey the sense, and some would argue the inherent inconsistency, of the Third World's goals. The Charter represents their effort to detail those measures which might be taken to achieve these goals.

THE CHARTER

The Charter consists of five parts: a preamble; and four chapters on the fundamentals of international economic relations, economic rights and duties of states, common responsibilities towards the international community, and final provisions.

The Preamble

After reiterating the fundamental purposes of the United Nations (international peace, security, friendly relations, and international cooperation), Preambular paragraph four declares that it is the fundamental purpose of the Charter:

> to promote the establishment of the new international economic order, based on equity, sovereign equality, interdependence, common interest and cooperation among all States, irrespective of their economic and social systems.

The theme of interdependence is underscored, and there is an implicit assumption that rich and poor nations alike have a mutual interest in the development of the less advantaged.   In the draft before the Second Committee, this paragraph had originally read that:

> ...it is a fundamental purpose of this charter to codify and develop rules for the establishment of the new international economic order... (54) (emphasis added)

Twelve developed countries offered an amendment to exclude this portion of the paragraph because the words "to codify and develop rules" would give the Charter the appearance of being a legally binding document, an unacceptable position to them. Their proposed amendment replaced these words with the assertion that the Charter's fundamental purpose was "to promote just and equitable economic relations among nations," (55) language which had previously been approved at the Fourth Session of the Working Group but subsequently replaced by the Group of 77; the amendment was rejected. (56) At the Second Committee, in an effort to gain general consensus on the Charter, Mexico introduced an oral revision on behalf of the Group of 77 to replace the words "to codify and develop rules for" with "to promote." (57) When a final vote was taken on each article of the draft Charter in the Second Committee, this fourth Preambular paragraph was approved with 10 abstentions and no negative votes. (58)

Preambular paragraph five enumerates some slightly more specific goals: wider prosperity among countries; higher standards of living for all peoples; economic and social progress; encouragement of cooperation based on mutual advantage and equitable benefits; overcoming the main obstacles to economic development; acceleration of economic growth; bridging the economic gap between developing and developed countries; and the protection, preservation, and enhancement of the environment. These are relatively cautious goals and point up the conservative elements of the Charter. What does it mean to "bridge" a gap? Why not "narrow" or "eliminate"? The implicit strategy seems to be to raise the living standards of the poorest without disturbing those of the richest. A disagreement did, nevertheless, arise over sub-paragraph (c) of the draft, which read as follows:

Desirous of contributing to the creation of conditions for:...

(c) the encouragement of cooperation, on the basis of mutual advantage and equitable benefits for all peace-loving states which are willing to carry out their obligations under the Charter, in the economic, trade, scientific and technical fields, regardless of political, economic or social systems. (59)

An amendment to replace the words "peace-loving states which are willing to carry out their obligations under this Charter" with the words "states concerned" (60) was rejected. (61) Just prior to the final vote in the Second Committee, Mexico proposed on behalf of the Group of 77 the phrase "their obligations under this Charter" be replaced by "the provisions of this Charter" (62) and in this revised form the paragraph found unanimous approval. (63)

The tone of the Preamble changes sharply in the sixth paragraph, which states that the General Assembly is:

Mindful of the need to establish and maintain a just and equitable economic and social order through:

(a) the achievement of more rational and equitable international economic relations and the encouragement of structural changes in the world economy,

(b) the creation of conditions which permit the further expansion of trade and intensification of economic cooperation among all nations,

(c) the strengthening of economic independence of developing countries,

(d) the establishment and promotion of international economic relations taking into account the agreed differences in development of the developing countries and their specific needs.

The existing economic order is considered to be neither just nor equitable, and to make it so, structural changes are needed, (64) trade must be expanded, and economic cooperation intensified. After stressing the interdependence of all states in the fourth Preambular paragraph, here the obverse - strengthening the independence of the LDCs - becomes a means to a just order.

The seventh was the only Preambular paragraph to receive a negative vote in the Second Committee when the final vote on the draft Charter took place. It reads:

Determined to promote collective economic security for development, in particular of the developing countries, with strict respect for the sovereign equality of each State and through the cooperation of the entire international community. (65)

As originally proposed by Brazil, the concept of "collective economic security" had been qualified as being "based on a shared responsibility of the international community which is essential to the sustained development and the expansion of the economies of all countries." (66) In the Fourth Session of the Working Group, the above cited wording, which singles out LDCs for particular attention, evolved and was incorporated into the draft presented to the Second Committee. (67) The EEC had been willing to accept the earlier more balanced version, and, together with other developed countries (except for the Netherlands), reintroduced that language as a proposed amendment which read:

Determined to promote collective economic security, with full respect for the sovereign equality of each State and through the cooperation of each State, in order to provide a favourable environment for all countries to pursue their development and well-being... (68)

The amendment was rejected 94-14-14. (69) In the final vote in the Second Committee, three negative votes and seven abstentions were recorded on this paragraph. (70) Perhaps in 1974, at the height of the raw materials shortage scare, developed countries dependent on primary products imports were not ready to accept as part of an economic charter a provision which did not promote equal economic security for all.

Preambular paragraphs eight through twelve were noncontroversial general statements relating to cooperation among states; ensuring appropriate conditions for the conduct of normal economic relations among states; strengthening of instruments of international economic cooperation; the need to develop a system of international economic relations; the responsibility for development resting primarily on each country, while recognizing that concomitant and effective international cooperation is an essential factor for full achievement of development goals; and the urgent need to evolve a substantially improved system of international economic relations.

The final Preambular paragraph, thirteen in the original draft before the Second Committee, had read that the General Assembly:

> Solemnly adopts the present Charter of Economic Rights and Duties of States as a first step in the codification and pregressive development of this subject.... (71)

The developed countries offered an amendment to excise the phrase "as a first step in the codification and progressive development of this subject." (72) The amendment was defeated, (73) but prior to the final vote on the revised draft Charter, Mexico introduced an oral revision on behalf of the Group of 77 striking the phrase, and this version was adopted. (74)

In conclusion, the Preamble stresses equity, sovereign equality, and interdependence, and calls for a just and equitable economic and social order to be brought about through unspecified structural changes. There was a sense of universal approval on this part of the Charter. (75) However, carrying this consensus forward to translate equity and interdependence into concrete rights and duties in subsequent chapters of the Charter would prove far more difficult.

Chapter I: Fundamentals of International Economic Relations

Chapter I contains a list of fifteen fundamentals of international economic relations which "shall" govern economic as well as political and other relations among States, as follows:

(a) Sovereignty, territorial integrity, and political independence of States

(b) Sovereign equality of all States

(c) Nonaggression

(d) Nonintervention

(e) Mutual and equitable benefit

(f) Peaceful coexistence

(g) Equal rights and self-determination of peoples

(h) Peaceful settlement of disputes

(i) Remedying of injustices which have been brought about by force and which deprive a nation of the natural means necessary for its development;

(j) Fulfillment in good faith of international obligations

(k) Respect for human rights and fundamental freedoms

(l) No attempt to seek hegemony and spheres of influence

(m) Promotion of international social justice

(n) International cooperation for development

(o) Free access to and from the sea by landlocked countries within the framework of the above principles

Although there was some disagreement over the use of the mandatory "shall," most of the principles have a long history, tend to be repeated often, and form a part of accepted international customary law. (76) The main areas of controversy related to provisions (f), (i), and (o).

While the LDCs had stressed points (a) and (c) through (f) continuously since the Afro-Asian Bandung Conference in 1955, when they were known as the Panchsheel or five principles, (77) "peaceful coexistence" (f) had never been universally accepted. Although seemingly innocent, the concept has been interpreted by the Soviet Union as permitting support for national revolutionary movements, and this has resulted in its rejection by many governments. (78) "Peaceful coexistence" did not appear in any of the three preliminary outlines of the Charter submitted by the Asian, African, and Latin American LDC blocs, nor even in their later collective effort. (79) It initially appeared in the draft outline produced during the First Session of the Working Group, at which time the Dutch immediately suggested that it be deleted, and the French proposed to substitute it with the phrase "the duty of States to practice tolerance and live together in peace with one another as good neighbors." (80)   These alternatives were retained through all four Working Group Sessions, but the Group of 77 draft to the Second Committee used the Soviet expression. The developed countries offered an amendment to change the phrase to "peaceful cooperation" (81) but by the final vote in the Second Committee only five developed countries voted against the inclusion of "peaceful coexistence," while five others abstained and several (including Japan, Sweden, Canada, and the United States) voted in favor of it. (82)   Chinese-Soviet antagonism surfaced on this matter, with China and Albania opposing the Soviet principle on the grounds that it represented "a smokescreen... [for]...a superpower's pursuing the policies of aggression and expansion infringing upon the sovereignty of other countries, interfering in their internal affairs and contending for world hegemony with the other superpower." (83)

Provision (i) "Remedying of injustices which have been brought about by force and which deprive a nation of the natural means necessary for its normal development was sponsored by Egypt, Iraq, and the Soviet Union. Primarily directed against Israeli occupation of Arab land, it was, together with Article 16(2) on a similar subject, (84) among the more controversial provisions of the Charter. Eleven countries called for the deletion of (i) (85) and, although the amendment was defeated, (86) it obtained 16 supporting votes and 10 abstentions.

Provision (o) "Free access to and from the sea by landlocked countries within the framework of the above principles" aroused some disagreement among LDCs. (87) The general principle has received the support of the world community since UNCTAD I, when a series of eight principles related to this issue were adopted. (88)   However, many of the neighbors of landlocked countries have been less than eager about surrendering part of their territorial sovereignty to guarantee the right of transit.   India's response typified that of other coastal states with landlocked neighbors, arguing that the Charter was not the appropriate place to set forth the principle, and that access to the sea was not an absolute right but rather one which must be established by bilateral or multilateral accord.   India stated further that it was its understanding that the "fundamentals" in Chapter I were not elevated to the level of rights under international law, but that these provisions, including (o), were "simply one of several formulations of what is considered necessary to promote international economic cooperation." (89)   Other transit states voted for the principle as an "expression of solidarity" but agreed with India that it could best be achieved within the framework of bilateral or regional agreements. (90)   This provision was one of only two to be voted on in the General Assembly Plenary prior to final passage of the Charter. (91) More than half of the abstentions on this point were cast by transit states. (92)

Three other of the fundamental principles of Chapter I are deserving of mention, in that they were relatively new to international agreements: (1) No attempt to seek hegemony and spheres of influence; (m) Promotion of international social justice; and (n) International cooperation for development.   Provision (1) appeared for the first time in the Group of 77 draft introduced in the Second Committee. China had authored it and has used it in a number of bilateral accords; (93) it met with no opposition. Provision (m), introduced by Venezuela, was incorporated without dissension. (94)   The principle of "cooperation in accordance with the [U.N.] Charter" has appeared in international documents and was included in the draft outline of the Charter. (95)   At the Second Session of the Working Group, Mexico proposed that the language be changed to read "international cooperation for development" (n). (96) This reformulation was accepted, and, in the succeeding Sessions of the Working Group, all mention of the United Nations Charter was dropped from the Preamble. (97)

In summary, while there were some abstentions in the votes on Chapter I in relation to the mandatory "shall," "peaceful coexistence," "landlocked countries," and "the remedying of injustices," only the last mentioned provision received a substantial number of negative votes, i.e. sixteen. (98) Up to this point in the Charter, one could argue that, while there was no strong consensus among rich and poor countries, there did appear to be the possibility of their working out an agreed text. The apparently insurmountable problems would not arise until Chapter II of the Charter.

Chapter II: Economic Rights and Duties of States

This is the heart of the Charter where the general principles of Chapter I are applied to specific issues in 28 articles. Rather than treating Chapter II sequentially, interrelated articles have been brought together under the general categories of private foreign investment; transfer of technology; shared resources; international trade; international organizations; regional groupings; East/West economic relations; foreign aid; and miscellaneous matters.

Private Foreign Investment [Articles 2 and 16(2)]

Article 2. No set of issues generated more dissension than did those in Article 2 on private foreign investment (permanent sovereignty over natural resources, transnational corporations, nationalization, jurisdiction over foreign investment disputes and compensation). Most agree that consensus on these points would have made possible an overall consensus on the Charter. Due to its importance, Article 2 is discussed more fully below in Chapter 6. Here only the main issues are highlighted.

During the nineteenth century, foreign investors, working with the governments of capital exporting countries, established a series of rules and regulations which have guided foreign investment until the early 1960s. Economically dependent countries, such as those in Latin America, frequently either did not fully understand the implications of the agreements into which they entered or the rights they granted, or felt that they lacked power to bargain for better arrangements with foreign investors. (99) Citizens of colonies and political dependencies had little or no participation in the colonial powers' allocation of rights and privileges to foreign investors. With the end of colonialism, the former colonies entered into an informal coalition with other politically sovereign but economically dependent countries in seeking to change the "rules of the game" governing foreign investment. Of primary concern was the issue of sovereignty over natural resources. Many LDC delegations to the United Nations from the early 1950s on aimed:

> ...to secure an international recognition of their right to nationalize and re-establish effectively their sovereignty over the natural resources contained in their territories, regardless of the necessity or adequacy of compensation. On the other hand, the developed nations were willing to recognize this right only on the condition that the underdeveloped nations should abide by established rules of international law providing for the payments of adequate compensation... (100)

In 1962, after protracted debate, the General Assembly passed a resolution (101) on permanent sovereignty over natural wealth and resources which permitted nationalization of foreign investments "on grounds or reasons of public utility, security, or the national interests." Nationalization under this Resolution brought with it the duty to pay "appropriate compensation" in accordance with national rules and "in accordance with international law." In case of controversy relating to compensation, "national jurisdiction of the State taking such measures shall be exhausted." Preference was stated for "arbitration or international adjudication" on agreement by "sovereign states and other parties concerned." The Resolution received the overwhelming support of both LDCs and developed countries, except for the Soviet Union, the Eastern European socialist countries, and France.

In the years intervening between the 1962 Resolution and the drafting of the Charter, the LDC members of the United Nations, which now constituted a two-thirds majority, stepped up their efforts to coordinate policies on foreign investment within the framework of the newly formed Group of 77. Foreign investment increased rapidly and the international companies spread throughout the globe; as a group they were renamed "multinational corporations." (102) Complaints were raised about their pervasive power, and demands for regulation and control increased. In 1973 ECOSOC requested the United Nations Secretary General to appoint a:

> group of eminent persons... to study the role of multinational corporations and their impact on the process of development, especially that of the developing countries, and also their implications for international relations, to formulate conclusions which may possibly be used by governments in making their sovereign decisions regarding national policy in this respect, and to submit recommendations for appropriate international action. (103)

Hearings were held in New York and Geneva, at which leading personalities from governments, business, trade unions, special and public interest groups, and universities testified. Following these hearings, the Group of Eminent Persons issued a report (104) on ownership and control, financial flows and balance of payments, technology, employment and labor, consumer protection, competition and market structure, transfer pricing, taxation, and information disclosure.   The report suggested the creation of various institutions to monitor these problems and to propose specific reforms (i.e. both the Commission and the Center on Transnational Corporations, 1974). Similar investigations into the activities of multinational corporations were carried out by the United States Congress. (105)

Article 2 of the Charter makes fundamental changes in the 1962 General Assembly Resolution on Permanent Sovereignty as follows:

1. The coverage of permanent sovereignty is expanded from a nation's "natural wealth and resources" to all its "wealth, natural resources, and economic activities" [Article 2(1)] .

2. Foreign investment, capital and earnings, which were formerly governed by "the national legislation in force, and by international law," are now to be regulated "in accordance with [the host country's]laws and regulations and in conformity with national priorities and objectives" [Article 2(2)(a)].

3. Multinational corporations, not mentioned in the 1962 Resolution, are specifically referred to in Article 2(2)(b) of the Charter where they are renamed "transnational corporations" (TNCs). States have the right:

> to regulate and supervise the activities of transnational corporations within the[host country's] national jurisdiction and take measures to ensure that such activities comply with [the host country's] laws, rules and regulations and conform with [the host country's] economic and social policies.

The TNCs are specifically prohibited from intervening in the internal affairs of host states.

4. Nationalization, previously based on "grounds or reasons of public utility, security or the national interest," is now an unqualified right under Article 2(2)(c).

5. The 1962 Resolution read that, in the event of nationalization, "the owner shall be paid appropriate compensation in accordance with the rules in force in the state taking such measures... and in accordance with international law." In 1962 the United States negotiator had argued that the words "international law" meant that in the event of nationalization, compensation would be "prompt, adequate, and effective," (106) although such language was not in the Resolution. Article 2(2)(c) of the Charter removed any doubts on this count by providing that "appropriate compensation should be paid by the state adopting such measures taking into account its relevant laws and regulations and all circumstances that the state considers pertinent." Thus the mandatory "shall" has been replaced by "should," all reference to international law is excluded, and the expropriating state determines which circumstances are pertinent.

6. On the subject of jurisdiction over compensation disputes, the 1962 Resolution provided that:

> the national jurisdiction of the State taking such measures shall be exhausted. However, upon agreement by sovereign states and other parties concerned settlement of the dispute should be made through arbitration or international adjudication.

Article 2(2)(c) of the Charter states instead that:

> In any case where the question of compensation gives rise to a controversy, it shall be settled under the domestic law of the nationalizing state and by its tribunals unless it is freely and mutually agreed by all states concerned that other peaceful means be sought on the basis of sovereign equality of states and in accordance with the free choice of means.

The Charter provision modifies the 1962 Resolution in two important respects. First there is a shift in emphasis: instead of exhausting local remedies and then proceeding to arbitration and international adjudication, cases are to be decided nationally (in the host country) or possibly by other peaceful means. Secondly, any agreement to utilize other peaceful means must be between "states concerned" rather than "upon agreement by sovereign states and other parties" (emphasis added), thus excluding private companies as parties to such agreements.

7. There was strong pressure from the developed countries to include in Article 2 the following language from the 1962 Resolution: "foreign investment agreements freely entered into by or between sovereign states shall be observed in good faith." The LDCs refused, although they did agree to include the principle "fulfillment in good faith of international obligations" in Chapter I of the Charter, without reference to foreign investment. LDCs construe the phrase "international obligations" to apply only to agreements between states, thereby excluding agreements between governments and foreign investors.

To summarize, there has been an expansion of the concept of permanent sovereignty; nationalization is now an unqalified right; transnational corporations have become a special category of institutions subject to particular rules; the standards for compensation are determined by national laws based upon what the nationalizing state considers pertinent; and disputes over compensation are to be decided by national tribunals utilizing national laws, unless states agree on other peaceful means.

Article 16(2). The only other Article concerned with private foreign investment is Article 16(2), which reads:

No State has the right to promote or encourage investments that may constitute an obstacle to the liberation of a territory occupied by force.

This provision was introduced late in the negotiations. Like provision (i) under Chapter I of the Charter, (107) its primary purpose was to prohibit investments in Israeli-occupied sections of Arab countries, although it could have much wider application to, inter alia, South Africa, Namibia, and Rhodesia. In the Second Committee, 12 developed countries proposed an amendment to delete Article 16(2) (108); the amendment was rejected, receiving only 17 affirmative votes and eight abstentions. (109)

Transfer of Technology (Article 13)

An extremely complex subject, the transfer of technology is covered by the very general Article 13, which received unanimous support only because of its cautious and non-controversial approach. Actually, transfer of technology will be one of the key international issues over the coming years. The LDCs know that they need modern technology if they are to increase their rate of development, but since they will be unable to pay market prices, they would like special arrangements to provide them with technology at a lower cost.

Early international discussions on development paid little attention to the issue of technology transfer, which was usually subsumed under "technical assistance" as a part of foreign assistance. This approach is exemplified by Special Principle Ten adopted at UNCTAD I, which met with no abstentions or opposition. At UNCTAD II, the issue was on the agenda, but no resolution was adopted. Paragraph 62 of the International Development Strategy for the Second United Nations Development Decade (1970) emphasizes cooperation between research centers. According to the Secretary General of UNCTAD, UNCTAD III represented the "decisive breakthrough" on the subject. (110) The Sixth and Seventh Special Sessions of the United Nations General Assembly both placed importance on transfer of technology, with the Seventh calling for a United Nations Conference on Science and Technology for Development. (111) This Conference, now scheduled for 1979, is being coordinated by the United Nations Committee on Science and Technology for Development with inputs from UNCTAD. A key demand on the part of the developing countries was for a code of conduct on the transfer of technology. The developed countries want any code on the subject to be purely voluntary in nature, whereas some LDCs would like it to be legally binding. Developed countries are unwilling to consider a legally binding code partly because, in most of them, technology is privately owned and its transfer on any concessional basis raises very real practical problems. The battle lines have been drawn but the struggle has not yet begun in earnest. By the time that UNCTAD IV met in 1976 in Nairobi, a draft code of conduct for the transfer of technology was under preparation. (112)

Although Article 13 of the Charter was unanimously approved in the Second Committee, negotiating positions were initially far apart. On the one hand, China called for free or low-cost transfer, and on the other, a group of developed countries put forward language which simply stated that the right to benefit from advances in science and technology "should not be curtailed." (113) Wording from a draft proposed by Yugoslavia served as the basis for negotiations within the Second and Third Sessions of the Working Group, leading to agreed wording in the Fourth. (114)

Paragraph (1) of Article 13 provides that:

Every State has the right to benefit from the advances and developments in science and technology for the acceleration of its economic and social development.

The right to benefit from science and technology is qualified by having as its objective economic and social development, unlike an earlier LDC proposed test which had provided that the right was absolute.

Paragraph (2) of Article 13 provides that:

All States should promote international scientific and technological co-operation and the transfer of technology, with proper regard for all legitimate interests including, inter alia, the rights and duties of holders, suppliers and recipients of technology. In particular, all States should facilitate the access of developing countries to the achievements of modern science and technology, the transfer of technology and the creation of indigenous technology for the benefit of the developing countries in forms and in accordance with procedures which are suited to their economies and their needs.

This formulation cites the responsibility of "all states," whereas the Yugoslav text had placed the burden on developed states to provide LDCs with technological advancements on concessional terms, had made specific reference to the rights and duties of holders and suppliers of technology, as well as to the recipients, and had included the duty to create "technologies adapted to the needs and realities of [developing countries]." (115)

Paragraph (3) incorporates the concept of improving scientific and technological infrastructure, which had appeared in Resolution 39(III) of UNCTAD III, (116) but which had surprisingly been absent from all proposed drafts put forward prior to the Fourth Session of the Working Group.

Accordingly, developed countries should cooperate with the developing countries in the establishment, strengthening and development of their scientific and technological infrastructures and their scientific research and technological activities so as to help to expand and transform the economies of developing countries.

Paragraph (4) of Article 13 touches directly on the sensitive issue of implementation of transfer of technology.

All States should cooperate in exploring with a view to evolving further internationally accepted guidelines or regulations for the transfer of technology taking fully into account the interests of developing countries.

Although the developed countries had accepted Resolution 39(III) which provided for a "study of the possible bases for new international legislation" to regulate technology transfer, (117) they were still generally opposed to proceeding with negotiations on a binding code of conduct.

Shared Resources (Article 3)

Ironically, Article 2, on which the developing world found the most cohesion, is followed by Article 3, also on natural resources, which provoked more disagreement among LDCs than did any other article of the Charter. This short article, which was introduced by Argentina, reads:

In the exploitation of natural resources shared by two or more countries, each State must cooperate on the basis of a system of information and prior consultations in order to achieve optimum use of such resources without causing damage to the legitimate interest of others.

International rivers, fish and other maritime resources, and land based petroleum are examples of natural resources which move between nations and whose exploitation has strong implications for neighboring users. (118)

Some 39 countries abstained or voted against Article 3 in either the Second Committee or the Plenary of the General Assembly, where it was one of only two articles to be voted on separately. (119) Most of those opposing it argued that Article 3 would impinge on a state's permanent sovereignty over its natural resources. For example, Brazil saw in the phrase "shared resources" a lack of clarity leading to conflicts between states over resources which were either exclusively within the jurisdiction of a state or were shared. Paraguay was troubled with the words "prior consultation," arguing that they could be construed to mean that a "prior agreement" was necessary before exploitation of a resource could begin. Brazil, discussing the same words, argued that for Argentinian jurists the words meant that exploitation could not be undertaken while views were still being exchanged, a position which limited state sovereignty. Another phrase in Article 3 which posed difficulties was "to achieve optimum use of such resources without causing damage to the legitimate interests of others." "Optimization," according to the Brazilian delegate, "is often associated with the obligation of studying the exploitation of the natural resources in its totality... so as to make [development projects] more favourable to the whole, even at the sacrifice of the national convenience of any of them." Brazil recognized that the resource exploiting state was obliged not to cause significant damage to third parties "and was responsible for such damages." This did not, however, give the neighboring state a veto over specific development projects. Argentina, the initiator of the resolution, had already stated that the neighbor did not have a veto. (120)

Opposition to Article 3 was not limited to Latin American states. Ethiopia, Afghanistan, Turkey, China, Tanzania, and Australia expressed either outright opposition or significant reservations about the article. Australia, for example, had reservations about the "apparent inflexibility in providing information and prior consultations on the sharing of the natural resources." (121) The East European states argued for the right to choose any form of cooperation in the joint exploration of shared natural resources, other than the system of information and prior consultation. (122) Seven abstaining Western European countries failed to explain their objections. (123)

International Trade

The Charter could, in some respects, be considered primarily a trade charter. Approximately one-half of the articles in Chapter II deal directly or indirectly with some aspect of trade, including producer associations, commodity agreements, price adjustments in relation to terms of trade, invisibles, general system of preferences, and trade with Socialist countries. The bias is natural in a Charter on International Economic Rights and Duties of States, and it reflects the predominant interest of LDCs, since the establishment of UNCTAD in 1964, in trade rather than aid as a source of foreign capital. (124) About 80 percent of foreign exchange flows into LDCs arise from trade, not aid. Also, the declining real volume of aid during the 1970s has underscored the fact that aid is far from automatic. Finally, aid, which often has had political and other conditions attached to it, is seen as engendering dependency, whereas trade tends to involve more of an independent indigenous effort to mobilize resources, and thus is more consistent with the Third World's goal of generating self-reliant growth.

A. Trade expansion and liberalization (Articles 14, 18 and 19).

Article 14. The system of world trade reflected in the Charter is ambiguous. On the one hand, the liberal free trade order envisaged in the post-World War II Bretton Woods agreements comes out clearly: Article 14 calls for the promotion, expansion, and liberalization of world trade by the "progressive dismantling of obstacles to trade and the improvement of the international framework for the conduct of world trade..." On the other hand, the Charter suggests that, at this stage of history, LDCs cannot rely exclusively on the market to improve their revenues from trade (i.e., the liberal philosophy of equality for all is recognized as being nothing more than the powerful and the weak competing under the same rules). Accordingly, Article 14 also emphasizes the special needs of LDCs:

... States shall take measures aimed at securing additional benefits for the international trade of developing countries so as to achieve a substantial increase in their foreign exchange earnings, the diversification of their exports, the acceleration of the rate of growth of their trade, taking into account their development needs, an improvement in the possibilities for these countries to participate in the expansion of world trade and a balance more favourable to developing countries in the sharing of the advantages resulting from this expansion, through in the largest possible measure, a substantial improvement in the conditions of access for the products of interest to the developing countries and, wherever appropriate, measures designed to attain stable, equitable and remunerative prices for primary products.

Two developed countries suggested that the phrase," [E]quitable opportunities for all in the conduct of world trade," be added to Article 14, (125) but this proposal was not accepted. (126)

Article 18. Historically many colonial powers accepted the principle of preferential treatment for their dependencies. They have, however, been cautious in extending the same privileges across the board to all LDCs. As early as 1958, in the Haberler Report on Trends in International Trade, (127) the developed countries made special reference to the need for expansion of LDC trade. These ideas eventually led, in 1966, to the adoption of Part IV of GATT, in which three new articles were added to the text of the Agreement. They dealt with the need for improved market access for all LDC products; undertakings by developed contracting parties to refrain from increasing barriers to products of particular export interest to LDCs; high priority to be given to reduction of existing barriers to trade in such products; various forms of joint action to promote, through trade, the development of LDC contracting parties; and the establishment of an international trade center in Geneva to provide trade information, market research facilities, and technical assistance in training of trade policy officials from LDCs. (128)

In the midst of these events, the LDCs were pursuing their own approach to the problem. They have been pressing for preferential tariff schedules for their exports at least since 1964, when UNCTAD I adopted General Principle Eight, stating that developed countries should not only give better than most-favored-nation (MFN) treatment (i.e., should discriminate in favor of LDCs), but also should not require any reciprocal concessions from LDCs. Both discrimination and nonreciprocity conflicted with the fundamental principles of GATT, (129) and, therefore, all the capitalist developed countries abstained or voted against General Principle Eight. In the 1967 Charter of Algiers, 71 LDCs called on developed countries to put into effect a general system of preferences (GSP). (130) In late 1967, the OECD sketched out en gros a GSP for manufactures and semi-manufactures; however, little was accomplished the following year at UNCTAD II, as developed and less developed countries both fought over the coverage (products and countries) and longevity of the GSP. Finally, in 1970, UNCTAD's Special Committee on Preferences agreed on the general outline of a system; but the OECD countries were still unable to agree among themselves on the type of GSP they wanted, with the result that a series of different systems were individually adopted. The Eastern European countries voiced support for a general system of preferences in 1970, but since the pricing policies of Socialist countries differ fundamentally from those in use in market economies, it is generally felt that such oral support for trade concessions has little impact.

Despite the fact that GSPs are now in effect in all major developed countries, they are generally recognized as less than optimal. The nondiscrimination clause in GATT was waived for a period of only ten years, although many LDCs will not have significant manufacturing capability before then. Almost all GSPs have special categories of "sensitive" products which are excluded from the system - often those items from whose export the LDC could most benefit - and quantitative restrictions exist in many of the schemes. (131)

Article 18 provides that:

Developed countries should extend, improve and enlarge the system of generalized nonreciprocal and nondiscriminatory tariff preferences to the developing countries... [and consider] ... the adoption of other differential measures, in areas where this is feasible and appropriate and in ways which will provide special and more favorable treatment, in order to meet trade and development needs of the developing countries... [and] endeavor to avoid measures having a negative effect on the development of the national economies of the developing countries, as promoted by generalized tariff preferences and other generally agreed differential measures in their favour. (emphasis added)

This nonmandatory language proved acceptable to the developed countries and the article was adopted unanimously. (132)   Presumably the "other differential measures" include reductions of nontariff barriers (i.e., rules of origin, health or safety standards, labeling requirements, customs formalities, and administrative procedures). Import quotas are the most important type of nontariff barrier, and although illegal under GATT, "voluntary" restrictions on imports have come into increasing use to protect, for example, domestic agriculture and textiles. In fact, new quotas are often aimed against LDCs because they cannot retaliate, whereas similar quotas if applied to developed countries would be reciprocated in kind. (133)

Article 19. In the Fourth Session of the Working Group, LDCs went a step further to universalize the concept of preferences by proposing the following language in Article 19:

With a view to accelerating the economic growth of developing countries and bridging the economic gap between developed and developing countries, developed countries should grant generalized preferential, nonreciprocal and nondiscriminatory treatment to developing countries in all fields of international economic cooperation wherever feasible. (134) (emphasis added)

The Group of 77, hoping to achieve consensus prior to the meeting of the Second Committee, modified the above version of Article 19, attenuating the force of "all fields" to "those fields... where it may be feasible." This did not, however, sway the developed countries, 15 of whom proposed the deletion of Article 19; (135) the amendment to delete was rejected 102-17-5 and Article

19 was approved with the Group of 77 modified language. (136)

There was, in fact, considerable uncertainty as to the purport of Article 19.   Greece interpreted it to include technology cooperation agreements and development loan programs. (137)   Others construed it to mean the selling of patent rights at preferential rates. (138) Italy suggested that nondiscriminatory treatment for LDCs would prohibit a developing country in very grave circumstances from receiving special assistance. (139) Denmark, the United Kingdom, and the United States all declared it to be too imprecise, or too general and broad in scope. (140)

B. Trade in commodities (Articles 5, 6 and 28).

Primary commodities account for 80 percent of total export earnings of the developing countries, most of which export only one, two, or perhaps three such products in any substantial quantities. (141)   In the commodity area, LDCs have two basic goals: the elimination of wide price fluctuations and the arrest of any further deterioration in the terms of trade. Over the years, they have supported various institutional devices to achieve these goals, including, inter alia, international commodity agreements, (142) producer associations, (143) supplementary financing, (144) compensatory financing, (145) and indexation. (146)   Before analyzing the relevant Charter articles, it would be useful to place these institutional devices in some historical perspective and to differentiate them conceptually.

Both prior to and after World War II various schemes were advocated to reduce price fluctuations in commodities. In 1942, John Maynard Keynes set the problem in these terms:

> The extent of the evil to be remedied can scarcely be exaggerated, though it is not always appreciated. A study of the violence of individual price fluctuations and the inability of an unregulated competitive system to avoid them is given in an appendix. It is thereshown that for the four commodities - rubber, cotton, wheat and lead - which are fairly representative of raw materials marketed in competitive conditions, the average annual price range over the decade before 1938 was 67 percent. An orderly program of output, either of the raw materials themselves or of their manufactured products, is not possible in such conditions. (147)

In 1951 (148) and 1954 (149) United Nations studies concluded that artificial price maintenance of commodities would be unwise. The first proposed that "rather than direct action on prices, a series of measures in the field of commodity arrangements, international investment, and foreign exchange reserves would improve international economic management." The second study concluded that it would be "preferable in general that prices should be left free to perform their function of allocating productive resources and that 'unfairness' should be compensated by direct income transfers" either through IMF loans or by way of automatic compensation schemes involving unconditional transfers between nations on a grant basis. The emphasis has been on the short-run stabilization of prices. The short-run stabilization idea became institutionalized in the IMF's compensatory financing scheme. (150) There is, however, little acceptance by either LDCs, or indeed by producers generally, that the latter scheme can by itself contribute even to short-run stabilization (e.g., in the event of collusive bidding or other circumstances causing a long-term depressive effect on prices).

There is no standard definition for either international commodity agreements or producer associations. The former are usually agreements between producers and consumers to bring about price stabilization. They have taken three forms: buffer stock schemes, where a scheme manager buys and stores the commodity when prices are below a floor price level and sells when they are above a price ceiling (e.g., the International Tin Agreement); long-term contracts, where the buyer prevents widespread fluctuations through contractual provisions (e.g., United States steel companies' long-term agreements to purchase iron ore from consortia in which they participate); and quota agreements, which specify export quotas for producers in order to minimize price fluctuations (e.g., the International Coffee Agreement).

Supplementary financing was an abortive proposal to provide financial resources to LDCs under specified conditions, in cases of sudden unforeseen falls in export income. Compensatory financing, on the other hand, is an operative IMF facility to help countries finance deficits arising out of short-term export shortfalls attributable to circumstances beyond the member's control and resulting in balance-of-payments difficulties.

Indexation was brought forth as a device by the developing countries to arrest any further deterioration of the terms of trade of LDCs by establishing and maintaining an index of import and export prices through market intervention. When a similar result is obtained without affecting the terms of trade - by a transfer of resources to fill the gap between the market and the indexed price - the process is called indirect indexation.

The United States, reflecting the position of most developed countries, has been wary of any scheme which tampers with the price mechanism. At a United States Congressional hearing on international commodity policy, an Assistant Secretary of the Treasury had this to say:

> I think that central to the discussion of international commodity policy is an appreciation of the challenge that the developing countries have now put to the industrial world. They have called for a basic redistribution of wealth through increasing the prices of raw materials and protecting those higher prices against increases in the price of other goods. This redistribution can be accomplished either through unilateral producer cartel action, as we have seen in the oil area, or by agreement among producers and consumers to fix prices and index them.

> ... joint efforts between consumers and producers are the appropriate means of coping with specific commodity problems. Such efforts should be aimed at improving and strengthening the market oriented system. And we must resist any generalized system of commodity agreements aimed at fixing prices. (151)

At the same hearing, Edward Fried, a Senior Fellow of the Brookings Institution, voiced a different viewpoint:

The danger that the commodity trade will be organized into a host of OPEC-like cartels is wildly overdrawn. With few if any exceptions, the prospects that producer cartels would be durable are small. Furthermore, if, contrary to my expectations, the producers of coffee, cocoa, bananas, or even tin and manganese should be able by themselves to sustain prices above the long-term competitive level, I would consider this one way of transferring limited amounts of resources to countries which probably need them. Certainly it would not cause me to lose any sleep over the consequences to the United States or the world economy. (152)

The three articles of the Charter which concern themselves with these issues each brought forth strong arguments and disagreements: Article 5 (producer associations), Article 6 (international commodity agreements), and Article 28 (price adjustments related to the terms of trade - popularly referred to as indexation).

Article 5. Article 5 provides support for state member (i.e., public) producer associations:

All states have the right to associate in organizations of primary commodity producers in order to develop their national economies to achieve stable financing for their development, and in pursuance of their aims assisting in the promotion of sustained growth of the world economy, in particular accelerating the development of developing countries. Correspondingly all states have the duty to respect that right by refraining from applying economic and political measures that would limit it.

Almost as long as man has been involved in commerce there have been varied forms of producer associations. Many have been little more than information clearing houses, while others have tended to be cartels, controlling prices and production. Although most have been managed by private parties, state cartels have not been unknown. Currently there are state producer associations for oil, copper, bauxite, iron ore, sulphur, uranium, mercury, and phosphate. (153) In addition, a banana exporters association has recently been formed. (154) (Coffee, cocoa and tin are covered by international commodity agreements, which are discussed under Article 6 below.) Some of the producer associations, such as those for oil and copper, have been in existence since 1960 and 1965, respectively. Others, like iron ore, came into existence only very recently. The goals of each association vary, but generally speaking they include both limiting price fluctuations and (at least implicitly) raising the price levels for the exported commodities. Today the best known state producer association is the Organization of Petroleum Exporting Countries (OPEC); OPEC's evolution is illustrative of one way in which producer associations may develop. (155)

In 1959, and again in 1960, the major oil companies cut the posted price (156) for crude oil. The oil-producing nations found their tax revenues seriously affected, which in turn reduced the potential foreign exchange available for investment. Following the second cut, five major oil-producing nations founded OPEC as an intergovernmental, interregional organization aimed at stabilizing prices by the regulation or production through mutual

consultation and exchange of information. With the passage of time, tax
issues (i.e., the expensing of royalties (157) and establishment of a tax rate
based on posted rather than sales prices) assumed more importance. In recent
years, negotiated participation of the producer governments in ventures with
the private companies, the development of national oil companies, nationalization, service contracts, and coordinated pricing policies have emerged as
the major issues. OPEC decisions are voluntary, with members acting
collectively so long as they find it advantageous to do so. (158) OPEC has had
a marked success in raising the revenues for member countries; in increasing
members' knowledge about exploration, exploitation, transport and marketing
of oil; and in enabling members for the first time to become the owners of
their oil facilities. Consuming countries have reacted against OPEC
collectively, by forming the International Energy Agency, (159) and, in the
case of the United States, by excluding OPEC members from the GSP
instituted under the 1974 United States Trade Act. (160)

Whether or not other producer associations will prove as successful as
OPEC depends on a number of variables, some of which have been succinctly
outlined by one authority in the field:

> In international trade, collusion is difficult. The success of any attempt
> to control the world market price will depend on how big the association's
> combined share of the market is, how easily nonmembers and producers of
> substitutes can increase their production, and how competitive the world
> market structure is. Each member's financial position, the political and
> economic orientations of the participating countries, and the cohesiveness
> and discipline of the members in carrying out joint policies are also
> important factors. (161)

Nevertheless, one can expect that similar groups will be founded; the
underlying reasons were perceptively observed by two World Bank economists
as follows:

> A sense of disappointment at their overall treatment by the industrial
> countries is almost universal among developing countries. For the
> producers of minerals, there is moreover (as for oil) the keen sense that
> their minerals are nonrenewable, an asset that should produce the greatest
> possible return and if possible have its useful life stretched out. Hence, it
> is only natural that producers should seek to change a situation in which,
> by and large, the sellers of nonfuel minerals are competing, diffuse, and
> unorganized in the face of relatively few and well-organized buyers on
> behalf of the consuming countries. (162)

When the Second Committee convened to discuss Article 5, only one year
had passed since the dramatic rise in oil prices and the OAPEC oil embargo.
During this period, the public was assaulted by a large number of publications
on producer associations, which were extolled, (163) attacked, (164) reviewed
historically, (165) considered inevitable, (166) or dismissed as limited in their
effect. (167) It should be noted that under Article 5 only "states" are
specified as having the right to form producer associations, leaving open the
quesiton of private groupings. The Article also fails to define "primary

commodity producers," nor is it instructive as to the nature of the organizations.

It was predictable that the developed countries would have little enthusiasm for a series of institutions modeled after OPEC. They offered an amendment to delete Article 5, (168) but it received only 15 affirmative votes and eight abstentions, and failed. (169) During the post-mortem when the votes were explained, opponents generally argued that Article 5 failed to take into account the interests of both producers and consumers. (170) The Netherlands would have supported Article 5 if the last sentence had been deleted. (171) Sweden noted for the record that its support for Article 5 "did not necessarily imply that [its] government supported all the measures which might be taken by associations of the kind referred to in Article 5." (172)

Article 6. A parallel approach to producer associations is that of the international commodity agreements. Much discussion and effort have gone into the examination of these agreements, as described below by one United States authority on the subject:

> The true issue in the commodity agreement debate, it seems to me, is not whether the United States should join international commodity agreements - for this converts the issue into an ideological debate over the efficacy of free markets - but what kind of commodity agreements the United States should be prepared to join. There are at least two sides to a description of an "ideal" commodity agreement system. The first question is that of the appropriate operating technique for regulation of the commodity market in question - export quotas, buffer stocks, or multilateral contracts. This is just one set of issues you have to deal with. The correct answer to this question will depend largely on the type of product that is involved. Bananas, for example, spoil rapidly, and hence would be less appropriate for a buffer stock arrangement than, for example, a metal such as tin. The more difficult question is the structure of the agreement once the technique for regulating the market has been selected. A viable agreement is a dynamic form of international organization that must possess certain systemic attributes in order to be successful, including the following:
>
> (a) a flexible market reallocation system;
>
> (b) flexible pricing arrangements;
>
> (c) a sound enforcement system; and
>
> (d) a program for structural reform of the market involved. (173)

To some extent, international commodity agreements have their counterparts in the protective arrangements which many countries have applied over the years towards their domestic agricultural sectors. Three of the most well-known commodity agreements have included the buffer stock International Tin Agreement; (174) the quota-type International Coffee Agreement discussed below; and the International Cocoa Agreement, which combines elements of the buffer stock and quota systems. (175) Although the high prices of coffee, tin, and cocoa have made all three Agreements of limited importance for the present, it is likely that they will assume more significance once prices begin to follow traditional cyclical patterns and decline again.

The first International Coffee Agreement came into force in 1963, (176) in response to a situation of widely fluctuating supplies and prices. Its membership was comprised of virtually all the world's key coffee producers and consumers. The market was to determine the price, but quotas would be adjusted to influence that price. Although most participants were willing to accept the principle of such a quota-type agreement, they found it difficult to agree on either the overall quota or each exporting country's relative share of that quota. Eventually separate quotas were established for four different qualities of coffee. Other major issues which had to be faced included new markets; non-quota countries; policing of the quotas through certificates of origin; and nontariff obstacles of importing countries including quantitative restrictions, internal taxes and trade preferences (both the sterling area and the franc zone had preferential arrangements at the time). An interesting system of voting evolved, under which exporters and importers voted separately, and countries had weighted votes in proportion to their relative share in exports and imports. This was very much the kind of voting arrangement which the EEC and the United States had in mind when proposing their amendment to Article 6 of the Charter. (177)

The Agreement was renewed in 1968 for another five years. As the time for a second renewal approached, producers and consumers failed to agree on price objectives and export quotas, thus freeing each exporting country to ship as much coffee as it wished during the last nine months of the Agreement. Importing countries wanted to stem the tide of increasing coffee prices; they were prepared to accept a floor price, but if prices remained at the rollback price (at the time, a price below the prevailing market rate but above the floor price) or rose, they wanted the quota system to be abolished. (178) The principal confrontation was between Brazil and Colombia on the one hand, and the United States, United Kingdom, and West Germany on the other. It was not until 1975 that a new Agreement was finally signed, (179) under which price-supporting export quotas would be removed "every time a crop failure or other production crisis creates a shortage and causes prices to increase." (180) The theory behind this was that once quotas were lifted, increased competition would lower prices, and that quotas would be reinstituted once prices fell again to a specified level. In 1976, following a major Brazilian frost, (181) prices for coffee began to skyrocket. Within one year, the spot price for Brazilian coffee in New York had tripled, and there was no sign of a reversal in the price trend in the near future. The Brazilian frost, together with the switching from coffee to other better earning crops, all contributed to a rapid increase in prices. At this stage speculators entered the market and demand for the already short supplies soared further. It is presently estimated that, barring unforeseen circumstances, coffee production will not return to normal until 1979-80, (182) when newly planted coffee trees in Brazil begin to produce.

There was originally no mention of international commodity agreements in the draft of the Charter presented to the Second Committee, which read:

It is the duty of states to contribute to the development of international trade of goods particularly by means of arrangements where appropriate and taking into account the interests of producers and consumers. All states share the responsibility to promote the regular flow and access of all commercial goods traded at stable, remunerative and equitable prices, thus contributing to the equitable development of the world economy, taking into account, in particular, the interests of developing countries. (183)

Ten developed countries proposed the following amendment:

All states shall be prepared to study and negotiate as appropriate worldwide commodity agreements on a case by case basis, which should cover as many producers and consumers as possible and a substantial part of the trade involved. All states should endeavor to promote the regular flow of raw material supplies, including agricultural and industrial raw material supplies having regard to the particular economic circumstances of individual countries, at stable, remunerative and equitable prices, thus contributing to the development of the world economy while taking into account, in particular, the interests of developing countries. (184)

The amendment would have changed the ambiguous "by means of arrangements" into "worldwide commodity agreements" to be studied and negotiated "as appropriate... on a case by case basis." The amendment goes beyond the draft Charter's "taking into account the interests of producers and consumers," by stating that the agreements "should cover as many producers and consumers as possible and a substantial part of the trade involved." Turning to the coverage of Article 6, the draft Charter spoke in terms of "all commercial goods traded" while the amendment limited the goods to "raw material supplies, including agricultural and industrial raw material supplies." Both versions agreed that prices should be "stable, remunerative and equitable." The amendment received only 17 affirmative votes and 10 abstentions, and failed. (185) However, prior to the final vote in the Second Committee, Mexico offered the following amendment on behalf of the Group of 77:

It is the duty of states to contribute to the development of international trade of goods particularly by means of arrangements and by the conclusion of long-term multilateral commodity agreements, where appropriate, and taking into account the interests of producers and consumers. All states share the responsibility to promote the regular flow and access of all commercial goods traded at stable, remunerative and equitable prices, thus contributing to the equitable development of the world economy, taking into account, in particular, the interests of developing countries. (186)

This amendment, which became the final text, incorporated only the concept of commodity agreements from the earlier developed country amendment. Eight of the 10 developed countries which had offered the defeated amendment continued to oppose the new version of Article 6, and the other two countries abstained. (187) The Group of 77 was attempting to preserve its options by maintaining the all-encompassing word "arrangements" in addition to commodity agreements. The omission of the reference to countries having a "substantial part of the trade" could prove significant if any attempt were made to initiate new commodity agreements. The same point can be made in relation to "interests of producers and consumers" rather than "as many producers and consumers as possible."

France, speaking after the passage of the amended Article, explained the dissatisfaction of the EEC:

> With regard to Article 6, in view of the members of the EEC, its main purpose should be to emphasize the interdependence of all States in the promotion of a regular flow of trade in raw materials. Case-by-case commodity agreements would be a useful method of achieving that objective in appropriate cases. What had prevented most of them from voting in favour of Article 6 as it stood... was the fact, in their view, the wording used seriously distorted the basic idea. (188)

The real point at issue was that, from the outset, the EEC (and to a lesser extent Japan) wanted something written into Article 6 which would oblige producers of raw materials to ensure supply. This issue was not so much one dividing developed and developing countries, but rather one that divided producers and consumers. As long as the EEC and Japan (to name but two) continued to maintain, and insist on, the right to apply barriers to access for exports, notably of agricultural products of interest to Australia and Canada (even when these barriers were in contravention of GATT), the latter were unwilling to give any assurances in the form of supply commitments. The EEC and Japan, for their part, were prepared to include something in Article 6 to balance the supply commitment, but the debate at the end really turned on whether or not the language would refer specifically to a balancing obligation to guarantee access for agricultural products. When that was not acceptable, Australia simply refused to accept any supply commitment. Hence, the final text (and indeed the final sentence) of Article 6 represented an attempt to formulate language not compromising to the position of any of these countries.

Article 28. Article 28 was known as the "indexation" Article, for it related to "pricing through a formula whereby the price of a product is increased in proportion to the increase in price of some market basket of other products" (189) as follows:

> All States have the duty to cooperate in achieving adjustments in the prices of exports of developing countries in relation to prices of their imports so as to promote just and equitable terms of trade for them in a manner which is remunerative for producers and equitable for producers and consumers.

Although various forms of indexation are used by many developed country members of the United Nations within their domestic economies in the form of "escalation" clauses in building and wage contracts, or as "parity" prices for agricultural goods, (190) they objected strongly to inclusion of such a device in the Charter. Some of the technical objections cited were difficulties in agreeing on a representative base period, the proper composition of a basket of goods against which to index the commodity, qualitative changes in manufactured goods, productivity changes, and differences in grades of commodities.

UNCTAD, dominated numerically by LDCs, had expressed an interest in indexation from its first session in 1964. (191) It was not until 1973, however, that any specific action was taken on the problem. In December 1973, a General Assembly resolution requested the Secretary General of UNCTAD:

> ... to prepare, after consultation with the President of the International Bank for Reconstruction and Development, a comprehensive study on the indexation of prices of commodities produced in, and exported by, developing countries, and to examine ways and means whereby unit prices of manufactured imports of developing countries and unit prices of exports from developing countries could be automatically linked. (192)

The resolution explicitly limited the study to "commodities" exported by LDCs and "manufactured imports" of LDCs. Prior to completion of the UNCTAD study, in early 1974 the Sixth Special Session of the United Nations General Assembly, in its Programme of Action on the Establishment of a New International Economic Order, called more generally for the establishment of "a link between the prices of exports of developing countries and the prices of their imports from developed countries." (193)

The 1974 UNCTAD study (194) had six parts: the concept of indexation, the policy issues, practical problems of indexation, operational mechanisms, economic consequences of indexation, and conclusions. The major findings of the study were that:

(a) indexation is technically feasible, but only under certain conditions;

(b) indexation could provide an effective countermeasure to internationally transmitted inflation;

(c) indexation, being related to prices, could not offset variations in export earnings which were due to quantity changes;

(d) the mechanism for indexation would differ from one commodity to another; and

(e) present conditions of economic disorder may be propitious for the introduction of indexation for a more orderly arrangement of international trade. (195)

The Twenty-Ninth General Assembly reviewed the UNCTAD study in the Fall of 1974, and asked the Secretary General of UNCTAD:

> ... to convene a group of experts to examine the issue or indexation in all its aspects, with a view to identifying practical and feasible schemes for implementation; taking into account the discussion on the subject by the Committee on Commodities at its eighth session and by the Second Committee of the General Assembly at its twenty-ninth session and to

report to the Trade and Development Board at its fifteenth session for such action as the Board may deem necessary. (196)

The Secretary General convened the Group of Experts in Geneva from April 28 to May 1, 1975 (after passage of Article 28 of the Charter). Unable to reach agreement on the issue of direct indexation, the Group did not attempt to produce a consensus report, but instead summarized its conclusions in a private note to the Secretary General. (197)

A review of the Group of Experts' note indicates differences of opinion both on the premise of whether or not there had been a secular deterioration in the terms of trade of LDCs and, if so, how it might be rectified. Although the Group was divided on whether indexation was desirable in principle as an instrument for helping primary producers, a substantial majority considered that indirect indexation was preferable to direct indexation because it was (a) more feasible, (b) less likely to result in misallocation of resources, and (c) easily applied selectively to LDC exports only. Although support for direct indexation waned following publication of the UNCTAD study and the Group of Experts' note, it was still included in the policy issues for discussion at UNCTAD IV in May 1976. (198)   Indirect indexation and the Integrated Commodity Program have, however, now moved to center stage.   Their interrelationship is discussed below in Chapter 4.

At the time of the negotiations on Article 28, eight developed nations offered an amendment to delete this "indexation" article; (199) it failed, receiving only 12 affirmative votes and 11 abstentions, (200) and Article 28 was, therefore, approved. (201) Following the vote in the Second Committee, explanations and reservations were offered by various delegations. Some supported Article 28 as an effort "to improve the terms of trade of developing countries." (202) Finland qualified its general support relating to the terms of trade argument by advising that it had not "committed itself to any particular means of doing so." (203) Denmark and the United Kingdom, in their opposition, pointed out that the quesiton of indexation was "being studied in other bodies, and acceptance of the text of Article 28 as it stood would be prejudicial to the studies being carried out." (204)   Still others doubted the feasibility of linking the prices of LDC exports to their imports. (205) The basis of the United States opposition to Article 28 was set forth by an Assistant Secretary of the Treasury at Congressional hearings subsequent to the Charter's approval:

... We do not believe that indexation is viable from a practical standpoint, nor do we feel it is in the best interest of the developing countries. Such a rigid arrangement would not permit relative prices to adjust to reflect changes in supply and demand resulting from changes in consumer taste, substitutes, new sources of technology and the multitudinous other factors in a dynamic and changing world.

... Furthermore, to the extent that this proposal might shift the terms of trade in favor of the raw material producers it would benefit the resource rich developed countries more than the developing countries. Some 70 percent of the nonfuel raw materials traded are exported by the developed countries.

... the best argument against indexation may actually be the actual record of the purchasing power of commodity earnings. World market prices of most nonenergy commodities have in fact <u>risen</u> over the past quarter century. This is true both in terms of their nominal prices and in terms of the industrial products which developing countries need. (206)

As evidenced by the above-cited dispute of the Group of Experts on the question of whether or not there had been a secular deterioration in the terms of trade of LDCs, the last point made by the Assistant Secretary is by no means universally agreed.

In conclusion, the stabilization of commodity prices and attempts to transfer resources through commodity prices are complex, difficult, and controversial on a domestic basis, and the more so when raised to the international level. Nationally there are often legitimate institutions for initiating and implementing such programs; this is not the case internationally. Although pressures for international decision making increase, few, if any, states stand ready to permit international bodies to act on behalf of the world community. The most progress to date has been made in the area of monetary policy, but there has been little agreement on commodity policy, aside from the compensatory financing facility of the IMF. While attempting to cope with some of these same issues in 1941, John Maynard Keynes advised:

These questions are not easily answered. But it is fair to point out that most of them apply equally to <u>any</u> schemes for introducing order into international trade. We may throw our hands in at the start on the grounds that it is too difficult to improve this awkward world. But if we reject such defeatism - at any rate to begin with and before we are compelled to acknowledge defeat - then the quesitons to be asked at so early a stage of our work need only be whether this particular machinery for introducing international order is exposed to more difficulty on the above heads than alternative proposals directed to the same general purpose. (207)

Trade in invisibles (Article 27)

Trade in invisibles has been a conscious concern of the LDCs as a group since UNCTAD I, (208) when Raul Prebisch highlighted its importance by stating that $9 billion of the predicted $20 billion LDC trade gap in 1970 would arise in the area of invisibles. (209) With shipping, banking and insurance generally in the hands of foreign companies, LDCs see scarce foreign exchange flowing away. Over the years they have endeavored to stem this outflow: by <u>inter alia</u> encouraging joint ventures with nationals, (210) creating regional or binational shipping lines, (211) requiring insurance companies to invest a fixed proportion of locally acquired premiums within the host country, (212) and requiring banks to maintain substantial reserves with the local central bank. (213) To encourage inflows, many LDCs have attempted to stimulate the development of tourism. (214) Article 27 of the Charter, which claims the right of states "To enjoy fully the benefits of world invisible trade and to engage in the expansion of such trade," was adopted without dissent. (215)

International Organizations (Articles 10 and 11)

A number of articles are related to international organizations, including those on regional organizations discussed in the next section below. Each is general in language, but reflects a particular concern of the LDCs.
Article 10. The essence of the problem posed in Article 10 lay in the fact that in the most influential international financial organizations, such as the International Monetary Fund (IMF) and the World Bank Group (IBRD, IDA and IFC), policy is decided by the developed countries because voting is weighted in relation to the financial contributions of member states. For example, the 15 leading developed country members of the World Bank contribute 66.82 percent of the capital and cast 61.12 percent of the votes. (216) This situation contrasts with that of most other United Nations bodies where the general rule is that each nation has one vote. The LDCs' dependency on the financial support of the developed countries makes voting arrangements an extremely delicate area for discussion: in 1964, UNCTAD almost failed to come into existence because of opposing views on this matter. (217) Article 10 exhibits a sensitivity in this regard by qualifying the right of participation in international decision-making to be "in accordance with... existing and evolving rules":

All States are juridically equal and, as equal members of the international community, have the right to participate fully and effectively in the international decision-making process in the solution of world economic, financial and monetary problems, inter alia, through the appropriate international organizations in accordance with their existing and evolving rules, and to share equitably in the benefits resulting therefrom.

Soon after the Charter was approved, 25 experts (primarily from LDCs and the principal developed countries, the Soviet Union, Czechoslovakia and Yugoslavia), commissioned by the United Nations General Assembly, completed a report on "A New United Nations Structure for Global Co-operation." (218) The report, which was unanimously adopted by the experts, had the following recommendation on international monetary reform:

(b) The distribution of voting rights under the weighted voting system in the International Monetary Fund [should] be revised to reflect the new balance of economic power and the legitimate interest of developing countries in a greater voice in the operation of that institution. (219)

The report also commented on the "question of the power of the veto on decision making by a single member" (i.e., the United States) and "the possible increase of the share of developing countries to the range of 45-50 percent of the total [voting power] with a substantially greater access of developing countries to IMF credit." (220) The report's recommendations on voiting rights in the World Bank and its discussion of such issues as the exercise of the veto power by one member and "the possible increase of the share of developing countries to that of parity with developed countries" (221) paralleled those relating to the Fund. (222)

In recent years the Fund and the Bank have, both individually and jointly, sought ways to bring more members into their respective decision making processes. The Group of Ten, (223) formed by the OECD in 1961 "for protection against possible financial difficulties resulting from the liberalization at that time of controls over capital movements" served as a developed country forum for consultation on calls for Fund resources under the General Agreement to Borrow. In 1972, the Board of Governors of the Fund constituted an ad hoc Committee on Reform of the International Monetary System and Related Issues. (224) This Committee of Twenty, as it came to be known, includes both developed and developing country members. In addition, the World Bank and the IMF created the Joint Development Committee (225) (of developed and developing countries), and the Third World created its own Group of 24 (226) experts on international monetary problems.

The newly created International Fund for Agricultural Development (IFAD) devised a voting formula which is a compromise between one nation one vote and weighted voting. (227)

Article 11. Article 11 is very general and expresses the intent to support the strengthening, improved efficiency and adaptation of international organizations to the changing needs of international economic cooperation. The article was introduced by Romania, (228) which had proposed that it be the first provision in the Charter, and was adopted unanimously. (229)

Regional Economic Groupings (Articles 12, 21, 23 and 24)

Article 12. Regional integration or economic cooperation among geo-graphically proximate countries has been an important feature of interstate relations during the post-World War II period, and any economic charter was sure to sanction and encourage it, "especially for developing countries." (230) Nevertheless, defining the corresponding duties of countries adhering to subregional, regional, and interregional groupings turned out to be a complex matter, which was resolved only in the final sessions of the Second Committee.

Although the framers of the ITO and the GATT had envisaged a free-trade world, given expression in the universal most-favored-nation (MFN) clause, this pure economic principle was modified in practice. Under GATT, members of regional customs unions were permitted to extend preferential treatment to each other, (231) so long as the general intent of the group was to move towards zero tariff levels and the group's common external tariff was not on average higher than the individual preintegration tariffs.

A somewhat ambiguous proviso to that effect appeared in the draft outline, which stated that economic integration policies should be "rational and outward-looking." (232) Several delegations suggested more precise language, (233) but the final Article was actually a juxtaposition of the many different proposals put forward throughout the negotiations, with no attempt to reconcile the contradictions. The policies of groupings are (according to a Nigerian proposal) "to correspond to the provisions of the Charter," (234) (according to the draft outline) "outward-looking," (235) (according to a United States' proposal) "consistent with their international obligations," (236) (according to a modified version of a Mexican and United Kingdom-Netherlands proposal) "consistent with the needs of international economic cooperation," (237) and finally (reflecting general Third World philosophy) to "have full regard for the legitimate interests of third countries, especially developing countries." (238)

The EEC was very supportive of the Charter in this respect because it represented the first important international document which recognized the concept of state groupings. In fact, the EEC Commission suggested that the transitional paragraph (between the Preamble and Chapter I) read "The General Assembly solemnly declares (adopts) the following principles concerning the economic rights and duties of States and where applicable groupings of States" (239) (emphasis added), although this formulation was not accepted. Nevertheless, without prejudice to its general support for the Charter, the EEC had difficulty with Article 12 of the Group of 77 draft in the Third Session of the Working Group, which read that "those States shall ensure... that the groupings... act... in accordance with the provisions of this Charter." (240) Under the Treaty of Rome (241) certain competences were transferred from member states to the Community as such; and, therefore, since these rights had been given up to the supranational body, EEC states were not legally able to "ensure" that the grouping would follow any particular policies. Mr. Maes, representative of the EEC, explained that "such a provision was not only contrary to the letter and spirit of the Treaty of Rome, but was incompatible with the very existence of any regional grouping to which States might have transferred certain competences." (242)

The controversy was symptomatic of one of the conceptual problems underlying the Charter of Economic Rights and Duties of States - that between state sovereignty and interdependence. Compromise language was finally found which declares that:

2. In the case of groupings to which the States concerned have transferred or may transfer certain competences as regards matters that come within the scope of this Charter, its provisions shall also apply to those groupings, in regard to such matters, consistent with the responsibilities of such States as members of such groupings. Those States shall cooperate in the observance by the groupings of the provisions of this Charter.

The EEC was ready to "cooperate in" where it had not been prepared to "ensure" observance of the Charter.

Article 21. This article allows LDCs to grant trade preferences to each other, without having to extend them to developed countries as well. It arose late at the Fourth Session of the Working Group (243) and was eventually approved unanimously. (244) In the past, preferential trading arrangements among LDCs have tended not to develop much beyond the subregional level. (245) Movement towards regional integration has often failed, primarily because of relative differences in levels of economic development of member countries, competitive rather than complementary economies, lack of intraregional transport and communications networks, and lack of mechanisms for clearing trade accounts. Hence, the comparatively more developed regional members have tended to gain disproportionately from the integration schemes. (246) Also, multinational corporations, which can often supply much of the missing infrastructure due to their global natures, have further complicated the integration issue. Integration, like commodities, although assumed to be an area for South/South cooperation, has frequently become yet another facet of North/South relations. (247)

Incorporated in Article 21 are provisos that inter-LDC trading preferences be "in accordance with the existing and evolving provisions and procedures of international agreements where applicable" and "not constitute an impediment to general trade liberalization and expansion." While the latter reflects the GATT free trade-cum-regional exceptions philosophy, the former apparently sanctions the continuation of "reverse preferences" for EEC products into the 46 ACP states. This contrasts with the Sixth Special Session Programme of Action's call upon LDCs "to ensure that no developing country accords to imports from developed countries more favorable treatment than that accorded to imports from developing countries." (248)

Article 23. Article 23 calls for developed countries and international organizations to assist in strengthening trade among Third World nations. (249) "Support" from developed countries is generally seen as one of two kinds, as spelled out in the International Development Strategy: (a) financial and technical assistance and (b) action in the field of commercial policy (preferential treatment for LDC exports). Economic cooperation among LDCs themselves has recently developed a new elan, being viewed as a concrete example of "collective self-reliance." This call for a lessening of dependence sits rather uneasily together with the appeal for increased support from developed countries. An acceptable balance was found in Article 23 by adding the qualifier that developed country and international organization support should be "appropriate and effective." Besides trade, "economic cooperation" in general is to be strengthened. Here UNCTAD has developed proposals for cooperation in production, including joint ventures among LDCs. Development finance, particularly from capital surplus oil-exporting countries, is another facet of LDC economic cooperation, which may vary from balance-of-payments support to project and program financing. (250)

Article 24. From the earliest Charter outlines submitted, LDCs had included a provision that regional groupings of industrialized countries should not adversely affect the interests of third countries. Special protection, particularly when offered to agricultural products, had long been a source of contention between the EEC and LDCs, only partially offset for some of the latter by the Yaoundé Conventions. (251) General Principle Nine of UNCTAD I (252) made it incumbent on regional economic groupings not to "cause injury to or otherwise adversely affect" imports from LDCs. The Charter of Algiers repeated this and went further to call for measures from regional economic groupings of developed countries to ensure freer access to LDC exports. (253) Two different developed country proposals would have countenanced the duty of all states to "take into account," instead of the much stronger Philippines' formulation of "not prejudicing or adversely affecting" third country interests. (254) By the Fourth Session of the Working Group, compromise language was agreed upon.   Once again, the dilemma was resolved by juxtaposing the two formulae. In the final Article 24, states are to "take into account" other countries' interests, as well as "avoid prejudicing the interests of developing countries." (255)

East/West Economic Relations (Articles 4, 20 and 26)

The Charter has thus far been characterized primarily as a North/South document.   There are, however, a few articles dealing with East/West economic relations, including Article 4 on the right to engage in trade "irrespective of any differences in political, economic and social systems"; Article 20 which calls on LDCs to "grant socialist countries conditions for trade not inferior to those granted normally to the developed market economy countries"; and Article 26 which explicitly states that "international trade should be conducted... on the basis of... the exchange of most-favored-nation treatment."

Article 4. This article evolved from an earlier formulation of 12 LDCs, Romania, and Yugoslavia (256) which was designed to prohibit such Cold War economic policies as the Hallstein Doctrine, whereby West Germany refused to recognize any country trading with East Germany, or the United States-instigated boycott of Cuba by the Organization of American States (OAS). The real debate on Article 4 was linked to the fact that Western developed countries have long opposed any automatic granting of MFN status to all countries, and in particular to the socialist bloc. After an early Philippines' proposal (257) specifically incorporating the MFN principle met with strong opposition, all mention of MFN status was dropped from Article 4, but retained in Article 26.

The question of MFN status has been a long-standing source of contention between the EEC and CMEA, the former claiming that MFN treatment can only be accorded to countries with similar economic systems. CMEA, on the other hand, often points to the discrimination that it faces with the EEC's common external tariffs and quotas. (258) In an effort to avoid any reference to "discrimination" (and thus, indirectly, to MFN), the EEC supported the wording in Article 4 "irrespective of any differences in political, economic and social systems" (emphasis added).   The Group of 77 accepted this formulation, but appended a new sentence stating that "No state shall be subjected to discrimination of any kind based solely on such differences" (259) (emphasis added). In the Fourth Session of the Working Group, and again as an amendment to the final Group of 77 draft, the EEC proposed an addition to the second sentence, i.e., "States in similar situations should not be given different treatment." (260) When this qualifying language was rejected, all but one of the EEC members voted against Article 4, as did six other developed nations, while the United States, Japan, and the Netherlands abstained. (261) France, speaking on behalf of the EEC, explained that "the benefits deriving in certain cases from regional arrangements could apply only to countries in similar legal and economic circumstances." (262)

A second objection of Western states (particularly the United States) to Article 4 related to whether or not the right to enter into bilateral or multilateral arrangements should be qualified by reference to international obligations. The LDC draft proposal to the Fourth Session of the Working Group stated that such arrangements would be "consistent with the needs of international economic cooperation." (263) Although the EEC was ready to consider omitting any reference to international obligations, for the sake of reaching consensus, (264) the United States wanted it included. (265) The Group of 77 draft submission to the Second Committee accommodated both the United States and LDC positions by providing that bilateral and multilateral arrangements would be "consistent with [every State's] international obligations and with the needs of international economic cooperation." (266)

Article 26. Article 26 was closely linked to Article 4 in the Working Group discussions. Article 26 could be construed as expressing the duty "to facilitate trade between States having different economic and social systems," thus complementing the right in Article 4 to trade "irrespective of differences in systems." Expansion of the meaning of the Article 4 provision that "no State shall be subjected to discrimination of any kind" was provided by the statement in Article 26 that "international trade should be conducted... on the basis of mutual advantage, equitable benefits, and the exchange of most-favored-nation treatment."   This greater degree of precision in Article 26 aroused 10 more states to oppose it or to abstain from voting than had done so in respect to Article 4. (267)

To understand fully the opposition of the West to including the MFN principle in the Charter, it is necessary to look beyond the Charter negotiations to the Conference on Security and Cooperation in Europe (SCSE), which was taking place simultaneously in Helsinki. Preparatory talks and the first stage of the SCSE were held between November 1972 and July 1973, that is, during the period in which the First and Second Sessions of the Working Group took place. At the time that the SCSE agenda was established in July 1973, it was assumed that SCSE would be finished by mid-1974. West European states were not prepared to "give away" long-sought-after MFN status to CMEA members in the Charter negotiations until they had received reciprocal and equivalent concessions from the East European nations at SCSE.   When it became obvious in the Spring of 1974 that the Helsinki Conference was not making any progress on the freer flow of information and contacts, this, in turn, blocked progress on the MFN clause in the Charter. Consequently, EEC members were not ready to go further in the Second Committee (268) than the following language which they had first introduced at Mexico City during the Fourth Session of the Working Group and subsequently reintroduced in the Second Committee as an amendment to Article 26: "In the pursuit of their trading relations States may, as a general rule, exchange most-favored-nation treatment through bilateral or multilateral arrangements" (269) (emphasis added).

Of course, LDCs also are opposed to generalized most-favored-nation treatment, to the extent that it prohibits "discrimination" in favor of their own exports. The general system of tariff preferences was included in Article 18, and even more extensive preferential treatment provided in Article 19. At the Third Session of the Working Group, LDCs added, in the discussion of Article 26, that nondiscrimination should, nevertheless, be "without prejudice to generalized nondiscriminatory and nonreciprocal preferences in favor of developing countries."

The United States voted against UNCTAD General Principles Two and Eight in 1964, and has since continued to insist that the MFN clause be applied on a case-by-case basis, and that there is no obligation to extend it either in customary international law or under United States municipal law. (270)

The Group of 77 saw themselves as producing a compromise formula between the CMEA and EEC members, (271) but their compromise did not go far enough to please the latter. China militated unsuccessfully against the Soviet position and encouraged the Group of 77 to drop the MFN clause, arguing along lines similar to those of the United States that the granting of MFN treatment was a sovereign right and should be obtained only via bilateral or multilateral agreements. (272) The specific duty to conduct international trade "on the basis of... the exchange of most-favored-nation treatment" remains in Article 26 of the Charter. The final text garnered 14 negative votes, including all of the EEC, the United States, and Canada, and 10 abstentions, including five from LDCs. (273)

Article 20. Also concerning trade with socialist countries, Article 20 is another specific case of the general principle of nondiscrimination in trade enunciated in Article 4. Since its Second Conference in 1968, UNCTAD has endeavored to expand trade between Eastern Europe and LDCs; resolutions adopted at UNCTAD II and III were balanced, encouraging LDCs and socialist countries to expand trade with each other. (274) However, Article 20, which appeared during the Fourth Session of the Working Group, placed the onus on LDCs in their trade with socialist countries to "grant these countries conditions for trade not inferior to those granted normally to the developed market economy countries." Although Article 20 was approved, 12 LDCs abstained, eight (including China) did not take part in the vote, and Chile cast a negative vote. (275) China condemned Article 20 as "espousing a doctrine of open door and equal opportunity for all within the framework of the struggle between the newer and the old style imperialist spheres of influence." (276) Many LDCs stated that both LDCs and socialist countries should make every effort to facilitate their trade relations; (277) others stated that if LDCs were giving concessions, then the socialist countries should increase their development assistance. (278)

Foreign Aid (Articles 17, 22, and 25)

Although trade is the predominant theme of the Charter, foreign aid is treated as well in Articles 17, 22 and 25.

Article 17. This article originated in the draft outline as a simple exhortation to states to cooperate in development, (279) but it later evolved into a slightly more detailed statement of how such cooperation should proceed:

International cooperation for development is the shared goal and common duty of all States. Every State should cooperate with the efforts of developing countries to accelerate their economic and social development by providing favourable external conditions and by extending active assistance to them, consistent with their development needs and objectives, with strict respect for the sovereign equality of States and free of any conditions derogating from their sovereignty. (emphasis added)

"[P]roviding favourable external conditions" presumably includes tariff and other trade preferences which fall beyond the scope of aid, reflecting once again the Charter's emphasis on trade as the principal instrument of economic development.   This formulation represented a compromise between one proposed article which would merely have repeated point (n) of Chapter I, i.e., "international cooperation for development," and several more explicit proposals made in the Second Session of the Working Group regarding duties to promote economic growth and provide aid.   Although China's original demand that "no conditions shall be attached and no privileges demanded" (280) in exchange for aid was not retained in the final text of Article 17, aid is to be "free of any conditions derogating from [the recipient's] sovereighty." (281) Australia attached a reservation that it "interpreted its general support for Article 17 as not derogating from the right of States to put such conditions on development assistance as might be required by their obligations to account for the expenditure of public funds." (282) No country abstained or voted against Article 17 in the Second Committee, (283) although Netherlands did not participate in the vote in the belief that the article could be interpreted as requiring cooperation with all LDCs in contravention of Dutch policy not to extend aid to Chile. (284)

Article 22.   The many disputes surrounding foreign aid in recent years reemerged during the negotiations of Article 22.   Proposed language on how strongly the developed countries' duty to give aid should be expressed ranged from "shall provide" (obligatory) to "should facilitate," or the very mild "should endeavor to facilitate." (285) Bulgaria claimed that aid "must be carried out also as a form of compensation by the former colonial powers for the damage sustained or being sustained by the developing countries as a result of colonial rule and of activities of foreign capital." (286)   The resulting Article 22, which was adopted unanimously, (287) read:

1. All States should respond to the generally recognized or mutually agreed development needs and objectives of developing countries by promoting increased net flows of real resources to the developing countries from all sources, taking into account any obligations and commitments undertaken by the States concerned, in order to reinforce the efforts of developing countries to accelerate their economic and social development.

2. In this context, consistent with the aims and objectives mentioned above and taking into account any obligations and commitments undertaken in this regard, it should be their endeavor to increase the net amount of financial flows from official sources to improve the terms and conditions.

3. The flow of development assistance resources should include economic and technical assistance.

Although no specific aid volume is targeted, the phrase "taking into account any obligations and commitments undertaken by the States concerned" in subsections 1 and 2 probably refers to the recommendations of UNCTAD I (288) and II (289) on public and private financial resources, as well as the various resolutions and policy statements of the OECD's Development Assistance Committee (DAC), relating to the volume, terms, and conditions of foreign aid. (290)   UNCTAD I recommended that each advanced country supply "financial resources to the developing countries of a minimum net amount approaching as nearly as possible to 1.0 percent of its national income..."   UNCTAD II retained the 1.0 percent standard, but applied the ratio to the gross national product rather than to national income. Later in 1968, when adopting the International Development Strategy, the United Nations General Assembly set a 0.7 percent of GNP target for "official development assistance"; thirteen DAC members accepted this figure, but at varying target dates. (291)   Throughout the post-1964 period, DAC members have made serious efforts to standardize their definitions and disaggregate their aid flows into three agreed categories: the concessional "official development assistance" (ODA); "other official flows" (OOF);   and "private flows." (292)   DAC also concerned itself with measuring the element of concessionality in total aid flows, and developed special criteria for the least developed countries. (293)

Total net flows from DAC countries to LDCs have increased from $10.1 billion (1964-66 average) to $39.9 billion (1975), (294) or from 0.75 percent to 1.05 percent of GNP.   DAC countries as a group first surpassed their 1.0 percent target in 1975.   However, the bulk of the increase over this period was accounted for by private flows (58.4 percent of the total); (295) hence, the record for the more important concessional official development assistance was not nearly so successful as the statistics cited above might indicate: 0.44 percent of GNP in 1964-66, dropping to 0.36 percent in 1975, compared with the stated International Development Strategy goal of 0.7 percent. (296)   Following the 1973-74 oil embargo, OPEC countries also became important aid donors, although neither the volume nor the direction of OPEC assistance has compensated for the increased cost of fuel imports to non-oil producing LDCs: (297)

OPEC aid for long term economic development was relatively small and amounted to between $40 and $60 million until 1973 when it exceeded the $100 million mark for the first time. It was mainly provided by Kuwait, and to a lesser extent, Libya and Saudi Arabia, and largely directed to Arab states, along with small and sporadic aid for some African countries. (298)

Total OPEC aid commitments rose to $8.1 billion in 1974 and $9.0 billion in 1975, (299) with the official development assistance component equal to 1.35 percent of their 1975 GNP. (300) Over the same period, net disbursements of total OPEC aid went from $4.7 billion to $6.0 billion.

Subsection 1 of Article 22 emphasizes "increased net flows of real resources," thus focusing on the one percent target for total flows, adjusted for inflation.   Subsection 2 concentrates on increasing the "net amount of financial flows from official sources," making no reference, perhaps as an oversight, to "real" flows.   The delegates satisfied themselves with an admonition "to improve the terms and conditions," rather than deal specifically with such problems as tied aid, automaticity of transfers, linkages between aid and development plans, project versus nonproject aid, local currency financing, debt servicing, and repayment schedules, and the like.   Finally, subsection 3 asserts that "development assistance resources should include economic and technical assistance." This has been the normal pattern of aid over the years, with technical assistance usually providing a relatively small percentage of the total (e.g., slightly more than 7 percent in 1975). (301)

Article 25. In 1972 the members of DAC issued new recommendations on the terms and conditions of aid, urging that a group of least developed countries should receive "the softest possible terms of aid":

> ... Official development assistance to [the least developed] countries should preferably be in the form of grants and the average grant element of all commitments from a given donor should either be at least 86 percent to each least-developed country over a period of three years, or at least 90 percent annually for the least-developed countries as a group. (302)

Article 25 encompasses many more countries than the 29 designated by the United Nations as being "least developed." (303)   The Lomé Convention between the EEC and the 46 African, Caribbean, and Pacific (ACP) countries exemplifies the application of special provisions for all categories of countries specified in Article 25. (304)

The need for special measures in favor of the poorest LDCs has long been recognized and no objections arose over the general topic during the Charter working sessions.   The discussion on the operative sentence turned on two different formulations using the mandatory predicate that "the international community shall give" or "must pay" (emphases added) special attention to these groups of developing countries. The compromise consisted in taking the United States-proposed auxiliary verb "shall" and the Philippines formulation "pay special attention" to render "shall pay special attention."   In the final version, the phrase "international community" is supplemented by "especially its developed members":

> ...the international community, especially its developed members, shall pay special attention to the particular needs and problems of the least developed among the developing countries, of landlocked developing countries and also island developing countries, with a view to helping them to overcome their particular difficulties and thus contribute to their economic and social development.

Despite the apparent solidarity on the issue of the plight of the poorest of the poor, measures to give preferential treatment to this group of countries have met with some resistance from among LDCs themselves, as expressed in Colombia's statement in the Second Committee, "... any special measures in favor of the least developed of developing countries should not injure or prejudice the interests of other developing countries." (305)

Miscellaneous (Articles 1, 7, 9, 15, and 16)

Articles 1, 7, and 9 of the Charter were noncontroversial provisions which, respectively, recognized the sovereignty and right of each state to choose its economic, political, social, and cultural systems; the responsibility of each state to promote the economic, social, and cultural development of its people; and the responsibility of all states to cooperate in the economic, social, cultural, scientific, and technological fields to promote economic and social progress, especially for LDCs.   All three articles were adopted unanimously.   However, Articles 15 and 16, relating to the utilization of resources freed by disarmament measures and to the elimination of various forms of external domination and discrimination, caused very heated debates.

Article 15.   The idea of linking resources freed from disarmament to the question of development was not new; this was the theme of one of the General Principles adopted by UNCTAD I in 1964, (306) and President Eisenhower had proposed a similar (but never adopted) scheme as early as 1953. (307) Although the Eastern European countries had supported the concept in 1964, they had since reversed their position with some reservations. (308)   United Nations General Assembly Resolutions had been adopted in 1969, 1970, and 1971 incorporating the idea that "progressively released resources [should] be used for economic and social progress for the welfare of people everywhere and, in particular, for the benefit of developing countries." (309)

As finally approved, Article 15 reads:

All States have the duty to promote the achievement of general and complete disarmament under effective international control and to utilize the resources freed by effective disarmament measures for the economic and social development of countries, allocating a substantial portion of such resources as additional means for the development needs of developing countries.

The developed countries offered an amendment to delete Article 15; (310) although the amendment was defeated, 22 votes were cast in its favor and there were 24 absentions. (311) Only one amendment proposed in relation to Article 2 (regarding compensation for foreign investment disputes) received fewer negative votes from LDCs.   Sweden, while abstaining, urged that "disarmament and development must be sought separately and development must not be made dependent on progress in disarmament." (312) China voted with West Germany, the United Kingdom, and the United States in opposing the article. (313)

China's criticism of Article 15, which it considered to be a thinly veiled Soviet public relations tactic directed at the LDCs, was very strong, and at one time, it appeared that China might succeed in having the article deleted. "If the Soviet representative insisted on having Article 15 stand, he would merely be revealing his real intention, which was to provoke controversy and disrupt the progress of the drafting work.   One could not expect the superpowers to become pacifists overnight." (314) China further pointed out that the Declarations adopted by the Sixth Special Session of the General

Assembly and by the World Food Conference had not included this subject. In fact, one of the many resolutions adopted en bloc at the Rome Food Conference called on states to implement the early Resolutions of the General Assembly pertaining to the reduction of military expenditures, and to "allocate a growing proportion of the sums so released to the financing of food production in developing countries and the establishment of reserves to deal with emergency cases." (315) There was, however, no reference to the issue in the Declaration on the Eradication of Hunger and Malnutrition. In private conversations with the Group of 77, China suggested that the paragraph be eliminated or, at the very least, that the word "disarmament" be qualified by the word "genuine." (316) The CMEA members also pressured the Group of 77 to modify Article 15 so that instead of "a substantial portion" of the resources freed by disarmament being allocated to LDCs, "resources... [would] be used for development of all nations, including the developing countries. (317) Neither proposal was incorporated in the Group of 77 draft Charter submitted to the Second Committee. (318)

Article 16.   Article 16 and Chapter I (i) were the most overtly political provisions in the Charter.   Particularly in its first paragraph, Article 16 appears to be consistent with the firmly established League of Nations and United Nations Charter principle of self-determination of all people. (319) Article 16 also expands on the important 1960 United Nations Resolution on Decolonization, (320) providing that:

1. It is the right and duty of all states, individually and collectively, to eliminate colonialism, apartheid, racial discrimination, neo-colonialism and all forms of foreign aggression, occupation and domination, and the economic and social consequences thereof, as a prerequisite for development.   States which practice such coercive policies are economically responsible to the countries, territories and peoples affected for the restitution and full compensation for the exploitation and depletion of, and damage to, the natural and all other resources of these countries, territories and peoples. It is the duty of all states to extend assistance to them.

2. No state has the right to promote or encourage investments that may constitute an obstacle to the liberation of a territory occupied by force.

Beyond calling for individual and collective struggles to eliminate obstacles to self-determination and development, Article 16 declares that "States which practice such coercive policies are economically responsible to the countries, territories and peoples affected." Restitution and full compensation for the natural and other (presumably human) resources is due to the victims.   Similarly, Chapter I (i) of the Charter lists as a fundamental principle of international economic relations the "remedying of injustices brought about by force and which deprived a nation of the natural means necessary for its normal development."

Separate drafts of Article 16 were originally submitted independently by Egypt and Iraq, (321) and the Soviet Union, (322) both aimed at Israeli-occupation of Arab land. References to apartheid also linked South Africa to the article. (323) The developed countries had two sorts of problems with

Article 16.   While the language is in the present tense and the Group of 77 gave assurances that they had no intention of demanding retribution for past colonial policies, the United States claimed that there was no clarification as to "whether [the article] is only prospective in effect or also retro-spective." (324) Moreover, the Article goes on to express the duty of all states "to extend assistance to [the countries, territories and peoples affected]," (325) while most developed countries consider it their prerogative to determine which countries they will assist. (326) Articles 17 and 22 of the Charter, which state the duty to provide aid to LDCs in general, do not mention all or even any particular group of LDCs. Even Article 25 on the least developed of the LDCs is worded in such a way as to leave room for the aid donors to be selective.

Finally, subparagraph 2 of Article 16 is actually a more generalized statement of the provision in the General Assembly Resolution on the Permanent Sovereignty over National Resources in the Occupied Arab Territories, which reaffirmed that Israel's measures to exploit "the human and natural resources of the occupied Arab territories are illegal." (327)   It is interesting to note that instead of outlawing all investment, the provision proscribes only that investment which may "constitute an obstacle to the liberation of a territory." Most Western countries voted to delete Article 16, which was, however, approved 98-17-8. (328)

Chapter III: Common Responsibilities Towards the
International Community (329)

The Seabed (Article 29)

Article 29 relates to the seabed and its resources beyond the limits of national jurisdiction.   Exploration and exploitation are to be carried out exclusively for peaceful purposes and the benefits are to be "shared equitably by all States taking into account the particular interests and needs of developing countries..."   In 1967, Ambassador Arvid Pardo of Malta had aroused the world to the prospect of the ocean's riches being appropriated by the technologically advanced few, raising the banner to make these resources "the common heritage of mankind." In 1969, the United Nations General Assembly passed a "moratorium" resolution calling on states and persons to refrain from all activities of exploitation, pending the establishment of an international regime with competence over the area. (330) The Declaration of Principles Resolution, (331) adopted by the General Assembly in 1970, specifically declared the resources of the seabed to be beyond national jurisdiction as the "common heritage of mankind."

Despite the fact that the proposed Article 29 of the Charter drew its inspiration from the latter General Assembly resolution, (332) which had been unanimously adopted, delegates could not agree on its inclusion in the Charter. First, on a general level, the United States wanted nothing in the Charter on the Law of the Sea, pending the results of the United Nations Conference on the Law of the Sea. Much of the EEC joined the United States in abstaining on Article 29 and reserved their position on the legal consequences of abstention until the outcome of the Law of the Sea Conference. More surprising, perhaps, were the abstentions of all Eastern European nations except Romania. The Soviet Union objected to the use of the general delimiting phrase "beyond the limits of national jurisdiction," since many LDCs consider their jurisdiction to extend 200 miles from the coast. (333) The CMEA countries informally submitted to the Group of 77 an amendment on Article 29 in which the phrase "with the Area to be established by an international treaty of an universal character, generally agreed upon" would have replaced "beyond the limits of national jurisdiction." A general proviso "within the framework and on the basis of provisions of such a treaty" would have modified the "common heritage of mankind." When these changes were rejected, the CMEA countries abstained on Article 29. After the vote, the German Democratic Republic, as spokesman for the CMEA, stated that it considered "national jurisdiction" to be confined to the 12-mile zone of the territorial sea and the continental shelf of the coastal States concerned. (334)

The Environment (Article 30)

"Preservation and enhancement of the human environment" was the second of the common responsibilities towards the international community originally included in the draft outline. However, with the Stockholm Environment Conference just having taken place, LDC negotiators were very attuned to this issue, which they all had not enthusiastically endorsed. In some cases, they were concerned that developed country interest in ecology threatened their development, as reflected in Brazil's suggestion in the First Session of the Working Group to add "effects of environmental policies on the development process of developing countries." (335) These two quite different approaches to the question of the environment were put forward in the Second Session of the Working Group, but were finally merged into a single paragraph on the recommendation of the Soviet Union. (336) Ultimately, at the Fourth Session of the Working Group, wording was found which was acceptable to both sides, except that the developed countries wanted to include the modifying phrase "in accordance with the Charter of the United Nations and the principles of international law"; (337) this was rejected. (338) Only eight of the usual 14 cosponsors of amendments joined together to propose an amendment in the Second Committee which would have referred to international norms. (339) In a gesture of compromise, the amendment read "in accordance with pertinent international norms, regulations, and obligations," instead of "international law." This amendment gathered the largest number of supporting votes of any amendment (22), including several from LDCs. (340) In the Second Committee final vote on Article 30, the issue was not considered important enough for any of the eight cosponsors to oppose it. (341) Only France, the United States, and the United Kingdom abstained; the Federal Republic of Germany and Paraguay did not vote. Article 30, in its final form, calls for the protection, preservation, and enhancement of the environment; but such environmental policies "should enhance and not adversely affect the present and future development potential of developing countries. All States have the responsibility to ensure that activities within their jurisdiction or control do not cause damage to the environment of other States or of areas beyond the limits of national jurisdiction."

Chapter IV: Final Provisions

There are four articles in Chapter IV. Two were approved unanimously (Articles 31 and 33) (342) and two received no negative votes but did incur . abstentions (Articles 32 and 34). (343)

In the draft outline prepared during the first meeting of the Working Group, the Charter was to have Chapters IV and V dealing respectively with Implementation (machinery; role of international organizations; reporting; consultation; and other ways of setting differences) and Final Provisions (adherence; other questions). (344) The developed countries wanted to delete the subject matter references in Chapter IV and change the title to "Concluding Section" and to delete Chapter V. (345) They opposed these provisions because they could be interpreted as giving the Charter formal attributes of a treaty. These issues were not discussed at either the second or third sessions of the Working Group. In a text submitted to the second session of the Working Group (346) the Philippines suggested the possible role of the Trade and Development Board in the implementation and review of the Charter. At the fourth session of the Working Group the LDCs developed the themes in the concluding paragraphs and submitted two general provisions which ultimately found their way into this part of the Charter. (347) The proposed concluding paragraphs linked the Charter of Economic Rights and Duties of States to the UN Charter by stating that it should not be construed "as impairing or derogating from the provisions of the Charter of the United Nations..." They also interrelated the interpretation and application of the Charter's provisions and provided for a "systemic and comprehensive consideration of the implementation of the Charter" by inscribing it on the General Assembly's agenda at specified intervals.

The general provisions which finally ended up in the last chapter of the Charter related to interdependence and to economic and political coercion. The developed countries favored the deletion of both the concluding paragraphs and the general provisions. (348) Following the meeting of the last session of the Working Group, informal meetings were held in Geneva by various Working Group members. This was during the time of a Trade and Development Board meeting. Their purpose was to attempt to achieve consensus on the Charter. Agreement was reached on the text concerning the principle of interdependence and on the text of the two provisions concerning the interpretation of the Charter. (349)

Article 31. Interdependency is the central theme of Article 31, in which it is asserted that "the prosperity of the international community as a whole depends upon the prosperity of its constituent parts." The developed countries proposed an amendment to this article to include the phrase "... all states have the duty... to maintain the appropriate balance between the interests of raw material producer and consumer countries," (350) but this was rejected. (351)

Article 32. This article prohibits the use or encouragement of "economic, political, or any other type of measure to coerce another state in order to obtain from it the subordination of the exercise of its sovereign rights." This was a slightly amended version of the original LDC draft which had included at the end "or to secure from it advantages of any kind," (352) before that phrase was omitted by an LDC amendment. (353) Eleven countries abstained on Article 32. (354)

Article 32 deals more specifically with the provision found in Chapter I (d) of the Charter: nonintervention. It continues the trend of the past twelve years, in international organizations, including within its definition "...economic, political or any other type of measure to coerce another State..." The UN Charter in Article 2 (4) uses the language "threat or use of force" and the general consensus is that this does not apply to economic force. (355) This consensus is based upon the rejection of a Brazilian amendment to the draft of this article to include "...the threat of use of economic measures..." (356) The first introduction of the broader language was introduced in the Charter of the Organization of American States signed in 1948 and effective in December 1951. (357) In addition to prohibiting intervention in Article 15, the Charter goes on in the next article to state:

Article 16

No State may use or encourage the use of coercive measures of an economic or political character in order to force the sovereign will of another state and obtain from it advantages of any kind.

In 1965 the OAS language was internationalized and expanded in a UN Resolution (358) which read

1. No State has the right to intervene, directly or indirectly, for any reason whatever, in the internal or external affairs of any other State. Consequently, armed intervention and all other forms of interference or attempted threats against the personality of the State or against its political, economic and cultural elements, are condemned.

2. No State may use or encourage the use of economic, political, or any other type of measures to coerce another State in order to obtain from it the subordination of the exercise of its sovereign rights or to secure from it advantages of any kind....

In 1970 (359) and 1972 (360) the 1965 language was repeated in new resolutions with the 1970 resolution deeming such acts to be in violation of international law. By the time of the Charter negotiations over Article 32 the issue of economic and political coercion was very familiar.

Following the Arab oil embargo of 1973, there was a great deal of scholarly interest on whether the embargo was in violation of international law. (361) Scholars took various approaches in analyzing the question. Some looked to the Charter of the UN and arrived at different conclusions. (362) Others rejected the UN Charter approach (363) because of their conviction that Article 2 (4) was inapplicable because it did not include economic measures. This latter group focused their attention on the various UN resolutions relating to nonintervention. These resolutions specifically prohibited certain forms of economic coercion. Before proceeding to test the boycott against the resolutions one other step had to be taken. Was a UN resolution binding as a source of international law? Opinions on this question range from those of Haight (364) who argues that they "cannot have legal pretensions. General Assembly resolutions do not in any way have the force of law," to the opinion of Lillich (365) that "While technically such resolutions are not regarded as binding obligations under international law, their authoritativeness, in that they reflect the expectations of the international community, certainly cannot be dismissed out of hand..." Even if one accepts the resolutions as determinative of international law, Lillich concludes, (366) along with Bowett, (367) "the emerging consensus is of little help, since the prohibitions found in the various UN resolutions are pitched on such a high level of abstraction as to be virtually meaningless." Many scholars agree that few economic actions would be labelled illegally coercive at first, but they hope that over a period of time a sophisticated body of case law will emerge. (368)

Articles on the Arab embargo influenced the LDCs and they amended their original version to exclude the phrase "or to secure from it advantages of any kind." Lillich speculates (369) that the omission "was to narrow the scope of Article 32, the success of the Arab oil embargo having convinced the developing States that they should retain the option of engaging in some of the economic pressures for which they so consistently had castigated the industrial countries in the pre-embargo period...."

Article 33. Article 33 integrates the Charter into the framework of the United Nations Charter by stating that nothing in it should be construed as "impairing or derogating from the provisions of the Charter of the United Nations." The second part of the article advises that the provisions of the Charter are interrelated and that each should be construed in the context of the other provisions.

Article 34. To permit the monitoring of the implementation of the Charter and its adaptation to evolving economic, social, legal, and other factors, Article 34 provides that the Charter will be an agenda item of the General Assembly every five years commencing with its Thirtieth Session (1975). Eight developed countries abstained on this article. (370)

The Legal Nature of the Charter

The adoption of the Charter has brought the issue of the legal nature of United Nations General Assembly resolutions to a position of prominence. Are countries bound by United Nations resolutions? Is the Charter a codification and restatement of existing international law? Does it create new international law? Is it a mixture of international law principles and proposals for new principles? How do voting patterns affect the answers to these questions? Is the total vote relevant? If an overwhelming number of countries endorses a resolution, does this have more weight than a resolution passed by a close vote? Does the economic and political power of countries modify a purely mathematical majority? What votes are relevant? For example, the Charter has a preamble and four chapters including thirty-four articles. Suppose a country votes against the Charter but votes in favor of all but two or three articles. Is this country bound by all of the articles which it voted for? Should the International Court of Justice look to United Nations resolutions as a source of international law?

The legal nature of General Assembly resolutions has been commented on over the years by scholars and jurists. (371)   The dominant opinion was summarized by Brierly in these terms:

> ..apart from its control over the budget, all the General Assembly can do is to discuss and recommend and initiate studies and consider reports from other bodies. It cannot act on behalf of all members, as the Security Council does, and its decisions are not directions telling the member states what they are or are not to do! (372)

This sweeping assertion on the limits of the General Assembly's power has been attacked on its periphery over the years. Parry has provided us with a good summary of these attacks. (373) He recounts that Sloan argued there were areas in relation to which the sovereignty of states was not established and where the "General Assembly acting as an agent of the international community may assert the right to enter the legal vacuum and take a binding decision." (374)   Kelsen argued that "a resolution in relation to peace and security might be binding." (375) Johnson, after asserting that resolutions are not binding on members who voted against them, finds, nevertheless, they "have... a 'legal effect'... in the sense that they may constitute a subsidiary means for the determination of rules of law capable of being used by an international court." (376)   Parry concludes his review with the following comment:

> ... The content of international law is very different now from what it was commonly understood to be at the beginning of the life of the United Nations - even after the entry into force of the Charter. Numerous factors no doubt have contributed to the change. But among these the resolutions of the General Assembly would seem to have been of no little importance. It would not seem, moreover, that the effect of these resolutions can be explained away, as it were, or rather brought under the accepted categories of the sources of international law, by any argument that they are only binding on states which vote in "favour" of them. (377)

With the entry of large numbers of new states into the United Nations, a growing number of scholars have been developing a theoretical basis for an enlarged role for the General Assembly in the formulation of international law. (378)   These scholars stress the importance of the will of the international community, rather than the sovereign rights of states. In a sense they are internationalizing a common law approach to law. Falk has summed up the approach succinctly in these words, "There is discernible a trend from consent to consensus as the basis of international legal obligations." (379)

The sponsors of the Charter intended to create a legally binding document (380) whose force would derive from the consensus of a majority of the United Nations members. The developed countries opposed this intention during early Working Group discussions and negotiations, and the question of the legal nature of the Charter was left to the General Assembly. (381) But the General Assembly never reached any determination on the legal nature of the Charter, and this left the Third World and developing countries free to try to bring the document into line with their preferences. The proponents of a binding document used the term "charter" to reflect its solemnity and to indicate that it was a source of norms much like a constitution. (382) The words "solemnly adopts" were employed in the body of the Charter; Article 33(1) linked it to the United Nations Charter. Article 34 made the Charter an agenda item of the General Assembly for the Thirtieth Session and for sessions every five years thereafter.

Those who argue for a nonbinding Charter stress the point that a resolution which failed to gain the support of the major economic powers of the world could hardly be expected to be binding on them. They also rely heavily on the argument that the General Assembly can make only recommendations, not binding decisions. They note that the General Assembly never exercised its authority to establish the Charter as a binding document. On the contrary, various changes made in the Group of 77 draft in the course of negotiations in the Second Committee did away with any presumption of a binding agreement. To wit:

(1) The fourth preambular paragraph originally declared "that it is a fundamental purpose of this Charter to codify and develop rules for the establishment of the new international economic order..." (emphasis added). The final draft of the Charter replaced the underlined words by the words "to promote." (383)

(2) Preambular paragraph five (c) originally spoke in terms of State "obligations" under the Charter. This was changed to read "States which are willing to carry out the provisions of the present Charter." (384)

(3) Preambular paragraph 13 of the draft Charter stated that the General Assembly "solemnly adopts the present charter of Economic Rights and Duties of States as a first step in the codification and progressive development of this subject..." (emphasis added). In the final version of the Charter the entire underlined clause was eliminated. (385)

(4) Early proposals to include dispute resolution and adherence provisions in the Charter, in order to give it some of the formal attributes of a treaty, were not pursued. (386)

No major legal commentator argues that the Charter is a legally binding document, but there is a divergence of opinion on its legal significance. Brower and Tepe (387) adopt the arguments set forth above by those opposed to the binding nature of UN resolution, and they agree with Brierly that the effect of these recommendations is only moral, not legal. Feuer (388) finds that the Charter expresses both traditional principles of international law (binding on all States) and new principles. He considers that the new principles represent a stage in the progressive development of international law, but gives them no more weight than an unratified treaty. New principles, in his opinion, can be introduced into the juridical order only through universal engagements of States or through conventional or customary means. New customary law can be made in a short or a long period of time. Feuer labels the Charter "une resolution infra-juridique," a "declaration - programme." It is a "declaration-programme" in the sense that, by Article 34 giving the General Assembly wide power of recommendations in matters concerning the application of the Charter, the LDC majority in the UN has the power to bring the issues in the Charter up for continual discussion. Feuer considers the Charter to have potential as an instrument allowing all States to work to improve the legal order.

Castañeda, (389) author of a leading text on the legal effects of UN resolutions (390) and the chairman of the working group on the Charter, emphasizes the norm-making rather than rule-making power of the Charter. These norms furnish a basis for the subsequent legal solutions to specific issues, thus equating it to a constitution. The Charter serves the dual purpose of codifying existing customary law and progressively developing new rules which satisfy the present and future needs of international society. (391) Castañeda says that the "binding character is not the same for some provisions as for others." (392) Some of the charter's provisions "express customery rules or long accepted general principles of law while others only reflect the wishes of the present international community (or in certain cases a considerable part of these) to find new solutions and means of bringing forth new principles or rules or simple recommendations which are contained in certain articles." (393) Some of the provisions of the Charter were approved unanimously while others were contested to a greater or lesser extent by some States, and, thus, there is no universal response to the binding nature of the Charter. Castañeda concludes that the juridical nature of the diverse provisions of the Charter, as well as the entire charter, requires a detailed study of the different articles: the relations between them, the pre-existing international law in relation to the contents of the provision under consideration, and the reasons and importance for disagreement in regard to them. To do this would require a study of the conditions under which the different articles were negotiated and accepted.

Dubitzky (394) finds the charter to be without immediate legal force, but argues that it may acquire meaning both as the view of the sources of international law change and as its provisions may be incorporated in practice. Relying on Judge Tanaka's opinion, (395) he finds the Charter may "evidence what States regard international custom to be." (396) He pursues this point and argues that the inclusion of Article 2 in the Charter has a negative evidentiary value which, although not in itself creating a new principle of international law, most certainly shows that the concept of "prompt, adequate and effective" compensation as a principle of compensation of nationalized assets can no longer be held out as a principle of customary international law. He also sees the repeated use of the language of legal obligations in the Charter as a challenge to the long-held position that the General Assembly cannot legislate. He concludes that it will be increasingly easy with practice to maintain that norms can indeed emerge from the Assembly floor.

Tiewul, (397) after a substantial analysis of the Charter, finds that in terms of aggregate outcomes, the Charter will contribute to the progressive development of international law and provide a basis for legitimating actions undertaken or contemplated by various international bodies. According to Tiewul, "some of the Charter provisions have received sufficient consensus to merit strong consideration as a source of common understanding on policy, perhaps even as a source of commitment. Others indicate areas in which the potential for agreement exists. Others yet embody issues on which the breadth and depth of controversy have at least been clearly identified."

The consensus of these scholars is that the importance of General Assembly resolutions is increasing. The Charter is not a statement of international law but it may become so with the evolution both of customary practice and of national views of the sources of international legal obligations. (398)

4 The Stalemate

In the two and one-half years following the adoption of the Charter of Economic Rights and Duties of States, the Group of 77 attempted in many different forms to implement and expand upon (1) its provisions. The major international forums for these negotiations were the Seventh Special Session of the United Nations General Assembly, the extended Conference on International Economic Cooperation (CIEC), and UNCTAD IV. (2) Negotiations tended to concentrate on energy, commodities, debt servicing, transfer of technology, and foreign private investment. Despite endless months of meetings, little agreement was produced on any of these issues. Although this period saw the gradual abandonment of the confrontational tactics of 1974, it did not see a change in substantive positions. The negotiations produced slight modifications in existing institutions rather than the restructuring of the international economic order sought by the LDCs.

The first part of this chapter traces a set of interrelated North/South negotiations in the Seventh Special Session, CIEC, and UNCTAD IV. The second part departs from the chronological narration to discuss the Second General Conference of the United Nations Industrial Development Organization, and the negotiations leading to the Lomé Convention on trade and aid relationships between the European Community and African, Caribbean, and Pacific (ACP) States.

MAJOR DEVELOPMENTS IN NORTH/SOUTH NEGOTIATIONS

The Conference on International Economic Cooperation
First Preparatory Meeting: April 1975

France was the first of many Western countries to revise its tactics in response to the growing public antagonism between the LDCs and the industrial states. In October 1974, the French President, Giscard d'Estaing, proposed a less public approach to the resolution of outstanding North/South issues. Perceptively arguing that the events of 1974 heralded an "enduring crisis" involving a redistribution of world resources, he asked for an oil conference in early 1975. (3)   It was to involve "a limited number of countries, 10 or 12," representing in equal numbers the oil-producing states, the developing consumer states and the developed consumer states, with the EEC treated as a single consumer. The goal of the President's initiative was "concentration," variously defined as cooperation, coordination, harmoniza- tion, or consensus. (4) The limited membership would make "concertation" possible. At the same time, the preponderant presence of the OECD, through the device of a single delegation representing the consensual position of the European Community, would strengthen the OECD bargaining position.

The OPEC countries responded to the French proposals in two OPEC meetings of early 1975. At the Ministerial Meeting in Algiers, January 24-25, they resolved that:

...negotiations between industrialized and developing countries, proposed by the President of the French Republic, should deal with the problem of raw materials as a whole and should take account of the interests of all the developing countries, which should be appropriately and duly represen- ted in accordance with their selection criteria... (5)

At a second Algiers meeting, March 4-6, the Heads of State of the OPEC countries made their attendance at the proposed conference conditional on an agenda broadened to include all North/South issues:

...the agenda of the aforementioned conference can in no case be confined to an examination of the question of energy; it evidently includes the raw materials of the developing countries, the reform of the international monetary system and international cooperation in favor of development in order to achieve world stability. (6)

The resolution went ever further in declaring:

...the necessity for the full implementation of the Programme of Action adopted by the United Nations General Assembly at its VIth Special Session. (7)

France invited ten delegations for a preparatory meeting in Paris on April 7, 1975, to negotiate the agenda and determine the participants for a world energy conference in the summer of 1975. The industrial consumers invited were the EEC, the U.S., and Japan; the oil producers were Saudi Arabia, Iran, Algeria, and Venezuela; and the non-oil producing LDCs were Brazil, India, and Zaire. (8)

The inflexibility of the United States negotiating stance largely predeter- mined the failure of the preparatory meeting. One day before the opening of the meeting in Paris, Unites States Assistant Secretary of State Enders declared in a British television interview that the strategy of consumer countries was to obtain enough market power to "hasten OPEC's demise." (9)

The leader of the United States delegation to the Paris meeting, Under-secretary of State Robinson, attempted the next day to minimize the impact of Ender's statement by saying that, "we are clearly here to work with OPEC countries and deal in a constructive way with common problems." (10) As the conference was to show, the United States was, in fact, not yet willing to effect any compromises in order to reach any agreement with OPEC countries. The United States hoped that the recession-induced slump would result in a sharp break in oil prices and lead to the demise of OPEC. Since time was perceived as a supporting factor in this scenario, the United States had no reason to compromise. (11) Japan and the EEC members, excepting France, reluctantly adopted the U.S. position. A factor which contributed to their rejection of a compromise on the agenda coverage was the lack of preparation by the industrial country delegations on any issues other than oil. (12)

The LDCs were equally steadfast in their insistence on broadening the agenda. When a similar issue had arisen in relation to the Sixth Special Session, the Group of 77 had prevailed against the industrialized countries. It was thus not prepared to settle for less now. (13)

Modification of the U.S. Negotiating Position: May 1975

Although the preparatory meeting in Paris ended in failure, it contributed to the United States decision, in the spring of 1975, to modify its intransigent approach to negotiation on North/South issues. Certain groups within the U.S. government came to realize that the Group of 77 would not let these issues lapse, but would reintroduce them again and again in subsequent international meetings. (14) Furthermore, there was growing appreciation that parts of the new international economic order were not necessarily inimical to the interest of the industrial nations. (15) It was feared that United States' intransigence could provoke the OPEC nations into using the oil lever to back even more radical Third World demands. (16) There was no evidence that the split, which the U.S. had both anticipated and encouraged, between oil-exporting countries and other LDCs would ever occur. (17) Instead, it was possible that a rigid United States position might produce a split among OECD countries. (18)

In the first part of 1975, groups within both the State Department and the Treasury began systematic analyses of the issues raised at the Sixth Special Session and the Twenty-ninth General Assembly, as well as those anticipated to be brought up at the Seventh Special Session. (19) The importance of these analyses is underlined by the fact that undersecretaries in both departments were put in charge of the analyses. (20) The State Department held bilateral consultations with selected LDCs both in New York and within 25 LDCs. (21) The Treasury set up a Task Force under the auspices of the Economic Policy Board and the National Security Council. (22)

Although the State and Treasury Departments shared the same economic philosophy, they did not agree on the best way to deal with the LDCs' demands. The State Department was conciliatory towards discussing the issues proposed by the LDCs and added another, the world food problem, as an issue of its own. It was concerned with short-term political goals. The Treasury Department, on the other hand, had no political goals which modified its strong stand against any external interference with the market mechanism. In a Congressional hearing held prior to the Seventh Special Session, Treasury attacked all the theses of the Group of 77. (23) It defended the current United States approach in the following terms:

First, our essentially open trading system, including free markets for commodity trade, has not failed. On the contrary, the efficient allocation of resources made possible by the market system has improved the living standards of all the world's people.

Second, the United States is not faced with the sole alternatives of unending confrontation with the developing world or agreement to jettison an international economic system which we feel has basically worked well. There is a sufficient middle ground where cooperative efforts between producers and consumers, developed and developing countries, can be productive without the United States abdicating its basic principles.

Third, excessive price fluctuations are costly to both producers and consumers. However, price fluctuations per se are not evil - in fact, they are part of the realities of the marketplace and we should not distort the functioning of the market in the interest of the short-run price stability.

Fourth, the solution to commodity problems does not lie in establishing high-fixed prices and attempting to maintain their value through indexing.

Fifth, joint efforts between consumers and producers are the appropriate means of coping with specific commodity problems. Such efforts should be aimed at improving and strengthening the market-oriented system. We must resist any generalized systems of commodity agreements aimed at fixing prices. (24)

Within a month after the inconclusive end of the preparatory meeting in Paris, and just prior to the Congressional Hearings, a speech by Secretary of State Kissinger in Kansas City publicly indicated that the United States would modify its rigid "free market" approach. (25) Speaking on May 13, 1975, the Secretary acknowledged that the Bretton Woods institutions and the philosophy underlying them were now "under serious stress." He characterized the existing system as one of open and expanding trade, free movement of investment capital and technology, readily available supplies of raw materials, and institutions and practices of international cooperation. In the first of a series of conciliatory remarks, he asserted that "no country - not even the United States - can solve its problems in isolation." He described the LDC position as one in which past exploitation had led to a challenge of the existing system, and the challenge was sustained by the view "that the current system is loaded against the interest of developing countries." Appreciation of the source of LDC discontent did not prevent him from questioning the Group of 77's solutions: Price-setting of primary products and indexation would lead to "a massive redistribution of the world's wealth" by making "the availability of vital natural resources depend on political decision." Promising that the United States would study the LDC demands, he added that "we are convinced that the present economic system has generally served the world well." Rivalry of blocs of nations would produce only instability and confrontation which would "prove disastrous to every nation." At the end of the sections of his speech on energy and just before addressing the issue of raw materials, the Secretary indicated the change in U.S. policy:

> The United States wants to say now that it is prepared to attend a new Preparatory Meeting. We believe that the meeting should be prepared through bilateral contacts between consumers and producers...Our own thinking on the issue of raw materials and the manner in which it can be addressed internationally, has moved forward.

This public announcement of a change in the United States approach to negotiations with the Group of 77 was instrumental in reopening channels of discussion in the French-initiated talks. It also signalled the new approach to Third World demands that the United States was to take in the Seventh Special Session.

Seventh Special Session of the United Nations
General Assembly: September 1-16, 1975

U.S. Secretary of State Kissinger prepared a 27-page speech on "Global Consensus and Economic Development" for delivery at the Seventh Special Session. (26) It emphasized the contributions that the U.S. had made and was planning to make to the development effort. The speech was a dramatic tactical reversal of the negative approach the United States had taken to Third World demands at the Sixth Special Session. The wealth of information and proposals that it marshaled impressed the Third World delegations and created a conciliatory atmosphere which lasted throughout the session.

In the area of international trade, the United States Secretary of State's major proposal was the creation of a Development Security Facility within the International Monetary Fund. This represented a restatement in new terms of U.S. support for the then current proposals for expansion and liberalization of the IMF Compensatory Finance Facility. This facility provides loans to countries to compensate for shortfalls in their export receipts. He also included a proposal for a trust fund to aid the poorest LDCs. The Compensatory Finance Facility, although important, was peripheral to the demand by LDCs for structural changes to stabilize the prices of their export commodities.

The Secretary's speech enumerated United States' efforts in trade with LDCs which were in line with longstanding U.S. policies. They included a Consumer-Producer Forum for every key commodity; the adaptation of nontariff barriers to provide special consideration for LDCs; the United States' intention to sign the Tin Agreement and to participate in coffee, sugar and cocoa negotiations for consumer/producer commodity agreements; support for the liberalization of IMF financing of buffer stocks to assure that drawings from this facility would not encumber other drawing rights; the intention of the United States to put into effect its generalized tariff preferences on January 1, 1976; and an effort by the U.S. to lower tariffs at the Multilateral Trade Negotiations on manufactured, processed, and tropical goods of the LDCs. As a quid pro quo the United States said that it would join other industrialized countries in negotiating supply access commitments.

Turning to the transfer of real resources, the Secretary's speech emphasized flows of private capital through a quadrupling of the capital of the International Finance Corporation and the creation of an International Investment Trust. The speech discussed the role of the World Bank Group in bringing together public and private investors to develop raw material resources. The United States Secretary assured the LDCs that technical assistance and expertise would be provided to those ready to enter long-term capital markets. He also promised to increase bilateral support for training and technical assistance to help developing countries find and exploit new sources of fossil fuel and other forms of energy.

With regard to public aid, the Secretary's speech reaffirmed the United States' commitment to seek Congressional authority to join the African Development Fund, to join in support of an increase of Inter-American Bank resources to $6 billion, to join in IDA replenishments, to participate in negotiations for Asian Development Bank replenishments, and to contribute to the United Nations Revolving Fund for Natural Resource Exploration.

Turning to the subject of science and technology, the Secretary's speech proposed the creation of a number of new institutions: an International Energy Institute, an International Center for Exchange of Technological Information, and an organization to coordinate and finance assistance to improve competitiveness with synthetics of nonfood, agricultural, and forestry products. It also proposed the expansion of multilateral support for community health programs in LDCs.

The United States' speech also pledged support for an International Industrialization Institute to accelerate industrialization in developing countries. To protect the rights of host countries as well as of multinational enterprises, the United States supported legislation to prohibit restrictive business practices, to harmonize tax treatment, and to promote arbitrational procedures to settle investment disputes. The Secretary's speech committed the U.S. to participate in bilateral consultation to identify and resolve potential investment disputes concerning transnational enterprises.

On the issues of food and agriculture, the Secretary proposed establishing a World Food Reserve System of which the United States would hold the major share. The Secretary supported an expansion of the capacity of the Consultative Group for International Agricultural Research and the International Agricultural Research Centers. He promised to increase university-based technical assistance and research in LDC agriculture, and to ask Congress to double bilateral agricultural assistance to $582 million. Finally, he proposed the creation of an international fund for agricultural development. The United States would seek $200 million from Congress provided that the combined goal of $1 billion from all countries was reached.

Kissinger supported the restructuring of the economic and social sectors of the United Nations, and proposed the formation of an intergovernmental committee to begin work immediately. He suggested that 1976 be dedicated as a year of review and reform.

The lengthy Kissinger speech was a tour de force creating a conciliatory atmosphere which was to last throughout the Seventh Special Session. However, it did not address any of the structural issues of primary concern to the developing countries. Many of the items in his speech were just a restatement of previously agreed U.S. initiatives collected together in one place. Rather than discussing the particulars discussed by other participants in earlier meetings, the Secretary of State presented an alternative way to view the problems under discussion.

Whereas the United States took the questions of the Group of 77 and then utilized its own framework in answering them, the Europeans argued and negotiated within the framework established by the Third World. The Europeans as a whole, and the French and British in particular, are more dependent than the United States on LDC commodities. They also tend more readily to accept planning and interventionist policies which they have pursued over the years in relation to their former colonies. With the exception of West Germany, they are much less concerned than the United States with "free market" rhetoric.

Speaking on behalf of the EEC the Minister of Foreign Affairs of Italy made a conciliatory speech which addressed the issues raised by the Group of 77 in the First Preparatory Meeting of CIEC and earlier meetings. (27) He called UNCTAD's integrated raw materials program a "useful basis for further work." The Community supported the diversification of LDC production and access of their products to developed countries' markets. The Community was prepared to examine "which products create problems for developing countries and the most appropriate instruments and means of solving such problems." The approach was to be on the basis of specific cases. The EEC supported the improvement in the IMF Compensatory Financing Facility and also the expansion of the Generalized System of Preferences. The Community reconfirmed the UNIDO Lima Declaration's "industrial" paragraphs. (28) The EEC agreed to participate in discussions on an international code of conduct on transfers of technology. As for transfers of financial resources, the Community "confirmed its determination to achieve the target of 0.7 percent of GNP for public aid set in the International Strategy for the Second Development Decade...." It supported both the "Third Window" facility proposed by the World Bank (29) and its Oil Facility. (30) It agreed to "undertake a careful examination of the debt problem arising in each case for developing countries...." (emphasis added).

To summarize the developed country positions, the United States was conciliatory but in essence followed the market economy approach to the solution of the development problems of the Third World. It emphasized the role of private investment capital and the potential of technical assistance. The Japanese and West Germans joined the Americans as strong supporters of the "free market" approach. The European Community as a whole was more willing to intervene in the market, particularly if it were done on a case-to-case basis.

The Eastern Europeans and the Chinese played a minor role in the Session, as they had throughout the debates on the NIEO. Although they did not cooperate with one another at the Session, their approach was based on a shared assumption expressed by the Chairman of the Soviet Delegation in these words:

It is not the Soviet Union who for ages used to plunder the national wealth of former colonial possessions which nowadays have come to be sovereign states. It is not the Soviet Union who used to exploit their population for centuries. Therefore, the Soviet Union does not bear - I specifically underline it - does not bear any responsibility whatsoever for the economic backwardness of the developing countries, their present hard situation, particularly, under the conditions of the aggravation of the economic crisis of the world capitalist economy. (31)

After the various United Nations delegations had outlined their public positions in the opening speeches of the session, the Group of 77 presented its position paper. Introduced on August 19th and subsequently modified, this paper became the principal focus of discussion. (32) In response to the paper, the United States prepared a position paper which followed the LDC paper point by point, inserting either the U.S. view on each issue or incorporating the acceptable Group of 77 position. (33) In brief, the Group of 77 urged improvement in LDC terms of trade, the stabilization of export earnings, the preservation and increase of purchasing power of their exports, and insulation from the adverse effect of inflation in developed countries. These goals were to be reached through support for the integrated commodity program proposed by UNCTAD not later than the meeting of UNCTAD IV; substantial improvement in compensatory finance; a priority study by the Secretary-General of UNCTAD of indexation options with concrete proposals prior to UNCTAD IV; access to markets of developed countries for all exports; improvement of the General System of Preferences; removal on a preferential and non-reciprocal basis of tariff and nontariff barriers affecting LDC exports; the right of LDCs to use export incentives without the application of countervailing duties by importing countries; elimination of restrictive business practices; the granting to LDCs of preferential treatment in all areas of the Multilateral Trade Negotiations; increase of the flow of foreign aid of each donor up to the 1 percent of GNP target with 0.7 percent in the form of Official Development Assistance, net of reverse flows, by 1978; a link between SDRs and aid; a conference in 1976 to examine means of mitigating the LDC debt burden; early agreement on a Trust Fund within the IMF and consideration of other automatic aid schemes; the phasing out of national reserve currencies; a substantial increase in LDC participation in the decision making process within the World Bank and the IMF; liberalization of the Fund's Buffer Stock Facility; the establishment of an industrial technological information bank; increase of research and development on specific problems of primary interest to LDCs, and the creation of suitable indigenous technology for LDCs; a legally binding international code of conduct for the transfer of technology from developing countries to LDCs by the end of 1977; and revision of the international conventions on patents and trademarks to meet special needs of LDCs.

The negotiations took place in three small contact groups. (34) The first dealt with trade issues; the second handled finance and monetary issues; and the third was to negotiate issues relating to science, technology, industrialization, food, and the restructuring of the United Nations' system in economic and social sectors.   In fact, the issues of food and agriculture and industrialization had been debated recently and were not major preoccupations of the participants. (35) With respect to the restructuring of the United Nations' system in economic and social sectors, the third contact groups noted the report of the Group of Experts (Group of 25) (36) and shifted the matter to an ad hoc committee of the whole with instructions to report to the 31st General Assembly in 1976.

In each group, a single spokesman represented the Group of 77. Other principal negotiators were from the United States, the EEC, Japan, Sweden, Australia, Canada, and New Zealand. The socialist countries and China met with the Group of 77 outside of the three contact groups. The goal of the negotiators was to achieve a generalized consensus and then have technical experts work out the details. (37)

The negotiators from developing and developed states were divided on all issues.   The LDCs sought comprehensive and frequently interventionist measures to regulate and direct the market mechanism. The United States, Japan, and the EEC (with some internal disagreements) insisted on a market approach to problems. The latter group argued that it had little control over such factors as terms of trade, purchasing power, shares in world industrial output, and R & D investment decisions. (38)

Although the Special Session was scheduled to end on September 12, it had to be extended until September 16, ending only hours before the opening of the Thirtieth General Assembly. No definitive agreement could be reached between the industrialized and developing states on the substance of the issues, but a general consensus was achieved on all points. (39) On some issues it was achieved by shifting the elaboration of general conclusions to other forums. Such issues as the integrated commodity program, direct and indirect indexation, the LDC debt problems, and a code of conduct for technology transfer were shifted to UNCTAD. On other issues agreement was reached only on very generalized language. The negotiators agreed that the General System of Preferences was to be continued beyond the original ten years on improved terms with wider coverage, and that the Multilateral Trade Negotiations (MTN) were to take effective steps to reduce and remove nontariff barriers. Maximum restraint was to be exercised in relation to the imposition of countervailing duties on LDC exports. Developed countries were to try to meet specified aid targets. The establishment of an International Investment Trust and the expansion of IFC capital were to be considered. Consideration was also to be given to an SDR aid link and the establishment of a Trust Fund. There was to be a reduction in national reserve currencies, and SDRs were to become a central reserve asset. The IMF's Compensatory Financing Facility was to be expanded and liberalized. The Fund's Buffer Stock Facility was to be liberalized along with a study of possible amendments to IMF rules to permit the provision of assistance to international buffer stocks. The process of decision making in international organizations was to be fair and responsive "in accordance with existing and evolving rules." There was agreement on the establishment of an industrial technological information bank and possibly regional and sectoral banks. Consideration was also to be given to the establishment, within the United Nations' system, of a center for the exchange of technological information and sharing of research information relevant to LDCs.

After studying the Session two scholars concluded that:

> In brief, the proceedings of the Seventh Special Session indicate that although there is no agreement between rich and poor countries on the substance of fundamental issues there now exists an explicit commitment to negotiate....(40)

> ...

> The occurrence of a new order is not guaranteed by the existence of a new context but by the same token, neither will a new order of relations be prevented simply by the fact that opposition remains. (41)

The Seventh Special Session demonstrated the institutionalization and unity of the Group of 77. It kept differences within the Group and treated them as family matters. It established a united front to pry concessions from the less than united OECD countries.

In terms of their approach to LDC demands for change in the international economic order, the United States, West Germany, and Japan were at the free market end of a continuum. Most of the Europeans accepted limited forms of intervention and occupied the middle ground of the continuum. The Scandinavians, Australia, New Zealand, and Canada were the countries most sympathetic to the interventionist goals, if not to all the specific methods proposed by the LDCs. (42)

The Kissinger initiative created goodwill and bought time for the industrial countries to reappraise their strategy and tactics, but it merely delayed another confrontation on ideological grounds. It remained to be seen if a viable compromise could be reached by moving the negotiations out of the public forums of the United Nations and into the Conference on International Economic Cooperation (CIEC) in Paris.

The Reconvened CIEC Preparatory Meeting: October 13-16, 1975

Following Kissinger's Kansas City speech on May 13, diplomatic talks began in Paris and resulted in the drafting of an aide-memoire, made public in September. (43) This provided the basis for reconvening the French-initiated meeting on October 13. (44) The meeting reached a formal agreement to convene the Conference on International Economic Cooperation on a ministerial level in Paris for two or possibly three days commencing on December 16, 1975. (45) The meeting of ministers was to be composed of 27 delegations (19 from developing countries and eight from developed countries, with the EEC represented by one delegation). The participants in the reconvened preparatory meeting assumed responsibility within their respective groups for the designation of the full complement of delegations.

The CIEC preparatory meeting resolved the agenda disagreement of April through a provision for the creation of four commissions: on energy, raw materials, development, and financial affairs. (46) Each commission was to have 15 members, ten from developing countries and five from industrialized countries. The commissions would be co-chaired by a member from each group. It was agreed that they would respect the jurisdiction of the international financial institutions and, thus, not discuss matters legally the concern of the IMF and the World Bank. The four commissions were to function in parallel, according to guidelines established by the Ministerial Conference. The United States (with support from Japan) and the Group of 77 each submitted lists of proposed subjects for the commissions. (47) They agreed, however, that any delegation could raise any subject relevant to the themes of the dialogue for discussion in the commissions. (48) The United States showed interest in oil prices, which it felt were too high, and their relationship to the long-term supply and demand for energy, and to world economic growth. The United States was also interested in security of supply. The LDCs' concern focused on protection of the purchasing power of export earnings from oil, access to the markets of developed countries, the transfer of technology, and the reform of the international monetary system.

In order to broaden participation in these discussions, the preparatory meeting arranged to invite intergovernmental functional organizations to the Ministerial Conference. They were to have the right to speak but not vote. (49) Members of the Conference who were not members of a particular Commission were to be permitted to participate as observers without the right to speak. English, Arabic, Spanish, and French were chosen as the working languages. It was further agreed that the Conference should have an international secretariat with an "exclusively administrative and technical function" which was meant to keep the control of the agenda items in the hands of the delegations.

The preparatory meeting chose the principle of consensus rather than voting as the procedure for the Conference and the Commissions. It recommended that a second Ministerial Conference be held 12 months from the first one, and that a meeting of government officials take place at least six months after the first meeting of the Conference on the ministerial level. (50)

The December Conference was almost delayed by a United Kingdom demand for representation separate from the EEC. (51) The British stand reflected internal pressure to adopt an independent energy policy which would maximize benefits from its newly discovered reserves in the North Sea. It created major problems for the industrial countries because the inclusion of a separate United Kingdom delegation, aside from creating antagonisms within the EEC, would mean the exclusion of one of the five regional countries already agreed on - i.e., a country of northern Europe, a country of central Europe, one in southern Europe, one to Canada, and another to a non-European country (Australia or New Zealand). The British gave up their demand in early December in return for concessions to ensure the profitability of new British oil from the North Sea. (52)

The Ministerial Meeting of CIEC: December 16-19, 1975

The delegations to the Ministerial Conference represented all of the principal capital-exporting countries in the world. (53) There were only eight developed country delegations, but one of these represented the nine countries of the European Economic Community.   Thus, a total of 16 industrialized countries were represented. Among these there were diverse opinions. Australia, Canada, the Netherlands, and Sweden tended to be more sympathetic to developing countries' points of view on commodity and development issues.   France, the only EEC country not a member of the International Energy Agency, tended to maintain a somewhat independent stand from other EEC members both on commodities and on energy policy. The United States, West Germany, and Japan tended to argue most strongly for the preservation of the existing economic order.

The developing countries attending the preparatory conferences were Algeria, Brazil, India, Iran, Saudi Arabia, Venezuela, and Zaire. Four of these members of OPEC (Algeria, Iran, Saudi Arabia, and Venezuela) and one is a member of CIPEC and IBA (Zaire). Brazil is extremely rich in raw materials; and India, the most populous non-communist country in the world, is traditionally a Third World leader.   These seven invited 12 additional countries to the Ministerial Meeting of CIEC: Argentina, Cameroon, Egypt, Indonesia, Iraq, Jamaica, Mexico, Nigeria, Pakistan, Peru, Yugoslavia, and Zambia.   The inclusion of Indonesia, Iraq, and Nigeria brought the total number of OPEC members to seven. With Indonesia, Peru, and Zambia, the final number of CIPEC members was four. The addition of Jamaica and Indonesia increased IBA members to three. The delegations included some of the key members of the nonaligned group (India, Egypt, and Yugoslavia). It also included the country which both took the lead in managing the Charter of Economic Rights and Duties of States and had recently made substantial new oil discoveries, Mexico. Dominant powers from each geographical area of the developing world were included: Latin America - Brazil, Argentina, Jamaica, Mexico, Venezuela, and Peru; Africa - Egypt, Algeria, Cameroon, Nigeria, Zambia, and Zaire; the Middle East - Iran, Iraq, Saudi Arabia; South Asia - India and Pakistan; Southeast Asia - Indonesia.   The remaining LDC was Yugoslavia, an independent usually considered in UNCTAD to be a member of the Asian bloc. Recapitulating the geographical breakdown, we have Latin America - six; Africa - six; Middle East - three; South Asia - two; Southeast Asia - one; and independent - one. These countries contained 1,243 million of the Third World's population.

It is interesting to note that, although all of the developing countries which attended can be classified as less developed countries, the list contained none of the 25 countries designated as least developed of the less developed countries (54) - but it does include four of the 41 countries classified as Most Seriously Affected (MSA) countries. (55)

The delegations chose Allan J. MacEachen of Canada and Manuel Perez-Guerrera of Venezuela to be the co-chairman of the Conference. (56) The agreed membership and co-chairman of the Commission were as follows: (57)

Energy Commission.   United States and Saudi Arabia (Co-Chairmen)
Algeria, Brazil, Canada, Egypt, EEC, India, Iran, Iraq, Jamaica, Japan,
Switzerland, Turkey, Venezuela, Zaire.

Raw Materials Commission. Japan and Peru (Co-Chairmen)
Argentina, Australia, Cameroon, EEC, Indonesia, Mexico, Nigeria, Spain,
United States, Venezuela, Yugoslavia, Zaire, Zambia.

Development Commission.   European Economic Community and Algeria
(Co-Chairmen)
Argentina, Cameroon, Canada, India, Jamaica, Japan, Nigeria, Pakistan,
Peru, Sweden, United States, Yugoslavia, Zaire.

Finance/Commission.   European Economic Community and Iran (Co-
Chairmen)
Brazil, Egypt, India, Indonesia, Iraq, Japan, Mexico, Pakistan, Saudi
Arabia, Sweden, Switzerland, United States, Zambia.

Table 4.1 summarizes the membership of each Commission.

Thus, the delegates of the European Community, the United States, and
Japan sat on all four of the Commissions. In contrast, only two developing
countries sat on as many as three Commissions (India and Zaire), with 17 on
two Commissions.

The CIEC Commissions: January 1976

The operational aspects of CIEC began after the completion of the
Ministerial Meeting when, on January 26, 1976, the Co-Chairmen of the
Conference met with the designated Co-Chairmen of the Commissions. At
this time specific dates were agreed on for forthcoming meetings. (58)
     Agenda and work programs were the order of business of the first
meetings of the Commissions with decisions based on proposals by both the
LDCs (Group of 19) and the United States. As will be seen below, the topics
listed for examination were extremely broad and virtually precluded any but
the most general conclusions.
     The Energy Commission was to focus on a general review of the energy
situation, the price of energy, availability and supply of energy, and
international cooperation in the energy field. (59)   Notwithstanding the
expansion of the CIEC agenda to include nonenergy subjects, this remained
the Commission of most interest to the developed countries. It, alone of the
Commissions, had an integrated agenda.
     The Commission on Raw Materials came up with a broad program
beginning with the trends and conditions of supply and demand of raw
materials, including food. This was followed by the problems of commodity
markets and trade expansion. Next they were to study export earnings with
special emphasis on developing countries. International cooperation in the
areas of production, investment, and technology were next on the list.
Special problems of the developing importing countries and producer and

TABLE 4.1 Memberships on CIEC Commissions

	Energy	Raw Materials	Development	Finance	Total
United States	x*	x	x	x	4
EEC	x	x	x*	x*	4
Japan	x	x*	x	x	4
India	x		x	x	3
Zaire	x	x	x		3
Algeria	x		x*		2
Argentina		x	x		2
Brazil	x			x	2
Cameroon		x	x		2
Canada	x		x		2
Egypt	x			x	2
Indonesia		x		x	2
Iran	x			x*	2
Iraq	x			x	2
Jamaica	x		x		2
Mexico		x		x	2
Nigeria		x	x		2
Pakistan			x	x	2
Peru		x*	x		2
Saudi Arabia	x*			x	2
Sweden			x	x	2
Switzerland	x			x	2
Venezuela	x	x			2
Yugoslavia		x	x		2
Zambia		x		x	2
Australia		x			1
Spain		x			1
TOTAL	15	15	15	15	60

*Co-Chairmen of the Commissions

consumer cooperation rounded out the list. (60)

The Commission on Development concerned itself with a number of general topics: trade, balance of payments, agriculture and food, infrastructure, transfer of resources, industrialization including the transfer of technology, foreign investments and transnational corporations, and the problems of the most disadvantaged LDCs. (61)

The fourth body, the Commission on Financial Affairs, began its activities with a general survey of the global economic and financial situation, with the developed countries concentrating on short-term issues and the LDCs' long-term problems. Other agenda items covered balance-of-payments problems, private capital flows including investments in LDCs, the assets of oil exporting countries including terms and conditions of their investment, the external debt of developing countries with special attention to the most seriously affected, and matters referred to the Commission by the other three Commissions. (62)

These top-heavy agendas resulted in extremely slow progress within the Commissions. Each Commission disaggregrated the general topics and held lengthy discussions primarily defining issues and their interlinkage with those before other Commissions. In order to develop concrete action-oriented programs, a second series of Commissions was scheduled to follow the July Conference of Senior Officials.

In May many of the CIEC participants left Paris to attend UNCTAD IV in Nairobi.

UNCTAD IV: May 5-31, 1976 (63)

The Group of 77 made intensive efforts to limit the agenda and to streamline procedures in order to enable the Conference to focus on what it considered to be the key issues at UNCTAD (64) - the International Commodity Program, the increasing debt burden of developing countries, and the transfer of technology. Following procedures initiated in connection with UNCTAD II, (65) the Group of 77 held first a series of separate continent-wide meetings in Asia, Africa, and Latin America, (66) and then the three groups met together in Manila to coordinate their positions. The Manila Declaration and Programme of Action (67) catalogued the increasingly refined goals of the Group of 77. The nine areas of interest fit neatly within the four commissions established by CIEC. (68)

Both OECD and COMECON countries held meetings to coordinate member positions prior to Nairobi. (69) In spite of these preparations, the OECD countries were severely criticized for devoting "very little effort toward reaching an agreed position prior to the Conference." (70) The lack of consensus within the OECD bloc was attributed to the failure of the United States' delegation to develop and communicate a coherent position on commodities to other members, and to the inability of the European Community to reach an agreed position. The LDCs maintained that the major concern of the OECD members was "to limit economic concessions without suffering political damage." (71)

In a number of pre-Conference meetings, the Trade and Development Board prepared a much more selective agenda than had been the case for earlier UNCTAD conferences. As a result of the limited agenda and various procedural innovations, only 12 substantive resolutions came up in UNCTAD IV, compared with 48 at UNCTAD III and 32 at UNCTAD II. (72) The drama of this Conference centered on the resolutions for the Integrated Commodity Program and the International Resources Bank. The first was a well known issue, (73) and a variation of the second had been introduced for the first time by the U.S. Secretary of State in his speech to the Seventh Special Session. (74)

Resolution on the International Commodity Program (75)

The International Commodity Program was the mechanism by which the Group of 77 proposed to stabilize commodity prices for its exports at an equitable level. It cassed for the creation of institutional arrangements for 18 commodities, (76) either through buffer stocks (77) or long-term contracts, (78) to narrow price fluctuations in specified commodities of fundamental importance to developing countries. The buffer stocks were to be funded through a common fund (79) financed and managed by some combination of importing and exporting countries. (80) In addition, the ICP called for the expansion and improvement of the IMF's compensatory finance facility. (81)

All issues pertaining to international commodity agreements, discussed above in relation to Article 6 of the Charter of Economic Rights and Duties of States, (82) surfaced once again. What kind of agreements should there be? Which commodities should be covered? Would supplies be guaranteed? Would market access be included? Should negotiations be commodity-by-commodity or should there be an overall agreement covering all of the commodities? As important as these issues were, still more important and controversial were the issues surrounding the common fund. (83) It had been estimated that $3 to 6 billion would be needed to set up buffer stocks for covered commodities. (84) Was this the best use of financial resources? Were prices really the problem, or was it revenue? Should voting in the common fund be weighted? If so, in relation to financial contributions, volume of trade, a mixture of the two, or some other criteria? Where should the commodities be stored, at a central location for each commodity or decentralized in the countries of origin? In cases of commodity shortages, what would be the allocation criteria? Until the very last moment it appeared that no resolution could achieve consensus. High level officials from the United Kingdom and Germany flew to the Conference in its closing days (85) and, together with the other delegates, achieved a consensus on an Integrated Programme for Commodities in Resolution 93 (IV).

The four parts of the resolution dealt with objectives, commodity coverage, international measures of the program, and procedures and timetable. The objectives, expressed in ambiguous language so that they might be acceptable to all parties, focused on the achievement of stable conditions in commodity trading including elimination of excessive price fluctuations at levels which would:

(a) be remunerative and just to producers and equitable to consumers;

(b) take account of world inflation and changes in the world economic and monetary situation;

(c) promote equilibrium between supply and demand within expanding world commodity trade. (86)

The commodities covered were 18 in number, (87) divided between food and beverages (bananas, cocoa, coffee, meat, sugar, tea, and vegetable oils), minerals and metals (bauxite, copper, iron ore, manganese, phosphates, and tin), and agricultural raw materials (cotton, hard fibers, jute, rubber, and tropical timber).

The international measures provided for in the resolutions reflected more agreement to agree than any firm commitment. The major concession of the developed countries was to agree that "steps will be taken...towards the negotiation of a common fund." (88)   This was compromise language.   The developed countries wanted to limit their commitment to "discussions" of a common fund, while the LDCs insisted on "negotiations" of a common fund. Once consensus was reached on this point, approval of the resolution was certain.

The stocking arrangements avoided the issue of commodity-by-commodity negotiations versus overall negotiations by permitting either course of action, (89) and elaborated a number of other important issues. (90)   The resolution exempted the least developed countries from financial contributions to implement the ICP. (91)

The final part of the resolution established the procedures and timetable for the ICP.   It set March 1977 as the outside date for a "negotiating conference" on a common fund, to be open to all members of UNCTAD. Preparatory meetings for this Conference were to discuss: (92)

(a) Elaboration of objectives;
(b) The financing of a common fund and its structure;
(c) Sources of finance;
(d) Mode of operations;
(e) Decision making and fund management.

The resolution provided not only for common fund negotiations, but also for international negotiations on individual products, to begin on September 1, 1976, and to be completed not later than February 1978. These preparatory meetings were to: (93)

(a) Propose appropriate measures and techniques required to achieve the objectives of the Integrated Programme;

(b) Determine financial requirements resulting from the measures and techniques proposed;

(c) Recommend follow-up action required through the negotiation of commodity agreements, or other measures;

(d) Prepare draft proposals of such agreements for the consideration of governments and for use in commodity negotiating conferences.

The resolution requested the Secretary-General to convene an over-all commodity negotiating conference at the conclusion of the preparatory meetings on individual commodities. It was to be concluded before the end of 1978.

Thus, approximately 18 months after the Secretary-General of UNCTAD presented his first relatively detailed proposal for an ICP, (94) UNCTAD IV approved the program without dissent. However, this consensus may prove to be more illusory than real. There was no agreement on how to implement the resolution other than to establish a forum where these issues could be discussed, i.e., where steps could be taken "towards the negotiation of a common fund" (95) and "preparatory meetings for international negotiations on individual products held." (96) The developed countries' reservations to the resolution revealed that major differences between the developed and developing countries had yet to be faced. Illustrative was the United States' reservation (97) that the vote in favor of the resolution was not to be interpreted that it would enter into negotiations on the establishment of specific commodity agreements or of the common fund, but only that it would discuss the nature of the problems affecting various commodities and the appropriate measures for financing buffer stocks.

Resolution on Debt Servicing

A major concern of the Group of 77 at its Manila meeting was the increasing debt burden of developing countries. (98) Between 1965 and 1972, debt outstanding rose by 15 percent per annum, and stood at $100 billion at the end of 1972. By the end of 1975, it had climbed to $174 billion, of which $70.2 billion came from bilateral official sources, $37 billion from multi-lateral public sources, and $67 billion from private sources. The World Bank estimated that debt service of LDCs would reach $18 billion in 1976. (99)

The Manila Conference proposed the waiver or postponement of interest payments and/or amortizations and the cancellation of the principal of official debt by bilateral donors to "developing countries seeking such relief." (100) For the poorest countries (least developed, developing land-locked and developing island countries), the Manila Conference advocated the cancellation of official debts. (101) The conference proposed the same treatment for other "most seriously affected" countries, "or, as a minimum, have their official debts waived until they cease to be regarded by the United Nations as most seriously affected countries." (102)

The Manila proposals differentiated multilateral public debt from bilateral public debt. This differentiation was based on recognition of the fact that multilateral institutions, such as the World Bank, rely on capital markets for most of their loan funds (103) and thus cannot write off a large group of loans without endangering their credit rating and the flow of capital from this source. The Manila Conference proposed that the burden of multilateral public debt on developing countries should be eased by the extension of program assistance to each developing country in an amount no less than its debt service payments to international institutions. In other words, these institutions should extend general development loans to cover the interest on outstanding debts. Although there was no discussion of terms, one can assume that the conference intended that the program assistance should be provided with low interest rates and long maturities and grace periods. It should be noted that if the World Bank and other international institutions are to give "soft" loans, i.e., loans for less than the market cost of money, then they must either subsidize these loans - which could affect their ability to raise money on capital markets - or else they must increase the contributions made to their soft loan funds (104) such as IDA, thus shifting the burden back to bilateral donors who would have to make the contributions.

With respect to the burden of commercial debts on developing country governments, the Manila Conference proposed that these debts should be consolidated and payments rescheduled over a 25-year period. As one way to handle debt to private creditors, the Conference suggested the establishment of a multilateral financial institution to fund short-term debts of interested developing countries. In order to "determine appropriate ways of implementing the principle and guidelines on the renegotiation of official and commercial debts," (105) the developing countries meeting at Manila recommended that UNCTAD convene a debtor/creditor conference in 1976.

After prolonged and difficult negotiations, (106) UNCTAD IV passed a consensus resolution (107) falling far short of the LDC's proposals. The agreed formula was for "quick and constructive considerations of individual requests" (emphasis added) within a multilateral framework "with a view to taking prompt action to relieve developing countries suffering from debt-service difficulties, in particular least developed countries and most seriously affected developing countries." "[A]ppropriate existing fora" were invited to "[p]rovide guidance in future operations relating to debt problems as a basis for dealing flexibly with individual cases." The developed countries thus maintained their position of dealing with the issue on a country by country basis. The Group of 77 failed in its efforts to obtain agreement on a debtor/creditor conference. The single concession to the long-term LDC interest in debt problems was the agreement that the Trade and Development Board would review action in pursuance of the resolution, and the Secretary-General of UNCTAD would "convene an inter-governmental group of experts to assist as necessary in that task."

Resolutions on Technology Transfer

A one-sided technological dependency has characterized the relationship between developing and developed countries. International action to correct this imbalance began at UNCTAD I where it was agreed that competent international bodies should explore:

possibilities for adaptation of legislation concerning the transfer of industrial technology to developing countries, including the possibility of concluding appropriate international agreements in this field. (108)

Many other bodies, both public and private, either continued or developed an interest in the general question of technology transfer. (109) Momentum on

the international level was increased when the Conference at UNCTAD III
passed a major policy resolution [39 (III)] on Transfer of Technology. (110)
Included within the resolution were detailed suggestions to the developing
countries to establish institutions, and to the developed market economy and
Eastern European socialist countries to facilitate an accelerated transfer of
technology on favorable terms for developing countries; and requested the
Secretary-General of UNCTAD to carry out with others:

> a study of possible bases for new international legislation regulating the
> transfer from developed to developing countries of patented and non-
> patented technology, including related commercial and legal aspects of
> such transfer. (111)

Also included in the resolution were various recommendations to improve the
scientific and technological infrastructure of the developing countries. This
part of the resolution called for action by the developing countries at the
national, regional, and interregional levels. In addition to a series of general
recommendations to the developed countries, there were two specific requests
of the developing countries to the developed countries with strong financial
implications:

> 17. Takes note of the wishes of the developing countries that the
> developed countries should: (a) Devote 0.05 percent per annum of
> their gross national product to the technological problems of develop-
> ing countries; (b) Allocate at least 10 percent of their research and
> development expenditure to programmes designed to solve problems of
> specific interest to developing countries generally, and as far as
> possible devote that expenditure to projects in developing
> countries. (112)

In order to implement the many suggestions of the Intergovernmental
Group on Transfer Technology, these issues were given higher priority in the
UNCTAD work schedule; and the Intergovernmental Group was replaced and
upgraded by a Committee on Transfer of Technology which became a
principal Committee of the Trade and Development Board. (113) In a report
of its first session (24 November - 5 December 1975), it was stated that a
representative of the Secretary-General of UNCTAD "observed that, owing to
the limitation of resources, only a few of the provisions of Resolution 39
(III)...had actually been implemented." (114)
   This was the setting when the Group of 77 met in Manila in February 1976
to prepare for UNCTAD IV. They proposed an updated elaboration of
Resolution 39 (III) including a compulsory code of conduct for the Transfer of
Technology. (115)
   The developing countries were advised to formulate technology plans as an
integral part of their national development plan and to establish appropriate
institutional machinery including national centers for the development and
transfer of technology. These national efforts were to be supplemented by
subregional, regional, and interregional cooperation. (116)
   The developed countries were asked to implement various provisions of

Resolution 39 (III) including paragraph 17 quoted above. In addition they were asked to "grant the developing countries unrestricted access to existing technology irrespective of the ownership of such technology." Cooperation was also solicited for the "establishment of industrial technological information banks, centers for the development and transfer of technology, and for other viable information centers." Finally, they were asked to refrain from "pursuing policies which might encourage the exodus of trained personnel from developing countries." (117) A Technological Advisory Service within UNCTAD and close collaboration with UNIDO were other suggestions included in the Manila Declaration. (118)

The proposal which was to generate the most controversy was the one calling for a compulsory code of conduct for the Transfer of Technology. Although this was not a new proposal, it was now gathering momentum following the establishment of the Intergovernmental Group of Experts on an International Code of Conduct on Transfer of Technology. (119) The Group of 77 had already submitted a proposal to the Intergovernmental Group, and it was this proposal which they wanted to use as a basis of negotiations at a suggested plenipotentiary conference under UNCTAD's auspices in 1977. (120) They argued that a multilateral, legally binding code is "the only way of efficiently regulating transfer of technology, taking into consideration the particular needs of the developing countries." (121)

With respect to industrial property, the Manila Conferees wanted UNCTAD to play a major role in the ongoing revisions of the Paris Convention for Industrial Property. (122) The LDCs asserted that patent legislation "should be designed to serve their public interest...and should basically be geared to creating conditions for optimal use as well as for the creation of knowledge and technology to further the social objectives of industrialization." (123) Property rights should be "accompanied by corresponding obligations on the part of the patentee"; " [a] dequate exploitation of the patents granted would contribute towards fulfilling the developmental needs...." (124)

The Manila proposals formed the basis of the Group of 77's negotiation position at UNCTAD IV. The industrial countries opposed a legally binding code of conduct, and reasserted that the private sector alone could decide questions of how it would share its industrial property. While they supported the strengthening of the technological capacity of developing countries, they did not agree with the Group of 77 as to how it should be done and who should pay for it. After protracted debate, UNCTAD IV passed three separate resolutions on the transfer of technology, each without dissent. (125)

The first resolution dealt with national and cooperative measures to strengthen the technological capacity of developing countries. (126)   It followed the general lines of the Manila proposals and included an agreement to establish an advisory service on the transfer of technology. However, it excluded the provisions of resolution 39 (III) (para. 17) summarized above, and specified formulas for developed country financing of technology transfer. In its place the resolution specified that assistance should be rendered from the regular budget of UNCTAD. It proposed that UNCTAD urge the General Assembly to provide resources for financing projects and programs from the United Nations Regular Program of Technological Assistance. It proposed also that UNCTAD urge the UNDP, the World Bank, and "all countries" to make voluntary contributions. The resolution called for developed countries to consider measures to deal with the "brain drain," and recommended that UNCTAD coordinate its actions with other UN bodies, particularly the Committee on Science and Technology.

U.S. comments on sub-paragraph 5(b) (i) of the resolution pointed up the role of the private sector in technology transfer. (127) It affirmed that the appropriate exchange of information on technological alternatives available to nations "must be consistent with contractual agreements and, where relevant, must respect the confidentiality of technological information."

The second resolution on the transfer of technology concerned industrial property. (128) It followed very closely the positions adopted by the Group of 77 in Manila. Emphasis remained on resolution 3 (I) of the Committee on Transfer of Technology calling, in general, for improved conditions for adaptation of technology, the development of indigenous technology, training, "fair and reasonable terms" for transfers, the working of patents within developing countries, the need for technical assistance in the field of industrial property, in-depth review of provisions on trademarks, study of the possibility of giving preferential treatment to developing countries and reasonable conditions for universal membership in the Paris Union. It was recommended that UNCTAD "play a prominent role with regard to the economic, commercial, and developmental aspects of a review of that field, in particular the ongoing revision of the Paris Convention."

The final resolution which dealt with technology transfer related to an international code of conduct on transfer of technology. (129) The developed countries opposed a legally binding code as proposed at Manila. The compromise arrived at was a consensus on the development of a code of conduct by UNCTAD, but no consensus was reached on its binding effect. This latter issue was put off until a later date. Work was continued on the drafting of a code, and it was agreed that an intergovernmental group of experts would be established with a goal of completing it by the middle of 1977. The group of experts was to be free "to formulate the draft provisions ranging from mandatory to optional, without prejudice to the final decision on the legal character of the Code of Conduct." It was further recommended that the General Assembly at its Thirty-first Session convene a United Nations conference, under the auspices of UNCTAD, to be held by the end of 1977 to negotiate the final code.

Resolution on Transnational Corporations (TNCs)

The only adopted resolution failing to be passed without dissent dealt with transnational corporations and expansion of trade in manufactures and semi-manufactures. (130) It received no negative votes, but sixteen abstentions were recorded. Following very closely the text of the Manila Declaration and Program of Action, it recommended a "reorientation in the activities of transnational corporations towards more complete manufacture...and further processing...of raw materials" in developing countries "for both domestic and foreign markets." The developed countries were asked in this connection to adjust "their tariff and nontariff and fiscal and financial policies."

Canada supported the resolution but pointed out that the suggestion that national fiscal and monetary policies should be directed at increasing further processing and more complete manufacturing abroad, rather than the management of the national economy, was not in keeping with its policies. New Zealand also had reservations along these lines. (131)

The resolution went on to recommend measures to strengthen the participation of national enterprises of developing countries in activities undertaken by TNCs in their territories, particularly in the area of the import and export of manufactures and semi-manufactures.

Other parts of the resolution suggested specific rules should be developed to control restrictive business practices of TNCs likely to affect adversely the import and export of developing countries. Finally it was recommended that measures should be designed to ensure that the activities of the TNCs would become a positive factor in the export efforts of the developing countries. This was to be achieved by bringing about greater governmental control over the processing, marketing, and distribution of TNC manufactures and semi-manufactures.

The United States, Japan, and Switzerland, in explaining their abstentions urged developing countries which considered private investment to be a positive contribution for their development process to promote an appropriate investment climate. (132)   The United States went on to underline the importance of local national laws being stable and "consistent with international laws." It cautioned that in regulating the activities of the TNCs, "governments should be guided by an understanding of the legitimate methods of an entity that is often privately owned, otherwise positive contributions from such activities to development could be diminished." This is a rather cryptic comment, and it is somewhat difficult to do more than speculate on the reasons behind the United States' abstention. For the most part, it appears to be a fear that the developing countries may overregulate the TNCs, and, thus, either limit or destroy their effectiveness. The EEC abstained without comment, but one could speculate that the Community's reasoning was similar to that of the United States.

The abstentions of Turkey (133) and Spain (134) were based on the fact that the Commission on Transnational Corporations was engaged in a study on these problems, and Turkey believed that the resolution was premature, while Spain believed that the issues would be prejudged in the Commission by this resolution.

In summary, the developing countries were attempting to increase their local manufacturing and processing operations with the support of the TNCs. Abstentions on the part of the developed countries appear to be based on the fear that the TNCs might be overregulated.

Resolution for the IRB

Only one resolution, that on a proposed International Resources Bank (IRB), was defeated at the Conference. (135) Introduced in the speech of the U.S. Secretary of State Kissinger, (136) it proposed a new institution to facilitate new investments in mineral exploitation in developing countries by reducing noncommercial risks. The vote was 31 in favor, 33 against, and 44 abstentions. (137)

The reason for advocating a new institution was directly related to the fact that private investors were becoming increasingly reluctant to invest in developing countries at a time when the demand for mineral resources was increasing. Mineral investments require large amounts of capital and in Kissinger's words, "[n]ationalization and forced change in the terms of concessions in some developing countries have clouded the general climate for resource investment in the developing world. Social and political uncertainties have further complicated investment prospects." He noted that this had resulted in the postponement, cancellation, or relocation of commercially viable projects to industrialized countries. Thus, the cost of minerals had escalated and the developing countries were not maximizing their export potential in this area. Kissinger noted that the requirements for resources would increase rapidly during the 1980s, and because of the long lag time between the investment decision and production, measures to increase production had to be made now.

The IRB was to have three functions: catalytic, financial, and insurance. It was proposed that it be capitalized at $1 billion. It was then to "participate with foreign investors and the host government in project agreements specifying the conditions of the investment on a basis acceptable to all parties." The bank would "support guarantees of both investor and host nation performance in accordance with conditions established in the project agreement." It was believed that this latter provision, by reducing noncommercial risks, would promote greater flows of investment capital.

Production-sharing was contemplated as an element of the agreements, with the foreign investor and host nation assured of an established percentage of total production. An interesting innovation was provided in the sale of IRB bonds in the international markets, pledging future output of resource projects as collateral. The trilateral agreement was also to provide for "the progressive acquisition of technology by the host country...." Kissinger suggested that the IRB "could be associated with the World Bank Group." It was assumed that its presence would make the foreign companies more acceptable to host governments and eliminate the threat of expropriation.

At the time of its presentation, this was not a detailed proposal. Instead, it set forth, in broad outline, a general approach to a complex problem. Subsequently, it was elaborated on and reviewed by the World Bank at the request of the United States Secretary of the Treasury. (138)

The public opposition to the proposal tended to be ideological and procedural. (139) Cuba argued that it ran counter to the principles and objectives of the New International Economic Order, the Democratic People's Republic of Korea argued that its sole purpose was to undermine the Integrated Commodity Program. Both Iraq and Libya saw it as a measure to strengthen the TNCs. Most opponents emphasized that it had not been the subject of any discussion or detailed study.

The report of the Congressional Advisors to the Conference believed that mostly tactical errors contributed to the defeat of the resolution. They elaborate four reasons for this judgment. (140) First, the United States attempted to negotiate a statement on reservations to the consensus resolution on commodities while the consensus resolution was still being negotiated, thus indicating a lack of good faith on the part of the United States. Thus many developing countries abstained on the IRB resolution. Second, the United States failed to inform other nations fully of the proposal for the creation of the IRB. For example, the United States' delegation failed to present a position paper to explain fully the IRB's purpose, possible functions, and structure. Third, they made it a separate resolution rather than tying it to the commodities resolution. Fourth, a factor over which the U.S. had no control, no black African had been included in the "president's" contact group. The Africans felt slighted and showed their pique by voting against, or abstaining on, the IRB resolution. The Congressional group rejected Secretaries Simon and Kissinger's joint statement, blaming the proposal's defeat on an "accidental majority" of countries inspired or created by the Socialist countries. (141)

However that may be, the conferees at UNCTAD IV passed all other resolutions without dissent. Given the substance of these resolutions, it is clear that the apparent unanimity did not reflect the achievement of consensus on these issues between developed and developing countries. It reflected, rather, their mutual desire to cooperate, even if only on noncommittal resolutions.

Conference at the Senior Officers Level (CIEC resumed)

Following UNCTAD IV, the North/South dialogue returned to CIEC. The senior officials' meeting took place in Paris from July 8-10, 1976. The co-chairman of the Conference announced that the Commissions would spend the second half of the year on specific areas of common concern with the objective of reaching concrete results satisfactory to all parties.

It was soon clear that there were serious differences of opinion between the two negotiating groups. (142) The LDCs, disappointed at the lack of results within the Commissions, presented a paper enumerating areas of concentration for them. The developed countries took issue with the Group of 19 paper on two grounds. First, they argued that the Commissions should determine their own work programs. Second, they opposed the formulation of the issues by the Group of 19; this group had assumed consensus on underlying policies when no such consensus existed. For example, the Group of 19 wanted agreed language in the work program that would have committed the industrial nations to implement a decision on reducing or eliminating public bilateral or international debt before the issue had been debated and agreed on. (143)

These differences could not be resolved, and CIEC was broken off. It took two months of quiet diplomacy to get the groups back together again in September. (144) A contributing factor in the reconvening of the conference was a fear, supported by OPEC statements, that if there were no progress in the talks, the price of oil might be raised at the OPEC meeting scheduled later in the year. Therefore, negotiations recommenced at CIEC. The Commissions accelerated their work schedules to meet the approaching deadline for the Second Ministerial Conference. They assigned contact groups the role of continuing the exchange of views and narrowing the gap between opposing positions.   These efforts resulted in no substantial consensus. The upcoming United States elections of November 1976 provided a rationale for putting off the Ministerial meeting until May 1977. (145) Both sides took advantage of the situation and agreed to postpone the final Ministerial meeting until May 30, 1977.

The Second Ministerial Meeting (CIEC): May 30-June 2, 1977

Four days of intense discussions and negotiations among the ministers produced the Final Communique of the Conference on International Economic cooperation. (146) It revealed that despite the six-month period of grace to finalize Commission reports, the countries had been able to reach few points of consensus on key issues. The Communique lists 20 items on which the participants agreed, and 21 on which they did not. This might lead to the conclusion that the Conference was a success. In fact, the 20 items of agreement were little more than broad statements of intent without procedures for implementation.

Given the divergence between the goals of the industrialized and developing countries, the failure to achieve substantive consensus might have been expected. The LDCs seek a restructuring of the international economic order.   The United States rejects this approach completely; its general strategy is to redirect the North/South dialogue, in CIEC and other fora, toward an emphasis on improving, rather than restructuring, the existing international economic system, and on enabling the developing countries to participate more fully in this system.   The other OECD countries are in general accord with the U.S. negotiating strategy.

Two concrete proposals to come out of CIEC were the "Special Action" Program to provide an additional $1 billion of aid to the poorest countries, and the establishment of priority lending by the World Bank for the development of energy resources. All other proposals in the Communique were extremely vague. What follows is a summary of these proposals by Commission heading.

Energy

Agreement on general guidelines that:

1. recognize that adequate and stable energy supplies are essential to global growth, and that it is the responsibilities of all nations...to ensure that such supplies are available;

2. call for intensified national and international cooperative efforts to expand energy conservation and accelerate the development of conventional and nonconventional energy supplies during the energy transition period and beyond;

3. affirm that special efforts should be made to assist oil importing LDCs to alleviate their energy burdens;

4. recommend that the IBRD, in the context of a general capital increase, establish a new priority lending for LDC energy developments;

5. call for new international efforts to facilitate the transfer of energy technology to LDCs wishing to acquire such technologies;

6. endorse enhanced international cooperation in energy R & D, which will probably lead to participation by some oil exporting and other developing countries in ongoing R & D work in the international energy agency; and

7. recognize the desirability and inevitability of the integration of the downstream processing industries of the oil exporting countries into the expanding world industrial structure as rapidly as possible.

No agreement was reached on the pricing of energy, purchasing power of energy export earnings, the utilization of accumulated revenues from oil exports, and continuing consultations on energy. The last point was considered to be of major importance to the developed countries, especially the European Community, inasmuch as there was no existing international forum for such consultations. Energy was the only issue at the Conference which was not explicitly within the province of other North/South forums.

Raw Materials

The Commission on Raw Materials agreed, in an inconclusive fashion, on the establishment of a common fund, its "purposes, objectives and other constituent elements to be further negotiated in UNCTAD" (emphasis added).

General agreement was reached on the principles of research and development and some other measures for natural products competing with synthetics; measures for international cooperation in the field on marketing and distribution of raw materials; measures to assist importing developing countries to develop and diversify their indigenous natural resources; agreement for improving a generalized system of preference schemes; identification of areas for special and more favorable treatment for developing countries in the multilateral trade negotiations; and certain other trade questions.

put into effect. There was disagreement on the issue of indexation, the right of UNCTAD to participate in discussions on modification of the IMF's compensatory finance scheme, along with the IMF/IBRD Development Committee, and aspects of local processing and diversification. Disagreement was also recorded on world shipping tonnage and trade, representation of LDCs on commodity exchanges, and a code of conduct for liner conferences. Production controls and other measures concerning synthetics and investment in the field of raw materials were still other areas of no consensus.

Development

There was agreement that the volume, quantity, and quality of official development assistance (ODA) should be increased. The developed countries made a specific commitment to provide $1 billion in a special action program for poorer LDCs, i.e., those eligible for IDA credits. The United States' contribution was to be in the form of $375 million of additional bilateral assistance. The European Community agreed to contribute $385 million to a special account of IDA, and other developed country participants agreed to split the remaining $240 million, some of which was to be in the form of debt relief.

There was general support for various food and agricultural policies already approved in other forums, including the General Assembly decision to make available within the World Food Programme an international reserve for emergencies, with the aim of a target of not less than 500,000 tons of cereals. There was also general agreement on infrastructure development in developing countries, with particular reference to transportation and communication systems in Africa.

Various LDC proposals for adjustment assistance to encourage domestic industries in developed countries to move progressively out of lines of production in which they are less competitive internationally were not acceptable to the Group of 8. Nor were their proposals to eliminate policies and measures designed to protect their uncompetitive industries and to provide unrestricted access to developed country markets for manufactured and semi-manufactured goods from developing countries.

There was no agreement on a compulsory code of conduct for transnational corporations.

Finance

Although there was general agreement on the importance of foreign investment and the need for a positive investment climate, there was no agreement on criteria for compensation, transferability of income and capital, and jurisdiction and standards for the settlement of disputes.

There was general agreement on improving the access of LDCs to private capital markets in developed countries. In this regard the work of the IMF/IBRD Development Committee was supported, and the speedy implementation of its recommendations was urged.

There was general endorsement of the work of the Interim Committee of the IMF with strong support expressed for the initiative taken to establish a supplementary credit facility in IMF.

There was no agreement on either the source of inflation or the way to deal with it.

There was no agreement on the handling of the financial assets of oil exporting developing countries.

The participants viewed the results of the Conference from their respective positions. The LDCs "noted with regret that most of the proposals for structured changes in the international economic system and certain of the proposals for urgent actions on pressing problems have not been agreed upon." (146a) The developed countries "welcomed the spirit of cooperation in which on the whole the Conference took place and expressed their determination to maintain that spirit as the dialogue between developed and developing countries continues in other places." (146b)

Summary

By mid-1977 it was obvious that the momentum generated by the LDCs in 1974 had been lost. In the two-and-a-half-year period following the Charter, the LDCs brought about no structural changes in the international economic order. By the conclusion of CIEC, the only positive achievement was an agreement by the developed countries to provide $1 billion of additional aid. The integrated commodity program, codes for the conduct of transnational corporations and the transfer of technology, indexation, and indebtedness were still being discussed without any consensus.

The developed countries were successful in slowing the advance of LDC proposals during the period. Concessions on compensatory finance and increased foreign aid operate very much within the existing structural framework. However, the developed countries failed in their efforts to return to the status quo ante of the 1974 resolutions. They did not repeal Article 2 of the Charter on private investment. They concluded no agreement on the price of energy or continuing consultations with OPEC. Perhaps most important, and related to these previous points, they achieved no agreement on investment in the field of raw materials.

CIEC was dissolved after the second Ministerial Meeting. It was an experiment in quiet diplomacy on an international level concerning issues of fundamental importance to all members of the world community. The issues did not die. The dialogue continues within UNCTAD, the United Nations, the World Bank, the IMF, GATT, and the Specialized Agencies.

OTHER NEGOTIATIONS

In addition to the negotiations discussed above, international negotiations on industrial development also took place during the period 1975-77. On the regional level, this period witnessed the conclusion of negotiations between the EEC and 46 developing countries, which led to the Lomé Convention. These developments are discussed here so as not to break the continuity of the more interrelated meetings discussed above.

The Second General Conference of the United Nations Industrial Development Organization (March 12-26, 1975)

The Second General Conference of UNIDO, meeting in Lima, Peru, continued the momentum and style generated by the Group of 77 at the Sixth Special Session and the Twenty-Ninth General Assembly. It adopted, after much debate, a Declaration and Plan of Action on Industrial Development and Cooperation (147) (the Lima Declaration) based upon a draft drawn up by the Second Ministerial Meeting of the Group of 77 held at Algiers from February 15-18, 1975. (148) The vote was 82 in favor, 1 against (U.S.), and 7 abstentions.

After reviewing recent resolutions including the Resolution on the Declaration and Programme of Action on the Establishment of a New International Economic Order and the Charter of Economic Rights and Duties of States, the Lima Declaration discussed the importance of industrialization in economic development and outlined a series of specific measures to achieve the goal of increasing the share of developing countries in world industrial production from 7 to 25 percent by the year 2000. (149) Among other things the Declaration recommended that UNIDO be converted into a specialized agency and that an Industrial Development Fund be established. (150)

The discussion of industrialization policy was comprehensive including, inter alia: (151) national industrial plans; financing; increased role for women, nationalization when necessary; the special problems of least developed countries; processing, consultation, and cooperation among producer associations; a code of conduct for technology transfer; linkage between industrial and agricultural sectors; the development of basic industries within LDCs; adaptation of the educational system; creation of research institutions and training programs; preferences for exports; and increased technical and financial assistance from the developed countries.

The Plan of Action (152) set forth the measures to be taken singly by developing and developed countries, as well as measures to increase cooperation among developing countries and between developing and developed countries. It concluded with a series of measures directed to the least developed, landlocked and island developing countries.

The Lima Declaration represented the consolidation of proposals made over the years in many forums. As such it provided a useful checklist for LDCs in formulating industrial policies. One of the new suggestions to improve the negotiating position of the LDCs was important, but peripheral to industrial development. It called for the LDCs to: (153)

> Consider all possible means of strengthening the action of producer associations already established, encourage the creation of other associations for the principal commodities exported by them, and establish a mechanism for consultation and cooperation among the various producer associations for the purpose of the coordination of their activities and for their mutual support....

The decision to recommend to the General Assembly of the United Nations that UNIDO should be converted into a specialized agency was taken with the idea of increasing the autonomy of UNIDO. (154) However, this was an approach fraught with dangers. UNIDO is a subsidiary organ of the General Assembly, and, as such, it is funded by the United Nations' budget. The United Nations' budget is funded by assessments on its members. Thus it has a certain automaticity. However, the creation of a specialized agency meant that current members of the United Nations would have to make two closely related judgments: whether their legislators would agree to funding a new international organization, and whether to join the new specialized agency. This is one of the few recent instances when the Group of 77 relied on their voting power without considering the financial consequences. The

LDCs agreed on the following provision in the draft constitution (155) to assuage fears that those funding the new Specialized Agency would not control it:

> The approval of the Programme of work and the corresponding budgetary estimates shall also require the affirmative vote of Members that are to contribute, through contributions assessed or voluntarily pledged without restrictions, at least one half of the resources to be spent by the Organization during the period concerned.

Discussions with the involved parties suggest that the Group of 77 believed that even if the United States and other developed countries refused to join and fund the new specialized agency, the OPEC countries would provide the necessary funds. Following the Lima Conference, ECOSOC reviewed the draft constitution of the proposed organization (156) and by resolution (157) transmitted it to the Seventh Special Session and Thirtieth Regular Session of the General Assembly for consideration. The Seventh Special Session endorsed the recommendation to convert the organization into a specialized agency and established an intergovernmental committee of the whole to meet in Vienna (headquarters of UNIDO) to draw up a constitution for UNIDO as a specialized agency. Although a number of meetings have taken place to date (July 1977) no decisions have been concluded. One of the barriers to agreement has revolved around funding the organization. To date the OPEC countries have not agreed to fund shortfalls resulting from the decision of particular countries not to join the new organization.

Two additional issues were discussed at the Conference: an industrial development fund, and the primacy of UNIDO over other international organizations in the field of industrial development. The Lima Declaration called for the establishment of an Industrial Development Fund (158) to both increase the resources of UNIDO and enhance "its autonomy and ability to meet, promptly and flexibly, the needs of developing countries." It was proposed that the Fund be established through voluntary contributions. No specific reference was made to the Fund in the resolutions passed at the Seventh Special Session.

The issue of the primacy of UNIDO as executing agency and central coordinator in the field of industrial development is an attempt to improve the position of UNIDO vis-à-vis the World Bank and the International Finance Corporation (IFC). To date the latter organizations have been much more important in financing industry and as executing agencies for the UNDP. Through June 30, 1976, the World Bank has loaned $2.6 billion for industrial projects plus another $3.2 billion to development finance companies. (159) In addition, the Bank has been a principal provider of funds to the capital and social infrastructure projects necessary to begin industrialization. Following behind the Bank in importance is the IFC, which was specifically established to supplement existing funds for industrialization. UNIDO has

> concentrated on technical cooperation in the preinvestment phase. The major part of the field activities of UNIDO is devoted to the provision of advisory services of various kinds; the carrying out of prefeasibility and

feasibility studies; assistance in establishing and strengthening national industrial institutions; the preparation of industrial development programmes and policies; and, last but not least, the training and upgrading of skills and the transfer of know-how. (160)

The problems of industrialization in LDCs is sufficiently complex to engage the attention of both UNIDO and the World Bank Group, and they have already entered into a cooperative program. (161)

The Lima Declaration and Plan of Action is a broad based controversial document touching on most of the major industrialization issues.   To be successful, it will require the support of both LDCs and developed countries. As presently worded, the achievements of the specified goals may be delayed due to ideological conflicts between the LDCs and the industrial states over how to achieve these goals. The latter argue for development through private capital, and the former for an increase both in publicly directed investment and public enterprises.

Negotiations Leading to the Lomé Convention:
July 1973-February 1975

The Lomé Convention, (162) signed on February 28, 1975, between the nine (163) members of the expanded European Economic Community and 46 African, Caribbean, and Pacific (ACP) states, (164) is the latest in a series of trade and aid arrangements which date back to the formation of the Community. (165)   The entry of the United Kingdom into the Community (166) resulted in the application, with some modification, to many Commonwealth LDCs (167) plus a few other countries (168) of long-held EEC policies towards members' former dependencies.   The most innovative aspect of the Lomé Convention is STABEX, an arrangement for the stabilization of LDC export earnings. (169) There is some controversy, however, over the significance of this measure, and of the Convention as a whole.   Some have hailed Lomé as indicative of new directions for other North/South relationships, (170) and suggested STABEX as a promising alternative to the controversial integrated commodity program proposed by the Group of 77. (171) Others have judged it to perpetuate a neo-colonial relationship and to be divisive of the Group of 77. (172)

At the formation of the Common Market in 1957, France insisted on provision in the Treaty of Rome of special trade and aid measures for associated members (colonies and territories).   Trade between associated members and the Common Market was to be "as free as possible." (173) Development aid was provided for through the establishment of the European Development Fund (EDF), initiated with $581 million of grant aid funds. (174)

By 1961, all of the associated members had become independent. This led to a revision of the special provisions in the Treaty of Rome for the 18 Associated African and Malagasy States (AAMS). (175)

In the Yaoundé Convention (176) of July 20, 1963, the EEC and AAMS agreed to the establishment of reciprocal non-discriminatory preferences and the progressive abolition of tariffs, export duties, and quantitative restrictions with appropriate escape clauses for AAMS based on "development needs, or its industrialization requirements or which are intended to contribute to its budget." (177)   The most important provision of the Convention from the perspective of the Associated States was Annex III, which phased out arrangements by which the former French colonies had entered into quantitative sales agreements over the years with the French at guaranteed, subsidized prices. (178)

The importance of these agreements may be illustrated by Senegal whose main export, peanuts, accounted for 85 percent of its export revenues. French subsidies in some years had run as high as 30 percent. (179) But with Yaoundé, a schedule was established for the marketing of certain previously subsidized products at world prices.   To soften the blow resulting from the ending of this institutional device, the EEC provided $230 million of total EDF aid of $666 million for diversification and production. (180) In addition, up to $50 million of EDF funds were earmarked for "advances for the purpose of helping to alleviate the effects of temporary fluctuations in world prices." (181) Aid modalities were varied in this Convention by instituting "loans on special terms," i.e., up to $46 million (182) subsidized from the EDF, and loans at market rates from the EIB. (183)

Other provisions of the Convention assured nationals and companies of EEC countries that they would all be placed on equal footing in Associated States. (184)   Thus lawyers, engineers, architects, dentists, and companies from any one of the EEC states were to be treated equally within the Associated States.   For example, Senegal permitted French professionals to operate within the country if they were licensed in France. Following the convention they had the option of permitting either all properly licensed professionals within the EEC to operate within Senegal or none.

In 1969, the term of the Convention came to an end.   A Second Convention, known as Yaoundé II, was signed on July 29, 1969 and came into force on January 1, 1971. It was not significantly different from Yaoundé I. Yaoundé II raised EDF aid from $666 to $828 million, (185) and EIB aid from $64 to $90 million (186) over a five-year period.

The Treaty of Rome and the two Yaoundé Conventions acted as transitional institutions created by former colonial powers to lessen the impact of ending favorable bilateral relationships with their present and past colonies.   However, the reciprocal nondiscriminatory, free trade provisions were not very important to the Associated States. From the beginning, they permitted specified tropical and industrial exports of the Associated States into the EEC duty free, but were more restrictive, through preferential tariffs, in relation to food products in competition with the Europeans. The elimination of tariffs on industrial imports had little effect on an Associated State which had very limited industrial production. Moreover, the reduction in the common external tariffs of the EEC through the establishment of new preferential trading relationships, (187) including the General System of Preferences with 91 LDCs, (188) meant that the ACP states were forced to compete with more industrially advanced LDCs for limited EEC markets.

The nondiscriminatory trade relations with members of the EEC had one positive by-product; it introduced a great variety of lower-priced European goods into the formerly high-priced and exclusive French market in the

Associated States. (189) The abolition of French agreements to import fixed quantities of Associated States' products at guaranteed, and usually subsidized, prices had a serious effect on the economies of various Associated States. The attempt to soften these effects through foreign aid fell far short of balancing the losses. Nevertheless, to the extent that EDF and EIB funds were additional to bilateral flows, they were both welcome and useful.

The British entry into the EEC in 1973 presented the Community with the same kinds of problems in relation to Commonwealth countries as those which had been faced by the EEC "six" in 1975 with regard to future economic relations with their historical trading zone. One major problem concerned the Commonwealth countries to which to extend Associate Status. The EEC and the United Kingdom agreed (190) that 20 independent Commonwealth countries had economic structures and production patterns comparable to those of the Associates under Yaoundé. They, thus, came within the Declaration of Intent of April 1963, which offered to such countries the opportunity to join the Yaoundé Convention. (191) Under the Declaration of Intent, they would be able to enter into any one of three relationships: become an Associate State in the Convention to follow Yaoundé II, enter into one or more Special Conventions with the EEC, or conclude a trade agreement. (192) Those countries wishing to become Associated States were invited to participate in the negotiations scheduled to begin August 1, 1973. (193) Countries which did not come within the 1963 Declaration of Intent were Ceylon, India, Malaysia, Pakistan, and Singapore. (194) In the Treaty of Accession a new Joint Declaration was made on the development of trade relations between these states and the EEC. (195)

Other problems involved products to be covered by special treaty provisions, and compensation, if any, to be granted to the 20 Commonwealth developing countries which would now share trade privileges with the 18 Associated States.

When the negotiations for Lomé commenced in July 1973, the LDCs consisted of 46 countries: the 19 Associated States; (196) 21 Commonwealth states (Grenada and Bahamas had just become independent and been added); (197) and six other African states (Guinea, Ethiopia, Liberia, Sudan, Equatorial Africa, and Guinea-Bissau). They were known as the African, Caribbean, and Pacific States (ACP). In 1977, six more countries signed the Convention: Papua New Guinea, Cape Verde, Comoros Republic, Sao Tome et Principe, the Seychelles, and Surinam.

In spite of their diverse stages of development and colonial heritages, the ACP states coordinated their negotiations. They selected a single spokesman for the African group in Brussels, and an OAU Secretariat was established there to work with existing Yaoundé and Arusha groupings. (198) The formal negotiations were delayed three and one-half months to give the ACP states adequate time for preparation. (199) The Nigerian Ambassador to Belgium, Mr. Olu Sanu, became the ACP spokesman. (200)   In July 1974, at a ministerial-level meeting in Jamaica, consensus was reached on three major sections of the Convention: (201) the EEC dropped any reciprocity requirements in regard to trade; there was to be a scheme for stabilization of exports; and, industrialization and technical aid was to be given priority. Disagreement continued on the amount of financial aid and the question of sugar exports. The question of sugar trade was of crucial importance to the economies of several of the ACP countries, the Caribbean states in particular. (202) Ministerial-level talks on January 13 and 30, 1975, led to an agreement on the text. (203) The signing of the Convention took place on February 28, 1975.

One commentator on Lomé (204) found that the relations between the "industrial states and the LDCs continue to be asymmetric," but was extremely impressed with the "organization, sophistication, skill, patience, and fortitude of the ACP states throughout the negotiations leading to Lomé." Nigeria and the six Caribbean Commonwealth countries were given high marks for the dynamism and skill of their experienced negotiators. (205) They were aided by the Yaoundé countries' familiarity with the EEC bureaucracy. (206) Gruhn argues, in essence, that a coordinated approach to the negotiations appreciably improved the bargaining power of the ACP states. (207)

Important changes in the trade cooperation provisions of Lomé compared to earlier Conventions are those ending reverse preferences, (208) i.e., requiring reciprocal preferences from the Associated States for EEC preferences, the redefinition of the rules of origin (209) to include all 46 ACP states as one unit, and a compensatory finance facility known as STABEX. (210) In addition, Protocol No. 3 of the Convention commits the EEC "for an indefinite period to purchase and import, at guaranteed prices, specific quantities of cane sugar" from ACP states. This is a form of concession which the Yaoundé states never obtained in relation to any of their exports. It guarantees, for at least seven years, the annual importation of up to 1.4 million tons of sugar into the Community from ACP states at an annually negotiated and guaranteed price indexed to the annually set support price for Community-produced beet sugar. The price is, in essence, a floor price. ACP exporters will sell their production to buyers within the Community. If the price or demand falls below the guarantees, the Community will intervene and buy the guaranteed production at the guaranteed price. National quotas have been allocated to sugar-producing ACP states, and if they fail to export amounts equal to their quota for reasons other than force majeure, their quota in future years is cut by the amount of the shortfall and can be reattributed by the Community to another producing country.

The Lomé Convention continued to utilize the aid institutions created under earlier agreements. Financial and technical assistance through the European Development Fund (EDF) and the European Investment Bank (EIB) was set at 3.39 billion units of account (u.a.) ($4.2 billion) over the five-year life of the Convention. (211) This was 269 percent above the Yaoundé II figure, and it was to service a population which had risen by 243 percent. If one uses current prices, per capita aid increased from 11.83 u.a. to 12.75 u.a. However, if inflation is taken into account, per capita aid is 40 percent below that offered under Yaoundé II. (212) The ACP states had requested 8 billion u.a. ($9.92 billion), but relented on their demands when the EEC argued that in light of the worldwide recession such a request could not be met. (213)

The EDF received 3 billion u.a. ($3.72 billion) (214) broken down as follows: 2.1 billion u.a. ($2.6 billion) grants; 430 million u.a. ($532.2 million) for special loans (40 years, 10 years' grace, 1 percent interest); 95 million u.a. ($117.8 million) for risk capital; up to 100 million u.a. ($124 million) to subsidize interest on EIB loans; and 375 million u.a. ($465 million) for STABEX. The EIB will authorize up to 390 million u.a. (215) ($483.6 million) of loans at commercial rates, some of which will receive interest subsidization from EDF resources.

There is no provision to allocate fixed amounts of aid to particular ACP states. There is, however, a specific article of the Convention requiring special attention to the needs of 24 least developed ACP states. (216) Approximately ten percent of the aid is reserved for financing regional projects. (217) An elaborate procedure has been devised to involve the ACP states in the various stages of a project. However, the ultimate decision on aid allocations remains with the EEC. (218)

Under Lomé, reverse preferences have been eliminated; a compensatory finance facility instituted; special arrangements have been provided for sugar producers; aid per capita in current, but not real, prices has increased; and the new ACP states have access to the Community under limited preferences. The Convention is, at best, a lateral move on the part of 46 states towards the New International Economic Order which they all supported in 1974. At worst, it may prove to be a stumbling block to LDC unity. When more universal approaches to the NIEO are initiated, the 46 will be required to decide on whether to give up comparative advantages for the good of the larger group of states.

CONCLUSIONS

From January 1975 through June 1977 a downturn in the international economy coupled with a perceptive appraisal by the U.S. government of the weakened position of developing countries' bargaining power all but brought to a halt initiatives for a New International Economic Order.

The United States Secretary of State broke off the early CIEC talks by withdrawing his delegation. Then, after a period of months, he modified the U.S. stand and made it possible for the talks to be resumed after the Seventh Special Session. His speech at this Special Session, sandwiched between the CIEC meetings, was well drafted and friendly and appeared to have the goal of making the recently chastized developing countries feel that the United States was once again willing to be on good terms with them. The speech had a secondary goal of shaking the Europeans out of their self-imposed impotency, and galvanizing them into a less maleable force vis-à-vis developing country demands. He was successful in both goals. By December 1975, the fears which had immobilized the developed countries for almost two years had been replaced by a self-confidence which enabled them to stand united against undesired structural changes.

The drop in commodity prices during this period seriously affected many of the developing countries and contributed to a toning down of confrontational tactics. Movement for new initiatives, or the implementation of old ones, relating to the New International Economic Order was considerably slowed.   The pattern at the CIEC talks, the Seventh Special Session, and UNCTAD IV appeared as much talk, many pieces of paper, and virtually no change in the status quo.

In spite of the lack of concrete results, the developing countries continued to articulate their demands for change. These were the countries which drew up the agendas at international meetings, they saw to it that reports and studies continued to be written on topics of interest to them, and the developed countries were continuously sensitized to their demands. Over time it is reasonable to anticipate that many of the problems raised by developing countries will be solved, though not necessarily in the manner deemed appropriate by them at this time.

Major structural reforms in the international economic order were not instituted during the two and one-half years following the adoption of the Charter of Economic Rights and Duties of States. There were, however, some reforms instituted and it is to these which we now turn.

5 Reforms— Not Restructuring

During the eighteen-month stalemate discussed in the previous chapter, it was quite evident that the developed countries opposed measures to restructure the international economy. Compulsory codes of conduct for transnational corporations and the transfer of technology, although discussed at length, brought forth no consensus. The same can be said for debt moratorium, international stocking of commodities, and a common fund. Agreements to agree were the order of the day.

Although restructuring was rejected, some innovations were initiated in the Lomé Convention such as the elimination of reverse preferences (1) and the agreement to buy specified quantities of sugar from ACP states. (2) Perhaps the most important reforms instituted were those relating to compensatory finance schemes under Lomé and within the IMF. In addition, a trust fund within the IMF and an International Fund for Agricultural Development were created to assist the developing countries.

CREATION OF THE IMF COMPENSATORY FINANCE FACILITY

There is substantial instability associated with commodity exports. Prices fluctuate widely and production, particularly of food crops, does the same. Being far more dependent on commodity exports than the developed countries, LDCs are more seriously affected by this instability. Reductions in export earnings affect import capacity and investment planning, and generate multiplier effects which have an adverse impact on national income, employment, and government revenue. (3)

At the suggestion of the United Nations Commission on International Commodity Trade, the IMF carried out a study and issued a report entitled Compensatory Financing of Export Fluctuations, which resulted in the creation of a compensatory finance facility in 1963. (4) The facility was designed to finance deficits arising from short-term export shortfalls attributable to circumstances beyond the member's control and resulting in balance-of-payments difficulties. In order to create the facility, a number of questions had to be answered: Should only the poorer members of the IMF be able to use the facility? What would be the source of funds? Would it be necessary to raise IMF quotas? What would be the limit on individual country drawings? What should be the terms and conditions of the drawings and repurchases? How should one determine and measure a short-term export shortfall? Should the focus be on export receipts, export prices, terms of trade, or the importing power of exports? Should there be exclusions for artificially induced shortfalls? What relationship should there be with others drawing from the IMF and the new facility?

After study and consultation, the following standards were established: (5) There would be no increase in members' quotas. All members would have access to the facility, and the amount of permissible drawings would "normally" be up to 25 percent of the member's regular quota. Repurchases (6) would be made within three to five years, thus maintaining the concept of a short-term facility. Eligible shortfalls had to result in balance-of-payments difficulties, be of a short-term character, and be attributable to circumstances beyond the member's control, i.e., not based on interference with the market by devices such as export controls. The member also had to cooperate with the IMF to find solutions. The shortfall would be measured by averaging export revenue for a five-year period and comparing that average with the shortfall year, the difference being the compensable shortfall. Calculations were based on actual revenue for the shortfall year and the two preceding years, plus estimates for the two following years. The average level of export forecasts for the post-shortfall years could not exceed 110 percent of the average level in the two years prior to the shortfall, and could not be assumed to be less than the level of exports experienced in the shortfall year itself. Whenever compensatory finance repurchases were made, the amount for additional drawings was increased pro tanto. Regular quotas were waived in relation to compensatory finance drawings, although the latter were counted against future regular drawings.

An improvement in the trend of commodity prices following the creation of the facility restricted drawings to only three between 1963 and 1966. (7)

UNCTAD I - Geneva 1964

In 1964, the first United Nations Conference on Trade and Development (UNCTAD) was held in Geneva, leading to the establishment of a permanent organization reporting directly to the United Nations General Assembly. Dominated by LDCs, it quickly became the intellectual and organizational center for these countries, with commodity problems a central concern. During the 1964 session, a resolution (8) on compensatory finance was passed without dissent. After acknowledging the IMF facility as "a definite step towards the solution of short-term financing problems," the resolution proceeded as follows:

[UNCTAD]

1. Recommends that Government members of the International Monetary Fund study the following measures:

(1) To increase, as soon as possible, the amount allocated by the Fund to compensatory financing, over and above its current transactions, from 25 percent to 50 percent of a member country's quota;

(2) To replace compensatory credits entirely outside the structure of the gold and successive credit tranches, so that the drawing of compensatory credits would not directly or indirectly prejudice a member's ability to make an ordinary drawing;

(3) To explore ways to secure possible refinancing of compensatory financing obligations of the developing countries in the event of persistent shortfall in export receipts beyond the control of the country affected.

2. Requests that the International Monetary Fund, in its determination of the shortfall in export receipts, consider giving greater weight to the actual experience of the preceding years.

In addition to the above, a related resolution (9) was passed requesting the World Bank to conduct a study of the feasibility of a scheme "to deal with problems arising from adverse movements in export proceeds which prove to be of a nature or duration which cannot adequately be dealt with by short-term balance-of-payments support. Its purpose should be to provide longer term assistance to developing countries which would help them to avoid disruption of their development programmes."

The 1966 Amendment of the IMF's Facility

As noted earlier, only three countries utilized the IMF facility during 1963-66. Although the principal factor was the improvement of commodity prices, many believed that the poorest countries with very low quotas were not sufficiently provided for by the 1963 facility. The IMF took two steps which dealt with this concern. (10) Since paragraph 3 of the 1963 decision permitted an upward adjustment of quotas of certain primary exporting countries, more than 20 quota increases were approved and 15 other countries appeared to be eligible for similar action. Secondly, in February 1966, there was a general quota increase in the IMF. In addition, in 1965, the Governors of the IMF recommended certain changes in the facility which were ultimately adopted in September 1966: (11)

(1) The drawing limit was raised from 25 to 50 percent of quotas in all circumstances, and this was not qualified, as in the 1963 decision, by the word "normally." Except for shortfalls due to disasters or major emergencies, the net amount outstanding could not increase by more than 25 percent of the quota during any twelve-month

period; requests which would increase drawings beyond 25 percent would be approved only if the IMF was satisfied that the member "had been cooperating with the Fund to find appropriate solutions for its balance of payments difficulties."

(2)   Regular and compensatory drawings were made independent of one another.

(3)   Repurchase policy was modified. In order to ensure the short-term character of the facility, the outside limit of five years was retained. Under the 1963 decision, regular repurchase policy had been followed, i.e., one-half was made in the fourth year and one-half in the fifth year. Under the 1966 decision, the IMF maintained the old rule and recommended that "as soon as possible after the end of each of the four years following a drawing under paragraph (5), the member repurchase an amount of the Fund's holdings of the member's currency equal to one-half of the amount by which the member's exports exceed medium-term trend of its export."

(4)   A reclassification procedure was instituted. (12)   It had been IMF practice to require that requests for compensatory finance be related to "an export shortfall over the latest twelve-month period for which, at the time of the request, a reliable estimate of actual exports can be made." It is obviously desirable that "the time lag between the shortfall and compensatory financing should be as short as possible." Because of delays in developing a "reliable estimate" the IMF decided to permit the "use of the standby and ordinary drawing facilities for the month period of any drawing to reclassify all or part of it as a compensatory drawing." The drawing had to satisfy the conditions for which it was made, i.e., regular or stand-by, and when reclassified it would have to satisfy the conditions for a compensatory drawing.

UNCTAD II - New Delhi 1968

Reactions to the 1966 decision were generally favorable, although the LDCs did not believe that it was far-reaching enough. First, in the Charter of Algiers (13) issued by the Group of 77 prior to UNCTAD II and subsequently during the 1968 New Delhi Conference itself, (14) they urged a further review and liberalization so that: (1) drawings would be immediately available up to 50 percent of the member's quota and not subject to any conditions; (2) repurchases would be linked to the recovery of exports rather than a rigid outer time limit of three to five years. If this could not be done, they asked for the inclusion of a refinancing provision in cases where exports did not recover; (3) account be taken of the fact that IMF quotas were inadequate in light of the magnitude of some LDCs' needs; (4) interest charges should be calculated separately from those employed in respect of ordinary drawings and should not attract the IMF's normal progressive interest provisions; (5) export shortfalls should be calculated in real terms; (6) adverse movements in import prices should render an LDC eligible for a compensatory drawing; (7) as suggested in the 1964 UNCTAD resolution, the formula for calculating shortfalls should be modified by taking as a basis a country's average exports during three or more normal years preceding the drawing.

The IMF representative to the UNCTAD II conference argued that the short-term nature of the facility prevented the IMF from refinancing and/or extending the repurchase period, and that the IMF's method of calculating shortfalls yielded a volume of assistance as great as that proposed by the LDCs. (15) Inasmuch as the 1966 decision was still relatively new (18 months), members were urged to give it a chance to operate. Answers to some of the other objections may be found in IMF publications. (16)

UNCTAD III - Santiago 1972

When UNCTAD III convened in Santiago in 1972, the concerns over the effects of the 1971 international monetary crisis dominated the meeting. Although no specific resolution on compensatory financing was issued, there was a resolution (17) on utilizing the World Bank to assist in price stabilization, along with discussions of supplementary financing.

Sixth Special Session of the United Nations General Assembly

At the end of the Sixth Special Session of the United Nations General Assembly, which met to discuss the OPEC-induced crisis of 1973-74, resolutions were passed concerning a Declaration (18) and a Programme of Action (19) on the establishment of a New International Economic Order. Article II.1.(i) of the Programme of Action provides for a "Review of the methods of operation of the International Monetary Fund, in particular...the system of compensatory financing...so as to enable the developing countries to make more effective use of [it]." This very general provision was expanded on in An Integrated Programme for Commodities, (20) a report by the Secretary General of UNCTAD published on December 9, 1974, which noted that compensatory financing would serve a role in the integrated program and asserted that "the expansion and liberalization of IMF assistance would probably be of significant help." (21) While problems would still exist, they would be greatly alleviated if "appropriate changes could be made in the IMF facility to enlarge the amounts transacted and the number of countries using the facility." (22) These changes included: (23)

(i)   more flexible conditions as regards the balance of payments criterion for assistance;

(ii)   relaxed limits on the amounts available, as determined by IMF quotas, to take account of the size of shortfalls;

(iii)   easier requirements on the completion of detailed export statistics within a relatively brief period of the shortfall in exports;

(iv)   extension of the repayment period beyond five years, by linking it more closely with export recovery; and

(v)   greater attention to the import purchasing power of a country's exports.

LOMÉ CONVENTION (24)

The IMF compensatory finance facility remained the only such international mechanism until February 1975, when the Lomé Convention between the European Economic Community (EEC) and 46 African, Caribbean, and Pacific (ACP) states was signed. Title II of the Convention provides for the stabilization of export earnings of the ACP states and has become known as STABEX. Under this scheme any ACP state exporting specified raw materials (12 principal products and certain subproducts for a total of 29) to the Community receives compensation for shortfalls in export revenues from EEC countries, provided the exports meet two independent standards. First, during the year preceding the application, export earnings on one or more of the specified commodities must equal 7.5 percent of total export earnings, although poorer and specially situated states need show only 2.5 percent. Thus, the first test relates to the importance of the product in total exports. Second, each eligible commodity has a moving reference level equal to the average earnings derived from the export of the commodity to EEC countries over the preceding four years. An ACP country may request a transfer when export earnings of the commodity to EEC states have decreased by 7.5 percent or, in the case of poorer and specially situated states, 2.5 percent. The difference between the reference level and actual earnings constitutes the basis of the transfer, which bears no interest.

The ACP states, excepting a list of the 34 poorer countries, (25) are expected to contribute to the reconstitution of resources to the extent they have received them over a five-year period. This is to be done each year that "the unit value of the exports is higher than the reference unit value" and "the quantity actually exported to the Community is at least equal to the reference quantity." If these two conditions fail to prevail sufficiently over the five-year period to equal the amount of the transfer, the Council of Ministers has the right to either request all or part of the amount outstanding or waive the right to repayment.

Approximately $413 million, equal to 375 units of account, (26) are available to STABEX over the five-year period of the agreement. The money has been divided into five equal installments, but there is provision for drawing up to 20 percent of the following year's installment.

KISSINGER'S DEVELOPMENT SECURITY FACILITY

The call for a development security facility highlighted Secretary Kissinger's speech to the Seventh Special Session of the United Nation's General Assembly. Its purpose was to be the stabilization of export earnings. It was in two parts. The first called for an expansion and modification of the IMF's compensatory finance facility. The second, for the creation of a trust fund to provide finance for developing countries. He described the facility in these terms:

> Let me set forth our proposal: The United States proposes creation - in the International Monetary Fund (IMF) - of a new development security facility to stabilize overall export earnings.

> The facility would give loans to sustain development programs in the face of export fluctuations - up to $2.5 billion, and possibly more, in a single year, and a potential total of $10 billion in outstanding loans.

> Assistance would be available to all developing countries which need to finance shortfalls in export earnings, unless the shortfalls are caused by their own acts of policy.

> The poorest countries would be permitted to convert their loans into grants under prescribed conditions. These grants would be financed by the proceeds of sales of IMF gold channeled through the proposed $2 billion trust fund now under negotiation.

> Eligible countries could draw most, or under certain conditions all, of their IMF quotas in addition to their normal drawing rights. Much of that could be drawn in a single year, if necessary: part automatically; part subject to balance-of-payments conditions; and part reserved for cases of particularly violent swings in commodity earnings.

> Shortfalls would be calculated according to a formula geared to future growth as well as current and past exports. In this way the facility helps countries protect their development plans.

> This facility would replace the IMF's compensatory finance facility; it would not be available for industrial countries.

> The United States will present its detailed proposals to the board of directors of the IMF this month.

The suggested changes in the Fund's facility are threefold:

1. Industrial countries are excluded from the use of the facility. Inasmuch as they have made only one drawing from the facility, this is largely a suggested codification of existing practice.

2. Although no figures are used, there is an implicit raising of permissible drawings to 'most, or under certain conditions all, of their IMF quotas in addition to their normal drawing rights' from the 50 percent limit. The language 'part automatically;

part subject to balance-of-payments conditions; and part reserved for cases of particularly violent swings in commodity
earnings' appears to be a reaffirmation of the 1966 standards.

3. The most important change is the provision permitting poorer
countries to 'convert their loans to grants under prescribed
conditions' with funds coming from the proceeds of sales of IMF
gold channeled through a trust fund.

At the conclusion of the Seventh Special Session, the final resolution on
international trade contained the following statement on compensatory
financing: (27)

International trade:
I.3.(d) Substantially improve facilities for compensatory financing of
exports revenue fluctuations through the widening and enlarging of the
existing facilities. Note has been taken of the various proposals regarding
a comprehensive scheme for the stabilization of export earnings of
developing countries and for a Development Security Facility as well as
specific measures for the benefit of the developing countries most in
need;

In the week following the Kissinger speech, the United States presented
the detailed provisions of its proposal to the IMF. (28) It suggested (1)
modifications of the 1966 compensatory finance facility in respect to the
computation of shortfall, limitation on access to the facility, the size of
permissible drawings, and the timeframe for the full compensatory finance
drawing; and (2) linkages with the approved, but not yet established, Trust
Fund.

MODIFICATION OF THE 1966 COMPENSATORY FINANCE FACILITY

The compensable shortfall was, as explained earlier, based on a five-year
average, including the two years following the shortfall year, for which the
IMF had to project commodity revenues. Since projections could not exceed
110 percent of average past export earnings, the facility had only limited
usefulness in times of high inflation. The United States now proposed to raise
the limit to 120 percent. In light of the new facility created under the Lomé
Convention, the United States also proposed that the IMF deduct compensatory financing available to a country under international arrangements
outside the IMF, on the grounds that this was "a simple, more equitable, and
economically sounder way of dealing with, and taking account of, the
inflation problem than complex attempts to compensate for shortfalls in 'real'
export earnings."
With respect to the size of the drawing, the United States announced that
if the facility were limited to LDCs, it would support a drawing limit equal to
100 percent of the quota instead of the existing maximum of 50 percent. Or,
if not, the United States would still support an increase to 75 percent. In

addition, the United States advocated an increase from 25 to 50 percent for drawings on the facility within any twelve-month period.

The IMF had established a buffer stock facility (29) and limited combined drawings from this and the compensatory finance facility to 75 percent. The United States supported the elimination of the combined quota limit.

ESTABLISHMENT OF A TRUST FUND

At the 1973 Annual Meeting of the IMF, it had been agreed to establish a Trust Fund to assist LDCs with the proceeds from the sale of a designated portion of the IMF's gold reserves. It was estimated that this Trust Fund would have approximately $2 billion. The United States proposed that Trust Fund resources be used (a) to provide grants for the repayment of compensatory financing drawings from the IMF by the poorest LDCs (income per capita below $200) in the event such countries were unable to complete payments within a five-year period; and (b) as a source of additional compensatory financing loans to LDCs dependent on export earnings from a specified list of commodities. To be eligible, a country would have to demonstrate the existence of a serious balance-of-payments problem arising from a shortfall in total export earnings from specified commodities. The first 25 percent of the country's compensatory finance would come from the IMF's regular facility, after which the member could utilize either the regular facility or the Trust Fund.

The Unites States suggested differentiated terms and sources of funding for compensatory financing loans from the Trust Fund based upon the per capita income of the borrowing countries. Those with incomes below $375 per capita could borrow at concessional rates (2 to 3 percent) over 10-12 years. The funds would come from the sale of IMF gold, donor country contributions, and borrowed funds. For those countries with per capita incomes of $375-1,000, drawings would be financed by medium-term borrowings, and the country would repay over five to eight years with interest at a rate to cover the cost of financing.

The United States proposal was an attempt to liberalize the existing IMF facility by redefining the compensable shortfall, increasing the amount which could be drawn, and by linking the IMF's compensatory finance facility to the proposed Trust Fund to ease the financial burden on poorer countries and increase the amount of funds available to all LDCs in relation to specified commodities.

IMPLEMENTATION OF MODIFICATIONS TO THE IMF'S COMPENSATORY FINANCE FACILITY

On December 24, 1975, the IMF modified the conditions of the compensatory finance facility, (30) adopting most of the Kissinger proposals as well as others proposed by the developing countries. (31) The size of the drawings was increased, but these drawings were not limited to LDCs and, thus, the limit was increased to only 75 percent of quotas rather than 100 percent. Up to 50 percent could be drawn in a twelve-month period. The common limitation on outstanding drawings under the compensatory financing and buffer stock financing facilities was abolished, and the computation of the compensable shortfall was modified. This last point had posed serious problems because of the rampant inflation in the 1970s. Different approaches to this problem were considered. "One solution was to measure shortfalls in real terms by dividing nominal earnings by a price index taken as unity in the shortfall year. This solution was studied but not adopted. Instead, it was decided to conduct, as in the past, all calculations in nominal terms, but to eliminate any forecast limit." (32) The modification was more liberal than the United States' formula and will permit larger drawings during periods of inflation. The language in the decision reads: "Earnings in the two post-shortfall years will be deemed equal to earnings in the two pre-shortfall years multiplied by the ration of the sum of earnings in the most recent three years to that in the preceding years." If the IMF finds the result not reasonable it will employ a "judgmental forecast." Provisions were made to review this formula. If the drawings in any twelve-month period exceed SDR 1.5 billion (approximately $1.8 billion) or outstanding drawings exceed SDR 3 billion (approximately $3.6 billion) the rules of the entire facility will be reviewed.

The Kissinger proposals relating to the Trust Fund were not adopted at the same time because the IMF had not worked out the procedures for its gold sales. Subsequently, the Interim Committee of the IMF Board of Governors met in Kingston, Jamaica, on January 7 to 8, 1976. As stated in the press release on this meeting: (33)

6.(a) it was agreed that the necessary steps should be taken to establish the Trust Fund without delay. Its resources would be derived from the profits of the sales of the Fund's gold, which should be augmented by voluntary national contributions. It was agreed that the amount of gold available for sale in accordance with the agreement reached by the Committee at its fourth meeting should be disposed of over a four-year period. The resources of the Trust Fund should be used to provide balance of payments assistance on concessionary terms to members with low per capita incomes. Initially, eligible members would be those with per capita incomes in 1973 not in excess of SDR 300.

On May 6, 1976, the IMF announced that the Trust Fund had been established and that the first gold auction would be held in Washington, D.C., on June 2, 1976. (34) Auctions for the sale of one sixth of the Fund's gold (25 mission ounces) were scheduled over a four-year period. Profits from these sales, equal to the difference between SDR 35 per ounce (approximately $41) and the auction price, go into the Trust Fund. Sixty-one countries with 1973 per capita incomes of SDR 300 or less, listed in an Annex to the decision, are eligible for Trust Fund loans on concessional terms to carry out balance of payments adjustment programs. Repayment will be in ten equal semi-annual installments - beginning not later than the end of the first six months of the sixth year after the drawing. Payment must be completed at the end of the tenth year after the date of the initial disbursement. Interest is to be charged at the rate of one-half of one percent per annum on the outstanding loan balance in simi-annual installments. Eleven gold auctions were held between June 2, 1976, and July 6, 1977, with auction prices ranging between a low of $109.40 per ounce and a high of $149.18 per ounce providing SDR 402 million (35) to the Trust Fund. During the January through June 1977 period, 24 loans totaling SDR 152.9 million were made to 24 countries. (36) Further loans were scheduled in six-month intervals.

The Trust Fund provides an additional source of low-cost funds to poorer developing countries. It does not go as far as the Kissinger proposal in permitting loans to be converted into grants. However, the low interest rate and long repayment periods may make it even more attractive than the Kissinger proposal.

STABEX AND THE FUND'S FACILITY COMPARED

STABEX differs from the IMF's compensatory finance facility in a number of ways. First, only ACP members may draw on STABEX. Second, STABEX compensates for a shortfall in earnings for each commodity, not all commodities. Third, STABEX limits the commodities covered both in particular and on the basis of their importance in the trade of the affected country with the EEC. Fourth, the STABEX reference level is based on an average of the four preceding years, whereas the IMF facility looks both to the past and the future. Fifth, STABEX applies different standards of eligibility for funds and repayment among ACP countries. Sixth, STABEX funds are much more limited than those of the IMF. Seventh, STABEX payments do not incur interest.

Thus, STABEX includes a number of features which were originally sought for the IMF facility by the LDCs, including automaticity, a reference level based on an average of the four years preceding the reference year, and the repayment provisions mentioned above. However, only $413 million is available to STABEX over the five-year period of the agreement.

The expansion and modification of the IMF facility and the creation of STABEX occurred at a propitious time: the worldwide recession had just reached its bottom. (37) The effect of the recession was evident when, in 1976, 48 countries drew on the IMF facility. (38) On the average, their export earnings were 13 percent lower in the shortfall year than in the preceding year. (39) The liberalization, in 1975, permitted drawings of SDR 2.35 billion whereas only SDR 0.48 billion could have been drawn under the 1966 decisions. (40) During the same period, 25 ACP countries used the two compensatory finance facilities as follows: STABEX alone (nine countries), STABEX plus IMF (eight countries), IMF alone (eight countries). (41) The amounts drawn were: (42)

	STABEX $ million	IMF Compensatory Financing Facility $ million
ACP countries drawing on both STABEX and IMF facility	$ 30	$ 143
ACP countries drawing on STABEX only	49.4	-
ACP countries drawing on the IMF facility only	-	185.9
TOTAL	$79.4	$328.9

With competing schemes in existence, scholars (43) have speculated on their relative merits. There is agreement, in which I concur, that "a significantly reformed IMF facility would be preferable to a new scheme based on the STABEX model," (44) the major reason being that the Fund's shortfall formula more accurately estimates the trend of export earnings. However, neither scheme deals adequately with the problem of inflation, and both require some form of indexation if the total impact of the shortfall is to be taken into consideration. A number of more conventional changes would also ease the burden on the poorer countries including: increasing IMF quotas (now underway); increasing the amount of LDC drawings within a twelve-month period from 50 percent to 75 percent, plus an additional 25 percent following consultations with the Fund; lower charges; and the conversion of outstanding drawings after five years to grants or long-term concessional loans, if balance of payments requirements so warrant. The Trust Fund could be used as a source of funds for the subsidies, and there is precedence in the Fund for a subsidy approach. (45) From the perspective of the developing countries, a liberalized international facility will be less divisive than a regionally oriented institution.

In conclusion, both the European Community and the IMF recognize the need for an institutional device to hlep countries with balance-of-payments problems due to temporary shortfalls in commodity revenue. These schemes, which do not interfere with the price mechanism, are considered preferable to the more complex and less predictable International Commodity Program. The developing countries accept the need for the compensatory finance facilities at the present time, but their preference is still for the more comprehensive International Commodity Program. The reason is that the stabilization of prices is only half of what they seek. The other half is higher price levels. The higher prices are required not to improve their relative position, but, rather, to prevent a further deterioration in their terms of trade. Indexation of industrial imports against developing country exports is one of the ways the developing countries intend to achieve this result. As we have seen, this is unacceptable to the industrial countries. (46) As of June 1977, compensatory finance reforms represent the limits of consensus.

CREATION OF THE INTERNATIONAL FUND FOR
AGRICULTURAL DEVELOPMENT (IFAD): 1974-1976

One of the major accomplishments of the 1974 World Food Con-
ference (47) was the agreement in principle reached between the OECD,
OPEC, and non-oil exporting developing countries on the creation of a new
International Fund for Agricultural Development. (48)

Chronic food shortages, increased demand, higher energy and fertilizer
costs, along with a 1974 food grain deficit of 25 million tons projected to rise
to 85 million tons in 1985 (49) inspired the OPEC countries, 22 other LDCs,
and three developed countries (50) to initiate a resolution (51) to establish a
fund to bring about a massive increase in LDC food production. The fund was
to funnel additional capital into agricultural development. Many developed
countries were skeptical about the need for a new institution, and others were
reluctant as they were still smarting from the aftermath of the Sixth Special
Session. (52) The General Assembly of the United Nations endorsed the
proposal (53) and, on the initiative of the Secretary General, a series of
Meetings of Interested Countries on the International Fund for Agricultural
Development were held in Geneva and Rome from early May 1975 through
early February 1976. (54) The idea received a substantial boost when
Kissinger stated, at the Seventh Special Session on September 1, 1975, that
the United States would support IFAD with a $200 million contribution,
provided that the other $800 million was forthcoming from OECD and OPEC
countries. (55) The General Assembly, following the recommendation of the
Meeting of Interested Countries, requested the Secretary-General to convene
a Conference of Plenipotentiaries as soon as the Meeting of Interested
Countries finished its preparatory work. (56) He convened a meeting in Rome
from June 10-13, 1976. (57) At that meeting the major issues concerning the
management, financing, and operations of IFAD were resolved, and an
Agreement establishing the Fund was initiated by 91 countries. (58) The
Agreement called for a Fund with initial capital of $1 billion to be used for
projects and programs to increase food in developing countries, with
particular emphasis on the poorest food deficit countries, and, within them,
the welfare of the poorest segment of the population.

The negotiations leading to the establishment of the Fund have been
discussed elsewhere. (59) Here only the highlights will be touched on. IFAD
will be a specialized agency relying heavily on other international financial
institutions for assistance to achieve its objectives. (60) Its initial capital is a
little over $1 billion. (61) It has three categories of members: (62) I)
developed country contributors, II) OPEC contributors, and, III) developing
country recipients. Like IDA, it will give grants and concessional loans. (63)
Its financial structure follows along the lines of IDA, i.e., Category I and II
countries will provide initial voluntary contributions in the form of
convertible currency, and Category III countries may give either convertible
or nonconvertible currency. (64) It was estimated that the initial contribution
would last for three years, and, as in IDA, replenishments would be necessary
for the institutions to continue their operations. Contributions from
nonmember countries and organizations may be accepted.

The organizational pattern is the familiar Governing Council (65) composed of all members, an 18-member Executive Board, (66) and a President (67) and staff.   Lending policy and regulations emanate from the Governing Council, while the Executive Board is charged with directing the regular operations of IFAD. Members of the Executive Board are representatives of governments and the 18 seats are divided equally among the three categories of countries - a new departure in international decision making - with each category deciding on the manner of selecting its six members.

The Fund has 1,800 votes divided equally among the three categories of countries (68) with each category authorized to determine a method for the distribution of its 600 votes. Countries in Categories I and II have decided on weighted voting, (69) in proportion to financial contributions added to basic votes which vary in each category. Category III countries have allocated all of their votes equally to members within the category, (70) an approach which they urged the other categories to follow.

Voting in the Governing Council (71) is by a simple majority of the total votes, and in the Executive Board, (72) by three-fifths of votes cast, provided that this includes at least one-half of the votes of each category. These provisions give effective protection to each category of countries.

IFAD's operational procedures make it a hybrid financial institution. It proposes and approves loans. However, it was the intention of its initiators to avoid the establishment of a new large international bureaucracy, and, to that end, it was decided that IFAD is to rely in large part on existing international institutions in identifying projects, loan appraisals, and in loan administration. (73)   In addition, it was agreed that national institutions of LDCs may be used for project appraisals and are eligible to receive lines of credit from which they may make subloans. (74)

The respective contributions of Category I and II countries turned out to be the most difficult problem of the negotiations. The OECD countries understood initially that they would provide 50 percent of the contributions for IFAD and the other 50 percent would come from OPEC countries. (75) However, just prior to the 1976 Rome meeting, OPEC announced that the OPEC Special Fund would contribute $400 million to IFAD, "inclusive of all amounts previously declared by some OPEC member countries." (76) The United States' contribution of $200 million was based on two conditions: first, that total commitments would equal $1 billion, and second, that there be an equitable burden sharing among the different categories of contributors. (77)   By the end of the Rome meeting, the equivalent of approximately $935 million in convertible currencies was pledged, including $527 million from OECD countries, $400 million from OPEC, and $9.1 million from Category III countries. (78)   After a great deal of negotiations and manipulation of commitments to other funds, the $1 billion goal was reached. (79)   OECD countries provided $560.1 million (56.6 percent) and $430.5 million (43.4 percent) came from the OPEC countries. In addition, the Category III countries provided $8.8 million in freely convertible currency and $10.3 million in non-freely convertible currency.   The total of freely convertible currency equalled $999.8 million, and if the non-freely convertible currency is added, the grand total amounted to $1.01 billion.

During the June 1976 meeting, it was decided to establish a Preparatory Commission charged with the preparation of bylaws and regulations to permit

IFAD to begin operations as soon as possible after the requirements for entry into force of the Agreement had been fulfilled. (80)   Among the topics considered by the Preparatory Commission was the relationship with other international financial institutions required in the Agreement.   The World Bank, FAO, UNDP, and the regional development banks were contacted and draft agreements between IFAD and each of these institutions were prepared to be discussed at a meeting in Rome, mid-July 1977. (81)

IFAD had not begun its operations as of June 1977. It is an unusual hybrid international organization. It has no unique function. Other multilateral and bilateral aid organizations have been doing similar work for years. It does, however, serve a number of LDC, OPEC, and OECD goals.   First, IFAD money is meant to be in addition to existing aid funds. Second, it has created a new organizational voting structure, and, thus, increased the decision making role of the LDCs in an international financial organization. Third, an LDC desire to play a bigger role in the aid process is provided for in relation to the role of national institutions in appraising loans and in making subloans. Fourth, all of these political gains were achieved without a great loss of efficiency, provided IFAD utilizes other international financial organizations to do its loan appraisals and administration. Fifth, through IFAD OPEC can point to a positive financial contribution to LDCs and claim credit for pressuring OECD countries to provide additional aid funds. Finally, from the point of view of the OECD, it helps to recycle petrodollars and it maintains one more operational contact between OPEC and OECD countries.

CONCLUSIONS

The major reforms instituted in the international economic order during the post-Charter period through June 1977 related to the modification, expansion, or creation of institutional devices to increase the flow of financial resources to developing countries with special emphasis on the least developed countries.   Within both the IMF and European Community institutions effective control over distribution of the increased and new funds remained with the developed countries.   IFAD deviated from traditional voting patterns by allocating one-third of the votes in both the Governing Council and Executive Board to developing countries. In addition, another third of the votes were allocated to the OPEC countries, slightly more than their contributions warranted.   Thus, in IFAD a coalition of OPEC and developing countries can decide on the allocation of funds. One should not, however, make too much of this, for IFAD funds must be replenished triannually and, thus, the consensus of developed countries will be required on all major decisions if they are expected to continue to provide new funds to IFAD.

These increased and new financial resources play an important role in the economic life of many of the developing countries. However, they fall far short of the measures proposed by the developing countries in their call for a new international economic order.

6 Foreign Private Investment

The series of confrontations which have taken place in the last two decades between developing countries and foreign private investors reflects the change in Third World attitudes towards foreign investment. In the years immediately following the accession to independence, most Third World countries welcomed foreign investment, which they considered to be an important factor in the development process. Later, Third World countries became less interested in maximizing the inflow of foreign direct investment into all sectors of their economy. Instead, they wanted to maintain (or regain) national control over key sectors including agriculture, mining, banking, insurance, and public utilities. They considered joint ventures to be preferable to wholly-owned subsidiaries of foreign corporations, even in manufacturing. (1)

Article 2 of the Charter represents the most comprehensive and up-to-date consensus in the Third World on permanent sovereignty over natural resources, the regulation of foreign investment, the supervision of trans-national corporations, and the resolution of disputes resulting from nationalization or other takings. (2) The provisions of Article 2 are consistent with most national (3) and regional approaches (4) to foreign investment, although the former are less detailed and, in some cases, less antagonistic to foreign investment than the latter. The evolution of the thinking represented by the Charter has raised questions about the future of foreign investment in developing countries. Will this way of thinking persist in the Third World? Or will countries such as Brazil, Mexico, Argentina, Iran, Saudi Arabia, and Kuwait find the need for foreign investment and all that comes with it in the form of technology and "know-how" so necessary that they will reverse their ideological position and make an all out effort to improve the investment climate in their countries? Are the new legal standards set forth in Article 2 really disincentives to investing? Is there a role for private investment even in an era of economic nationalism? Is it in the economic interest of developed country industry not to be involved abroad in both extractive industry and manufacturing? Can they take the risk of being without formal links which will provide necessary raw materials? Will the oil-rich nations become the financiers of the future supplying the financial needs of the developing countries and buying the necessary technology and "know-how"? If so, would the perceived problems of investments from developed countries recur in relation to new sources of capital?

This chapter analyzes investment flows to less developed countries and evaluates current and proposed institutions to regulate foreign direct investment. The first section of the chapter reviews foreign investment flows to developing countries. The current statistics cover only the period through 1976. Thus, it is somewhat early to evaluate changes in investment flows which occurred in direct response to passage of the Charter in December 1974. It is also difficult to isolate the effects on foreign investment of actions and attitudes of developing countries. The state of the world economy, widely fluctuating exchange rates, and the relative costs of the factors of production at home and abroad are as important in the complex decision making process underlying foreign investment as the investment climate in particular developing countries.

The second section of the chapter reviews current developing country initiatives to refine and implement permanent sovereignty over natural resources. After reviewing nationalizations by the developing countries from 1960 through mid-1974, this section focuses on four extractive industries - oil, copper, bauxite, and iron ore. I examine fiscal and other measures adopted by host governments to regulate natural resource investments. I also examine current proposals for financing mineral production in developing countries to ensure that supplies keep up with demand.

The third section of the chapter analyzes proposals to regulate trans-national corporations. In the final section of the chapter, I look at Article 2 once again, and discuss the barriers it raises to foreign investment in the developing countries.

THE CURRENT FLOW OF DIRECT FOREIGN
INVESTMENT TO DEVELOPING COUNTRIES

Over the past ten years, there has been a substantial increase in the nominal value of direct investment to developing countries from OECD countries. From an average of $2.25 billion during the period 1965-67, it climbed to a high of $10.33 billion in 1975, and leveled off to $7.56 billion in 1976. However, if we take into account inflation, the increase over the years would be slight. Table 6.1 recapitulates the flows from the principal capital-exporting OECD countries.

Direct investment from all OECD countries except France increased substantially over the ten-year period. The largest source of investment throughout the period was the United States, accounting for at least 50 percent of total direct investment in all years. In 1975, U.S. investment represented 75 percent of the total from the OECD, but in 1976 it dropped back to 50 percent. The drop in 1976 has been variously attributed to a lagged effect from the worldwide recession, the volatile foreign exchange market, proposed changes in United States' tax regulations, the rapid

TABLE 6.1 - Direct Investment to Developing Countries

(Disbursements)   (Billions of U.S. Dollars)

Country	(1965-67)	1970	1974	1975	1976
Canada	.03	.06	.19	.30	.43
France	.34	.24	.24	.27	.25
Federal Republic of Germany	.15	.32	.70	.82	.77
Japan	.08	.26	.71	.22	1.10
United Kingdom	.20	.34	.72	.80	.72
United States	1.15	1.74	3.80	7.10	3.28
Six country total	1.95	2.96	6.36	9.51	6.55
Total of all OECD direct investment	2.25	3.54	7.10	10.33	7.56

Source: Development Cooperation: 1977 Review (OECD) Tables A.9-A.17.

---

escalation of production costs abroad compared to the United States, and host country policies. (5) Unfortunately, the aggregation of the statistics does not permit comparison of the flows to individual countries with their vastly different investment climates.

Given the preponderance of United States' share in total OECD investment, it is useful to examine the more detailed publicly available United States data. As of year end 1976, the net book value of U.S. direct investors' equity in, and outstanding loans to, foreign affiliates was $137.2 billion. Petroleum accounted for 22 percent of the position, manufacturing for 44 percent, and "other industries" - in which the positions in finance and insurance, trade, mining and smelting were the largest - for 34 percent. By area, developed countries accounted for 74 percent, developing countries for 21 percent, and "international and unallocated" for 5 percent. Within developing countries, $23.5 billion of total investments of $29 billion, or 81 percent, was in the Western Hemisphere with 72.7 percent in Latin America. United States' investment in developing countries was, until 1974, fairly evenly divided among petroleum, manufacturing, and "all others." Following the oil nationalizations, discussed below, radical rearrangement of the sectoral distribution of investment occurred. By the end of 1976, only 10 percent of U.S. investment was in petroleum, while 39 percent was in manufacturing, and 51 percent in other industries. (6)

Table 6.2 furnishes a detailed sectoral breakdown of U.S. direct investment position at year end 1976.

TABLE 6.2 - Sectoral Breakdown of U.S. Investment Position in Developing Countries at Year End 1976 (percentage)

Manufacturing		39.2
Chemicals and allied products	9.8	
Machinery	9.5	
Transportation equipment	9.0	
Food products	4.3	
Primary and fabricated metals	3.4	
Other	3.2	
Finance and Insurance		20.6
Trade		11.1
Petroleum		9.9
Mining and smelting		7.9
Transportation, communication and public utilities		1.9
Other		9.3

Source: Derived from Survey of Current Business, Vol. 57, No. 8, August 1977, reprinted in Aspects of International Business, U.S. Department of Commerce, p. 45.

Manufacturing and finance and insurance make up close to 60 percent of U.S. foreign investment, while less than 18 percent is in petroleum, mining and smelting. This contrasts sharply with the sectoral distribution of United States' investment in the 1960s. As late as 1971, petroleum alone accounted for 33.9 percent of investments in developing countries, and manufacturing was only 29.1 percent.

Foreign investment in developing countries has been a very profitable business. Table 6.3 compares the receipt of income as a percentage of direct investment over the years 1970-76.

In summary, foreign investment flows have increased over the past ten years. This has been true despite the changing attitudes of developing countries towards foreign investment. It is too soon to know whether the Charter will either stop or even slow down the flow. If past experience is any indication then it is unlikely. There has been a change in the sectors in which investment takes place. Investment in extractive industry has been reduced, whereas manufacturing and financial investment has increased. Foreign investment in developing countries continues to provide a substantially higher return than investment in developed countries.

TABLE 6.3 – Receipts of Income as a Percentage of Direct U.S. Investment (millions of dollars)

	1970	1971	1972	1973	1974	1975	1976
Developed countries							
Direct investment position	51,819	56,950	62,060	72,214	83,025	90,923	101,150
Receipts of income	2,436	2,775	2,911	3,875	4,892	4,609	5,217
Percentage return	4.7	4.9	4.7	5.4	5.9	5.1	5.2
Developing countries							
Direct investment position	19,192	20,719	22,274	22,904	19,812	26,222	29,050
Receipts of income	2,340	2,712	3,079	4,272	6,086	3,619	5,763
Percentage return	12.2	13.1	13.8	18.6	30.7	13.8	19.8

Source: Survey of Current Business (U.S. Department of Commerce), August 1977, Table 12.

PERMANENT SOVEREIGNTY OVER
NATURAL RESOURCES

Beginning in 1952 with the first resolution on permanent sovereignty over natural resources, (7) the developing countries have stressed their "right to determine freely the use of their natural resources" and the need "to utilize such resources in order to be in a better position to further the realization of their plans of economic development in accordance with their national interest." They have broadened the concept of permanent sovereignty over natural resources by including wealth and economic activities within the definition spelled out in Article 2 of the Charter. (8) Strategies which the developing countries have adopted to assert their right of permanent sovereignty include nationalization and other takeovers, the regulation of natural resource ventures, and fiscal measures. These strategies have, in turn, forced the consideration of alternative arrangements to provide capital for the development of extractive industries.

Nationalizations and Takeovers

From 1960 through mid-1974 there were 875 nationalizations or takeovers of foreign enterprises by 62 different developing countries. The bulk of them, 591, took place in ten countries. (9)   There were an average of 60.3 per year. (10) African states south of the Sahara led the way with an average of 23.7 cases per year (39 percent). They were followed by West Asia and Africa north of the Sahara with an average of 15.7 cases (26 percent), South and Southeast Asia with 13.0 cases (22 percent) and the Western Hemisphere with 8.0 (13 percent). (11) The African states south of the Sahara accounted for an average of only 13.8 cases per year during the period 1960-69. However, these members increased sharply to an average of 45.6 cases per annum during the 1970-74 period. (12)

The sectoral breakdown of nationalizations and takeovers yields no surprises. Mining, agriculture and petroleum account for 38 percent, and another 30 percent were in banking and insurance. Table 6.4 provides the sectoral breakdown of nationalization.

TABLE 6.4 - Nationalization or take-over of foreign enterprises, sectoral distribution, 1960 to mid-1974 (percentage)

Mining, petroleum and agriculture		38
mining	7	
petroleum	16	
agriculture	15	
Banking and insurance		30
Manufacturing		16
Public utilities		6
Trade		4
Others		7

Source: United Nations General Assembly Document A/9716, 20 September 1974 - Annex p. 10, Table 5.

British investors, involved in 42 percent of the cases, were the most seriously affected by the takeovers. United States investors followed with 25 percent and the French with 11 percent. (13)   United Kingdom enterprises accounted for the bulk of takeovers in agriculture, banking, insurance, and, to a lesser extent, trade. (14)   Most of these investments had been made while the countries were under colonial rule.   In contrast, U.S. enterprises accounted for most of the take-over in mining, petroleum, manufacturing and public utilities. (15)

Seventy-eight percent of the cases of take-overs were in sectors previously discussed in relation to permanent sovereignty, i.e., extractive industries, agriculture, banking, insurance, and public utilities. (16)   Raw materials headed the list with 38 percent of the cases, followed by banking and insurance (30 percent), public utilities (6 percent) and trade (4 percent). Only 16 percent of the cases involved manufacturing. This may be accounted for by the fact that manufacturing has never been perceived as being the same kind of a threat to national sovereignty as raw material industries. Moreover, the nationalization of factory buildings does not provide the host country with either the technology or the know-how to continue the innovative processes which keep the products competitive internationally. The effect of this differentiated treatment by host countries may very well limit the capital inflows into raw material production but permit it to continue in manufacturing ventures.

Oil Naturalization and Takeovers (17)

By the end of 1976, member states of OPEC had obtained control over virtually all of the hydrocarbon resources within their respective territories. In many cases the government ownership was at, or approaching, the 100 percent level. The central importance of oil to industrial countries made it a likely industry for takeovers; on the other hand, this unique characteristic made it difficult for other producer associations to emulate OPEC successes.

The evolution from concession agreement to service contract has been discussed at length elsewhere. (18)   Briefly, oil companies began major foreign exploration and exploitation, with the D'Arcy concession of 1901. (19) Early agreements, usually written by the companies, were extremely favorable to the investor. They were made for long periods of time, and frequently covered an entire country. (20)   As the demand for oil grew, competing companies began to cooperate (21) and host governments began to demand a larger number of provisions to protect their own interests. (22) But it was not until 1948 that the next major change in the concession agreements took place in the form of the Venezuelan initiative for 50/50 revenue sharing between the host government and the companies. (23) This approach was not accepted without disagreement by some companies. When the oil companies in Iran refused the 50/50 formula, the entire industry was nationalized by Mossadegh. When he was subsequently displaced, the 50/50 formula became a part of the revised concession. (24)

The large increase of newly independent states in the late 1950s and 1960s, each eager to draft and implement a development program, affected the terms and name of the concession agreements. They were now called economic development agreements, and the companies undertook to provide new social services including education, health facilities, and housing. (25) By the end of the 1950s oil supplies were exceeding demand, and the oil companies cut the price of crude oil without prior consultation with the host governments. This action was fully within their legal rights, but it was to prove costly to them. It provoked the oil-exporting countries, deeply involved in development programs based upon oil revenues projected at the old rates, to band together to form OPEC. (26)

OPEC's initial impact was slight. In its formative years it acted as a center in which information was collected and exchanged. One of its first revenue-producing acts was to require the expensing of royalties, which the host governments had formerly treated as a credit against taxes. (27) The fruits of many years of information exchange and consultation became clear in June 1968, when the OPEC member governments adopted the Declaratory Statement of Petroleum Policy in Member Countries. (28) It embodied policies for fundamental structural changes in the industry. Government initiatives were to become primary, with foreign investors serving in a supplementary role. Foreign capital was to be supervised "to ensure that it is used in the interest of national development and that returns by it do not exceed reasonable levels." When foreign capital was utilized, it was agreed that "Government shall seek to retain the greatest measure possible of participation in and control over all aspects of operations." Participation was not limited to new investments alone. Old relationships were to be revised under the legal principle of rebus sic stantibus (changed circumstances). Other points in the OPEC Declaration were equally sweeping, and some foreshadowed provisions of Article 2 of CERDS: Oil prices which were to be "determined by the Government and should move in such a manner as to prevent any deterioration in its relationshjp to the prices of manufactured goods traded internationally"; there was to be accelerated relinquishment of acreage of existing contract areas; renegotiations were to be held in case of "excessively high net earnings"; operator's income, taxes, and other payments were to be assessed on the basis of government-determined posted or tax-reference prices; and disputes were to be settled exclusively by competent national courts or projected regional courts.

Participation by the host government in the equity of the foreign-owned companies produced dissent by those who believed that the proposal went too far (29) and those who believed it didn't go far enough. (30) The companies argued that rebus sic stantibus was not a justifiable legal basis for forcing participation upon the companies. On the other side, leaders such as Abdullah H. Tariki, former Saudi Arabian Minister for Oil, believed that nationalization was the only proper policy. These differences soon became academic as both enlargement of participation and nationalizations became the order of the day.

In 1971, Algeria nationalized all pipelines and gas fields and 51 percent of all French oil concessions. In the same year, Venezuela enacted into law the gradual takeover of the oil companies by 1983. In early 1972, Saudi Arabia, Kuwait, Qatar, and Abu Dhabi began negotiations for 25 percent participations, with increases to reach 51 percent in 1982. When the Shah of Iran nationalized the Consortium's holdings in 1973, Kuwait and Saudi Arabia reviewed their position and demanded an immediate 60 percent participation by the end of 1974. Between 1971 and 1974, Libya nationalized 50 to 100 percent of the equity of all the oil companies within its borders. Iraq nationalized the Iraq Petroleum Company's Kirkuk field in 1972, and followed this up in 1973 by nationalizing the Basrah Petroleum Company. In 1974 the Nigerian Government acquired a 55 percent participation share in the assets of the companies operating within that country.

In a brief span of four years, control of oil production by national governments was complete. (31) The takeovers provided, in most cases, compensation of a magnitude "somewhat more than the book value of the above-ground assets according to an accounting formula known as 'updated book value,' but obtained the recognition that unproduced oil reserves were national assets not subject to compensation." (32) The companies were by no means eliminated. They continued to market the petroleum and were entitled to purchase the crude under "buy back" formulas at prices somewhere between the tax-paid cost and the posted price. (33)

Today, ownership of producing facilities and control of production is firmly in the hands of the producing countries. The movement from concession to contract has been completed. There still remains the question of whether the producing countries will opt to do their own refining, shipping, and marketing. Indications are that they will become increasingly involved in the first two and put off for some time their involvement in marketing.

The effectiveness of OPEC in raising the price of oil and in securing control over its production and price acted as an incentive to those in copper, bauxite, and iron ore. However, the experience was not to be as readily transferred to other minerals as some had hoped.

Bauxite Nationalizations, Takeovers and Production Levies

Bauxite-exporting countries grouped together in the International Bauxite Association (IBA) have been second only to members of OPEC in increasing their revenue. (34) There have been some takeovers (35) but the major emphasis has been on revenue-increasing measures. Bauxite exporters have been developing joint ventures with one another and with other developing countries in the processing of bauxite.

The IBA was established in March 1974, and was the outcome of discussions among bauxite-exporting countries beginning in 1970. The government of Jamaica set the direction for other IBA members in May of 1974 with a five-point proposal: (36)

a) The formula for revenue should be linked not as customarily has been the case, to the price of the raw material, but to the price of the finished product (aluminum);

b) Means should be found to increase the contributions made by Jamaica's bauxite and alumina exports to its balance of payments;

c) All lands currently owned by the companies should revert to the government so that control of the surface rights would return into Jamaican hands;

d) The government should reacquire control of the bauxite ore;

e) National participation in the ownership of the bauxite and aluminum operations in Jamaica should be negotiated.

Jamaica achieved all of its stated goals. In the negotiations with Kaiser Aluminum, for example, the company accepted a much increased production levy linked to the price of aluminum ingots, agreed to sell 51 percent of its bauxite mining operations in Jamaica (to be paid for over a period of ten years with 8.5 percent interest per annum), and to sell back 40,000 acres of land to the Jamaican government. (37) Kaiser agreed to full and equal participation by the government on the board of the new corporation and entered into a management contract for a seven-year period.

IBA members, each negotiating on a bilateral basis, have increased revenues, participations, and nationalizations. They have also been developing joint ventures with one another. Guyana, Jamaica, and Trinidad and Tobago have decided to enter into joint venture processing arrangements by constructing two aluminum smelters. (38) The first is to be in southern Trinidad and the second in Guyana. Mexico and Jamaica have agreed to establish an integrated aluminum project consisting of three companies (39) for bauxite production, aluminum production, and aluminum smelting. The first two are to be in Jamaica with control in the hands of a Jamaican majority. The third is to be in Mexico with 51 percent Mexican equity.

Australia, the only developed country member of IBA, has won a radical increase in its royalties from bauxite. (40) The state government of Queensland increased royalties to $A1 per ton for exported ore and $A.50 per ton for ore processed in the country, compared with previous rates of $A.10 and $A.05 respectively.

The IBA, after a slow beginning, appears to be moving in the direction that OPEC did. First, there was the exchange of information which permitted members to compare one another's arrangements with the companies. In at least one instance IBA permitted cost saving "swaps." (41) It has pursued strategy of price leadership rather than price agreement. Participations are continuing, and it is quite possible that in the next few years bauxite production will become solely a governmental function. To date, no pricing standards differentiated on ore quality and transportation have emerged, nor has there been any attempt at the coordination of production levels. The IBA has achieved a large measure of success, and it is doubtful that its members will wish to jeopardize this success by precipitous action. However, over time IBA will certainly attempt to extend its control over bauxite production and processing with a view to further increasing national revenue.

Copper Nationalizations and Takeovers

The Inter-Governmental Council of Copper Exporting Countries (CIPEC) was established in 1967 by the four major copper exporters - Chile, Peru, Zaire, and Zambia. It has not achieved the success of OPEC and the IBA in increasing members' revenues. On the other hand, its members had, by January 1, 1974, established national control over copper production. (42)

Zaire was the first of the four countries to nationalize the copper facilities located in its territory when it took over Union Miniere du Haute Katanga in 1966-67. (43) Chile began its takeover of the copper industry in 1967 and completed it in 1972. Initially the government obtained majority control in the major mines within the country, and by 1972 all large-scale copper mining companies were nationalized. Following the demise of Allende and his government, the nationalized companies were compensated, but the mines were not denationalized. In 1970, Zambia asked for, and received, a 51 percent participation in the two major companies operating in the country. The companies continued to maintain substantial control through sales and management contracts.   In August 1973, governmental powers in the companies were increased by providing the government a greater role in management through the abolition of special privileges preserved by the company, and through the creation of a government-owned copper-marketing company.   In 1974, Peru nationalized Cerro, one of its major copper companies.   The United Nations has summarized CIPEC members' nationalizations through mid-1974. (44)

In spite of these actions, one authority in the field, Stephen Zorn, has noted (45) that the balance in bargaining power may have shifted in recent copper negotiations between developing countries on the one hand and transnational corporations and international financial institutions on the other. He argues that features of recent agreements "appear to contradict the tendency toward greater host government control of mining operations and a greater share for the host government of the surplus produced by mining operations." (46) In his opinion, the shift in bargaining power resulted from extremely low copper prices, large stocks of copper, the general debt problem of developing countries, and setbacks and delays in many copper projects in developing countries. The key characteristics noted by Zorn in the only major copper agreement negotiated during 1976 were: (47)

(a) expressions of sovereignty, in which the principles repeatedly stated in United National General Assembly resolutions on permanent sovereignty over natural resources and the New International Economic Order, are recognized in a formal, legal sense, although not necessarily in a practical sense;

(b) staged development of the project, with opportunities for both the foreign investor and the host government to rethink their initial decision to proceed:

(c) financial provisions that substantially reduce the risk to the foreign investor and to the foreign providers of finance, by accelerating returns in the early years of production;

(d) higher government 'take' in the later years of a project's life, either through higher taxes or greater government equity, after the foreign investor has had an opportunity to earn a reasonable return;

(e) decision making procedures related to major aspects of the project which retain effective control for the foreign investor, regardless of the nominal distribution of shareholding between the government and the investor; and

(f) <u>dispute-settlement procedures</u> that preserve the host country's position of legal sovereignty but that give effective arbitral authority to a person or body outside the host country.

In addition to these provisions in the 1976 agreements, Zorn also notes that, with the exception of the Sar Cheshmeh mine in Iran, "all major copper projects underway in developing countries involve substantial foreign participation." (48)

In November 1974, in order to stem falling prices, EIPEC members attempted unsuccessfully to institute a quota system by agreeing on a 10 percent reduction of copper shipments in all forms. In June 1976, the cutback schemes were abandoned when they failed to spur a rise in the price of copper. (49)

From 1974 on, there have been discussions between CIPEC and other producer associations about the possibility of bringing about cooperation among producer associations whose products compete, e.g., copper, aluminum, and stainless steel. (50) As of July 1977, nothing concrete had developed out of these talks.

Papua/New Guinea, an associate member of CIPEC since 1975, has decided on a 70 percent excess profits tax on the major company within its territory, rather than the nationalization and participation tactics of other members. (51)

In sum, control of copper facilities within the major CIPEC countries has passed to these governments. Prices continue to fluctuate widely and quotas have not been successful in preventing price declines. A suggested plan of cooperation between CIPEC and producer associations of competing materials has not as yet materialized. Unlike the case of oil, recent agreements suggest that there has been a shift in bargaining power away from the host governments towards the transnational corporations and international financial organizations.

Iron Ore Nationalization and Takeovers

Iron ore exporting countries signed an agreement on April 3, 1975, establishing the Association of Iron Ore Exporting Countries (APEF) and it came into force on October 12, 1975. (52) Both Australia and Sweden are members. Canada remained outside of the Association because consumer countries were not permitted to become members. Up through mid-1974, there were six nationalizations or takeovers in five countries, only three of which are members of APEF. (53)

Conclusions

There have been substantial nationalizations and takeovers in the developing countries, primarily in the extractive industries, banking and insurance, public utilities, and trade. Manufacturing has been less seriously affected. Wholesale nationalizations in minerals may very well deter large-scale investments in this sector. There has already been a suggestion that the United States should no longer continue to offer specific or extended risk insurance, or any other kinds of incentives, to its nationals investing in the extractive industries due to the high risk involved in such investments. Such admonitions have not been directed towards manufacturing investments.

Government Regulation of Natural Resource Ventures

Not all developing countries have favored the route of nationalizations and/or participations. However, virtually all of them have taken legal and administrative steps to ensure that companies operate in a manner consistent with national development priorities. A recent United Nations report listed a series of steps taken by various countries: (54)

Those steps may relate inter alia to the provision of information on the companies' activities, representation on their boards of directors or supervisory committees, prevention of tying up of reserves, utilization of domestic manpower and domestically produced goods and services, technical and managerial training of nationals down-stream integration and diversification and strengthening of the domestic industrial base.

Some of these provisions have appeared in the investment codes of individual developing countries by years. Today these principles are being accepted as minimum standards by transnational corporations desirous of operating in developing countries.

During the 1950s codes were drafted to encourage foreign investment. (55) They frequently included tax incentives, and there was a general competition between developing countries to bring in foreign investors. Today, developing countries are, in general, more circumspect. They no longer believe that development, as they desire it, will automatically flow from the introduction of private investment. They fear both the economic and political power of the transnational corporation.

Governments have become much more specific in their regulations over the last 20 years. This reflects their greater understanding of their own development goals. However, weak legal and administrative structures make many of the rules and regulations more illusory than real. (56) For example, the filing of large amounts of information on company operations becomes meaningful only if some official examines the data and develops policies to modify company behavior not in accord with development goals. Tax laws are important only if tax administration is good enough to implement the laws and apply sanctions when they are not obeyed. Governments are becoming increasingly aware of the need for implementation and enforcement mechanisms.

While governments in many developing countries have weak legal-administrative systems, they are not without ways and means to overcome perceived inequities. They have a whole array of instruments at their command, including visas for company officials and skilled staff, and control over electricity, water, railroads, harbors, customs, import and export licenses, local credit facilities, and foreign exchange. When pressed, they are extremely adept at utilizing these time-honored administrative devices to bring about their objectives.

Most of the steps mentioned in the U.N. report (57) are obvious and straightforward.   It is however useful to expand upon a few of them. Governmental representatives on boards of directors and/or governmental supervisory committees permit governments to audit, and subsequently influence, company policies without requiring any financial investment by the government.   So long as governments utilize this approach to maximize development, and not as a technique of intimidation, it can be extremely useful, for it demonstrates to governments how corporations function and it underlines government policy to the companies at an early stage of policy making.

The concern over the tying up of potential, or proved, reserves by foreign-operated natural resource companies is based upon the actions of some companies which have attempted either to maintain prices by limiting worldwide output or to limit production from one country while seeking cheaper reserves elsewhere. (58) A series of measures has been devised to limit or prevent these actions. Thus, a company may be required to relinquish a fraction of its concession within a fixed time period. (59) If exploration had not begun, the company would not know which area to relinquish.   Some governments require a fixed schedule of annual investments. (60)   Various penalties may be imposed if production does not begin within a fixed time period after deposits are discovered. (61)   Once production is underway, quotas may be established, and, if they are not reached, company taxes may be based upon targeted rather than actual production. (62)   The particulars vary   from country to country and from resource to resource.   With for formation of UNCTAD, the Group of 77, and the various producer associations, the companies can be quite certain that the knowledge of unsatisfactory company policies, the host country techniques to combat them, will be known by virtually all developing countries within a very short period of time.

The use of local manpower, goods, and services has been a condition of doing business in any developing country for years. Everyone recognizes that matching manpower with actual needs is difficult. The developing counries' goal is to see that within a limited time period all unskilled jobs will be filled with nationals and, with training, semi-skilled, skilled, and managerial jobs will follow suit. (63)   Again, enforcement is the key.   Companies have less trouble with buying local goods than they do local services, provided the cost and quality of the local goods are competitive.   Local services are more difficult because local companies or groups such as engineers, contractors, architects are, for the most part, just beginning to gain the experience necessary to carry out a major job. This should be a passing pheneomenon.

The development plans of some countries call for the "establishment of viable   mineral   plants"   and/or   for   the   "diversification   of   mineral products." (64) Concession agreements for timber, oil and gas, and minerals may require the building of saw mills, plywood factories, fertilizer plants, refineries, smelters, or other processing facilities.   These may not be profitable operations.   In each case, it is essential for the government concerned to do a cost/benefit analysis.   What may be profitable for a transnational corporation controlling an integrated operation and serving a large market may not necessarily be the best use of capital for a developing country.   Once the decision is made to develop processing facilities, it is relatively simple to draft appropriate clauses for investment codes, or concession agreements, to achieve the goal.

Recognizing that they need help to broaden their industrial base, some countries require that petroleum producing companies invest a percentage of their after-tax profits in either related or other industries, thus providing capital and drawing upon the investment and managerial skills of the large companies. (65)

Governments of developing countries continue to grow more sophisticated in their regulation of natural resources ventures.   Their ultimate goal is to develop and control their own integrated industries.   For some, this may well become a possibility.   For others, with limited human and physical resources, it appears to be less likely.

Taxation of Natural Resources Ventures (66)

Regardless of the name of the agreement between developing countries and mineral companies, one cannot evaluate it unless one has a clear understanding of how much of the revenues derived from the resource ventures is to go to the host government.   Thus a concession agreement could conceivably give the host government a larger return than a service contract. This highlights the problem of establishing standards of interpretation for such nebulous concepts as gross profits, net profits, and expenses.   Accounting practices are almost as differentiated as languages.   What is crucial is that both parties to an agreement have a clear idea of the standards applicable to each particular venture.   As we have seen above, oil royalties at one time were credited against producing-country taxes.   Now they are treated as an expense, thereby increasing host government revenues. Arguments continue on many other points including: the allocation of parent company overhead costs to the foreign subsidiary; the "fair market value" of exports, such as bauxite (for which there is no independent market price); the deduction of interest on loans from parent companies to subsidiaries; and the proper allocation of costs to patents and trademarks of the parent utilized by the subsidiary.   These are some of the issues raised in the report (67) of the "Group of Eminent Persons" and they are currently being studied by the Centre of Transnational Corporations. (68)   Even when these definitional issues are resolved, the organization of the tax collection and tax administration will remain for the development of these institutions.

Financing Non-Fuel Mineral Investments

In order to satisfy the demand for non-fuel minerals during 1976-1985, one group of economists has estimated, in 1977, that $179 billion of investment will be needed: $73 billion for the first five years and $106 billion for the next five. (69)   It was judged that approximately 50 percent of this investment must be made in developing countries ($95.5 billion), with 80 percent of the total allocated for three commodities alone - copper, iron, and bauxite (including alumina and aluminum). (70)   Foreign financing requirements in developing countries, extremely difficult to predict, have been estimated at $4.6 billion per annum for the first five years, and $7.3 billion per annum for the second five years. (71)

Developing country initiatives to ensure control over their natural resources, coupled with the uncertainties of future energy costs and environmental legislation, have raised questions about whether these goals will be met, as in the past, by the large mineral companies and, if not, by some other source of capital. These questions are raised at a time when mineral prices are depressed, costs are rising rapidly, and the era of self-financing within the sector has come to an end. Currently, both the mineral companies and the international financial institutions favor investments in developed countries (the United States, Canada, Australia, and South Africa) where, for the most part, infrastructure is in place, public/private ownership questions are not an issue, and external debt problems are manageable. (72) However, these countries alone will not be able to meet the projected demand.

The shortage of capital and the shift away from self-financing has given the mining companies a like-minded ally in the international financial institutions. (73) The strength of this alliance was apparent during the negotiations of recent copper agreements discussed above. It will be recalled that these agreements have reversed the trend towards greater host government control of mining operations and a greater share for the host government of the surplus produced by mining operations. Whether this new shift will occur in future agreements involving bauxite, iron ore, and nickel is unknown, but there is little doubt that both the companies and financial institutions will press for a continuation of this trend.   The outcome of particular negotiations will depend upon the need which each of the parties has for the investment in question, and on the availability of alternate sources of financing or supply. The existence of alternate sources of finance will not, however, relieve the developing countries of the need for mineral company management and technology.

Most developing countries must seek capital for mineral development abroad. Few have access to capital markets because of the general weakness of their economies and their high debt burden relative to export earnings. If the funds are to come from the private sector, the most likely source will be the mineral companies which can, in turn, secure funds from financial institutions. There has been a suggestion that some of the capital-surplus oil companies may have some interest in investments in this sector. (74) In order to increase private flows of investment, there have been suggestions that capital-exporting countries might create an international insurance scheme to guarantee noncommercial risks. (75) Similar schemes already exist within individual countries. (76) Another idea in an early stage of development is for the establishment of an international minerals investment trust (IMIT). (77) Initial capital would come from capital-exporting countries and would be used to purchase debt and equity securities of companies established under the laws of the host countries to exploit the national ore deposits. Subsequent financing would come from sales of new shares of IMIT. These shares would be sold to public and private agencies and be fully negotiable. As a part of the proposal, it has been suggested that sales on the open market might be matched by equal sales to participating governments. One of the main purposes of the trust, in addition to providing a new source of capital, would be to provide a degree of risk diversification not possible for investors in particular projects. On a government-to-government basis, there have been suggestions that OPEC countries with capital surpluses might be interested in moving into nonfuel mineral investments. (78) As of June 1977, however, OPEC members had not done so. Public financial institutions, such as the regional development banks and the World Bank, have been considered as possible sources for increased capital. The World Bank has made loans in the mineral sector and will continue to do so. (79) However, it would require a substantial reorientation of its development strategy to increase its loans to this sector to anywhere near the level of anticipated investment needs. (80) A major shortcoming of public international financial lending is its orientation towards project development funding, since this has excluded the use of such funds for mineral exploration. Part of this problem could be solved by an expansion of the United Nations Revolving Fund for Natural Resources Exploration. (81) Finally, there is the proposal of the United States for an International Resources Bank. (82) This tripartite arrangement bringing together private investors, host governments, and the World Bank was rejected at UNCTAD IV but may, with changing circumstances, be revived.

The problem of financing mineral investments is a continuing problem. There are many options open to both the producers and users of minerals. The particular approach utilized will be dependent upon the shifting bargaining power of the host countries and the mineral companies over time.

REGULATION OF THE TRANSNATIONAL CORPORATION

The increase in the activities of transnational corporations during the 1960s produced mixed feelings within host countries, both developed and developing. These large business entities were seen as a source of capital, technology, "know-how," and management with ready access to worldwide markets. They were highly capitalized, very powerful, and ubiquitous. Many were more powerful and wealthier than the governments of various of their hosts. These facets of the transnationals tended to create uneasiness, dislike, and fear among host-country officials. The growing awareness of the transnationals by governments and scholars resulted in an outpouring of books and articles, some favorable (83) and others critical. (84) Disagreement over the role of the transnationals in economic development did not moderate the general consensus of their pervasiveness and their economic and political power. One of the most influential books on the subject, Sovereignty at Bay by Harvard Business School Professor Raymond Vernon, (85) clearly delineates why governments believed that their sovereignty was threatened by the transnationals.

The probing analyses of scholars and the fears of governments spilled over into national and international forums. National legislators held their own investigations and wrote lengthy reports. (86) The United Nations, at the request of its Economic and Social Council, appointed its own group of Eminent Persons which surveyed the transnationals and made its report. (87)

Other official and non-official bodies followed this lead. (88)

After approximately ten years of studies and reports, there has emerged a wide range of suggestions on what should be done about transnational corporations. Some believe that they should police their own activities through discussions in informal fora; (89) others would like to see an international regulatory institution both to cover those jurisdictional areas beyond the control of national governments and to bring about uniformity in conflicting national laws. (90) In this section we will review briefly the ideas and proposals of scholars and international organizations relating to these issues. Special attention will be given to the United Nations's Commission on Transnational Corporations and its Centre on Transnational Corporations, as well as the OECD's Declaration and Guidelines for Multinational Enterprises.

Scholarly Views on the Regulation of Transnational Corporations

Focus within the scholarly community has varied from proposals for an overall approach to the issues to suggestions on how to deal with particular problems. Included in the first category are proposals for an international company law, (91) a GATT-like institution for international investment (92) and an International Corporation Consultative Center (ICCC). (93) Proposals in the second category cover, inter-alia, harmonization of national laws on the provision of information by transnationals to governments, (94) accounting procedures, (95) taxation, (96) security regulations, (97) anti-trust (98) and export controls. (99)

We will limit our attention to the three general proposals which predated the report of the Group of Eminent Persons and a conference which preceded the Eminent Persons' report. (100)

Scholars and practitioners within the capital-exporting countries saw that the growth of economic and political power of transnational corporations might create friction both at home and abroad. In the late 1960's, they began to discuss the problems and suggest ways to eliminate or minimize them.

An International Company Law

While the Harvard Business School was formulating its six-year major research project on multinationals, George Ball, a practitioner, scholar, and former diplomat, put forth his proposal for an international company law. As early as 1967, he proposed the establishment by treaty of an international company law, administered by a supranational body, including representatives drawn from various countries. (101) It was envisioned that the supranational body would exercise not only normal domiciliary supervision but also enforce anti-monopoly laws and administer guarantees with regard to uncompensated expropriation. Ball left to others both the specifics of the laws and the ways in which they would dovetail with national company laws. Widespread shared owhership was urged for the global corporations so that they could not be regarded as the exclusive instrument of a particular nation. Ball said that his proposal was but an extension of the call for a Common Companies law for the European Economic Community. His proposal has received some support, but was generally considered unachievable in the foreseeable future.

A GATT for Investment

Goldberg and Kindleberger concluded, in 1970, that there are substantial and recurring problems involving the international corporation in regard to taxation, antitrust policy, balance-of-payment controls, export controls, and security regulations. (102)   Each is found to have a common denominator: "the international corporation is either unregulated, having slipped between the cracks of national jurisdiction, or is cabined by the overlapping regulation of two countries having varying political or economic goals." (103)

Their review of scholarly literature reveals a range of opinion from those who see "a trend towards natural harmonization of national policies" (104) to those who seek an internationally agreed approach. (105) Between these two broad approaches are those that involve the utilization of international agreements on specific matters. (106) Goldberg and Kindleberger remind the reader that the only serious prior attempt to reach an agreement which was both multilateral in format and comprehensive in scope, the draft Charter of the International Trade Organization, failed when the United States withdrew its support. (107)

According to Goldberg and Kindleberger, the problem of TNCs stems from the fact that private corporate decisions may be perceived by a host or home country to be in conflict with national policies. (108)   These conflicts are serious, in the opinion of the authors, in only five areas: taxation, antitrust policy, foreign exchange, export controls, and security regulations. (109) Arguing that these conflicts are universally recognized, the authors are optimistic that "meaningful progress towards the resolution of multiparty disputes can be made in the near future." (110) They see little hope for the resurrection of the ITO-type code, and propose instead a contractual arrangement, much like the GATT, developed from agreement on a few fundamental principles and procedures. As accepted principles begin to emerge, they envision broader and deeper agreement as to foreign investment practices leading to "an international treaty of substantial coverage...accepted by the nations of the world." (111) They are cautionary, and note that one of the pitfalls to avoid is attempting too much too soon. (112)

To prepare the way for the formation of a General Agreement for the International Corporation, Goldberg and Kindleberger urge governments to agree to the formation of a preparatory Commission "to draft in detail the few principles on which agreement is needed, and establish the limited international machinery it requires." (113) They go on to suggest that "an international group of experts and staff be impaneled for a period of up to two years to consider the problem of regulation of the international corporation" with the goal of creating an international agreement. (114) Once an agreement is drafted and signed, questions could be submitted to the agency by either countries or companies. The agency would then investigate the facts and the issues presented. "Recommendations to take or cease action would be issued, but there would be no compulsion to abide by them." (115)   They see the agency developing into an ombudsman for corporations and countries seeking relief from oppressive policies. The issues of sponsorship, budgeting, and other administrative matters they leave to others. They conclude with the opinion that "international supervision is a much more preferable solution than complete laissez-faire or a return to nationalism," but they believe that it is necessary to start nearer the laissez-faire position and to evolve a system through trial and error and the establishment of precedent. (116)

An International Corporation Consultative Center

Seymour Rubin, one of the leading lawyers writing on and advising transnational corporations, remains one of the leading skeptics on the threat to national sovereignty posed by transnational corporations. (117)   In his opinion, "extraterritoriality is essentially a non-issue" of "little more than polemic significance." (118) He does, however, find that there is a political psychological issue in a foreigner having the power to affect one's national economy. (119)   In some cases, this issue may involve the fear of concentrating economic power in private hands, irrespective of whether they are national or foreign.   In such cases, he suggests that "the issue of foreigners [can be] turned to account by the advocates of democratic socialism." (120)

Rubin believes the most important problem posed by TNC's to be the economic one: Is the multinational enterprise an expensive way for nations to acquire capital and/or skills?   Are these enterprises, with their ability to reallocate production across countries, a threat to home countries where labor and other costs may be comparatively higher? (121)

Rubin is skeptical about the "something must be done approach."   He considers Ball's proposal for an international company law to be "a reasonable way of incorporating a multination enterprise" but concludes that it is likely to be too little or too much. (122)   In addition he finds there "is little chance that regulation of the alleged excesses of either domestic or international corporations could be written into a statute acceptable to all states...."(123) He prefers Dunning's cost/benefit approach to the analysis of TNC's to Ball's, i.e., "what does the host country get; what does this cost; is there a better alternative?" (124)

Rubin, in general, does not believe that the costs of foreign investment are too high, that there should be a progressive denationalization, or that there is a need to establish a disinvestment corporation. He is not convinced that fade-out provisions should be included in agreements, or that technology transfers should be made via centralized coordinating agencies. The merit of most of these proposals has not been "adequately demonstrated, or indeed, [shown to] respond to provable needs." (125)

Arguing that "there is surely no near prospect of an organization that will administer an international agreement or agreements" in respect to multinational enterprises, Rubin proposes an institution with powers which he believes to be more appropriate, an International Corporation Consultative Center (ICCC). (126)   The work program of ICCC would "put primary emphasis on the implication for conventional concepts of national sovereignty of the growing phenomenon of internationalized production." He questions whether national sovereignty is an ideal, and considers "possibilities of a World Interstate Commerce Clause, like that of the United States Constitution." (127) It should be noted that, within the United States, the Interstate Commerce Clause has encouraged trade and investment between the states, and has centralized regulatory power over corporations at the national level.

Rubin would like to see the ICCC linked to an existing organization rather than established as a new autonomous institution. (128)   The OECD, UNCTAD, and UNIDO each are seen as too committed to be acceptable to both developed and developing countries.   The World Bank remains a possibility in his mind, but its system of weighted voting might make it objectionable to the developing countries.   Regional institutions are also seen as a possibility, with the Organization of American States and the Inter-American Bank prototypes of institutional linkage.

As Rubin sees it, the ICCC would engage in research and analysis and make recommendations on a wide range of issues: extra-territoriality, an international company law, the effect of the growth of international production on traditional trade theory, the pros and cons of national versus foreign ownership in particular fields of special interest (natural resources) and for particular periods of time (various disinvestment schemes), and national private versus national public ownership.

Rubin sees the need to establish a number of procedures and principles to make the research more useful. (129) He wants to separate the problems of multinational enterprises in developed and developing countries and disaggregate the developing countries into more meaningful subgroups. He also wants more comparative work to be done on the manner and style of different capital-exporting countries. Lastly, he wants special relations, such as those between the United States and Mexico and the United States and Canada, to be seen as such and not form the basis for universal generalizations.

Rubin sees the ICCC's greatest potential contribution to be the encouragement and sponsorship of objective and careful analysis and the establishment of a forum for regular and informed discussion.

The Dusseldorf Conference on Multinational Corporations

In January 1973, a group of scholars, practitioners, and officials of international organizations and governments from both developed and developing countries met for two days in Dusseldorf, Germany, to inquire into the "desirability and feasibility of some sort of international governmental body that would affect the multinational operations of international corporations." (130)

The Conference agreed with considerable unanimity of opinion that "a GATT for Investment, much less a disinvestment agency would be neither feasible nor desirable at present." (131)

Panel II concerned itself with developing countries and grappled with the question, "Can international controls, either in the form of a code creating enforceable rights and remedies or in the form of an international regulatory body, help the less developed countries?" (132)   The universal negative response was based on two arguments: (133)

1. [I]nternational approaches are either ineffective or biased in favor of the developed world; and

2. Arrangements on the fundamental issue...must come from ad hoc or bilateral negotiations in which the developing nations participate directly.

Access to more information and the provision of technical assistance and training to less developed countries involved in negotiating with potential investors were the only international steps desired by the developing countries.

Apparently the multinational corporations were both pleased and relieved at the conclusions of the Conference participants. Seymour Rubin, however, saw neither "benevolent approval nor benign neglect for the MNEs" in the Conference's decisions. (134) Noting the suggestions of the numerous studies and reports emanating from developed nations and their economists, it was his personal opinion "that some movement towards a new international organization or towards increasing the powers and role of existing organizations is likely." (135) Rubin appeared prophetic when, before the end of 1973, the United Nations created the Group of Eminent Persons to look into the activities of the multinationals.

Rubin's belief that both international and increased national regulation would become a reality was strengthened by the various revelations made before the Church Subcommittee investigating the activities of multinationals. (136) He referred specifically to the desire of ITT to overthrow the Allende government in Chile and the efforts of the oil companies to hold down production when a glut of oil on the world market was feared. One means used was drilling wells to the wrong depth and covering up others by bulldozers to hoodwink the Iraqi Government. Finally, he cites reports of a Standard Oil of California memorandum which proposed dealing with the anticipated threat to stable oil prices "by reducing U.S. production, cutting imports into the United States from Canada, and slicing production in various oil-producing nations to accommodate the expectations of increased revenues of Iran and Saudi Arabia." (137) Although he suggests that these revelations can be "laid to the ineptitude and greed of some multinationals," (138) he is politically wise and realistic, and argues that the consequences of these actions could include "such administrative or legislative actions as movement towards deconcentration by use of existing or new anti-trust laws, revision of previously advantageous tax treatment, and, almost certainly, by more stringent requirements for reporting than now exist." (139) Rubin concludes his 1974 article with the repetition of his proposal for the ICCC. He suggests regular meetings of experts to discuss issues on a noncrisis and regular basis. Starting with those issues where there is a mutuality of interest, he hopes that, over time, broader proposals will be discussed.

Almost before the ink was dry on Rubin's July 1974 article, the United Nations voted to accept the recommendations of the Group of Eminent Persons as to the establishment of both a Commission and a Centre on Transnational Corporations. (140)

The United Nations

The principal bodies within the United Nations' system responsible for policies, studies, and other activities concerning transnational corporations are the Commission and the Centre. Both were created in 1974 following the recommendations of the Group of Eminent Persons earlier that year. (141) As of May 1977, the Commission had held three annual meetings and had set into motion an extensive program of research, information-gathering, and technical assistance with the purpose of formulating policies concerning transnational corporations. On a day-to-day basis, the Centre acts as the administrative, research, and technical assistance arm of the Commission. (142)

Presently, the highest order of priority of the Commission and Centre is the development of a code of conduct for transnational corporations. (143) In order to provide member governments with information on which to base a mutually agreed code of conduct, the Commission and Centre are developing a comprehensive information system on the activities of transnational corporations. (144) The research program is concerned with political, legal, economic, and social aspects of TNCs' activities. (145) After collecting data from governments and other sources, they analyze, store, and disseminate it to governments on request. The Centre also provides technical assistance and training in the form of experts and courses. (146) The aim is to strengthen the capacity of host countries, particularly developing ones, to negotiate with transnationals.

The Commission and Centre have recently established working groups on corrupt practices and international standards of accounting. (147) Work on the Code of Conduct has reached the stage of a topical outline which will now be disaggregated and annotated. (148) UNCTAD, the ILO, UNIDO, and various other UN institutions, such as the regional economic commissions, have included various transnational corporation issues on their agendas. (149)

The Organization of Economic Cooperation and Development (OECD)

The domination which the developing countries have achieved over most nonfinancial institutions of the United Nations system has encouraged the industrial countries to formulate their policies elsewhere. The OECD, with its 24 members, includes all of the major capital exporting countries of the world whose nationals are responsible for virtually all foreign investment. (150) Thus it came as no surprise that the OECD carried out its own study on international investment and multinational enterprises and issued both a Declaration (151) and guidelines for multinational enterprises. (152)

The OECD Council met at a ministerial level in June 1976 and issued a Declaration which stated that it was agreed that cooperation among member countries "can improve the foreign investment climate, encourage the positive contribution which multinational enterprises can make to economic and social progress, and minimize and resolve difficulties which may arise from their various operations." (153) To this end the Ministers adopted a set of guidelines for multinational enterprises. (154) The Declaration also dealt with national treatment of foreign-owned enterprises, concluding that they should be treated no less favorably than domestic enterprises; (155) international investment incentives and disincentives, agreeing that such measures should be as open as possible; and consultation procedures under which Members agreed to continue to consult with one another in relation to decisions of the Council on these matters. (156) It was also agreed that all of these matters would be reviewed in three years. (157)

The Guidelines for Multinational Enterprises are recommendations jointly addressed by Member countries to multinational enterprises operating within their countries. (158) International cooperation on these matters is extended to all states, and specific reference is made to developing countries "with a view to improving the welfare and living standards of all people..." (159) Observance of the Guidelines is "voluntary and not legally enforceable." (160) The sovereignty of each state is ensured by the right "to prescribe the conditions under which multinational enterprises operate within its national jurisdiction." (161) It is subject only to "international law and to the international agreements to which it has subscribed." (162) The Guidelines define multinational enterprises very broadly. The General Policies are encompassed in nine points: (163)

Enterprises should

(1) take fully into account established general policy objectives of the Member countries in which they operate;

(2) in particular, give due consideration to those countries' aims and priorities with regard to economic and social progress, including industrial and regional development, the protection of the environment, the creation of employment opportunities, the promotion of innovation and the transfer of technology;

(3) while observing their legal obligations concerning information, supply their entities with supplementary information the latter may need in order to meet requests by the authorities of the countries in which those entities are located for information relevant to the activities of these entities, taking into account legitimate requirements of business confidentiality;

(4) favor close cooperation with the local community and business interests;

(5) allow their component entities freedom to develop their activities and to exploit their competitive advantage in domestic and foreign markets, consistent with the need for specialization and sound commercial practice;

(6) when filling responsible posts in each country of operation, take due account of individual qualifications without discrimination as to nationality, subject to particular national requirements in this respect;

(7) not render - and they should not be solicited or expected to render -

any bribe or other improper benefit, direct or indirect, to any public servant or holder of public office;

(8) unless legally permissible, not make contributions to candidates for public office or to political parties or other political organizations;

(9) abstain from any improper involvement in local political activities.

An attempt has been made in the Guidelines to at least touch on the major concerns of the developing countries. Consideration was given to their "aims and priorities with regard to economic and social progress," and their desire that TNCs should provide "information relevant to the activities of those entities," and abstain from "any improper involvement in local political activities." These and other items are expanded on in paragraphs following the general listing of the nine points. Included are expanded statements on disclosure of information, competition, financing, taxation, employment and industrial relations, and science and technology. Within these paragraphs one finds still other controversial points covered. Thus, the transnationals are asked to provide information on research and development expenditures for the enterprise as a whole (but not within each country as desired by the developing countries); the policies followed in respect to intragroup pricing; and the accounting policies, including those on consolidation. Various restrictive and monopolistic business practices are to be avoided, and they are to observe the objectives countries set for balance-of-payments and credit policies. They are to "refrain from making use of the particular facilities available to them, such as transfer pricing, which does not conform to an arm's length standard." (164) In employment and industrial relations they are to observe national standards and "respect the rights of their employees to be represented by trade unions" and "to engage in constructive negotiations," plus a whole series of enlightened labor practices including the training and upgrading of local employees. (165) They are not to "threaten to utilize a capacity to transfer the whole or part of an operating unit from the country concerned in order to influence unfairly those negotiations or to hinder the exercise of a right to organize." (166) The rapid diffusion of technology and the transfer of technology on reasonable terms and conditions are also included.

The OECD Council decided that its Committee on International Investment and Multinational Enterprises shall "periodically or at the request of a Member country hold an exchange of views on matters related to the guidelines...."(167)

Major differences in approach have been noted between OECD and UNCTAD in attempts to create various codes of conduct. (168) The three most important differences are: (1) OECD's preference for general principles and UNCTAD's desire for general principles and specific rules; (2) whether the convention should deal with the actions of the transnationals only (preferred by UNCTAD), or with those of home and host governments' enterprises as well (preferred by OECD); and (3) the legal nature of such codes, with OECD preferring voluntary codes and UNCTAD preferring binding codes. As the authors point out, this last difference "may well be one over a matter of form rather than one of substance" (169) for it is unclear how a binding code would be implemented. The members of OECD have a number of ways to put pressure on transnationals to follow the Guidelines. For example, in the case of either nationalizations or other takeovers, the member government could conditon its diplomatic intervention on behalf of the transnational and/or its payment of investment insurance of conformance within the voluntary guidelines. (170)

Conclusions on the Regulation of Transnational Corporations

Ten years of discussion and studies among scholars, legal practitioners, and officials of governments and international organizations on the regulation of transnational corporations has encouraged two international institutions to try their hand at proposing regulations. The OECD, representing the principal capital-exporting governments of the world, put forth a non-binding set of guidelines agreed to in 1976 by its members. The approach is voluntary self-regulation. The Commission on Transnational Corporations and its Centre are hard at work on an elaborate code of conduct for transnational corporations. No decision has been made on its legal nature. Whether guidelines or a legally binding code becomes the order of the day seems to be much less significant than the fact that there is virtually universal governmental consensus that transnational corporations should come under some form of regulation.

CONCLUSIONS ON PRIVATE FOREIGN INVESTMENT

In general, it is difficult to ascertain whether Article 2 of the Charter has acted as an impediment to foreign investment. However, there can be little doubt that it has created additional apprehension on the part of new investors in developing countries. To those who are experienced investors in developing countries, the uncertainties are balanced by high profits; and the ambiguities of the wording in Article 2 are not very important to those who have many years experience working abroad. Article 2 is little more than the internationalization of conditions under which they have lived for many years.

Before closing this chapter, it is worthwhile to examine the provisions on compensation and dispute resolution. Compensation following takeovers is at best a speculative issue. How much is a nationalized asset worth? What standards should be employed in answering this question? Should the issues be based purely on accounting principles, or should other criteria be included in the judgment? Should compensation be measured on the basis of return on investment, book value of the company, or some other criteria? How much of a return on investment is equitable? Do unmined resources or unpumped oil represent compensatible assets of the investor? A recent three-volume study on various approaches to valuation points up the fact that there are no universally accepted answers to these questions. (171) Few would argue that the investor should not receive a fair return on investments. Needless to say, differences of opinion center on what is a "fair" share. If past experience provides any indication of future actions, one is forced to recognize that, in many instances, prevailing economic and political conditions, as well as the relationships developed over the years between representatives of the investor and the host government, will be key elements in the final decision on compensation.

When compensation disputes arise, the mechanism for resolving them becomes particularly important. This apparently procedural question is treated as a substantive issue by investors and host governments alike. On the one hand, investors fear unfair treatment if issues are decided under local law in local tribunals, for it is often assumed that such decisions will be subjectively nationalistic. Thus, they favor outside "objective" parties to resolve the disputes. The developing countries, on the other hand, fear that outsiders will reinforce the status quo and make subjective decisions favoring international investors. The assumption underlying this fear is that rules governing compensation issues were created by capital-exporting countries to protect their investors. These assumptions are reinforced by psychological memories of international law phrases such as "minimum standards" and "civilized countries," which tended to equate countries outside of Europe and North America with a lesser species of being.

In the final analysis, the desire to make and receive investments will be based on a balancing of interests of the investor and the host country. Once having made the investment, if the estimates of either party are very far off the mark, there will be a demand for a reformation of the agreements underlying the arrangements. This has occurred frequently over the past twenty years; for example, in concession agreements which have evolved through a series of intermediate steps towards service contracts. The sanctity of contract, a prevalent concept within many industrial countries, is no longer considered sacrosanct by many developing countries. When they discover that the arrangements which they have entered into are no longer equitable, either due to their ignorance at the time of signing the agreement or changing circumstances, they demand reformation. To maintain a feeling of good faith between the parties and a continuing sense of equity in relationships, it probably will be necessary to include provisions for a periodic review within long-term contractual arrangements. As virtually any government can harass a company through administrative means without violating the letter of the law, it is in the interest of both parties to attempt to maintain an equitable balance in pursuing their respective interests.

Over the years many attempts have been made to resolve these thorny issues. One interesting approach, with which the author was involved, was initiated by the India Council of the Business Council for International Understanding (BCIU). (172) In April 1964, recognizing that there were opportunities as well as deterrents to private investment in India, BCIU sponsored a conference in New Delhi for the specific purpose of opening a dialogue between top Indian government officials and key United States business representatives. The business delegation represented 30 United States' companies, ranging from those with already large investments and long operating experience in India, to those newly attracted to India. In order to invite free expression and exchange of thoughts and opinions, by government as well as business, the New Delhi Conference was developed as an opportunity to compare, side by side, the ten principal points which seemed to underlie India's industrial investment policy with ten corresponding points which the business delegation regarded as essential incentives for promoting foreign investor confidence.

Policy Objectives and Incentives for Investing in India

Industrial policy objectives for the developing Indian economy	*Incentives for promoting foreign investor confidence*
OVERALL OBJECTIVE	OVERALL INCENTIVE
Accelerated economic development to improve the standard of living consistent with resources available therefor.	A demonstrable intent and program on the part of the Indian Government to improve the climate for foreign private investment.
SPECIFIC OBJECTIVES	SPECIFIC INCENTIVES
1. Substantial contribution to foreign exchange earnings or savings.	1. Acceptable return on capital employed as compared to competitive opportunities outside India.
2. Acceptable level of local participation in equity consistent with availability of needed foreign exchange.	2. Acceptable level of foreign participation in equity and management control, commensurate with contribution of foreign exchange and know-how.
3. Reasonable equity to loan ratio and acceptable repatriation schedule for loans and dividends.	3. Reasonable amortization and divident policy with greater freedom to reinvest locally for expansion, technological and quality improvements.
4. Acceptable unit costs for project investment and operation consistent with safety, performance, quality standards.	4. Reasonable import duty and other controls, to assure minimum unit investment and operating costs.
5. Priority on manufacturing investments in locations acceptable to government.	5. Need for investment in both manufacturing and distribution, in relation to regional demand.
6. Competitive prices on imported raw materials, together with economic utilization of available local supplies.	6. Freedom to select raw material source consistent with commercially competitive pricing and impact on foreign exchange.
7. Reasonable ex-plant and consumer price levels, with safeguards against excessive profits.	7. Flexible product pricing policy consistent with acceptable return on investment.
8. Foreign and local private enterprise, subject to same controls, regulations, and tax treatment.	8. Stable, simple, and equitable tax and depreciation policy; avoidance of retroactive tax.
9. Creation of employment, together with accelerated training and development of Indian personnel.	9. Adequate staffing by foreign technical experts and managerial talent.
10. Development of certain industries designated as the exclusive responsibility of the State.	10. Expeditious approval procedures, based on well-coordinated planning with equitable allocation of capacity to the foreign private investor.

When put side by side, the ten points provided the basis for a dialogue which made explicit issues generally skirted by individual investors and host governments in their dealings. This was a serious effort to go beyond the rhetoric which clouds the issues in many such discussions. A more international systematic follow-through of this approach might yield impressive results in a large number of countries.

Although the international environment for investment has changed radically during the post-World War II era, the flow of investments has continued to increase. At the same time, the developing countries have become more skeptical about the benefits of foreign investment. Many extractive and plantation industries have been nationalized, though foreigners continue to play important technological and marketing roles in these sectors. Banking and insurance have become carefully regulated. In manufacturing areas, joint ventures have become the preferred policy option of many developing countries. The manufacturing industries will most likely continue to attract an increasing rate of foreign investment.   In this area, the developing countries are particularly in need of the technology, "know-how," management, and marketing skills of foreigners, and the foreign investor requires much smaller capital investments in manufacturing ventures than in the extractive industries.

What the businessman sees abroad today is reminiscent of events in industrial countries years ago - increased regulation of investments and fiscal policies which cut into profits.   Complaints about regulation, reporting systems, and taxes are normal responses of businessmen everywhere. Those who have filed registration statements with the United States Securities and Exchange Commission would be hard pressed to complain about "red-tape" and the time-consuming regulation in developing countries. The real changes in foreign investment are psychological. The easy days of working abroad are disappearing, and the developing countries are becoming as regulated as the developed countries. The foreign investor wishing to operate in a developing country is being asked more and more to demonstrate how his investment will lead to the development of the host country. No longer is it automatically assumed that investment equals development.

7 Concepts of International Equity in Transition

Since its inception, the developing countries have used the United Nations to pursue the goal of a more equitable distribution of power and wealth. The latest statement of measures to implement this goal is the Charter of Economic Rights and Duties of States. Its provisions call for changes in the institutional and legal order which would increase the access of developing countries to economic opportunities. The Charter is a comprehensive statement which consolidates a large part of the resolutions initiated by the Third World in various fora over the last 30 years, and most of its provisions were unanimously approved by the United Nations General Assembly in December 1974.

The institutional and conceptual framework which has permitted the developing countries to win a hearing for their demands for the new international economic order has its origin in the post-World War I decisions of the Western industrial countries. When the allies established the League of Nations and the International Labour Organization, they created organs for the internationalization of issues which formerly had been the exclusive preserve of nation-states. The activities of the Economic and Financial Organization of the League and the international economic conferences which it sponsored were dramatic evidence of the high level of international concern with national policies. By the mid-1930s, the League was spending 65 percent of its budget on economic and social issues.

The number of international organizations and the level of their activities increased after World War II. The Bretton Woods Agreement established the International Monetary Fund, the World Bank, and indirectly, the GATT. Decolonization increased membership within international organizations from 51 in 1945 to 149 in 1977. The large influx of new developing states greatly accelerated the involvement of international organizations in the development process. It also changed the approach of many of these organizations as voting control of all but the financial organizations moved from the developed to the developing countries.

In 1964, the developing countries created the United Nations Conference on Trade and Development. It was here that they organized themselves into

173

the Group of 77, which has acted as a negotiating bloc to initiate, research, and pursue their diverse objectives.   Drawing intellectual leadership from Latin American developmentalists, it has become a central training ground and meeting place.

Implicit in the approach of the developing countries is the thesis that the majority of countries in the world, containing a majority of the world's population, should determine the kind of world in which they wish to live. This approach elevates the democratic ideals of the French and American revolutions to the international level.   The 1973 Arab oil boycott provided the leverage to force a high-level discussion of development issues in the United Nations Sixth Special Session and the ongoing negotiations on the Charter of Economic Rights and Duties of States.   Given the very general nature of much of the Charter, most of its provisions received unanimous approval. However, those provisions which made a frontal attack on existing international trade and investment institutions were rejected by the industrialized and capital-exporting countries.

The most controversial article of the Charter dealt with foreign private investment.   This was the only article which substantially modified an earlier international accord.   The 1962 United Nations Resolution on Permanent Sovereignty over Natural Resources had provided for state responsibility to pay "appropriate" compensation in cases of nationalization "in accordance with international law."   Since the developed countries had construed this to mean "prompt, adequate, and effective," they had approved the 1962 resolution.   They would not, however, approve the very different language of Article 2 of the Charter.   Article 2 excluded any reference to states' obligations under customary law to respect international agreements or pay adequate compensation.   Article 2 moved dispute resolution from international to national fora under national rules unless governments decided otherwise.   In addition, it singled out transnational corporations as special subjects of national supervision. Discussion on Article 2 continued up to the last moment, but no consensus was achieved.

Persistent wide fluctuations in commodity prices and deteriorating terms of trade set the stage for an article to establish state-run producer associations, a particularly sensitive issue for developed countries as the negotiations came on the heels of the 1973-74 oil boycott.   The principal argument which they directed against Article 5 was that it failed to take into account the interests of consumers as well as producers.

Price indexation was another policy which the developing countries proposed in the Charter as an instrument to prevent the deterioration of their terms of trade.   Article 28 called for the linking of the prices of exports of developing countries to the prices of their imports. The developed countries, wary about any scheme to tamper with the price mechanism, rejected the approach, but it was easily passed by vote of the developing countries.

Three main blocs negotiated the Charter: the Group of 77, the OECD countries, and the Soviet bloc. The Group of 77 maintained voting unity in spite of the great disparities among developing countries in income and ideology.   In no instance did a sufficient split occur in the voting bloc to defeat any of the proposed draft articles.

The OECD countries had more difficulty in maintaining unity.   Only six voted against the Charter as a whole, while ten others abstained, and eight voted in favor. The United States, West Germany, and Japan were the most unified in opposition during the debates. However, in the final vote of the Charter, Japan abstained. France pursued a maverick role and showed particular sympathy to Group of 77 positions on commodity policy. The Scandinavians (except Denmark), Australians, and Canadians gave strong support to many controversial developing country initiatives. Friction between the United States and European Community countries was at least partly based on a strong difference in resource endowments.

The momentum which the Group of 77 enjoyed in 1974 continued after the passage of the Charter into the Lima meeting of UNIDO. At UNIDO the Group of 77 reiterated the principles of the NIEO and the Charter and won the approval of the Conference for a declaration calling for an increase in the share of developing countries in industrial production from 7 to 25 percent by the year 2000.

The Seventh Special Session saw the end of the forward thrust of developing country initiatives. A speech by United States Secretary of State Kissinger isolated the hardliners from the moderates within the Group of 77 and gave new coherence to the bloc of OECD states. Kissinger rejected Third World proposals to restructure the world economy and proposed, instead, more traditional reforms. From 1976 on, the Group of 77 made no new advances. The CIEC talks ended in a stalemate with consensus on only the most general matters. Third World attempts in CIEC and UNCTAD to establish an integrated commodity program, debt moratorium, and a code for the transfer of technology elicited no more than an agreement to agree. The few gains which the developing countries reaped between 1974 and mid-1977 fell into the traditional framework of the past. The IMF expanded and modified its compensatory finance facility and created a Trust Fund to assist in balance-of-payment problems. In addition, United Nations members established a new International Fund for Agricultural Development, and the European Community put into operation STABEX to assist ACP states faced with balance-of-payment problems resulting from fluctuating commodity prices.

Many developing countries are concerned about their lack of success in moving rapidly towards their goal of a New International Economic Order. A more detached historical perspective should ameliorate their current state of depression. They have effected fundamental changes in aspects of their external relations which reflected past conditions but which were formerly protected by the international legal order. Virtually all colonies have gained independence, and foreign investors no longer exercise control over mineral and oil resources within developing countries. The terms of contractual relations between developing countries and foreign investors have been modified substantially in favor of the less developed countries.

In the process of subverting old political and contractual relations, the developing countries have also effected change in the value system underlying traditional international law. Their confrontation with developed countries has resulted in new perceptions of the sovereign prerogatives of states and the nature of equitable arrangements between the industrialized countries and the Third World. With the cooperation and support of OPEC, they have forced the OECD countries to discuss issues of their choosing and have created international pressure to solve their economic and financial problems.

Finally, the developing countries have established as law new principles and processes which work in their interest. Today, transnational companies must demonstrate that their investments will further the goals of the host government. Among the new processes are various institutional arrangements in the United Nations, including the establishment of UNCTAD, the United Nations Development Programme, UNIDO, and the International Fund for Agricultural Development. Even within the World Bank and IMF, where voting is weighted, the developing countries have benefited by new organs (the Development Committee and the Group of 24) and have increased their role in decision making.

The developing countries have used sophisticated tactics in their efforts to bring about a redistribution of wealth and power. Through the creation of a solid voting bloc and the use of democratic procedures in North-South conferences, they have made it difficult for developed countries to generate support for the maintenance of the status quo. Some consider the passing of United Nations resolutions to be a naive tactic because it is unlikely that such resolutions can replace customary international law. Nevertheless, the passage of international resolutions in support of Third World interests is a useful instrument by which weak countries can mobilize world opinion. To the extent that there is an ongoing movement from consent to consensus as the source of international law, as Falk suggests, (1) UN resolutions may take on the status of quasi-law.

The Group of 77 has developed an integrated approach to development problems, made possible through the establishment of UNCTAD, where they have been able to carry out research and sound out their ideas both with one another and with developed countries. The long experience of the Latin Americans in thinking and writing about development problems has provided a theoretical base for much of UNCTAD's work. The Group of 77 has also benefited enormously from the ideological and material support of the OPEC countries. Without OPEC countries as committed members of the Third World, the distribution of power capabilities between the industrialized countries and the Third World would have been little changed from the 1950s and 1960s, and the outcome of recent international conferences would have been much less favorable to developing countries.

Many of the Group of 77's proposals for the restructuring of the world economy have been attacked as inefficient interferences with the functioning of the market economy. However, these proposals are, for the most part, adaptations on the international level of institutions and interventionist policies long practiced by governments in the developed countries. For example, the integrated commodity program, with its proposals for stockpiles and a Common Fund, closely resembles United States government agricultural policies with respect to the Commodity Credit Corporation. Selective trade concessions and other preferences are extrapolations on national programs of affirmative action to assist long-disadvantaged individuals. Indexation of prices may be found in the escalation clauses of private contracts and the linkage in the United States of Social Security payments to the cost of living index. Producer associations differ from historical cartels only inasmuch as governments, rather than private companies, control them. What is new about the Charter and the New International Economic Order is not particular programs or provisions but rather the goals of redistributing wealth and power to the developing countries.

Change, both within states and on the international level, tends to be incremental except during periods of cataclysmic events such as wars, natural disasters, and major economic disruptions. Looking back over the past sixty years, it is clear that the conception of the proper role of international organizations in economic and social issues has consistently broadened over time. In the post-World War II period, the developed countries have, in addition, come to adopt the view that international law and international organization should, in certain instances, be used to foster the development of the poor countries. There are no important reasons to believe that these trends will not continue. (2) The developing countries are temporarily stymied in their attempts to shift the balance of rights and duties of states in favor of their own welfare claims and against the political and commercial interests of the developed countries. As international economic conditions improve, it is likely that Third World efforts will gain new momentum.

Appendix A

The Charter of Economic Rights and Duties of States

RESOLUTION ADOPTED BY THE GENERAL ASSEMBLY

[on the report of the Second Committee (A/9946)]

3281 (XXIX). Charter of Economic Rights and Duties of States

The General Assembly,

Recalling that the United Nations Conference on Trade and Development, in its resolution 45 (III) of 18 May 1972, (1) stressed the urgency to establish generally accepted norms to govern international economic relations systematically and recognized that it is not feasible to establish a just order and a stable world as long as a Charter to protect the rights of all countries, and in particular the developing States, is not formulated,

Recalling further that in the same resolution it was decided to establish a Working Group of governmental representatives to draw up a draft Charter of Economic Rights and Duties of States, which the General Assembly, in its resolution 3037 (XXVII) of 19 December 1972, decided should be composed of forty Member States,

Noting that, in its resolution 3082 (XXVIII) of 6 December 1973, it reaffirmed its conviction of the urgent need to establish or improve norms of universal application for the development of international economic relations on a just and equitable basis and urged the Working Group on the Charter of Economic Rights and Duties of States to complete, as the first step in the codification and development of the matter, the elaboration of a final draft Charter of Economic Rights and Duties of States, to be considered and approved by the General Assembly at its twenty-ninth session,

Bearing in mind the spirit and terms of its resolutions 3201 (S-VI) and 3202 (S-VI) of 1 May 1974, containing the Declaration and the Programme of

Action on the Establishment of a New International Economic Order, which underlined the vital importance of the Charter to be adopted by the General Assembly at its twenty-ninth session and stressed the fact that the Charter shall constitute an effective instrument towards the establishment of a new system of international economic relations based on equity, sovereign equality, and interdependence of the interests of developed and developing countries,

Having examined the report of the Working Group on the Charter of Economic Rights and Duties of States on its fourth session, (2) transmitted to the General Assembly by the Trade and Development Board at its fourteenth session,

Expressing its appreciation to the Working Group on the Charter of Economic Rights and Duties of States which, as a result of the task performed in its four sessions held between February 1973 and June 1974, assembled the elements required for the completion and adoption of the Charter of Economic Rights and Duties of States at the twenty-ninth session of the General Assembly, as previously recommended,

Adopts and solemnly proclaims the following Charter:

CHARTER OF ECONOMIC RIGHTS AND DUTIES OF STATES

PREAMBLE

The General Assembly,

Reaffirming the fundamental purposes of the United Nations, in particular the maintenance of international peace and security, the development of friendly relations among nations and the achievement of international co-operation in solving international problems in the economic and social fields,

Affirming the need for strengthening international co-operation in these fields,

Reaffirming further the need for strengthening international co-operation for development,

Declaring that it is a fundamental purpose of the present Charter to promote the establishment of the new international economic order, based on equity, sovereign equality, interdependence, common interest and co-operation among all States, irrespective of their economic and social systems,

Desirous of contributing to the creation of conditions for:

(a) The attainment of wider prosperity among all countries and of higher standards of living for all peoples,

(b) The promotion by the entire international community of the economic and social progress of all countries, especially developing countries,

(c) The encouragement of co-operation, on the basis of mutual advantage and equitable benefits for all peace-loving States which are willing to carry out the provisions of the present Charter, in the economic, trade, scientific and technical fields, regardless of political, economic or social systems,

(d) The overcoming of main obstacles in the way of the economic development of the developing countries,

(e) The acceleration of the economic growth of developing countries with a view to bridging the economic gap between developing and developed countries,

(f) The protection, preservation and enhancement of the environment,

Mindful of the need to establish and maintain a just and equitable economic and social order through:

(a) The achievement of more rational and equitable international economic relations and the encouragement of structural changes in the world economy,

(b) The creation of conditions which permit the further expansion of trade and intensification of economic co-operation among all nations,

(c) The strengthening of the economic independence of developing countries,

(d) The establishment and promotion of international economic relations, taking into account the agreed differences in development of the developing countries and their specific needs,

Determined to promote collective economic security for development, in particular of the developing countries, with strict respect for the sovereign equality of each State and through the co-operation of the entire international community,

Considering that genuine co-operation among States, based on joint consideration of and concerted action regarding international economic problems, is essential for fulfilling the international community's common desire to achieve a just and rational development of all parts of the world,

Stressing the importance of ensuring appropriate conditions for the conduct of normal economic relations among all States, irrespective of differences in social and economic systems, and for the full respect of the rights of all peoples, as well as strengthening instruments of international economic co-operation as means for the consolidation of peace for the benefit of all,

Convinced of the need to develop a system of international economic relations on the basis of sovereign equality, mutual and equitable benefit and the close interrelationship of the interests of all States,

Reiterating that the responsibility for the development of every country rests primarily upon itself but that concomitant and effective international co-operation is an essential factor for the full achievement of its own development goals,

Firmly convinced of the urgent need to evolve a substantially improved system of international economic relations,

Solemnly adopts the present Charter of Economic Rights and Duties of States.

CHAPTER I

Fundamentals of international economic relations

Economic as well as political and other relations among States shall be governed, <u>inter alia</u>, by the following principles:

(a) Sovereignty, territorial integrity and political independence of States;

(b) Sovereign equality of all States;

(c) Non-aggression;

(d) Non-intervention;

(e) Mutual and equitable benefit;

(f) Peaceful coexistence;

(g) Equal rights and self-determination of peoples;

(h) Peaceful settlement of disputes;

(i) Remedying of injustices which have been brought about by force and which deprive a nation of the natural means necessary for its normal development;

(j) Fulfillment in good faith of international obligations;

(k) Respect for human rights and fundamental freedoms;

(l) No attempt to seek hegemony and spheres of influence;

(m) Promotion of international social justice;

(n) International co-operation for development;

(o) Free access to and from the sea by land-locked countries within the framework of the above principles.

CHAPTER II

Economic rights and duties of States

Article 1

Every State has the sovereign and inalienable right to choose its economic system as well as its political, social and cultural systems in accordance with the will of its people, without outside interference, coercion or threat in any form whatsoever.

Article 2

1. Every State has and shall freely exercise full permanent sovereignty, including possession, use and disposal, over all its wealth, natural resources and economic activities.

2. Each State has the right:

(a) To regulate and exercise authority over foreign investment within its national jurisdiction in accordance with its laws and regulations and in conformity with its national objectives and priorities. No State shall be compelled to grant preferential treatment to foreign investment;

(b) To regulate and supervise the activities of transnational corporations within its national jurisdiction and take measures to ensure that such activities comply with its laws, rules and regulations and conform with its economic and social policies. Transnational corporations shall not intervene in the internal affairs of a host State. Every State should, with full regard for its sovereign rights, co-operate with other States in the exercise of the right set forth in this subparagraph;

(c) To nationalize, expropriate or transfer ownership of foreign property, in which case appropriate compensation should be paid by the State adopting such measures, taking into account its relevant laws and regulations and all circumstances that the State considers pertinent. In any case where the question of compensation gives rise to a controversy, it shall be settled under the domestic law of the nationalizing State and by its tribunals, unless it is freely and mutually agreed by all States concerned that other peaceful means be sought on the basis of the sovereign equality of States and in accordance with the principle of free choice of means.

Article 3

In the exploitation of natural resources shared by two or more countries, each State must co-operate on the basis of a system of information and prior consultations in order to achieve optimum use of such resources without causing damage to the legitimate interest of others.

Article 4

Every State has the right to engage in international trade and other forms of economic co-operation irrespective of any differences in political, economic and social systems. No State shall be subjected to discrimination of any kind based solely on such differences. In the pursuit of international trade and other forms of economic co-operation, every State is free to choose the forms of organization of its foreign economic relations and to enter into bilateral and multilateral arrangements consistent with its international obligations and with the needs of international economic co-operation.

Article 5

All States have the right to associate in organizations of primary commodity producers in order to develop their national economies, to achieve stable financing for their development and, in pursuance of their aims, to assist in the promotion of sustained growth of the world economy, in particular accelerating the development of developing countries. Correspondingly all States have the duty to respect that right by refraining from applying economic and political measures that would limit it.

Article 6

It is the duty of States to contribute to the development of international trade of goods, particularly by means of arrangements and by the conclusion of long-term multilateral commodity agreements, where appropriate, and taking into account the interests of producers and consumers. All States share the responsibility to promote the regular flow and access of all commercial goods traded at stable, remunerative and equitable prices, thus contributing to the equitable development of the world economy, taking into account, in particular, the interests of developing countries.

Article 7

Every State has the primary responsibility to promote the economic, social and cultural development of its people. To this end, each State has the right and the responsibility to choose its means and goals of development, fully to mobilize and use its resources, to implement progressive economic and social reforms and to ensure the full participation of its people in the process and benefits of development. All States have the duty, individually and collectively, to co-operate in order to eliminate obstacles that hinder such mobilization and use.

Article 8

States should co-operate in facilitating more rational and equitable international economic relations and in encouraging structural changes in the context of a balanced world economy in harmony with the needs and interests of all countries, especially developing countries, and should take appropriate measures to this end.

Article 9

All States have the responsibility to co-operate in the economic, social, cultural, scientific and technological fields for the promotion of economic and social progress throughout the world, especially that of the developing countries.

Article 10

All States are juridically equal and, as equal members of the international community, have the right to participate fully and effectively in the international decision-making process in the solution of world economic, financial and monetary problems, inter alia, through the appropriate international organizations in accordance with their existing and evolving rules, and to share equitably in the benefits resulting therefrom.

Article 11

All States should co-operate to strengthen and continuously improve the efficiency of international organizations in implementing measures to stimulate the general economic progress of all countries, particularly of developing countries, and therefore should co-operate to adapt them, when appropriate, to the changing needs of international economic co-operation.

Article 12

1. States have the right, in agreement with the parties concerned, to participate in subregional, regional and interregional co-operation in the pursuit of their economic and social devleopment. All States engaged in such co-operation have the duty to ensure that the policies of those groupings to which they belong correspond to the provisions of the present Charter and are outward-looking, consistent with their international obligations and with the needs of international economic co-operation, and have full regard for the legitimate interests of third countries, especially developing countries.

2. In the case of groupings to which the States concerned have transferred or may transfer certain competences as regards matters that come within the scope of the present Charter, its provisions shall also apply to those groupings, in regard to such matters, consistent with the responsibilities of such States as members of such groupings. Those States shall co-operate in the observance by the groupings of the provisions of this Charter.

Article 13

1. Every State has the right to benefit from the advances and developments in science and technology for the acceleration of its economic and social development.

2. All States should promote international scientific and technological co-operation and the transfer of technology, with proper regard for all legitimate interests including, inter alia, the rights and duties of holders, suppliers and recipients of technology. In particular, all States should facilitate the access of developing countries to the achievements of modern science and technology, the transfer of technology and the creation of indigenous technology for the benefit of the developing countries in forms and in accordance with procedures which are suited to their economies and their needs.

3. Accordingly, developed countries should co-operate with the developing countries in the establishment, strengthening and development of their scientific and technological infrastructures and their scientific research and technological activities so as to help to expand and transform the economies of developing countries.

4. All States should co-operate in research with a view to evolving further internationally accepted guidelines or regulations for the transfer of technology, taking fully into account the interests of developing countries.

Article 14

Every State has the duty to co-operate in promoting a steady and increasing expansion and liberalization of world trade and an improvement in the welfare and living standards of all peoples, in particular those of developing countries. Accordingly, all States should co-operate, inter alia, towards the progressive dismantling of obstacles to trade and the improvement of the international framework for the conduct of world trade and, to these ends, co-ordinated efforts shall be made to solve in an equitable way the trade problems of all countries, taking into account the specific trade problems of the developing countries. In this connection, States shall take measures aimed at securing additional benefits for the international trade of developing countries so as to achieve a substantial increase in their foreign exchange earnings, the diversification of their exports, the acceleration of the rate of growth of their trade, taking into account their development needs, an improvement in the possibilities for these countries to participate in the expansion of world trade and a balance more favourable to developing countries in the sharing of the advantages resulting from this expansion, through, in the largest possible measure, a substantial improvement in the conditions of access for the products of interest to the developing countries and, wherever appropriate, measures designed to attain stable, equitable and remunerative prices for primary products.

Article 15

All States have the duty to promote the achievement of general and complete disarmament under effective international control and to utilize the resources released by effective disarmament measures for the economic and social development of countries, allocating a substantial portion of such resources as additional means for the development needs of developing countries.

Article 16

1. It is the right and duty of all States, individually and collectively, to eliminate colonialism, apartheid, racial discrimination, neo-colonialism and all forms of foreign aggression, occupation and domination, and the economic and social consequences thereof, as a prerequisite for development. States which practise such coercive policies are economically responsible to the countries, territories and peoples affected for the restitution and full

compensation for the exploitation and depletion of, and damages to, the natural and all other resources of those countries, territories and peoples. It is the duty of all States to extend assistance to them.

2. No State has the right to promote or encourage investments that may constitute an obstacle to the liberation of a territory occupied by force.

Article 17

International co-operation for development is the shared goal and common duty of all States. Every State should co-operate with the efforts of developing countries to accelerate their economic and social development by providing favourable external conditions and by extending active assistance to them, consistent with their development needs and objectives, with strict respect for the sovereign equality of States and free of any conditions derogating from their sovereignty.

Article 18

Developed countries should extend, improve and enlarge the system of generalized non-reciprocal and non-discriminatory tariff preferences to the developing countries consistent with the relevant agreed conclusions and relevant decisions as adopted on this subject, in the framework of the competent international organizations. Developed countries should also give serious consideration to the adoption of other differential measures, in areas where this is feasible and appropriate and in ways which will provide special and more favourable treatment, in order to meet the trade and development needs of the developing countries. In the conduct of international economic relations the developed countries should endeavour to avoid measures having a negative effect on the development of the national economies of the developing countries, as promoted by generalized tariff preferences and other generally agreed differential measures in their favour.

Article 19

With a view to accelerating the economic growth of developing countries and bridging the economic gap between developed and developing countries, developed countries should grant generalized preferential, non-reciprocal and non-discriminatory treatment to developing countries in those fields of international economic co-operation where it may be feasible.

Article 20

Developing countries should, in their efforts to increase their over-all trade, give due attention to the possibility of expanding their trade with socialist countries, by granting to these countries conditions for trade not inferior to those granted normally to the developed market economy countries.

Article 21

Developed countries should endeavour to promote the expansion of their mutual trade and to this end may, in accordance with the existing and evolving provisions and procedures of international agreements where applicable, grant trade preferences to other developing countries without being obliged to extend such preferences to developed countries, provided these arrangements do not constitute an impediment to general trade liberalization and expansion.

Article 22

1. All States should respond to the generally recognized or mutually agreed development needs and objectives of developing countries by promoting increased net flows of real resources to the developing countries from all sources, taking into account any obligations and commitments undertaken by the States concerned, in order to reinforce the efforts of developing countries to accelerate their economic and social development.

2. In this context, consistent with the aims and objectives mentioned above and taking into account any obligations and commitments undertaken in this regard, it should be their endeavour to increase the net amount of financial flows from official sources to developing countries and to improve the terms and conditions thereof.

3. The flow of development assistance resources should include economic and technical assistance.

Article 23

To enhance the effective mobilization of their own resources, the developing countries should strengthen their economic co-operation and expand their mutual trade so as to accelerate their economic and social development. All countries, especially developed countries, individually as well as through the competent international organizations of which they are members, should provide appropriate and effective support and co-operation.

Article 24

All States have the duty to conduct their mutual economic relations in a manner which takes into account the interests of other countries. In particular, all States should avoid prejudicing the interests of developing countries.

Article 25

In furtherance of world economic development, the international community, especially its developed members, shall pay special attention to the particular needs and problems of the least developed among the developing countries, of land-locked developing countries and also island developing countries, with a view to helping them to overcome their particular difficulties and thus contribute to their economic and social development.

Article 26

All States have the duty to coexist in tolerance and live together in peace, irrespective of differences in political, economic, social and cultural systems, and to facilitate trade between States having different economic and social systems.   International trade should be conducted without prejudice to generalized non-discriminatory and non-reciprocal preferences in favour of developing countries, on the basis of mutual advantage, equitable benefits and the exchange of most-favoured-nation treatment.

Article 27

1. Every State has the right to enjoy fully the benefits of world invisible trade and to engage in the expansion of such trade.

2. World invisible trade, based on efficiency and mutual and equitable benefit, furthering the expansion of the world economy, is the common goal of all States. The role of developing countries in world invisible trade should be enhanced and strengthened consistent with the above objectives, particular attention being paid to the special needs of developing countries.

3. All States should co-operate with developing countries in their endeavours to increase their capacity to earn foreign exchange from invisible transactions, in accordance with the potential and needs of each developing country and consistent with the objectives mentioned above.

Article 28

All States have the duty to co-operate in achieving adjustments in the prices of exports of developing countries in relation to prices of their imports so as to promote just and equitable terms of trade for them, in a manner which is remunerative for producers and equitable for producers and consumers.

CHAPTER III

Common responsibilities towards the international community

Article 29

The sea-bed and ocean floor and the subsoil thereof, beyond the limits of national jurisdiction, as well as the resources of the area, are the common heritage of mankind. On the basis of the principles adopted by the General Assembly in resolution 2749 (XXV) of 17 December 1970, all States shall ensure that the exploration of the area and exploitation of its resources are carried out exclusively for peaceful purposes and that the benefits derived therefrom are shared equitably by all States, taking into account the particular interests and needs of developing countries; an international régime applying to the area and its resources and including appropriate international machinery to give effect to its provisions shall be established by an international treaty of a universal character, generally agreed upon.

Article 30

The protection, preservation and enhancement of the environment for the present and future generations is the responsibility of all States. All States shall endeavour to establish their own environmental and developmental policies in conformity with such responsibility. The environmental policies of all States should enhance and not adversely affect the present and future development potential of developing countries. All States have the responsibility to ensure that activities within their jurisdiction or control do not cause damage to the environment of other States or of areas beyond the limits of national jurisdiction. All States should co-operate in evolving international norms and regulations in the field of the environment.

CHAPTER IV

Final provisions

Article 31

All States have the duty to contribute to the balanced expansion of the world economy, taking duly into account the close interrelationship between the well-being of the developed countries and the growth and development of the developing countries, and the fact that the prosperity of the international community as a whole depends upon the prosperity of its constituent parts.

Article 32

No State may use or encourage the use of economic, political or any other type of measures to coerce another State in order to obtain from it the subordination of the exercise of its sovereign rights.

Article 33

1. Nothing in the present Charter shall be construed as impairing or derogating from the provisions of the Charter of the United Nations or actions taken in pursuance thereof.

2. In their interpretation and application, the provisions of the present Charter are interrelated and each provision should be construed in the context of the other provisions.

Article 34

An item on the Charter of Economic Rights and Duties of States shall be included in the agenda of the General Assembly at its thirtieth session, and thereafter on the agenda of every fifth session. In this way a systematic and comprehensive consideration of the implementation of the Charter, covering both progress achieved and any improvements and additions which might become necessary, would be carried out and appropriate measures recommended. Such consideration should take into account the evolution of all the economic, social, legal and other factors related to the principles upon which the present Charter is based and on its purpose.

2315th plenary meeting
12 December 1974

Appendix B

Explanation of Terms Used with Reference to Developing Countries

(Contents, cont'd.)

EXPLANATION OF TERMS USED WITH REFERENCE TO THE DEVELOPING COUNTRIES

The special interests of the developing countries have become a factor in international relations only in the last two decades. Before World War II, the few independent states of Asia and Africa had no recognition of common political and economic interests within their own continents or with the countries of Latin America. Neither collectively nor individually did these countries exercise any independent role in international affairs. It was, therefore, natural that the network of international organizations, as planned during and after the war by the Western industrial states, took no account of the concerns of these countries. The International Monetary Fund (IMF), the International Bank for Reconstruction and Development (IBRD, or World Bank), the General Agreement on Tariffs and Trade (GATT), and even the United Nations were conceived as agents of the interests of the Western industrial countries. (1) In the immediate post-war period, there were only two "worlds" - West and East.

The term Third World was first used in 1956 by a French scholar, Alfred Sauvy, in the title to a collection of writings on "underdevelopment and development." (2) In Sauvy's view, the widespread poverty of the states and territories of Africa, Asia, and Latin America set them apart from the Western industrialized countries of the "First World" and the Communist countries of the "Second World." Sauvy's basic criterion in delimiting the Third World was per capita income, but he also considered political factors and, in the case of South Africa, the factor of income distribution. Thus Sauvy's notion of the Third World included all of Africa, Asia except Japan, Latin America except Argentina, plus Yugoslavia. (3) Sauvy considered the Third World to be in a position reminiscent of that of the historical Third Estate, whose demands for liberty and equality had led to the French revolution. His phrase called attention to the appearance of a new force which refused the division of the world into blocs. While set apart economically by its poverty, this diverse group of states and territories was distinguished politically by the experience that most at one time had a subjugation to a foreign power, usually a Western one. When international developments in the 1960s led to the creation of the Third World as a united political entity, the basis for it was the determination on the part of the poor countries to prevent a recurrence of the humiliation suffered in the colonial period and to achieve respectable world status.

In chronicling Third World institutional developments, it is conventional to start with the Afro-Asian conference convened in 1955 in Bandung, Indonesia by Burma, Ceylon, India, Indonesia, and Pakistan. (4)   This conference established the principles for economic cooperation which have served as guidelines for the creation of a new economic order.   Among the recommendations adopted was a plea for collective stabilization of the demand for raw materials and of their international prices. (5)   The main achievements of Bandung, however, were political: it extended the basis of the solidarity of the Afro-Asian states and national movements against imperialism, and thereby laid the foundations for the future development of the non-aligned movement.

The non-aligned movement grew out of the desire on the part of the new states to avoid commitment to former colonial rulers and yet to exercise collective influence over the course of international events. The movement emerged as a reaction against the formation by Western countries of hegemonistic military alliances with Asian and African states, such as SEATO and CENTO, and also against the positions that Western countries were taking in the United Nations.

The first two summit conferences of the non-aligned states, at Belgrade in 1961 and Cairo in 1964, have been called "Bandungs without China and with the addition of Yugoslavia and Cuba." (6)   They represented an attempt by India, Egypt, and Yugoslavia to increase their influence over Third World states and to develop an Afro-Asian creed. However, the growth of divergent national interests among Third World states meant that Afro-Asianism as a political creed could not provide a basis for the continuation of the movement.   Over the course of two decades, the non-aligned movement transformed itself from a force against imperialism into a collective struggle by a majority of developing countries for full economic and political sovereignty.

The non-aligned movement is represented by the process of multilateral communication and feedback among non-aligned states. The regular holding of conferences has given it what institutional character it has; in particular, the preparatory conferences before the summits have played the fundamental organizational role in the evolution of the movement. The non-aligned states have also developed the practice, recently formalized in the institution of the Coordinating Bureau, (7) of organizing periodic meetings of their delegations at the United Nations to try to work out a common strategy.   The membership of the non-aligned movement more than doubled in the 1960s, a period in which a large number of African colonies achieved independence. In the 1970s, it nearly doubled in size again, to reach its present membership of eighty-five. (8)

Action taken at the non-aligned conferences spearheaded the developing countries' demand for the New International Economic Order. At the Lusaka

Summit Conference, held in 1970, the non-aligned states urged the United Nations "to employ international machinery to bring about a rapid transformation of the world economic system, particularly in the field of trade, finance, and technology." (9)   Against the background of the Libyan nationalization of foreign oil companies and an imminent war in the Middle East, participants in the Algiers Summit Conference in 1973 unanimously declared that the international strategy of development had failed, and requested the United Nations to adopt a "charter of the economic rights and duties of states" at the 28th session of the General Assembly. (10)

A second forum which has contributed to the development of a Third World strategy in international relations is the Group of 77. This group began as an ad hoc group of cosponsors of the first UNCTAD meeting. Led by Raul Prebisch, these developing countries caucused together, negotiated through common spokesmen, and voted as a bloc in UNCTAD.   In the "Joint Declaration of the 77 Developing Countries," the Group of 77 expressed its intent to maintain and strengthen its unity as an "indispensable instrument for securing the adoption of new attitudes and new approaches in the international economic field." (11) It has been observed that the formation of the Group of 77 made UNCTAD I the first major international conference in modern history in which the East-West confrontation was submerged by the confrontation between the North (the industrial market states of the OECD) and the South (the non-communist developing world). (12)

The Group of 77 holds meetings at the ministerial level prior to each session of UNCTAD in order to reach agreement on an agenda and common strategy. A major consequence of the emergence of this group has been the de facto institutionalization of the group system of negotiating in UNCTAD. This spilled over into other United Nations forums and is now the standard mode of interaction between rich and poor countries at international conferences.   The developing countries use the permanent secretariat of UNCTAD to produce studies and collect data and argumentations supportive of Third World claims which are sometimes contrary to the views and outputs of other international economic organizations like GATT, the International Monetary Fund, and the World Bank. This body of literature has given the Third World a systematic basis on which to challenge the postulates of the developed countries.

The group of 77 includes, but is not limited to, the membership of UNCTAD's Group A (Asia-Africa plus Yugoslavia) and Group C (Latin America). These blocs had a total membership of 115 countries in 1976. The other two groups in UNCTAD correspond to the notions of "First World" and "Second World." Group B includes the market economy developed countries and Group D includes the centrally planned economies, except China. (13) As of 1976, countries from Groups B and D which were members of the Group of 77 were Cyprus and Romania. (14)

Many of the developing country members of UNCTAD apply the General Agreement on Tariffs and Trade on either a de facto or full contracting basis. The GATT is the technical organization which negotiates binding trade agreements among states based, in general, on quid pro quo exchange of mutually equilibrated concessions. Since the system of negotiations works against poor countries, which have little to offer in return for tariff concessions by developed states, developing countries perceive GATT to be a "rich men's club." At the first UNCTAD meeting, the developing countries tried, but did not succeed, either in reducing GATT to some subordinate role vis-à-vis UNCTAD or in establishing a formal link between the two organizations. GATT, in turn, responded to the challenge presented by the establishment of UNCTAD by enlarging its competence in the trade problems of developing countries, particularly through the adoption of Part IV of the General Agreement. (15) This did not, however, change the fact that GATT is principally concerned with trade among developed countries. The developing countries have limited means of exerting pressure in GATT. Developing countries normally avoid choosing between GATT and UNCTAD: "they would like to be parties to all possible advantages that may stem from membership of both organizations, even though they generally disapprove of GATT and of what it stands for." (16)

With the establishment of UNCTAD in 1964 as a permanent organ of the General Assembly, (17) the developing countries were provided an organization capable of intensifying their efforts in the areas of trade and development. With the formal creation of the United Nations Industrial Development Organization (UNIDO) in the following year, (18) an institution was provided to intensify their efforts for industrialization. The developing countries thought that the World Bank Group did not do enough to promote their industrialization, and that a new agency would be able to carry out the research and raise the capital required for a large program of investment in industry. UNIDO was created to fill this need. Like UNCTAD, it is an organ of the General Assembly but functions as an autonomous organization. It is governed by the Industrial Development Board whose 45 members are elected by the General Assembly under a formula which gives 25 seats to Africa, Asia, and Latin America; 15 to Europe, North America, Australia, New Zealand, and Japan; and 5 to the socialist states of Eastern Europe. Its administrative and research activities are financed from the United Nations regular budget, and its operational activities are financed from voluntary contributions. (19)

The Second General Conference of UNIDO, held in Lima in March 1975, adopted a formal declaration calling for an increase in the share of the developing countries in total world industrial production from the present level of 7 percent to at least 25 percent by the end of the century. To accelerate the rate of industrial development, it recommended that UNIDO be converted into a specialized agency and that an Industrial Development Fund be established. (20)

There is no universal standard by which to classify a country as developing or developed. It depends on which organization and for what purpose the classification is made and used. The United Nations classifies countries according to political as well as economic criteria. Like Alfred Sauvy's conception of the Third World, the United Nations' definition of developing countries excludes the poor states of southern Europe, which are counted as "less developed countries in Europe." The United Nations also excludes China and Yugoslavia from its list of developing countries. (21) In contrast, the Development Assistance Committee (DAC) of the OECD includes Yugoslavia and four southern European states (Greece, Portugal, Spain, and Turkey) among the developing countries. Like the United Nations, but unlike

UNCTAD, the DAC excludes China from its list of developing countries. (22)

For purposes of analyzing financial and trade flows, the International Monetary Fund classifies member countries as industrial, more developed primary producing countries, and less developed primary producing countries. (23) The more developed primary producing countries, although widely scattered geographically and diverse with respect to a number of basic economic characteristics, are heavily dependent in most cases upon foodstuffs and crude or semiprocessed industrial materials for their export earnings. They also tend to be characterized by a balance-of-payments structure of current account deficits financed by capital imports. These characteristics cause this group of countries to share with the (non-oil) developing countries many of the effects of inflation and income fluctuations in the industrial world and of increases in oil and other import prices. (24)

Important changes in the relative economic positions among countries resulted from the increases in oil prices in the 1970s. The IMF charts of world trade and balance of payments distinguished the major oil exporters from other primary producing countries for the first time in 1972. (25) As of 1976, the major oil exporters comprise the 13 member countries of OPEC. (26)

The IMF gives increasing attention not only to the oil exporting countries, but also to major developing country exporters of other primary commodities. These countries were encouraged to form alliances by the successful cooperation of oil exporting governments. In general, they have in common with OPEC countries a heavy reliance on one or two primary commodities for foreign exchange receipts, fiscal revenues, national income, and socioeconomic development. Forces which spurred intergovernmental cooperation among developing country exporters included a sense of economic insecurity and dissatisfaction among host governments with respect to large fluctuations in prices, inflationary erosion of real earnings, and, in many cases, the existence of international oligopoly or oligopsony power. (27) The most important economic consultative organizations among developing country exporters are the Conseil Intergovernmental des Pays Exportateurs de Cuivre (CIPEC), the International Bauxite Association (IBA), and the Association of Iron Ore Exporters (AIOEC). CIPEC was established in 1967. In 1975, CIPEC countries accounted for about 35 percent of the total copper mine capacity outside Eastern Europe and China, and for 65 percent of world primary copper exports. (28) IBA was established, after several abortive attempts, in 1974. In that year, IBA members produced about 97 percent of the world's bauxite. (29) AIOEC was formed in 1975. (30) About two-thirds of the world trade in iron ore (including exports from the Soviet Union to other East European countries) represent intracompany transfers or long-term contracts fixing tonnages and prices. (31) Iron ore exporting countries hope to cooperate to take advantage of the countervailing power of nonintegrated sellers. It is noteworthy that developing country members of the AIOEC and IBA are joined by Australia, whose Labour Government shares the aspirations of developing countries for greater national control over its natural resources.

In some cases, exporter countries have sought importers' cooperation in fostering improved market conditions for a primary commodity. The tin and coffee agreements represent an attempt by a large group of exporter and importer countries to maintain a balance between world production and consumption and to prevent excessive price fluctuations. The International Tin Agreements have covered the periods 1956-61, 1961-66, 1966-71, and 1976-81. (32) Importer and exporter groups have an equal voting power in the International Tin Council, which administers and supervises the agreements. A similar arrangement holds in the International Coffee Organization (ICO). The ICO came into existence in 1962 when the first International Coffee Agreement was negotiated.   Since 1963, the ICO has administered three international coffee agreements, covering the periods 1962-68, 1968-73, and 1976 to date. (33)

The international classification of countries as developed or developing primarily according to per capita gross national product tends to imply that by achieving a higher per capita income, a country can achieve greater well-being and economic independence.   An additional assumption which is generally made is that this increase in per capita income can be hastened through foreign aid and investment, as well as more favorable economic and commercial policies on the part of developed countries.   These assumptions formed the basis for the establishment of the International Development Association (IDA) by the United Nations in 1960, and also for the elaboration of the international development strategies of the United Nations' Development Decades.

IDA was created in order to increase the flow of development loans on highly concessionary terms.   Developing countries in particular need of "soft" loans are those whose exports are unlikely to grow rapidly enough to provide the funds required for transferring abroad the interest and capital repayments on an increased volume of foreign debt.   At any given time, many poor countries are not eligible for World Bank loans because they have exhausted their creditworthiness for loans with the Bank.   The situation in 1960 was such that the low-income member countries of the Bank were paying out more in interest and repayments of principal on Bank loans than the Bank was disbursing on those loans.   This imbalance in the flow of resources to the very poor countries was corrected as a result of IDA loans. (34)

An additional reason for the establishment of IDA was that it was felt that an international institution, rather than an expansion of existing bilateral aid agencies, would be able to obtain a wide sharing of the burden of development aid. (35)   The IDA articles provide for contributions largely from the industrialized countries.   IDA negotiates replenishment agreements with donor countries at three-year intervals.   As of 1977, IDA was the largest single source of long-term development aid on highly concessionary terms. (36)

IDA is frequently referred to as the World Bank's "soft window." Though legally a distinct entity, it has the same management and staff as the World Bank.   With the exception of a few countries, all members of the World Bank are also members of IDA.   The difference between the two organizations is in their terms of lending.   World Bank loans have an average duration of 20-25 years and interest rates usually one percent above the rate at which the Bank can borrow, whereas the standard terms of IDA lending are no interest, but a service charge of .75 percent; and a final maturity of 50 years, with a grace period of ten years. (37)

Because of the small amounts of IDA funds available relative to global needs, IDA loans are normally made only to countries below a per capita income of $550, in 1976 terms. (38)   In fact, about 90 percent of IDA commitments during the period 1975-1977 were made to countries with a per capita income below $265, in 1975 terms. (39)   An additional criterion of eligibility for IDA loans is lack of creditworthiness for loans on commercial terms. (40) Even before a developing country "graduates" from IDA eligibility to creditworthiness for World Bank loans, it may also receive loans from the World Bank. For many of the countries with per capita income below $550, Bank loans and IDA credits are blended to provide terms commensurate with the capacity of the country to carry additional external debt. (41)

The same year which saw the creation of IDA also marked the declaration of the United Nations Development Decade. The 16th Session of the United Nations General Assembly designated the decade of the 1960s to be a period of intensified cooperation among all peoples on behalf of those living in developing countries. (42)   Resolution 1710 expresses the international strategy for developing countries in terms of targets for growth rates and transfers of aid and capital. Each developing country was to set its own target, with the objective of attaining a minimal annual growth rate of five percent at the end of the decade. This was to be made possible by the pursuit of policies by developed countries designed to enable developing countries to sell more of their products at stable and remunerative prices in expanding markets, and also by the increase in flows of development assistance and private investment capital to developing countries.

The United Nations General Assembly designated the Second Development Decade to begin January 1, 1971. (43)   Unlike the resolution for the First Development Decade, Resolution 2626 provided for a systematic monitoring mechanism at various levels to check performance against established benchmarks. The target for the average annual rate of growth in the gross product of the developing countries as a whole was set at six percent. Specific measures called for by the resolution were the achievement of international agreement on pricing policy to serve as guidelines for actions on individual commodities; the reduction of trade barriers to products of export interest to developing countries; official development assistance from each developed country of a minimum net amount of 0.7 percent of its gross national product; promotion of the earnings of developing countries from invisible trade; and the implementation by developing countries of population, education, agricultural, export diversification, and other programs.   The resolution also called for special measures in favor of the least developed and landlocked developing countries to ensure their sustained economic and social progress. (44)

This call for special measures in favor of the least developed among the developing countries was not new. Both the Final Act of UNCTAD I (45) and the 1967 Summit Conference of the Non-Aligned in Algiers (46) requested that special measures be provided to those developing countries which were not participating in the trend of sustained growth. While developing countries encounter similar problems on a regional and sectoral basis, it was felt that the least developed among them could not be expected to benefit fully or automatically from general measures adopted in favor of all developing countries. In response to these demands, UNCTAD II invited international bodies responsible for measures to benefit developing countries to elaborate special measures which might be taken in favor of the least developed, and to identify such countries. (47) In 1971, the expert Committee for Development Planning at the United Nations designated 25 hard-core least developed countries (LDLDC's) on the basis of criteria of per capita income, degree of manufacturing activity, and level of literacy. (48) In its 1977 revision of this list, the Committee for Development Planning added four countries to the original list. (49)

The average per capita income in the LDLDC's is less than one-half the average in all developing countries as a group. The LDLDC's may also be distinguished from the group of all developing countries by their limited ability to mobilize domestic resources and their consequent critical dependence on aid flows. Data collected in 1972 on the original 25 least developed countries show that net loans and grants represented 36.8 percent of total imports during that year, compared with 15.2 percent for all developing countries as a group. (50)

A critical problem common to the least developed countries is the rudimentary stage of development of their health, education, communications, and transportation infrastructure. The constraining effect on development of poor transportation facilities is particularly acute in those least developed countries which are landlocked. It is not surprising, therefore, that all but four of the landlocked developing countries are included among the hard-core least developed countries. (51) UNCTAD, from its inception, took an active interest in assisting the landlocked developing countries to overcome their difficulties regarding transit trade. (52) In 1975, the United Nations General Assembly decided to establish a special fund for the landlocked developing countries to compensate for their additional transport and transit costs. (53)

Another group of developing countries that is sometimes singled out in resolutions to the United Nations is the island developing countries. UNCTAD Resolution 65 (III) called upon the Secretary-General of UNCTAD to convene a panel of experts to identify and study their particular problems, "giving special attention to the developing island countries which are facing major difficulties in respect of transport and communications with neighboring countries as well as structural difficulties, and which are remote from major market centres." (54) This panel of experts, which met in 1973, decided to include in its discussion the dependent island territories, since many already enjoyed a large degree of self-government, and in several cases full independence could be foreseen in the near future. (55)

There is wide variation in per capita incomes among the developing island countries. Per capita GNP for some countries (and territories) in 1973 was in excess of $3,000 (Bermuda and the Virgin Islands), while the lowest did not exceed $140 (Haiti, the Maldives, Seychelles, and Western Samoa). Of the latter, Seychelles is a British colony and the other three are counted among the hard-core least developed countries.

The severe structural disequilibrium of the world economy in 1973-74 gave rise to a demand in the United Nations to identify and provide emergency financial assistance to the group of countries most seriously affected by the price increases in petroleum, fertilizer, and food. A resolution of the Sixth

Special Session of the General Assembly, which met in April 1974, called upon the Secretary-General to launch an emergency operation to provide relief to those developing countries which were expected to have significant shortfalls in their balance-of-payments in 1974 and 1975. (56) Criteria which were used in identifying these countries were (1) per capita income below $400, (2) sharp increases in the cost of essential imports relative to export earnings, (3) high level of debt service changes relative to export earnings, (4) insufficiency of export earnings, comparative inelasticity of export incomes, and unavailability of exportable surplus, (5) lower level of foreign exchange reserves, (6) adverse impact of higher transportation and transit costs, and (7) relative importance of foreign trade in the development process. (57)

Worsening economic conditions in some of the poorest developing countries is reflected in the periodic addition by the United Nations to the list of those most seriously affected (MSA's). There were 45 such countries as of 1977. (58)   This list overlaps with the 29 hard-core least developed countries, but omits those ten least developed countries which are so isolated from the world economy that they have been spared serious disturbances to their economies. The most seriously affected are the countries in need of emergency assistance to pay for minimum import requirements of food, fertilizer, and industrial inputs, whereas the least developed countries are defined in terms of their long-term need for special measures to deal with the root causes of poverty. In July 1976, the International Monetary Fund decided to establish a Subsidy Account to assist the most seriously affected countries to meet the cost of using the resources made available through the Find's oil facility for 1975. (59)

The increase in food prices in 1973-74 focused attention on the problem of world hunger and the inadequacy of the rate of growth of food production in developing countries. In order to find ways to tackle these problems, the United Nations created the World Food Council in 1974. (60)   Pursuant to General Assembly Resolution 3348 and to Resolution XIII passed in the first session of the World Food Council, the United Nations Secretary-General convened a meeting of 66 interested states at Geneva on 5-6 May 1975 to discuss the establishment of an International Fund for Agricultural Development (IFAD). The original proponents of Resolution XIII were 34 developing countries financially able to contribute funds to agricultural development, with sponsors who belonged to the Development Assistance Committee of the OECD.   The 66 countries meeting in Geneva agreed to finance a large increase in agricultural investment in poor developing countries. (61)   The Second Session of the World Food Council, held in Rome from June 10-13, 1976, cleared the way for the establishment of IFAD as a new United Nations specialized agency as soon as the target of $1 billion in contributions in convertible currencies was reached. (62)   Ninety nations at the four-day United Nations Conference on the Establishment of an International Fund for Agricultural Development adopted and initialled the IFAD Agreement on June 13, 1976. (63)

The purpose of the Fund is to accelerate the growth rate of food production in developing countries. It disburses resources mainly through concessional loans but partly through outright grants. The organizational structure is innovative, with three votes shared equally by three categories of states: developing donor (OPEC), developing recipient, and developed. (64)

The structure of IFAD testifies to the fact that the Third World no longer includes only poor countries. The recent term, Fourth World, was coined by the Overseas Development Council (ODC) to designate the poorest group of developing countries: the hard-core least developed countries and the most seriously affected countries. (65) The ODC's purpose in coining the term was to focus the attention of aid donors on the countries that were not perceptibly growing. The Council conceived the division between the Third and Fourth Worlds to be a fluid one: some Fourth World countries had only temporarily ceased to grow because of recent adverse international economic events, although others were separated from the Third World states by a widening gap. People outside the ODC have sometimes used the term Fourth World to designate all poor developing countries, in contrast to the developing countries which have gained sudden wealth.

The developing countries as a bloc have resisted efforts by developed countries to split them into a Third and Fourth World. There has been no salient cleavage between the least developed and other developing countries over issues involving changes in the international economic order. The chronic reliance of all developing countries on Western technology, equipment, and arms provides the economic rationale for the continuance of the Third World, broadly defined, as an entity in support of the creation of a New International Economic Order. (66) The weakness of developing countries in international institutions, and their interest in a shift in institutional power, provides the political rationale for Third World unity. The changes proposed by the NIEO would give all Third World states more decision making power.

A technical concept which has come to be used to distinguish the neediest group of people within a developing country, rather than to make distinctions among developing countries, is the notion of absolute poverty. Absolute poverty is a term which describes the conditions of human existence at the margin of physical needs expressed in terms of caloric and protein requirements. The World Bank estimates that there are at least 900 million people living in conditions of absolute poverty all over the developing world, and that national development has not so far appreciably affected their lives. (67) They own little or no land and suffer from high levels of malnutrition and disease. These factors impede their ability to profit from the new economic opportunities which development provides at the national level. To highlight the need to make the benefits of economic advancement accessible to the poorest people, the World Bank group has defined "target groups" in terms of per capita (and family) income appropriate for rural poor in each recipient country. In the case of most recipient countries, the target group is defined as having an annual per capita income of up to $40-$60 in terms of 1976 dollars. (68) Efforts to provide services to the target groups play a part in shaping World Bank and IDA projects in rural development, water supply, education, and other sectors. For example, IDA has shifted the focus of its lending in agriculture away from an increase in agricultural production in general to an increase in production and productivity of small farmers. As a device to monitor IDA success in implementing this policy, only projects with more than one-half of all direct beneficiaries in the absolute poverty groups are designated as "rural development projects." (69)

Unlike the policy of the World Bank group, it is the official policy of the United States Agency for International Development (AID) to avoid singling out the "neediest" population in developing countries. The legislation for AID makes no distinction between the "richest of the poor" and the "poorest of the poor." Rather, the legislation speaks of the "poor majority," that is, the majority of people in developing countries who are poor. In response to his observations that AID personnel tended to speak of Agency responsibility for helping "the poorest of the poor," the chief administrator of United States AID sent a memorandum to all assistant administrators and heads of offices that these terms should be banished from their lexicons. His rationale was that the concept of aiding only the poorest citizens of a country unnecessarily restricted AID's focus on the broad range of programs appropriate to the United States Congressional mandate, and made it seem as if "we are running a welfare scheme rather than an economic development program." (70)

In pursuit of Third World economic interests, developing countries have formed blocs not only in the United Nations General Assembly and UNCTAD, but also in the IMF and, most recently, in the Conference on International Economic Cooperation in Paris. Decision making in the IMF is subject to a system of weighted voting. Before the increase in IMF quotas in 1976, the ten countries participating in the General Agreements to Borrow, i.e., the Group of Ten, accounted for 58.1 percent of the total vote. The Group of Ten has been meeting regularly since 1964 in order to concert their views on the international monetary system. The Group's meetings take place outside the framework of the IMF, but are attended by the Managing Director of the Fund, as well as the Secretary-General of the OECD and the General Manager of the Bank for International Settlements. Since the members of the Group of Ten command a majority of the voting in the IMF, their agreed positions have tended to determine Fund policy. (71)

The developing countries have expressed concern from time to time regarding the manner in which major decisions affecting the international monetary system were adopted, and the extent to which the Fund membership as a whole could make an effective contribution to the decision making process. (72) They became especially concerned after the monetary crisis of 1971, as it became clear that the entire structure of the international monetary system would have to be reviewed. The Second Ministerial Meeting of the Group of 77, held in Lima in November 1971, declared that "It is entirely unacceptable that vital decisions about the future of the international monetary system which are of concern to the entire world community are sought to be taken by a limited group of countries outside the framework of the IMF."

In order to ensure "full participation of the developing countries in searching for a solution to the present international monetary crisis and to safeguard the interests of the developing countries," the Lima Declaration asserted the intention of the developing countries to establish an intergovern-mental group of Finance Ministers and Central Bank Governors. (73) This group became the Intergovernmental Group on Monetary Matters, whose membership of 24 gave it the name the "Group of 24." (74) The purpose of the Group is to coordinate the policies of the developing countries on financial questions important to them. It holds meetings at the ministerial level and meetings of deputies, to which other developing countries are permitted to send delegations. The Group of 24 has been instrumental in bringing the 100-odd developing countries that are members of the IMF behind a united front for the establishment of a link between SDR creation and development assistance. (75)

By 1972, there was widespread recognition in the IMF that the international monetary system required fundamental reforms and that an alternative to the forum of the Group of Ten was necessary to permit broader representation of members' interests. These circumstances converged to make possible the establishment in July 1972 of an ad hoc "Committee of the Board of Governors (of the IMF) on Reform of the International Monetary System and Related Issues" - popularly known as the Committee of 20. (76) The structure of membership corresponded to the IMF's Executive Board. Of the 20 committee members, five were appointed by the IMF member countries with the five largest quotas, three were elected from groups of countries in "the American Republics," and twelve were elected by groups of countries elsewhere in the world. Modeling the Committee of 20 on the Executive Board assured the developing countries of nine seats, while it also assured the developed countries that they would not be outnumbered. (77)

The Committee of 20 discussed the problems of payments-adjustment and liquidity creation between September 1972 and June 1974 without reaching final accord on a comprehensive plan for reform. Instead, the Committee concluded that the task of designing and implementing a reformed international monetary order would have to be a gradual process of evolution. (78) To carry forward this process, in October 1974 the IMF established an "Interim Committee of the Board of Governors on the International Monetary System." (79) The Interim Committee was, in fact, the Committee of 20 by another name, with many of the same countries participating in both. (80) At a special meeting in Kingston, Jamaica, in June 1976, the Interim Committee agreed that floating exchange rates should be legalized, and that the Fund's existing compensatory financing facility should be liberalized. (The latter would offset the scheduled phasing out of the Fund's oil facility.) In the Jamaica meeting it was also agreed to increase IMF quotas by one-third, with the OPEC countries' share in the total increased from 5-10 percent, and the share of industrial countries correspondingly reduced. As of 1976, when the Board of Governors of the IMF approved the Jamaica proposals, Third World countries together accounted for about one-third of Fund quotas, and thus one-third of the voting power. (81) The Interim Committee continues to have an advisory role to the Board of Governors pending the establishment, by amendment to the IMF Articles of Agreement, of a Council of Governors with decision making powers.

A notable success secured by Third World members of the IMF in 1974 was the agreement to create a joint IMF/IBRD Development Committee. The Development Committee is officially designated the "Joint Ministerial Committee of the Boards of Governors of the Bank and the Fund on the Transfer of Real Resources to Developing Countries." It was established under a resolution adopted by the Governors of the Fund and World Bank at their 1974 Annual Meetings. Its terms of reference are to maintain an overview of the development process, advise and report to the Boards of Governors on all aspects of the question of the transfer of real resources to developing countries, and give urgent attention to the problems of the least developed and most seriously affected developing countries. (82) As in the case of the Interim Committee, the constituencies from which the Development Committee was selected were those of the Executive Directors of the Fund. (83)

In June 1975, the Development Committee unanimously urged that "as a first concrete step" in meeting the serious difficulties faced by many developing countries, the World Bank should establish the "Third Window" for one year to provide an additional $1 billion in assistance at concessional terms. (84) In August, the Executive Directors of the World Bank authorized lending for one year at terms between those of standard Bank loans and the concessional loans of its affiliate, IDA. (85) Discussions held and understandings reached in the Development Committee were also instrumental in the IMF's decision in 1976 to establish the Subsidy Account and Trust Fund in order to channel special balance-of-payments assistance to developing countries. (86)

Despite the elaborate machinery which has been developed for discussions between industrial and developing countries, there is no North-South forum in which energy matters are central. Following the United Nations Seventh Special Session in September 1975, it was decided to pursue the issues of Energy, transfer of resources, trade, and development at a small conference of developed and developing countires. This was the Conference on International Economic Cooperation (CIEC), or North-South dialogue, held in Paris between December 1975 and June 1977. The "Group of 19" developing countries (87) came to Paris with the intention of implementing the recommendations of the Sixth and Seventh Special Sessions. The "Group of Eight" developed countries (88) came for the purpose of discussing matters relating to energy supply and availability, and setting up a new consultative forum on energy between oil-rich and oil-poor countries. The overestimation by each group of its negotiating power was a major reason for the failure of CIEC participants to reach significant compromises. The Group of Eight misjudged its power to lure the non-oil developing countries to its side by promising them controlled oil prices and cooperation for the development of new sources of energy. On the other hand, the Group of 19 put too much faith in the ability of Third World solidarity to exact concessions for an "equitable and comprehensive program" for international economic cooperation. (89)

A group of developing countries which has been prominent recently in special trade negotiations is the 46 African, Caribbean, and Pacific states (ACP), (90) which concluded the Lomé Convention with the European Economic Community on February 28, 1975. The convention covers trade and aid relations and replaces the Yaoundé Convention and the Arusha Agreement. It is for five years, dating from March 1, 1975. Despite the lack of any pre-existing institutional links, the Francophone African countries were able to make common cause with the Anglophone African, Caribbean, and Pacific countries. The ACP states obtained results in the form of a system of stabilization of export receipts (STABEX) and increased financial and technical cooperation. A major innovation of the Lomé Convention is the EEC's abandonment of its previous insistence on reciprocity in trade concessions. The Convention provides for the possibility of accession by every country with an economic structure comparable to the ACP countries, subject to the consent of the original signatories. (91)

Considering the range of interests to be accommodated, and also the economic competition among the developing countries, the measure of success that the Third World has achieved in forging common positions and forcing reforms in international organizations has been impressive. Over a period of about two decades, they created new organs within the United Nations system (UNCTAD and UNIDO), and won important reforms in the World Bank and the International Monetary Fund (IDA, Third Window, Compensatory Financing Facility, SDR link, Interim Committee, Development Committee). In the economic spheres, they used producers' associations to increase their bargaining power in markets for their raw materials (OPEC and IBA).

The outcome of these institutional developments was to modify Northern behavior as well as Northern perceptions of the Asian, African, and Latin American countries. This change can be seen in the emergence of development as one of the principal areas of concern in international organizations. It can also be seen in the gradual change in the way in which Northerners characterize these countries. Northerners tended to describe them as "backward" or "underdeveloped" prior to the mid-1960s. Beginning in this period, they increasingly referred to them as "developing" or "less developed," and reserved the term "underdeveloped" for the very poorest among the poor countries. (92) Since the quadrupling of oil prices in 1974, Northerners have set the OPEC states apart in a category of their own.

The spectacular increase in wealth by the oil-exporting developing countries points up the transformation that has occurred in the Third World since Alfred Sauvy coined the term in 1956. This transformation has led some people in the industrial countries to argue that the group of developing countries now constitutes two worlds - the Third as well as a poorer Fourth World. But there has been no salient cleavage between the least developed and other developing countries over issues involving the creation or the structure of the New International Economic Order. In spite of divergencies of economic interests, developing countries form a coherent bloc in international organizations and conferences. They share a past, in which they experienced formal or informal colonialism, and a present, in which they are impatient to gain power to influence the international system.

Notes and References

Chapter 1

(1) The terms "developing countries," "less developed countries (LDCs), and "Third World countries" are used interchangeably throughout the text. The earliest terms used to designate the poorer countries of the world were "backward" and "underdeveloped." Today the preferred term appears to be "developing countries." Generally speaking, the countries included are all countries in Asia except Japan, all countries in Africa except South Africa, and all countries in Latin America. See Appendix B for a discussion of various terms used throughout the text.

(2) UNGA Resolution 3201 (S-VI), 1 May 1974.

(3) UNGA Resolution 3202 (S-VI), May 1, 1974.

(4) UNGA REsolution 3281 (XXIX), December 12, 1974.

(5) Algeria, Behrein, Egypt, Iraq, Kuwait, Libya, Qatar and Saudi Arabia, Syria, and the United Arab Emirates. See Z. Mikdashi, The International Politics of Natural Resources (Cornell University Press, 1976), p. 72.

(6) See Appendix B for a listing of member countries. Z. Mikdashi, op. cit., Chapter 2, gives a brief summary of OPEC's origins and developments. D. Rustow and J. Mugno, OPEC: Success and Prospects (New York University Press, 1976) is an interesting and provocative study of OPEC and includes a chronology which goes through December 1976.

(7) For an excellent collection of articles on the crisis see "The Oil Crisis in Perspective," Daedalus (Fall 1975), and D. Rustow and J. Mugno, op. cit.

(8) D. Rustow and J. Mugno, op. cit., p. 24.

(9) New York Times, January 10, 1974, p. 1. The countries included were: United Kingdom, Canada, France, Italy, Japan, the Netherlands, Norway, and the Federal Republic of Germany.

(10) New York Times, January 11, 1974.

(11) "Global Aspects of the Energy Crisis Discussed by Secretary Kissinger and William Simon," January 10, 1974, Bureau of Public Affairs, Department of State.

(12) B. Gosovic and J. Ruggie, "On the Creation of a New International Economic Order," International Organization, (Spring 1976), pp. 309, 317.

(13) See Appendix B for a discussion of non-aligned countries and a list of countries included in this grouping.

(14) UN Document A/9541, February 5, 1974.

(15) UN Document A/9542, February 25, 1974.

(16) Washington Energy Conference Communique, February 13, 1974. The meeting took place from February 11 to 13, 1974.

(17) Ibid.

(18) New York Times, March 21, 1974, p. 36.

(19) Ibid.

(20) UN Document A/9556, April 30, and May 1, 1974, contains this proposal as A/AC.166/L.47.

(21) Thirty-Ninth Extraordinary Meeting of the Council, Annual Review and Record of OPEC, 1974, p. 30.

(22) Official Records of the General Assembly, Sixth Special Session, Plenary Meeting, 2208th Meeting, paragraphs 3-152. This speech was reported to have been drafted by the U.S. consulting firm Arthur D. Little. New York Times.

(23) Ibid.

(24) The recommendations are contained in Document A/9556 printed as an Annex to the official Records of the General Assembly, p. 27 et seq.

(25) See Appendix B for a definition and listing of members of the Group of 77.

(26) See note 20 supra for the Group of 77 submission. The Declaration and Action Program may be found in Fundamental Texts of the Fourth Conference of Heads of State or Government of Non-Aligned Countries, Algiers, 5-9 September 1973.

(27) UNGA Resolution 3201 (S-VI), May 1, 1974.

(28) UNGA Resolution 3202 (S-VI), May 1, 1974.

(29) A/AC.166/L.49, April 30, 1974.

(30) "U.N. Focus on Raw Materials," World Today, June 1974. The Group prepared two texts to submit to the plenary: a Group of 77 draft and a more moderate "consensus" draft. If a vote was forced by the developed countries, they threatened to vote for the Group of 77 draft. The United

States refrained from blocking the "consensus" and argued instead that it was not a genuine consensus.

(31) Speech by Ambassador John Scali of the United States before the United Nations, May 1, 1974, Department of State Bulletin, May 27, 1974.

(32) Proceedings, UNCTAD III, Vol. I (1972) Resolution 45 (III), p. 58.

(33) See Chapter 3 for details.

(34) UNGA Resolution 3202 (S-VI), May 1, 1974, p. 11.

(35) See Chapter 2 for a discussion of the background.

(36) A/9946, p. 26.

(37) The six opposed were: Belgium, Denmark, Federal Republic of Germany, Luxembourg, United Kingdom, and the United States. The ten abstaining were: Austria, Canada, France, Ireland, Israel, Italy, Japan, Netherlands, Norway, and Spain.

(38) Reprinted in "Review of the 1974 General Assembly and the United States Position in the United Nations," Hearings before the Subcommittee on International Organizations of the Committee on Foreign Affairs, 94th Congress, First Session, February 4-5, 1975, p. 10.

Chapter 2

(1) Name changed in 1878 to the Universal Postal Union.

(2) Name changed in 1932 to the International Telecommunications Union.

(3) For a more detailed discussion, see F.P. Walters, A History of the League of Nations, 2 vols. (London: Oxford University Press, Royal Institute of International Affairs, 1952).

(4) Martin Hill, The Economic and Financial Organization of the League (Carnegie Endowment, 1946), p. 17.

(5) Walters, op. cit., Vol. 1, Chapter III.

(6) The original membership of the League included: Union of South Africa, Argentine Republic, Australia, Belgium, Bolivia, Brazil, United Kingdom of Great Britain and Northern Ireland, Canada, Chile, China, Colombia, Cuba, Czechoslovakia, Denmark, France, Greece, Guatemala, Haiti, Honduras, India, Italy, Japan, Liberia, Netherlands, New Zealand, Nicaragua, Norway, Panama, Paraguay, Persia, Peru, Poland, Portugal, Romania, Salvador, Siam, Spain, Sweden, Switzerland, Uruguay, Venezuela, Yugoslavia. Twenty-one countries subsequently joined the League during its course of existence. Walters, op. cit., Vol. 1, pp. 64-65.

(7) See Article 22 on mandates, and Article 23(e) which used the phrase "equitable treatment for the commerce of Members of the League."

(8) Robert Asher, The United Nations and Promotion of General Welfare (Washington, D.C.: Brookings Institution, 1957), p. 159. Austria received a Ł 26 million loan in 1923 which was underwritten by 10 League members. Hungary received a Ł 10 million loan. The League also supervised loans and aid to Estonia, Danzig, and China. Additionally, loans were made to Romania, Greece, and Bulgaria to aid in refugee resettlement. Stephen S. Goodspeed, The Nature and Function of International Organization, 2nd ed. (New York: Oxford University Press, 1967), pp. 65-66.

(9) John McMahon, "The International Labour Organization," in E. Luard ed., The Evolution of International Organization (New York: Praeger, 1966).

(10) Ibid., p. 183.

(11) Ibid.

(12) Conference recommendations are also a means of influencing national policy, although they do not deal with "subjects which are to be implemented in municipal law." McMahon, op. cit., p. 185.

(13) The Convention was signed by 29 nations and ratified by 18 which was one less than needed for entry into force. Walters, op. cit., p. 428.

(14) Despite failures on the trade front, agreement was reached to establish the Bank for International Settlements (1930) which was to handle arrangements for German payment of reparations and to provide a forum for cooperation among central banks. See Roger Auboin, The Bank for International Settlements, 1930-55 (Princeton, New Jersey: Princeton Studies in International Finance No. 22, Department of Economics, Princeton University Press, 1955).

(15) Delegates from 64 countries attended. However, the Conference was destined for failure from the outset. In April 1933 the United States went off the gold standard, with the resulting uncertainty and instability of the monetary system. The political situation worsened throughout the period.

(16) This contradicted the Tripartite Declaration of 1936 (U.S., U.K., and France) which supported "equilibrium in the system of international exchange" and relaxation of tariff and exchange controls.

(17) Walters, op. cit., pp. 522-23.

(18) League of Nations, Council, Special Committee on Technical Problems, The Development of International Cooperation in Economic and Social Affairs (Geneva: August 22, 1939), A.23.1939.

(19) Ibid., p. 7.

(20) Key among these reports was The Transition from War to Peace Economy (League of Nations Publications II. A.3 1943) (1943).

(21) This portion of the Moscow Declaration is quoted by Goodspeed, op. cit., p. 79. Prior to this declaration, the Atlantic Charter (August 14, 1941) had called for the establishment of a "permanent system of general security." The United Nations Declaration (January 1942) also endorsed the program of the Atlantic Charter which included the "general security" concern.

(22) They expressed formal disapproval in Resolution XXX of the document produced by the Inter-American Conference, Mexico City, February 21-March 8, 1945.

(23) This is despite the fact that the General Assembly has authority over budgetary matters.

(24) A postwar planning group was established in the United States Department of State in 1939 immediately after the outbreak of war. For a detailed account, see Robert W. Oliver, International Economic Cooperation and the World Bank (Bristol, Great Britain: Macmillan Press Ltd., 1975) and his monograph Early Plans for a World Bank (Princeton, New Jersey: Princeton Studies in International Finance No. 29, Princeton University Press, 1971).

(25) Oliver, Early Plans for a World Bank, pp. 25-26.

(26) Robert E. Asher, et al., The United Nations and Promotion of the General Welfare (Washington, D.C.: The Brookings Institution, 1957), p. 178.

(27) See Oliver, Early Plans for a World Bank and International Economic Cooperation and the World Bank. For an account of planning within the State Department, refer to Department of State, Postwar Foreign Policy Preparation 1939-45, Department of State Publication 3580, General Foreign Policy Series 15 (Washington: Government Printing Office, 1950). The Treasury Department gained ascendancy in postwar international economic institution planning by the spring of 1943.

(28) The United States criticized Keynes' plan because it felt undue burden would be placed on countries with a surplus balance-of-payments situation. Keynes stated:

> I cannot emphasize this too strongly. This is not a Red Cross philanthropic relief scheme, by which the rich countries come to the rescue of the poor. It is a piece of highly necessary business mechanism, which is at least as useful to the creditor as to the debtor. A man does not refuse to keep a banking account because his deposits will be employed by the banker to make advances to another person, provided always that he knows that his deposit is liquid and that he can spend it himself whenever he wants to do so. Nor does he regard himself as a dispenser of charity whenever, to suit his own convenience, he refrains from drawing on his own bank balance.

Oliver, Early Plans for a World Bank, pp. 11-12. Oliver takes this quotation of Keynes from Seymour Harris, ed., The New Economics (New York: Alfred A. Knopf, 1948), pp. 365-66.

(29) Gerald M. Meier, Problems of a World Monetary Order (New York: Oxford University Press, 1974). Meier cites a portion of the text of White's Plan (1943), which includes the following statement regarding the role of the Fund in stabilizing disequilibria situations (p. 24):

The resources of the Fund would be available under adequate safeguards to maintain currency stability, while giving member countries time to correct maladjustments in their balance of payments without resorting to extreme measures destructive of international prosperity. The resources of the Fund would not be used to prolong a basically unbalanced international position. On the contrary, the Fund would be influential in inducing countries to pursue policies making for an orderly return to equilibrium.

(30) White also drew up the basic outline of the Bank.   His original conception was somewhat more unconventional than that of the IMF. In particular, several controversial aspects, later excluded, were proposed: issuance of noninterest bearing notes by the Bank; provision of loans for currency stabilization as well as reconstruction; equity investments; and organization and financing of an International Raw Materials Development Corporation and an International Commodity Stabilization Corporation. Oliver, Early Plans for a World Bank, pp. 46-47.

(31) Two percent of the subscription was due in gold, 18 percent in the member's currency, and the rest was on call. The member was obligated to maintain the value of his country's currency.

(32) Asher, op. cit., pp. 185-86.

(33) Paraphrase of Final Act and Related Documents, Havana Conference, United Nations Conference on Trade and Employment (March 1948). The Department of State of the United States published the Havana Charter for an International Trade Organization, March 24, 1948 (Publication 3206 Commercial Policy Series 114) which includes a study guide.

(34) For an explanation of the reasons for the United States' failure to ratify the Charter, see: William Diebold, Jr., "The End of the I.T.O." (Princeton, New Jersey: Essays in International Finance No. 16, Princeton University, October 1952). There was also strong opposition in the United Kingdom due to the Imperial Preferences issue.   Richard N. Gardner, Sterling-Dollar Diplomacy, Expanded Edition (New York: McGraw Hill, 1969).

(35) These were: Australia, Belgium, Brazil, Burma, Canada, Ceylon, Chile, China, Cuba, Czechoslovakia, France, India, Lebanon, Luxembourg, Netherlands, New Zealand, Norway, Pakistan, South Africa, Southern Rhodesia, Syria, United Kingdom, United States. In 1949 the Contracting Parties expanded to include: Denmark, Dominican Republic, Finland, Greece, Haiti, Italy, Liberia, Nicaragua, Sweden.   Asher et al., The United Nations and Economic and Social Cooperation (Washington, D.C.: The Brookings Institution, 1957), p. 112.

(36) ECOSOC Resolution 222.

(37) Asher, The United Nations and Economic and Social Cooperation, p. 457. For the period 1950-51, about $20 million was budgeted for an 18-month period; 60 percent was provided by the United States. The IBRD had provided $500 million in reconstruction loans and $16 million for

development loans by the end of 1948. Subsequently, $109.1 million in development loans was committed for two power plant projects in 1949.

(38) Ibid., Chapters X and XI.

(39) Martin Hill, "The Administrative Committee on Coordination," in E. Luard, ed., The Evolution of International Organization, Chapter 6.

(40) The United Nations' system did provide the following: (1) IMF provided dollar exchange; (2) IBRD made four reconstruction loans worth $500 million by the end of 1948; (3) information-gathering. In this period, the new international institutions were in their formative stages and were largely concerned with refining operating principles and resolving differing notions of purpose as defined in their respective Articles of Agreement. For example, the IBRD was concerned with establishing its credit-worthiness in the private capital markets.

(41) In large part the Marshall Plan (named for the then Secretary of State George C. Marshall) was motivated by fear of Soviet expansion - expressed in the Truman Doctrine - and the belief that a united Europe was a defense against such a threat.

(42) For a concise summary of United States' foreign aid efforts, see Evolution of Foreign Aid 1945-1965 (Washington, D.C.: Congressional Quarterly Service, 1966).

(43) Barbu Niculescu, Colonial Planning (London: Allen & Unwin, 1958), p. 75; Robert F. Meagher, Public International Development Finance: Senegal (New York: Columbia University Law School, 1963) p. 70.

(44) Niculescu, op. cit., p. 129. The Moyne Report and the CD & W Act (1940) represented a new policy of responsibility for colonial development. However, this was not implemented until after World War II.

(45) Report of the Ad Hoc Committee on Proposed Economic Commission for Latin America, United Nations, ECOSOC (New York, 1948), E/630/Add. 1. The Inter-American Conference (1945) discussed most of the concerns regarding the postwar situation of Latin America.   The Conference members expressed the fear that: resumption of normal trade patterns would result in a loss in their wartime industrial achievements, dollar balances currently held in Latin America would depreciate in value, Latin America would not "receive an 'equitable' share of available capital goods" after the war, and a decline in raw material prices would adversely affect the Latin American economies. Asher, The United Nations and Promotion of the General Welfare, p. 193. Asher further notes, in regard to the 1945 period, that: "The attention of the underdeveloped countries was concentrated on the removal of all possible obstacles to the early fulfillment of their development plans. Among these were the possible loss of purchasing power of their foreign exchange reserves in times of inflation and the instability of the prices of the primary commodities that were their principal exports," p. 197.

(46) Report of the Economic Commission for Latin America (Fourth Session), United Nations, ECOSOC (New York, June 1951), E/CN.12/266.

(47) However, Raul Prebisch warned against ECLA's being considered an organization whose sole purpose was theoretical and scientific research. Economic Commission for Latin America, Fourth Annual Report, United Nations, ECOSOC (New York, March 1952), E/CN.12/AC.16/15, p. 23.

(48) Prebisch is an influential figure in the international arena. He is an Argentinian economist (b. April 17, 1901) who taught at Buenos Aires University as well as serving in various government positions, most notably as Director-General of the Central Bank of the Republic of Argentina (1935-1943). In 1948 he worked as an adviser to ECLA and from 1950-1962 he served as its Executive Secretary. He subsequently became the Director of the Latin American Institute of Economic and Social Planning, and in 1964 was appointed the Secretary General of UNCTAD. New York Times, January 11, 1961, p. 2; Kathleen McLaughlin, "Warm Abrazo for Dr. Prebisch," Who's Who International, 1975). Prebisch encouraged the development of economic explanations for underdevelopment which diverged from standard explanations. He stated: "...only with the development of independent ways of thinking and of action could the Latin American countries accomplish their task in economic development and international cooperation." Report of ECLA (June 1951), E/CN.12/266, p. 38.

(49) Prepared in 1950 by Raul Prebisch, a consultant to ECLA before becoming its Executive Secretary. Report of the Economic Commission for Latin America (June 1951), E/CN.12/266. The Economic Development of Latin America and Its Principal Problems, Economic Committee for Latin America, United Nations, ECLA (April 1950), E/CN.12/89/Rev. 1.

(50) Report of the Economic Commission for Latin America, United Nations, ECOSOC (New York, June 1950), E/CN.12/190, p. 9.

(51) Prebisch, The Economic Development of Latin America and its Principal Problems.

(52) Ibid., pp. 8-10. Prebisch cites the report: Post War Price Relations in Trade between Underdeveloped and Industrialized Countries, United Nations, ECLA, 1949, E/CN.1/Sub.3/W.5. M. June Flanders in an article entitled "Prebisch on Protectionism: An Evaluation," (The Economic Journal LXXIV, June 1964, pp. 305-26) argues that there is not a single Prebisch model and that there are in fact at least two. The first is found in the 1950 article cited in the text, the second in the 1959 article "Commercial Policy in the Underdeveloped Countries," American Economic Review, Papers and Proceedings XLIV (May 1959): 251-73. The two are not necessarily consistent. See the Flanders article for an excellent exposition and critique of Prebisch's ideas regarding trade and development. These ideas are controversial and questioned both from the standard of empirical evidence and from a conceptual viewpoint. For representative critiques, see Harry G. Johnson, Economic Policies toward Less Developed Countries (London: Allen & Unwin, 1967); Gottfried Haberler, "Terms of Trade and Economic Development," in H. Ellis, ed., Economic Development for Latin America (London: Macmillan, 1961); W.

Arthur Lewis, Aspects of Tropical Trade 1883-1965 (London: Allen & Unwin, 1969); Werner Baer, "The Economics of Prebisch and ECLA," Economic Development and Cultural Change XI (January 1962): 169-82.

(53) J. David Edwards, Criteria for an Effective International Organization: The Case of ECLA (Muscatine, Iowa: The Stanley Foundation, 1975). The exposition of these ideas to the American academic community was largely through the writings of Hans W. Singer. For example: Hans W. Singer, "The Distribution of Gains between Investing and Borrowing Countries," American Economic Association, Proceedings 1949-50, pp. 473-85. Also, American Economic Review, 1951, pp. 419-21.

(54) Afghanistan, Burma, Cambodia, Ceylon, People's Republic of China, Egypt, Ethiopia, Gold Coast, India, Indonesia, Iran, Iraq, Japan, Jordan, Laos, Lebanon, Liberia, Libya, Nepal, Pakistan, Philippines, Saudi Arabia, Sudan, Syria, Thailand, Turkey, Democratic Republic of Vietnam, State of Vietnam, and Yemen.

(55) Per the Bogor Communique. See George McTurnan Kahin, The African-Asian Conference (Ithaca, New York: Cornell University Press, 1956).

(56) Ibid., p. 81.

(57) G.A. Res. 1991 A and B, December 17, 1963.

(58) Department of State Bulletin, October 16, 1961, pp. 619-625.

(59) Afghanistan, Burma, Cambodia, Ceylon, (Belgian) Congo, Cuba, Cyprus, Ethiopia, Ghana, Guinea, India, Indonesia, Iraq, Lebanon, Mali, Morocco, Nepal, Saudi Arabia, Somali Republic, Sudan, Tunisia, United Arab Republic, Yemen, Yugoslavia, and Provisional Government of Algeria. Observers: Bolivia, Brazil, Ecuador.

(60) See Appendix B for a discussion of the non-aligned states.

(61) Fundamental Texts IV Conference of Heads of State or Government of Non-Aligned Countries. Algiers, September 5-9, 1973, p. 63.

(62) G.A. Res. 1785 (XVII), December 8, 1962.

(63) Joint Declaration of 75 Developing Countries on UNCTAD; G.A. Res. 1897 (XVII), November 11, 1963.

(64) Ibid. and Branislav Gosovic, UNCTAD: Conflict and Compromise (Netherlands: A.W. Sijthoff, 1972), pp. 26-27.

(65) For a concise summary of the background and subsequent activities of UNCTAD I see Michael Zammit Cutajar and Alison Franks, The Less Developed Countries in World Trade (London: The Overseas Development Institute, 1967), especially Chapters 9 and 10.   For a more detailed account see Gosovic, op. cit., especially pp. 15-27.   For the list of participants, see p. 5 of Final Act. Preliminary meetings of the regional economic commissions were held prior to the Conference. The following documents state the position of the regional groupings: Charter of Alta Gracia March 1964, ECLA and Special L.A Co-ordinating Committee of OAS); Niamey Resolution (December 1963, ECA and Economic and Social

Committee of OAU); Teheran Resolution (March 1964, ECAFE). The ECE also met, but issued no resolutions. Reports on these meetings can be found in Vols. VI and VII of UNCTAD I Proceedings. At the Conference the Latin American, African, and Asian regional groups chose representatives to negotiate a common developing country position.

(66) E/Conf.46/3 (1964).   As others have noted, the analysis tends to concentrate on conditions characteristic of the Latin American situation, as if these were universal, for example, the concern with manufactured goods and the trade gap. Furthermore, there are extensive criticisms of Prebisch's analysis particularly within the scholarly economic literature. However, these are not examined here since our concern is not with the validity of his analysis, but with the important role which it played in shaping LDC arguments to restructure world trade relations. See Cutajar and Franks, op. cit. for summary and analysis of the Prebisch Report.

(67) Prebisch, Towards a New Trade Policy for Development, E/Conf.46/3 (1964), p. 6.

(68) Campos, Harberler, Meade and Tinbergen, Trends in International Trade (Geneva: GATT, 1958), popularly known as The Harberler Report, and the 1963 GATT decision not to require reciprocity from LDCs show GATT's examination of how its policies affected LDCs. However, a commitment to remove barriers to LDC exports of manufactures does not necessarily mean the implementation of such a commitment.

(69) For contrary opinions see Harry Johnson, Economic Policies towards Less Developed Countries.

(70) Prebisch, Towards a New Trade Policy, p. 117. It was largely the failure to import substitution policies designed to insulate infant industry and the domestic economy from external disturbances which led Prebisch to modify his earlier policy position. Concern for a new trade policy and emphasis on trade as an essential means to economic growth were the logical results of disillusionment with the import substitution strategy. This thesis is criticized on many grounds. First, it universalized from the Latin American experience. Second, it underestimated the importance of the agricultural sector and the adverse impact of import substitution policies on agricultural exports. Third, it overestimated the importance of export expansion for economic growth.

(71) Prebisch, Towards a New Trade Policy, p. 124.

(72) The representation on the Trade and Development Board was apportioned as follows:

Group A: 22 Afro-Asian countries (68 total in UNCTAD)
Group B: 18 Industrialized countries (Western Europe, United States, Canada, Japan—30 total in UNCTAD)
Group C: 9 Latin American/Caribbean countries (24 total)
Group D: 6 USSR/Eastern Europe (9 USSR/Eastern Europe total).

A two-thirds majority on substantive matters and a simple majority on procedural matters was specified.

(73) The Group of 77 included those that had signed the 1963 Declaration of 75 Countries, plus Kenya, South Korea and South Vietnam and minus New Zealand. They were: Afghanistan, Algeria, Argentina, Bolivia, Brazil, Burma, Burundi, Cambodia, Cameroon, Central African Republic, Ceylon, Chad, Chile, Colombia, Congo (Brazzaville), Congo (Leopoldville), Costa Rica, Cyprus, Dahomey, Dominican Republic, Ecuador, El Salvador, Ethiopia, Gabon, Ghana, Guatemala, Guinea, Haiti, Honduras, India, Indonesia, Iran, Iraq, Jamaica, Jordan, Kenya, Kuwait, Laos, Lebanon, Liberia, Libya, Madagascar, Malaysia, Mali, Mauritania, Mexico, Morocco, Nepal, Nicaragua, Niger, Nigeria, Pakistan, Panama, Paraguay, Peru, Philippines, Republic of Korea, Republic of Viet-Nam, Rwanda, Saudi Arabia, Senegal, Sierra Leone, Somalia, Sudan, Syria, Thailand, Togo, Trinidad and Tobago, Tunisia, Uganda, United Arab Republic, United Republic of Tanganyika and Zanzibar, Upper Volta, Uruguay, Venezuela, Yemen and Yugoslavia.

(74) Diego Cordovez, "The Making of UNCTAD," Journal of World Trade Law (1967). Cordovez provides a detailed account of the negotiations which resulted in agreement on the institutional form of UNCTAD.

(75) The Principles were voted on individually and only one was adopted unanimously. They are not binding.

(76) Final Act, pp. 18-19. The United States voted against this statement.

(77) Ibid., p. 19. The United States abstained.

(78) The United States, United Kingdom, and France did not support these latter principles. Cutajar and Franks, op. cit., p. 174.

(79) Gosovic, op. cit., p. 206, Footnote 22.

(80) General Agreement on Tariffs and Trade, Basic Instruments and Selected Documents, Thirteenth Supplement (Geneva: GATT, July 1965). This stemmed from concerns expressed in the Harberler Report to GATT in 1958, which were given new prominence due to UNCTAD. See B. Gosovic, op. cit., p. 22.

(81) The Charter of Algiers is contained in Vol. I, Proceedings, UNCTAD II, pp. 431-44. The Ministerial Meeting followed the regional meetings of the 88 members of the Group of 77. The Charter of Algiers was the product of negotiations based on agreements made at these regional meetings: the African Declaration of Algiers, the Bangkok Declaration, and the Charter of Tequendama. The OECD countries also met in December 1967, prior to UNCTAD II.

(82) See p. 123 et. seq.

(83) Summary Proceedings, Annual Meeting, the International Monetary Fund, 1969, p. 11.

(84) Final Act, UNCTAD II, p. 17.

(85) TD/3/Rev. 1, 1968.

(86) Final Act, UNCTAD II, p. 8.

(87) Proceedings, UNCTAD II, Vol. I, p. 423.

(88) Department of State Bulletin, May 8, 1967, pp. 707-708. For a characterization of the remarks and their linkage to preferences see the testimony of Assistant Secretary of State for Economic Affairs Solomon before the SubCommittee on Foreign Economic Policy of the Congressional Joint Economic Committee reprinted in American Foreign Policy 1967: Current Documents (Department of State) p. 1105 and p. 1111.

(89) Henry G. Aubrey, Atlantic Economic Cooperation: The Case of the OECD (New York: Praeger, 1967).

(90) Proceedings, UNCTAD II TD/97, Vol. I, resolution 21 (II), p. 38.

(91) The GSP schemes seemed to indicate that the developed countries were willing reluctantly to endorse the principle of preferences. In practice, however, they would make only minor concessions which did not threaten domestic producers.

(92) See for example "Evolution of the Generalized Use of Preferences of the European Communities: A Perspective," in Journal of World Trade Law 383 (1976).

(93) At the same time, the U.S. made a 10 percent cutback in its foreign aid.

(94) Declaration of Lima, Proceedings, UNCTAD III, Vol. I.

(95) Ibid., p. 374.

(96) UNCTAD III 1968, TD/180 Vol. I, Annex VIII, p. 377, para. 6.

(97) Y.S. Park, The Link between Special Drawing Rights and Development Finance (Princeton, New Jersey: International Finance Section, Department of Economics, Princeton University, 1973).

(98) In 1971 UNCTAD was granted participating agency status in the UN Development Program, which gave it more of an operational role in technical assistance.

(99) Proceedings, UNCTAD III, TD/180, Vol. I, p. 53 et. seq.

(100) Proceedings, UNCTAD III, TD/180, Vol. I, resolution 45, (III), pp. 58, 59.

Chapter 3

(1) For a discussion of this point, see p. 87 et. seq.

(2) The author is indebted to the Ministry of External Affairs of Mexico for this information.

(3) Proceedings UNCTAD III, Vol. Ia, pt. 1, p. 186 (1972).

(4) Proceedings UNCTAD III, Vol. I, pp. 35-36. Abstaining were: Australia, Austria, Canada, Denmark, Federal Republic of Germany, Finland,

Ireland, Italy, Japan, Liechtenstein, New Zealand, Norway, Paraguay, South Africa, Spain, Sweden, Switzerland, United Kingdom of Great Britain and Northern Ireland, United States of America. See Proceedings UNCTAD III, Vol. I, Annex I, pp. 117-133 for explanations of their votes by the abstaining states.

(5) Proceedings UNCTAD I, Vol. I, pp. 10-12 (1964).

(6) Proceedings UNCTAD III, Vol. I. (1964).

(7) A/C.2/L.1104/Rev.1.

(8) Issued by the first Ministerial meeting of the Group of 77 on October 24, 1967. It is reprinted in Proceedings UNCTAD II, Vol. I, p. 431.

(9) Issued by the second Ministerial meeting of the Group of 77 on November 7, 1971. It is reprinted in Proceedings UNCTAD III, Vol. I, p. 373.

(10) Since the establishment of UNCTAD in 1964, the LDCs have tended to prefer it to ECOSOC as a forum for discussion of major policy questions. This was because at the time of UNCTAD's establishment, ECOSOC was still dominated by the developed countries.

(11) Proceedings UNCTAD III, Vol. I, Annex I, p. 133.

(12) Resolution 45 (III) suggested that the Working Group be comprised of 31 members, and the discussion in the Plenary proposed five members each from the UNCTAD regional groupings, with six from Asia, of which one would be China. The list proposed by Secretary General Perez-Guerrero of UNCTAD followed this model exactly, but it was attacked by Iraq as having "a flagrant imbalance in the Asian Group," relating to the fact that no Asian-Arab nations were included. Morocco had, in fact, been on the first list, and in UNCTAD was in Group A (the Afro-Asian plus Yugoslavia Group), but this did not satisfy Iraq. Bolivia complained that none of the 18 landlocked LDCs were members, TD/B/SR.338, 341, pp. 294 and 308, respectively. G.A. Res. 3037 (XXVII) expanded the Working Group to 40 members. Egypt and Iraq were added, as were Bolivia and Zambia (landlocked LDCs). Switzerland withdrew at the First Session of the Working Group, and was replaced by Belgium. The final composition of the Working Group was: Brazil, Canada, China, Czechoslovakia, Denmark, France, Germany (Federal Republic of), Guatemala, Hungary, India, Indonesia, Italy, Ivory Coast, Jamaica, Japan, Kenya, Mexico, Morocco, Netherlands, Nigeria, Pakistan, Peru, Philippines, Poland, Romania, Union of Soviet Socialist Republics, United Kingdom of Great Britain and Northern Ireland, United States of America, Yugoslavia, Zaire, Australia, Bolivia, Bulgaria, Chile, Egypt, Iraq, Spain, Sri Lanka, Zambia, and Belgium.

(13) TD/B/AC.12/1, p. 26, para. 71. When the matter was discussed at the Thirteenth Session of the Trade and Development Board, the United States, France and Canada opposed having summary records for financial reasons. Board decision 98 (XIII) allowed for a summary of views "during the closing phases of the two sessions." This coverage was limited to only

two paragraphs in the Third Session of the Working Group report and without attribution, but was expanded in the final Fourth Session's report where nine countries' comments were summarized.

(14) International Development Strategy for the Second United Nations Development Decade, UNGA Resolution 2626 (XXV), October 24, 1970.

(15) TD/B/AC.12/1, p. 4.

(16) Ibid., pp. 9-14.

(17) TD/B/AC.12/R.11 and TD/B/AC.12/R.7, respectively. Both reproduced in Annexes to TD/B/AC.12/1.

(18) TD/B/AC.12/1, p. 16, para. 60.

(19) Canada, Denmark, Federal Republic of Germany, Italy, Netherlands, and the United Kingdom of Great Britain and Northern Ireland. Ibid., p. 24.

(20) TD/B/AC.12/a.

(21) Ibid., p. 2, para. 3.

(22) Ibid., p. 2, para. 4 and TD/B/AC.12/R.13.

(23) TD/B/AC.12/2, p. 2, para. 6. The draft is contained in TD/B/AC.12/R.17.

(24) TD/B/AC.12/2, p. 3, para. 8. See p. 65 for a membership list of each sub-group.

(25) Ibid., p. 45.

(26) Ibid., p. 64.

(27) Trade and Development Board Decision 98 (XIII).

(28) G.A. Res. 3082 (XXVIII).

(29) TD/B/AC.12/3.

(30) Ibid., pp. 3-7.

(31) Ibid., p. 8.

(32) Ibid., pp. 8-17.

(33) The centrally planned economies supported most of the LDC positions but did not take a major part of any articles other than those of direct interest to themselves, i.e. Articles 4, 20 and 26.

(34) TD/B/AC.12/3, March 8, 1974, p. 22.

(35) Ibid.

(36) See Chapter 1 above, pp. 38-41.

(37) See Chapter 1 above, pp. 38-41.

(38) G.A. Res. 3201 (S-VI), 3202 (S-VI). The Group of 77 had threatened to vote through even less acceptable documents, from the standpoint of the more developed countries, if the latter did not acquiesce to "adoption without vote" of the draft resolutions.

(39) The Contact group consisted of Chairmen of the negotiating groups: three members of Groups A and C (of the Group of 77), three members of Group B (developed economies), two members of Group D (centrally planned economies) and China. See TD/B/AC.12/4, p. 27.

(40) Manuel Tello, La Politica Exterior de Mexico 1970-74 (Mexico City: Fondo de Cultura Economica, 1975), pp. 196, 208.

(41) TD/B/528.

(42) Ibid., p. 51 and Annex IV.

(43) Ibid., p. 52.

(44) Decision 110 (XIV), in Ibid., Annex I.

(45) A/C.2/L.1386.   China and the East European countries presented recommendations for change before the Group of 77 draft was officially introduced in committee and did not submit official amendments thereafter. In most cases, the Group of 77 contact group did not heed the socialist countries' recommendations, although they were ready to accept the mention of "detente" or "relaxing of tensions" in the Preamble (as a concession to the Eastern European socialists) and the adding of the qualifier "genuine" to disarmament in Article 15 (as a concession to China). However, these modifications did not appear in the final Group of 77 draft submitted to the Second Committee.

(46) A/C.2/1.1398-1415. All of these amendments are collected in A/9946, December 9, 1974, pp. 14.

(47) A/9946, pp. 19-20.

(48) Ibid., pp. 23-26.

(49) A/C.2/1.1419.

(50) A/9946, pp. 22-23.

(51) Except for Chapter I (i) and Articles 5, 15, 16, 19 and 28, where the Chairman determined that the earlier vote on an amendment proposed by the more developed countries was indicative of the vote on the final Charter Article. See Ibid., pp. 23-26.

(52) Ibid., p. 26.

(53) Official Records of the General Assembly, Twenty-Ninth Session, Annexes, Agenda item 48, p. 31.

(54) A/9946, p. 3.

(55) Ibid., p. 14, para. 6(a)(i).

(56) Ibid., p. 22, para. 17(a). There were 89 affirmative and 17 negative votes, and 3 abstentions.

(57) Ibid., para. 8(a).

(58) Ibid., p. 23, para. 22. The United Kingdom abstained on the final vote on paragraph 4 because it opposed, in principle, a change in a formulation

which had been agreed by all. See Command Document 5907, February 1975, p. 82.

(59) A/9946, p. 4.

(60) Ibid., p. 15, para. 6(b).

(61) Ibid., p. 22, para. 17(b).

(62) Ibid., p. 19, para. 7(a).

(63) Ibid., p. 23, para. 22.

(64) In both the sixth Preambular paragraph and Article 8, China opposed the tenet of "promoting a just and rational international division of labor through the necessary structural changes in the world economy" and proposed instead simply "the achievement of just and rational international economic relations." See TD/B/AC.12/2, p. 5. The concept of changing the international division of labor was not a new one, and can be found in UNCTAD I, General Principle 5; the 1967 Charter of Algiers, part 2, section3.4; G.A. Res. 2626 (XXV) "International Development Strategy," para. 19; UNCTAD Resolution 46 (III); and "Programme of Action on the Establishment of a New International Economic Order," G.A. Res. 3202 (S-VI), I.3(a)(vii). In these past declarations the developed countries were called on to avoid taking protective measures, to help promote LDC industrialization and diversification, and to increase the flow of trade among LDCs. The 1975 UNIDO Lima Declaration and Plan of Action states as a goal the attainment by LDCs of 25 percent of total world production by the end of the twentieth century. Western Europe did not oppose the formulation "rational international division of labor" (but preferred adding "in the context of a balanced economy in harmony with the needs and interests of all countries," as appears in Article 8). In the end, both the sixth Preambular paragraph and Article 8 use" [more] rational and equitable international economic relations" together with "the encouragement of structural changes in the world economy," but do not mention attaining a "just and rational international division of labor," as had been proposed in the draft outline. See TD/B/AC.12/1, pp. 16 and 19.

(65) A/9946, p. 23, para. 22.

(66) TD/B/AC.12/2, p. 5. The Latin American Working Paper, the Joint Developing Country Working Paper, and the Draft Outline all contain the concept.

(67) TD/B/AC.12/4, p. 5.

(68) A/9946, p. 15, para. 6(c).

(69) Ibid., p. 22, para. 17(c).

(70) Ibid., p. 23, para. 22. Belgium, Federal Republic of Germany, and the United States. For a discussion of this concept, see J.S. Nye, "Collective Economic Security" in International Affairs, Vol. 50, No. 4, pp. 584-588; and TD/B/AC.12/R.15 "Collective Economic Security: Note by the UNCTAD Secretariat." It is curious to note that no exception was taken to similar language in sub-paragraph (b) of the fifth Preambular

paragraph, which reads "Desirous of contributing to the creation of conditions for: (b) The promotion by the entire international community of economic and social progress of all countries, especially developing countries."

(71) A/9946, p. 5.

(72) Ibid., p. 15, para. 6(a) (ii).

(73) Ibid., p. 22, para. 17(a).

(74) Ibid., p. 20, para. 8(b).

(75) In 13 paragraph-by-paragraph votes, only paragraphs four and seven were not approved unanimously. Paragraph four received 10 abstentions, while paragraph seven received seven. The only three negative votes were on paragraph seven. See A/9946, p. 23, for the paragraph-by-paragraph and Article-by-Article votes.

(76) Provision (i) was completely new, inspired by the Israeli-Arab problems, and apparently had its origin in a U.S.S.R. proposal for provision (n): "cooperation...on the basis of genuine equality, mutual advantage..." TD/B/AC.12/1, p. 18. See the discussion of Article 16, p. 82. The United Nations Charter G.A. Res. 2625 (XXV) "Declaration of the Principles of International Law Concerning Friendly Relations and Cooperation among States in Accordance with the United Nations Charter" contains (a), (b), (c), (d), (g), (h), (j), and (k). G.A. Res. 2542 (XXIV) contains (f). G.H. Jansen, Non Alignment and the Afro-Asian States (New York: Praeger, 1976), p. 129, says that "coexistence, is amply defined in the words of the Charter Preamble, 'to practice tolerance and live together in peace with one another as good neighbors.'" While this may suggest the spirit of peaceful coexistence, the term itself was apparently never used in the United Nations as long as Western Europe and the United States controlled the General Assembly. Provision (e) or "mutual and equitable benefit" also comes from the Panchsheel, which Jansen states equates with MFN status (p. 130). However, this could never have been the understanding of the Western Europeans, who accepted the provision unanimously in the Charter negotiations, at the same time that they fought hard to exclude any mention of most-favored-nation (MFN) treatment.

(77) The original formulation of the Panchsheel was: (1) Mutual respect for each others' territorial integrity and sovereignty; (2) mutual nonagression; (3) mutual noninterference in each other's affairs; (4) equality and mutual benefit; and (5) peaceful coexistence. Jansen discusses the legal and political significance of the Bandung Conference and the Panchsheel. G.H. Jansen, op. cit.

(78) For a discussion of "peaceful coexistence" and its United Nations-Western equivalent of "friendly relations," see E. McWhinney, "The 'New' Countries and the 'New' International Law: The United Nations' Special Conference on Friendly Relations and Cooperation among States," American Journal of International Law (1966), p. 1. See also note 83 of this chapter below.

(79) In Annex I, TD/B/AC.12/1.

(80) The Netherlands: TD/B/AC.12/1, p. 17; France: TD/B/AC.12/2, p. 6.

(81) A/C.2/L.1402.

(82) Belgium, Federal Republic of Germany, Ireland, Italy, and the United Kingdom opposed. The United Kingdom's policy has been not to accept Soviet attempts to codify the principle of peaceful coexistence as being equivalent to the fundamental principles of the United Nations Charter. The United States shared this position until 1972 when it was reversed with the signing of Basic Principles of Mutual Relations by the United States and the Soviet Union. See Stephen Schwebel, "The Brezhnev Doctrine Repealed and Peaceful Coexistence Enacted," American Journal of International Law (1972), p. 816 and sources cited therein.

(83) A/C.2/SR.1647, p. 13.

(84) See discussion of Article 16(2), pp. 107, 163.

(85) A/9946, p. 15, para. 6(f).

(86) Ibid., p. 22, para. 17(f).

(87) Although no state voted against provision (o), there were 12 abstaining countries in the Second Committee votes.

(88) Proceedings, UNCTAD I, Vol. 1, pp. 25-26. See also M. Dubey, "International Law Relating to the Transit Trade of Land-locked Countries," Indian Yearbook of International Affairs, Vol. XI, pp. 22-44.

(89) A/PV.231.6, pp. 3-5.

(90) Pakistan and Tanzania: A/C./SR.1649, p. 4; SR.1650, p. 8. Rights of landlocked states will be an important part of the treaty being drafted at the Third United Nations Law of the Sea Conference, where the 30 landlocked, the 20 shelflocked, and the other "geographically disadvantaged states" constitute a theoretical one-third blocking minority (the treaty must be approved by a two-thirds majority). Dissatisfaction with what they consider to be very poor guarantees for their "rights" has coalesced an otherwise very heterogeneous group at the Geneva, 1975, and New York, spring 1976, sessions. Article 109 of the Conference's "single negotiating text" gives the landlocked "the right of access to and from the sea" and "to this end, freedom of transit by all means of transport," but Article 110 states that the "terms and conditions...shall be agreed between the landlocked State and the transit States." A/CONF.62/WP.8/ Rev. 1/Part II. See Nepture, No. 8, May 1976.

(91) The other provision was Article 3.

(92) Two other transit states did not participate in the vote in the Plenary.

(93) See for example the Treaty of Peace and Friendship between Japan and the Peoples Republic of China, August 12, 1978, Article II, reprinted in Japan Report No. 17, September 1, 1978, p. 2 (Consul General of Japan, New York). The use of the word hegemony held up the conclusion of the Treaty for many years.

(94) A/9946, p. 24 para. 22.

(95) For example, "Declaration on Friendly Relations and Cooperation among States", G.A. Res. 2625 (XXV). See TD/B/AC.12/1, p.18.

(96) TD/B/AC.12/2, p. 19.

(97) The German Democratic Republic and the Soviet Union urged that such cooperation be modified by "genuine equality, mutual advantage, nondiscrimination and the most-favored-nation principles," but this suggestion was not adopted. TD/B/AC.12/2, p. 6.

(98) The only other negative votes were those cast against the "peaceful coexistence" provision.

(99) M. Mughraby, Permanent Sovereignty Over Oil Resources (Beirut: Middle East Research and Publishing Center, 1966). See also R. Barnet and R. Muller, Global Reach (New York: Simon and Schuster, 1974).

(100) Cf. Mughraby, op. cit., p. 15. To the United States and the United Kingdom, "established rules of international law" meant prompt, adequate, and effective compensation.

(101) Resolution No. 1803 (XVII), December 14, 1962.

(102) R. Vernon, Sovereignty at Bay (New York: Basic Books, 1971). Still later they were renamed Transnational Corporations. See Chapter 6 below.

(103) ECOSOC Res. 1721 (LIII).

(104) "The Impact of Multinational Corporations on Development and on International Relations" (United Nations Publications, Sales No. E.74.II.A.5, 1974) and Summary of Hearings before the Group of Eminent Persons (United Nations Publications, Sales No. E.74.II.A.9, 1974).

(105) Hearings before the Sub-Committee on Multinational Corporations of the Committee on Foreign Relations, United States Senate, 93rd Congress, 1st and 2nd Sessions on Multinational Corporations and United States Foreign Policy, 1973, 1974.

(106) S. Schwebel, "The Story of the U.N.'s Declaration on Permanent Sovereignty over Natural Resources," American Bar Association Journal (1963), p. 463.

(107) See the discussion of Chapter I (i) on p. 48.

(108) A/9946, p. 18, para. 6(n).

(109) Ibid., p. 23, para. 18(h).

(110) Surendra J. Patel, "Transfer of Technology and Third UNCTAD," Journal of World Trade Law (1973), p. 226. See also Resolution 39 (III) of UNCTAD III.

(111) G.A. Res. 3362 (S-VIII), Section III.

(112) Transfer of technology TD/190, December 31, 1975, is the UNCTAD Secretariat paper prepared for UNCTAD IV. See ftn. 46 of the document for references to a Code of Conduct and p. 29 for the current activities of the Intergovernmental Group of Experts on the Code of Conduct on Transfer of Technology. See also TD/B/AC.11/10Rev. 1, entitled "Major Issues Arising from the Transfer of Technology to Developing Countries," April 22, 1974.

(113) TD/B/AC.12/2, pp. 30, 55, respectively.

(114) Ibid., pp. 30, 55; TD/B/AC.12/3, p. 10.

(115) For a discussion of the differences between "appropriate" (Yugoslav text) and "indigenous" (Article 13(2) language) technology, see Development Centre, Low-Cost Technology: An Inquiry into Outstanding Policy Issues, OECD, 1975.

(116) Proceedings UNCTAD III, Vol. I, p. 110. See Section III of Resolution 39 (III).

(117) Ibid., para. 9.

(118) Migratory species of fish, such as tuna, are one of the problems whose solution has been particularly difficult during the current United Nations Law of the Sea Conference. See "The Resources of the Oceans - Protecting and Developing Them," Global-1, Development Issue Paper 8 (United Nation's Development Program, September 1975).

(119) The other Article was Chapter I (o) on free access to the sea for landlocked countries. See Official Records of the General Assembly, Twenty-Ninth Session, Annexes, Agenda Item 48, p. 31.

(120) The dispute between Brazil and Argentina involves the use of the Parana River and the construction of the vast hydroelectric complex at Itaipu which, according to Argentina, could damage the navigation and hydroelectric potential of the Parana further south in Argentina. Argentina, Brazil, Paraguay, Bolivia, and Uruguay are parties to the River Plate Basin Treaty, which defines an international river and the concept of shared natural resources arising from shared sovereignty. In March 1973, they had agreed to exchange information and advice on the use of the Parana; but in April, Paraguay and Brazil's signing of the Itaipu project brought Argentine protests. See Latin America, May 4, 1973, pp. 140-41. Uruguay and Argentina, affected by actions taken on the Parana, voted for the article, with Brazil, Paraguay, and Bolivia voting against it. Beyond the merits of the Itaipu case, Brazil felt that the idea of shared sovereignty of an international river was distinct from clearly defined sovereignty over natural resources in the territory of a single state. Before this article could be made operational, the extent of its coverage would have to be made clear. Argentina made no detailed presentation of its position (in meetings for which there are summary records), but see A/C.2/SR.1647, p. 3; A/PV.2315, p. 77. For Brazil's position see A/PV.2315, pp. 31-40 and A/PV.2316/Corr. 1. Paraguay's comments can

be found in A/C.2/SR.1647, pp. 10-11; A/PV.2315, p. 16. Finally, it should also be noted that the Parana River dispute had surfaced earlier at the Stockholm Environment Conference.

(121) A/C.2/SR.1650, p. 7.

(122) A/C.2/SR.1649, p. 7.

(123) Belgium, Federal Republic of Germany, Austria, Italy, Luxembourg, Spain, and United Kingdom. Japan was another abstaining developed country.

(124) See for example R. Prebisch, Towards a New Trade Policy for Development E/CONF.46/3, 1964.

(125) United Kingdom and Federal Republic of Germany, TD/B/AC.12/1, p. 21.

(126) It was excluded from the next draft.

(127) GATT (Geneva 1958) (The report was written by Professors Campos, Haberler, Meade, and Tinbergen). M. Z. Cutajar and Alison Franks, The Less Developed Countries in World Trade (Overseas Development Institute: London, 1967), p. 143.

(128) Cutajar and Franks, op. cit., p. 143.

(129) Ibid., pp. 132, 137.

(130) For a discussion of the relation of General Systems of Preferences (GSPs) to GATT, see "GATT: Accommodating Generalized Preferences," Journal of World Trade Law (1974), p. 341.

(131) The EEC system calculates import ceilings for "semi-sensitive" products, which trigger reimposition of MFN duties. Many of the articles receiving preferential rates are designated as "sensitive," i.e., whose massive import might "disrupt" home markets. These products are subject to even more limitations. The Japanese list of excepted products from preferential treatment includes textiles, footwear, and other products in which the LDCs presently enjoy a comparative advantage, and in which they could rapidly expand their exports. The Japanese also have quantitative limits on certain imports. See R. Benham, "Development and Structure of the Generalized System of Preferences," Journal of World Trade Law (1975), p. 442; T. Murray, "UNCTAD's Generalized Preferences: An Appraisal," Journal of World Trade Law (1973): 461; and Zubair Igbol, "The General System of Preferences Examined," Finance and Development (September 1975), pp. 34-39.

(132) A/9946, p. 23.

(133) See H.B. Malmgren, Trade and Development (Overseas Development Council, 1971).

(134) TD/B/AC.12/4, p. 17. Canada had originally introduced similar language; TD/B/AC.12/2, p. 43.

(135) A/C.2/L.1412.

(136) A/9946, p. 25, para. 22, ftn. 9.

(137) A/C.2/SR.1642, p. 8.

(138) Conversations with participants in the negotiations.

(139) A/C.2/SR.1650, p. 5.

(140) A/C.2/SR.1649, p. 10; SR.1650, p. 17.

(141) Export Earnings Fluctuations and Economic Development: An Analysis of Compensatory Financing Schemes (A.I.D. Discussion Paper No. 32, Bureau for Program and Policy Coordination, 1975), p. 1.

(142) "International Commodity Agreements," XXVIII Law and Contemporary Problems (Duke University, 1963); "International Commodity Stabilization Arrangements," Hearings before the Subcommittee on International Trade, Investment, and Monetary Policy of the Committee on Banking, Currency, and Housing, House of Representatives 94th Congress, 1st Session, July 9 and 10, 1975; W. Fox, Tin: The Working of a Commodity Agreement (London: Mining Journal Books, 1974); B. Fisher, The International Coffee Agreement: A Study in Coffee Diplomacy (New York: Praeger, 1972).

(143) See Agreement Establishing the International Bauxite Association, 1974; An Agreement to Establish the Intergovernmental Council of Copper Exporting Countries (CIPEC), June 8, 1967; Revision of CIPEC's Agreement, June 26, 1974; Agreement Establishing the Association of Iron Ore Exporting Countries, April 3, 1975; "Raw Material Producers Eye the OPEC Model: Who? Where? How?," Business International, (November 7, 1975), pp. 358, 359; C.F. Bergsten, "The New Era in World Commodity Markets," Challenge, (November/December 1974); C.F. Bergsten, "The Threat from the Third World," Foreign Policy, (Summer 1973); M. Mughraby, Permanent Sovereignty over Oil Resources (Beirut: Middle East Research and Publication Center, 1966).

(144) Proceedings UNCTAD I, E/Conf. 46/141, Vol. I (1964). Res. A.IV.18, p. 52, pp. 200-203; UNCTAD II TD/97, Vol. I (1968), Res. 30 (II), pp. 42, 43 and pp. 288-290, 437, 448.

(145) E/Conf. 46/141, Vol. I (1964), Res. A.IV.17, p. 52 and pp. 125, 139, 200-203. TD/97, Vol. I (1968), Res. 31 (II), p. 43 and pp. 290, 437, 438; TD/B/C.1/166/Supp. 4, December 13, 1974; TD/B/C.1/195, October 16, 1975; TD/189; March 1976; TD/184, March 4, 1976, pp. 14, 15: Compensating Financing of Export Fluctuations: A Second Report by the International Monetary Fund (no date); A.I.D. Discussion Paper No. 32, op. cit.; R.F. Meagher, "The Expansion and Modification of the IMF's Compensatory Finance Facility," International Lawyer (1977), p. 277.

(146) The Indexation of Prices TD/B/503/Supp. 1, July 30, 1974; TD/B/503/Supp. 1/Add. 1, July 5, 1974; TD/B/503, August 6, 1974; TD/B/563, July 7, 1975; TD/B/C.1/188, July 8, 1975, pp. 18-22.

(147) J.M. Keynes, "The International Control of Raw Materials," reprinted in Journal of International Economics (1974), p. 300.

(148) Measures for International Economic Stability (United Nations Publications, Sales No. 1951. II. A.2).

(149) Commodity Trade and Economic Development (United Nations Publications, Sales No. 1954.II.B.1).

(150) R.F. Meagher, "The Expansion and Modifications of the IMF's Compensatory Finance Facility," International Lawyer, (1977), p. 277.

(151) "International Commodity Stabilization Arrangements" Hearings before the Subcommittee on International Trade Investment and Monetary Policy of the Committee on Banking, Currency and Housing, House of Representatives 94th Congress, 1st Session, July 9 and 10, 1975. Testimony of Assistant Secretary Parsky, p. 9.

(152) Ibid., pp. 59-63.

(153) Z. Mikdashi, The International Politics of Natural Resources (Ithaca, NY: Cornell University Press, 1976), Chapter 3. See also K. Clarifield, S. Jackson, J. Feeffee, M. Noble, and P.A. Ryan, Eight Mineral Cartels: The New Challenge to Industrialized Nations (New York: McGraw Hill, 1975); A.D. Deloff, M.J. Frantz, and L.H. Richmond, "Non-Fuel Mineral Cartels-United States Economic Policy and Changing Resource Patterns," Law and Policy in International Business (1975), p. 89.

(154) L.H. Richmond, op. cit., p. 114.

(155) See Mikdashi, op. cit.; Mughraby, op. cit; D. Rustow and J. Mugno, OPEC Success and Prospects (New York: New York University Press, 1976); Z. Mikdashi, The Community of Oil Exporting Countries (Ithaca, NY: Cornell University Press, 1972); Daedalus (Fall 1975) - the entire issue is devoted to "The Oil Crisis in Perspective." See particularly Z. Mikdashi, "The OPEC Process" and G. Lenczowski, "The Oil Producing Countries." C. Barker and B. Page, "OPEC as a Model for Other Mineral Exporters," Institute of Development Studies Bulletin (October 1974), p. 82. For a clear statement of the activities of OPEC and the effect of the 1973 OPEC price increases during the two years after the action, see The Economist, September 20, 1975, pp. 13, 14, 83-86.

(156) The posted price is the price per barrel used by the host government to determine its share of revenue, regardless of the actual sales prices.

(157) Expensing of royalties meant that whereas in the past royalties could be deducted in toto as a credit, they would now be only partially offset as an expense deducted from gross revenue.

(158) At the end of 1976 there was a disagreement on a suggested price increase, with Saudi Arabia and the United Arab Emirates arguing for a five percent increase and other OPEC members opting for 10 percent. This led to a two-tier pricing system, but it did not result in the break-up of the Organization. New York Times, December 17, 1976, p. 1; J. Lichtblau, "OPEC's Price-Split Mixed Blessing?" in Business section of New York Times, January 2, 1977.

(159) See Agreement on an International Energy Program March 15, 1975 (International Energy Association); Long-Term Cooperation Programme, January 30, 1976 (International Energy Association); U. Lantake, "The OECD and Its International Energy Agency," Daedalus (Fall 1975); "The Future of Energy in OECD Countries," OECD Observer (January-February 1975); E. Davignon, "The Aims of the International Energy Agency," OECD Observer (January-February 1975).

(160) Public Law 93-618, Section 502. Discussed in R. Stebbins and E. Adams, American Foreign Relations 1974, p. 570; and American Foreign Relations 1975, p. 24 (New York: New York University Press, 1976 and 1977 respectively).

(161) R. Mikesell, "More Third World Cartels Ahead?" Challenge (November/December 1974). See also C. Barker and B. Page, "OPEC as a Model for Other Mineral Exporters," op. cit.

(162) B. Varon and K. Takeuchi, "Developing Countries and Nonfuel Minerals," Foreign Affairs, (April 1974), p. 505.

(163) J. Amuzegar, "The Oil Story," Foreign Affairs (July 1973); M. Mughraby, op. cit.

(164) Testimony of Assistant Secretary Parsky, cited in note 152.

(165) Z. Mikdashi, The International Politics of Natural Resources Chapters 2 and 3.

(166) F. Bergsten, "The New Era in World Commodity Markets," Challenge (September/October 1974); President Carlos Andres Perez, "Altering the North-South Collision Course," New York Times, December 15, 1976, on the Op Ed page.

(167) See Hearings noted in ftn. 152 above, pp. 59-63.

(168) A/9946, p. 17, para. 6(i).

(169) Ibid., p. 22, para. 17(d).

(170) Official Records of the General Assembly Twenty-Ninth Session, Second Committee (1974), p. 443, para. 24 (Norway); p. 444, para. 28 (Denmark); p. 446, para. 50 (Canada); p. 449, para. 4 (Belgium); p. 454, para. 50 (United Kingdom).

(171) Ibid., p. 453, para. 43.

(172) Ibid., p.447, para. 60.

(173) See Hearings referred to in ftn. 152 above, p. 57. This testimony was given by Bart Fisher.

(174) For a review of the operation of the International Tin Agreement, see William Fox, Tin: The Working of a Commodity Agreement (London: Mining Journal Books, 1974). In early 1977 the tin buffer stocks were exhausted and the price rose beyond control. An article in the New York Times (Peter Kilborn, "The International Tin Agreement Reported Near

Collapse," January 20, 1977) concluded that "the agreement today is effectively defunct and for the first time in years tin has become a target for international speculators." The breakdown of this long-standing Agreement came about when Bolivia, the world's second largest producer, withdrew rather than sign the fifth five-year Agreement. Being a relatively high-cost producer, Bolivia wanted higher price ceilings; it also wanted consumer countries to absorb a larger share of the buffer stock storage charges. Other producer countries, fearing the use of substitutes if prices rose too high, refused.

(175) After much discussion throughout the 1960's, a three-year International Cocoa Agreement finally came into force in 1973. The text of the Agreement can be found in United Nations Cocoa Conference, 1972: Summary of Proceedings (United Nations Publications, Sales No. E.73.II.D.9), p. 7. Annual export quotas and an indicator price range to be defended by quota adjustments and buffer stock operations were the main elements in the Agreement, but they were never utilized because the market price for cocoa always remained above the range within which they were to take effect. In October 1975 a conference was held to extend the pact for an additional three years following the expiration date (September 1976) of the first accord. Once again, the United States (which had not been a member of the first Agreement) declined to participate, primarily because it felt the price range was too high. The text of the second Agreement is included in United Nations Cocoa Conference, 1975 (United Nations Publications, Sales No. E.76.II.D.9). For a discussion of the United States' position, see the New York Times, October 25, 1975 and January 16,1976; and Journal of Commerce, January 16, 1976.

(176) 469 U.N. T.S. 170, September 28, 1962, 484 U.N. T.S. 416, December 27, 1963. For an excellent article describing the negotiations, see R. Bilder, "The International Coffee Agreement: A Case History in Negotiation," Law and Contemporary Problems (Spring 1963). See also Bart Fisher, International Coffee Agreement (New York: Praeger, 1972); "International Coffee Organization," Journal of World Trade Law (1967), p. 359; "National Legislation Concerning Coffee," Journal of World Trade Law (1967), p. 370; "International Coffee Agreement, 1968," Journal of World Trade Law, (1968), p. 359; "1972 Geneva Coffee Agreement," Journal of World Trade Law (1972), p. 612.

(177) A/C.2/L.1147. Producers, consumers, and amount of trade to be used as variables to determine voting rights.

(178) The Outlook for Coffee (Commodity Paper No. 2 (3/73), International Bank for Reconstruction and Development), Annex I, p. 1.

(179) New York Times, December 4, 1975.

(180) Ibid.

(181) New York Times, August 8, 1975. It was estimated that it would take four years to replace the damaged trees with seedlings.

(182) New York Times, January 12, 1977.

(183) A/C.2/L.1407.

(184) A/9946, p. 17, para. 6(j).

(185) Ibid., p. 23, para. 17(e).

(186) Ibid., p. 19, para. 7(d).

(187) Ibid., p. 25.

(188) Official Records (see note 171 above),p. 450, para. 7.

(189) See Hearings, p. 71, cited in note 152.

(190) Z. Mikdashi, The Community of Oil Exporting Countries (Ithaca, N.Y.: Cornell University Press, 1972), p. 175.

(191) See, for example, Recommendation A.II.8 of Proceedings UNCTAD I.

(192) G.A. Res. 3083(XXVIII).

(193) G.A. Res. 3202(S-VI).

(194) TD/B/503/Supp.1/Add.1.

(195) TD/B/503/Supp.1, p. 58, para. 154.

(196) G.A. Res. 3308(XXIX).

(197) TD/B/563, p. 1 and Annex II.

(198) TD/184.

(199) A/9946, p. 18, para. 6(p).

(200) Ibid., p. 23, para. 17(j).

(201) No vote was taken on Article 28 following the rejection of the proposed developed country amendment contained in A/C.2/L.1413. The vote on the amendment was 101-12-11. Official Proceedings of the General Assembly, Twenty-Ninth Session, Annexes, Agenda Item 48, p. 12.

(202) Official Records of the General Assembly, Twenty-Ninth Session, Second Committee, December 6, 1974, p. 442, para. 15 (Finland); and p. 443, para. 24 (Norway).

(203) Ibid., p. 442, para. 15.

(204) Ibid., p. 444, para. 28 (Denmark); and p. 454, para. 50 (United Kingdom).

(205) Ibid., p. 447, para. 56 (Canada); p. 450, para. 11 (Italy); p. 454, para. 50 (United Kingdom).

(206) See Hearings noted in 152 above, pp. 17-19.

(207) J.M. Keynes, "The International Control of Raw Materials," op. cit., p. 306.

(208) Proceedings UNCTAD I, Vol. I. See the following recommendations of the Conference: Annexes A.IV.21 through A.IV.24. For a summary of the

activities of the Committee on Invisibles and Financing Related to Trade, see Proceedings (1968), Vol. I, p. 6, para. 16, and the Committee on Shipping, para. 17. Resolution 42(III) of the Third Session dealt with insurance and reinsurance. Proceedings (1972), p. 54 and Report on the Fourth Committee (in the same volume), p. 244.

(209) See Cutajar and Franks, op. cit., p. 160.

(210) W. Friedmann and G. Kalmanoff, Joint International Business Ventures (New York: Columbia University Press, 1961) and W. Friedmann and J.P. Beguin, Joint International Business Ventures in Developing Countries (New York: Columbia University Press, 1971).

(211) For example, the Black Star Line created by Ghana and Israel and the efforts of Sudan and Yugoslavia, described in R.F. Meagher, Public International Development Financing in Sudan (New York: Columbia Law School, 1965).

(212) R.F. Meagher, "Industrial Financing in Five African Countries," in Industrialization and Productivity Bulletin (UNIDO), No. 11 (1965).

(213) Ibid.

(214) These programs may be found in the development plans of many countries (e.g., Kenya, Turkey, Tunisia, Greece). The World Bank maintains a Tourism Department which gives technical and capital assistance for programs in this sector. See the Annual Reports of the World Bank.

(215) The vote was 131 to none. Official Records of the General Assembly, Twenty-Ninth Session, Annexes, Agenda Item 48, p. 24.

(216) See the World Bank Annual Report, 1976.

(217) R.N. Gardner, "The United Nations Conference on Trade and Development," in R. Gardner and M. Millikan,eds., The Global Partnership, (New York: Praeger, 1968), pp. 99, 114-120.

(218) E/AC.62/9 (United Nations, 1975). See note 2 to Chapter 7 below for the resolution implementing this Report.

(219) E/AC.62/9 p. 56.

(220) Ibid., p. 56, para. 181(h).

(221) Ibid., p. 57, para. 183(d).

(222) In May 1976 the Executive Directors of the World Bank transmitted to the Board of Governors for vote a resolution (World Bank Annual Report, 1976, p. 6) "that up to $8,430 million of selective increases in subscriptions to capital stock be allotted to 125 members. Allotments are "made to those individual members which accepted increases in their quotas in the International Monetary Fund (IMF). This selectivity reflects a longstanding policy of the Bank that when increases in IMF quotes are accepted, members are also expected to request increases in their subscriptions to the capital of the Bank. A resolution to increase quotas

in the IMF, arising from its sixth general review of member countries' quotas was approved by the Fund's Board of Governors in March 1976." If approved, the World Bank's selective capital increase would lower the voting strength of the five largest shareholders (United States, United Kingdom, Germany, France, and Japan) by 2.18 percent to 42.56 percent, and lower the voting strength of other developed countries by 0.58 percent to 18.79 percent. There would also be a decrease in the voting power of nonoil producing LDCs by 1.38 percent to 29.43 percent. On the other hand, the combined voting strength of the OPEC countries would increase from 4.4 percent to 9.22 percent, in line with a similar agreement on shares of quotas in the IMF. A roughly similar reallocation of voting power took place in the IMF (see International Monetary Fund Annual Report, 1976, p. 47).

(223) J. Surr, "The Committee of Twenty: Its Origin, Evolution and Procedures," Finance and Development, Vol. II, No. 2 (June 1974).

(224) Ibid.

(225) Summary Proceedings of the 1976 Annual Meetings of the Boards of Governors of the IBRD, IDA and IFC, pp. 237-271.

(226) J. Surr, op. cit.

(227) See the International Fund for Agricultural Development, discussed in Chapter Five.

(228) TD/B/AC.12/C, p. 41. For a Romanian view on international organizations, see C. Morsue, "The Contribution of International Organizations to the Establishment of a New World Economic Order," Revue Romaine d'Etudes Internationales 9, no. 2: 119-137.

(229) Official Records of the General Assembly, Twenty-Ninth Session, Annexes, Agenda Item 48, p. 22. The vote was 129-0-0.

(230) See discussion of Articles 21 and 23.

(231) Article XXIV of the GATT.

(232) The draft outline was inspired on this point by the Asian Working Paper, borrowing from the International Development Strategy, G.A. Res. 2626(XXV), para. 39.

(233) Two EEC countries suggested that trade policies be "outward-looking and consistent with the general norms of international trade." (United Kingdom/Netherlands TD/B/AC.12/2, p. 29). The Soviet Union and Czechoslovakia worked in their standard theme of nondiscrimination, as did the United States its theme on "full regard for their international obligations" (TD/B/AC.12/2, p. 28). Mexico suggested that "rational and outward-looking" be supplemented by "consistent with the general norms of international trade and shall not limit the development of economic relations and trade exchanges of all countries, in particular those of developing countries." (TD/B/AC.12/2, p. 29). This reflected a general LDC worry about increased protectionism imposed against their products by regional groupings.

(234) TD/B/AC.12/2, August 8, 1973, p. 28.

(235) TD/B/AC.Add.1, August 9, 1973, p. 12.

(236) Ibid., p. 49.

(237) Ibid., p. 66.

(238) TD/B/AC.12/2, p. 29. These comments were made by Mexico.

(239) Commission of the European Community, SEC(74)1500 final, April 23, 1974, p. 2.

(240) A/9946, December 9, 1974, p. 9.

(241) Articles 111, 113, 116, 228, 237, and 238.

(242) A/C.2/SR.1640, p. 7.

(243) TD/B/AC.12/4, p. 17.

(244) A/9946, p. 25.

(245) See Report by the Secretariat for UNCTAD IV, TD/192, "Economic Cooperation among Developing Countries," p. 7.

(246) See "Dimensions Internationales de l'Integration Regionale dans le Tiers-Monde," Proceedings of the 5th International Conference of the Institute for International Cooperation, 1975; Towards a New International Economic Order, Commonwealth Secretariat, London, 1975.

(247) For a further development of this theme, see H.J. Rosenbaum and W. Tyler, "South-South Relations: The Economic and Political Content of Interactions among Developing Countries," International Organization p. International Organization p. 243 (Winter 1975).

(248) G.A. Res. 3202(S-VI), Section VII, I(e).

(249) Some disagreement arose over whether the Article should state directly that it was the developed countries' duty to support LDC economic groupings or more indirectly, as the United States proposed, that "developing countries should strengthen their mutual relations...with the support of the developed countries and the international community." TD/B/AC.12/2, p. 35. The Third Session of the Working Group used the common technique of compromise by juxtaposing the two formulations.

(250) See Report by the Secretariat for UNCTAD IV, TD/192, "Economic Cooperation among Developing Countries."

(251) See p. 267.

(252) Proceedings UNCTAD I, Vol. I, p. 20. The European Six abstained at the time.

(253) Proceedings UNCTAD II, Vol. I, p. 439, part two, section E.3.

(254) TD/B/AC.12/2, p. 36.

(255) Another disagreement concerned whether states should avoid prejudicing "the interests" of third countries, or simply their "legitimate interests." The EEC favored the latter formulation only if there was included in Article 2 a provision on reliable and steady supplies of raw materials. EEC Commission memorandum, op. cit., p. 21 (see note 240 supra). Apparently the feeling was that "legitimate interests" was a more powerful expression, whereas "interests" was more vague and hence less binding. In any case, no provision appeared for reliable and steady supplies of raw materials, and apparently, according to EEC wishes, in Article 24, states are to avoid prejudicing only the "interests" of LDCs. On the other hand, as discussed above in connection with Article 12, paragraph 1, all states are to ensure that their groupings "have full regard for the legitimate interests of third countries, especially developing countries" (emphasis added).

(256) TD/B/AC.12/R.11, Chapter II, A, 2 in TD/B/AC.12/1, Annex 1, p. 14.

(257) TD/B/AC.12/2, p. 24.

(258) Until June 1977, few substantive discussions have been agreed between the East and West European organizations because CMEA does not legally recognize the EEC, and individual East European members will not agree to deal bilaterally with the EEC. On the other hand, the EEC prefers trade discussions to be between the Community, as a whole, and individual East European countries, maintaining that the CMEA state-trading systems make commercial negotiations between groupings difficult. Furthermore, the EEC does not consider CMEA to be a legitimate legal equivalent to the Community. Any bloc-to-bloc negotiations can only make "equivalent" commitments. In 1976 CMEA submitted a new set of proposals for EEC consideration. See Europe, May 10, 1976, p. 4. The German Democratic Republic (GDR) exports to the Federal Republic of Germany (FRG) without facing tariffs, on the basis of a special protocol adopted in 1957 at the same time as the Treaty of Rome. Now that the GDR has been internationally recognized, this could perhaps provide a precedent for CMEA arguments of EEC discrimination, as well as increasing EEC demands for isolating the Community's markets from nonmembers.

(259) TD/B/AC.12/4, p. 11.

(260) A/C.2/L.1405.

(261) Even the Netherlands, which abstained, commented that the article could not be supported because the second sentence was not clear. A/C.2/SR.1650, p. 14.

(262) A/C.2/SR.1650, p. 4.

(263) TD/B/AC.12/4, August 1, 1974, p. 11.

(264) Ibid.

(265) Ibid.

(266) A/9946, p. 7.

(267) General Principles 2 and 8 of UNCTAD I are somewhat analogous to Articles 4 and 26. General Principle 2: "There shall be no discrimination on the basis of differences in socioeconomic systems. Adaptation of trading methods shall be consistent with this principle," was opposed in 1964 by Canada, the Federal Republic of Germany, and the United States. General Principle 8, which states that international trade should be conducted to mutual advantage on the basis of most-favored-nation treatment, mustered 11 negative votes and 23 abstentions. However, some of the negative votes were due to the issues of general preferential concessions to LDCs as well as special concessions enjoyed by the Commonwealth LDCs and the Yaoundé "associated" states. See, Proceedings UNCTAD I, Vol. I, pp. 18, 20.

(268) A/C.2/SR.1650, p. 4.

(269) A/C.2/L.1405.

(270) The United States did extend MFN status to the Soviet Union from 1935 through 1951 and again in 1972, but the Jackson Amendment to the Trade Reform Act tied the already relatively low level of export credits ($300 million) and MFN status to the Soviet-Jewish emigration issue, and led the Soviet Union to refuse the agreement on those terms. It seems that the MFN clause may not actually have been the deciding factor for the Soviet Union, so much as the extremely low level of export credits. See Michael Kaser, "Soviet Trade to Europe," Foreign Policy, No. 19 (Summer 1975). This could explain CMEA's recent change in dealing with the EEC, explained above.

(271) A/C.2/SR.1638, p. 7.

(272) A/C.2/SR.1639, para. 22 and A/C.2/SR.1647, para. 35.

(273) A/9946, p. 25.

(274) Proceedings UNCTAD III, TD/180, Vol. 1 (1972), Resolution 53(III), which also refers to Resolution 15(II) of UNCTAD II.

(275) A/9946, p. 25.

(276) A/C.2/SR.1634, p. 10.

(277) These sentiments are contained in the Charter of Algiers and in the Declaration of Lima, Group of 77 position papers released prior to and appearing in Vol. I of the Proceedings of both UNCTAD II and III respectively.

(278) A/C.2/SR.1650, p. 13.

(279) TD/B/AC.12/2/Add.1, p. 13, para. 13.

(280) TD /B/AC.12/2, p. 33.

(281) This more general qualifier differs from the Sixth Special Session's "Declaration" (G.A. Res. 3201(S-VI), which at paragraph 4(k) states specifically that assistance must be "free of any political or military conditions" (as taken from General Principle 11 of UNCTAD I).

(282) A/C.2/SR.1650, p. 7.

(283) A/9946, p. 25.

(284) Netherlands did not vote on this article. Official Records of the General Assembly, Twenty-Ninth Session, Annexes, Agenda Item 48, p. 23.

(285) TD/B/AC.12/2, p. 35.

(286) Ibid.

(287) Sweden, however, remarked that a distinction should have been made between commercial transactions and development assistance. A/C.2/SR-.1649, p. 19.

(288) Proceedings UNCTAD I, Vol. I, Annex A.IV.2, p. 43.

(289) Proceedings UNCTAD II, Vol. I, p. 38.

(290) The major resolutions may be found in Development Assistance Efforts and Policies (Development Assistance Committee of OECD) for the following years: 1965 Review, pp. 115-122; 1969 Review, pp. 267-270; 1972 Review, pp. 207-210.

(291) Belgium, Netherlands, Norway, Sweden without reservation; Australia, Denmark, France, and New Zealand with a target date after 1975; Canada, Finland, Federal Republic of Germany, Japan, and the United Kingdom without a target date. International Development Strategy for the Second Development Decade, G.A. Res. 2626(XXV) (1968).

(292) These terms are defined in the 1969 Development Cooperation (DAC Review), pp. 239-245.

(293) See the 1972 Development Cooperation (DAC Review), pp. 207-210.

(294) See the 1976 Development Cooperation (DAC Review), p. 206, Table 1.

(295) Ibid., p. 209, Table 4.

(296) Ibid., p. 207, Table 2.

(297) Ibid., p. 100.

(298) Ibid., p. 99.

(299) Ibid., p. 100.

(300) Ibid., p. 101.

(301) Ibid., p. 216, 217, Table 10.

(302) The Charter of Algiers in 1967 first recognized the need for special action. See 1972 Development Cooperation (DAC Review), p. 209.

(303) Countries designated "least developed countries" were Botswana, Burundi, Chad, Dahomey, Ethiopia, Guinea, Lesotho, Malawi, Mali, Niger, Rwanda, Somalia, Sudan, Uganda, Tanzania, Upper Volta, Afghanistan, Bhutan, Laos, Maldives, Nepal, Sikkim, West Samoa, Yemen, Haiti. (From G.A. Res. 2768(XXVI) of November 27, 1971). Bangladesh, Central African Republic, Republic of Democratic Yemen, and Gambia were added to the original list in 1975. The landlocked states had been recognized as having special development problems, and a set of principles

relating to their transit needs had been voted in 1964 at UNCTAD I. (Proceedings UNCTAD I, Vol. I, pp. 25-26.) Developing island countries had been recognized as a separate category at UNCTAD III. Of course, these categories overlap: 16 of the least developed countries are landlocked and another three are islands.

(304) In the export stabilization scheme of the Convention, for 34 of the 46 LDC members only 2.5 percent of their total commodity export earnings need to have been accounted for by the individual commodity. Earnings from exports to the EEC need to have been 2.5 percent below their reference values, instead of the 7.5 percent figures for the other members. The EEC further recognized that for 24 of the poorest 46, repayment of the transfers made under the stabilization scheme need not be repaid.

(305) A/C.2/SR.1640, p. 3. Nor did adoption of the detailed "wish list" of the Special Program, part of the Sixth Special Session's Programme of Action. But implementation of measures, such as linking the creation of SDRs to a distribution formula in inverse proportion to the level of development, was fought by some of the more developed LDCs. Others, including the OPEC nations, have opposed the notion of a "Fourth World" to represent the least developed or resource poor nations, because of the political implications for the solidarity of the Third World in its struggle with the more developed countries.

(306) The United States had voted against General Principle 12 in 1964 and other developed countries (East and West) had abstained. Proceedings UNCTAD I, Vol. I, pp. 21, 80.

(307) Department of State Bulletin, April 27, 1953. Following a suggestion for disarmament he said, "This government is ready to ask its people to join with all nations in devoting a substantial percentage of the savings achieved by disarmament to a fund for world aid and reconstruction..."

(308) A/C.2/SR.1649, para. 21.

(309) G.A. Res. 2542(XXIV), 2734(XXV), 2880(XXVI).

(310) A/9946, p. 18, para. 6(m).

(311) Ibid., p. 23, para. 17(g).

(312) A/C.2/SR.1649, p. 19.

(313) A/C.2/SR.1639, p. 391, para. 20.

(314) Ibid.

(315) 28 Yearbook of the United Nations (1974), p. 486.

(316) Ibid., p. 490.

(317) A/C.2/SR.1693, p. 393.

(318) A/9946, p. 10.

(319) "Self-determination" is itself a part of Chapter I of the Charter.

(320) G.A. Res. 1514(XV) "Declaration on the Granting of Independence to Colonial Countries and Peoples."

(321) TD/B/AC.12/2, p. 43.

(322) Ibid. The Soviet attitude on foreign aid has been that it should represent "compensation for damages caused by colonial domination and neocolonialist policies." "The Right to receive compensation for economic damage" was a part of the African Group Working Paper, TD/B/AC.12/1, Annex I, p. 5.

(323) On the importance of the Middle East dispute and the South Africa situation for all LDCs, see T. Farer, "The United States and the Third World: A Basis of Accommodation," Foreign Affairs, p. 79 (October 1975). Andreas Leitolf ("International Law and the New World Economic System," Review of International Affairs, December 5, 1975, p. 79) believes that the importance of Article 16 transcends these two specific disputes. "Article 16 is grounded in the economic decolonialism principle of international law. The right to development assistance, then, is based on a new principle of compensation. Colonial and neocolonial injustices have to be set right. The compensation model based on Echeverria's doctrine, derived from the principle of strict economic decolonialization, reveals a far-reaching turning-point in modern theory of international law. Political decolonialization entails economic decolonialization...Thus the problem of the economic sovereignty of the developing countries is resolved in a theoretically impeccable manner in Article 16, that is, by confirming the principle of decolonialization itself." However, this interpretation rests firmly on a retrospective application of Article 16, and it implies a well-established understanding of "neocolonial injustices."

(324) Department of State memorandum, op. cit., p. 6.

(325) This had been a separate point in the Sixth Special Session's "Declaration on the Establishment of a New International Economic Order," G.A. Res. 3201(S-VI), 4(i).

(326) Canada, for instance, expressed its reservation on this provision. A/PV.2315, pp. 59-60.

(327) G.A. Res. 3175(XXVII), para. 2.

(328) A/9946, p. 23, para. 18(h).

(329) Mexico had proposed another common responsibility; "outer space, the moon and other celestial bodies also form part of the common heritage of mankind and should be used exclusively for peaceful purposes. Their exploration and use should be carried out for the benefit of all nations." TD/B/AC.12/2, p. 44.

(330) G.A. Res. 2574 (XXIV).

(331) G.A. Res. 2749 (XXV).

(332) Paragraphs 1, 7, 8 and 9.

(333) In early sessions of the Law of the Sea Conference, the United States and U.S.S.R. resisted claims to "exclusive economic zones" of 200 miles.

Both superpowers have since accepted "resource zones" with limited coastal state sovereignty beyond 12 miles while maintaining their own claims to free passage for submarines and other military craft through and above these zones.

(334) A/C.2/SR.1649, pp. 7-8.

(335) TD/B/AC.12/2, p. 24.

(336) Ibid., p. 40.

(337) TD/B/AC.12/4, p. 20.

(338) A/9946, p. 13. The Group of 77 draft to the Second Committee. An amendment was offered at the meeting of the Second Committee which called for the insertion of the words "in accord with pertinent international norms, regulations and obligations" between the words "All states have" and "the responsibility" in the fourth sentence of Article 30. This Amendment was rejected. (A/9946, p. 23, para. 18 (k).)

(339) A/C.2/L.1414, in A/9946, p. 18.

(340) A/9946, p. 23, para. 18(k).

(341) Ibid., p. 25, para. 22.

(342) A/9946, pp. 25, 26, para. 22.

(343) Ibid.

(344) TD/B/AC.12/1, p.24.

(345) Ibid.

(346) TD/B/AC.12/R.17.

(347) TD/B/AC.12/4, pp. 20-22.

(348) Ibid., p. 21.

(349) Summary Records of meetings of the Second Committee, 18 September -11 December 1974, p. 383, para. 5.

(350) A/9946, p. 18, para. 6(1).

(351) Ibid., p. 23, para. 18(f). The vote was 97-15-10.

(352) Ibid., p. 14.

(353) Ibid., p. 20, para. 7.

(354) Ibid., p. 25, para. 22.

(355) Richard Lillich, "Economic Coercion and the 'New International Economic Order': A Second Look at Some First Impressions," Virginia Journal of International Law (Winter 1976), pp. 232, 235.

(356) Ibid.

(357) Reprinted in Legislation on Foreign Relations, Committee on Foreign Relations and Committee on Foreign Affairs, U.S. Congress.

(358) G.A. Resolution 2131 (XX) Declaration on the Admissability of Intervention into the Domestic Affairs of States (1965).

(359) G.A. Resolution 2625 (XXV) Declaration on Principles of International Law Concerning Friendly Relations and Cooperation Among States in Accordance with the Charter of the United Nations (1970).

(360) G.A. Resolution 3016 (XXVII) Permanent Sovereignty Over Natural Resources of Developing Countries (1972).

(361) Richard Lillich has edited a volume entitled, Economic Coercion and the New International Economic Order (Charlottesville, Virginia: Michie, 1976), which contains fifteen of the leading articles on this subject.

(362) Lillich, "Economic Coercion and the 'New International Economic Order'," op. cit., p. 235, fn. 9.

(363) Ibid., pp. 235, 236.

(364) "The New International Economic Order and the Charter of Economic Rights and Duties of States," International Lawyer, (1975), pp. 591, 597.

(365) Lillich, "Economic Coercion and the 'New International Economic Order,'" op. cit., pp. 232, 237.

(366) Ibid., p. 238.

(367) Ibid., p. 238, fn. 29.

(368) Ibid., p. 240.

(369) Ibid., p. 237, fn. 21.

(370) A/9946, p. 26, para. 22. The United Kingdom explained its abstention as flowing from the difficulties it saw in the Charter as a whole and to the attitude it had been constrained to adopt in the voting. For these reasons it had felt unable to endorse the reference in the second sentence of the paragraph to consideration of the implementation of the Charter. See Summary Records of the Second Committee (op. cit.), p. 454, para. 50.

(371) See for example J.L. Brierly, The Law of Nations (London: Oxford University Press, sixth edition 1963), p. 110; C. Parry, The Sources and Evidences of International Law (Manchester, England: Manchester University Press, 1965), pp. 19, et seq., 113; W. Friedmann, The Changing Structure of International Law (New York: Columbia University Press, 1964), pp. 135, et seq.; Max Sorenson (ed.), Manual of Public International Law (New York: St. Martin's Press, 1968), p. 157, et seq.; A.A. Fatouros, "The Participation of the 'New' States in the International Legal Order," in R. Falk and C. Black (eds.) The Future of the International Legal Order, Vol. I (Princeton, N.J.: Princeton University Press, 1969); J. Castañeda, Legal Effects of United Nations Resolutions (New York: Columbia University Press, 1969); R. Falk, "On the Quasi-Legislative Competence of the General Assembly," American Journal of International Law (October 1966), p. 782; R. Higgins, The Development of International Law Through the Political Organs of the United Nations (London: Oxford University Press, 1963); and W. Jenks, Law, Welfare and Freedom (New York: Oceana, 1963).

(372) Brierly, op. cit., p. 110.

(373) Parry, op. cit., pp. 19, et seq.

(374) B. Sloan, "The Binding Force of a Recommendation of the General Assembly of the United Nations," British Yearbook of International Law, XXV (London: Oxford University Press, 1948), p. 1.

(375) H. Kelsen, The Law of the United Nations (London: Stevens, 1950-51), p. 195.

(376) D. Johnson, "The Effect of Resolutions of the General Assembly," British Yearbook of International Law, XXXII (London: Oxford University Press, 1955-56), pp. 97, 121, 122.

(377) Parry, op.cit., p. 21.

(378) See C. Parry, op. cit.; W. Friedmann, op. cit.; W. Jenks, op. cit.; A.A. Fatouros, op. cit.; J. Castañeda, op. cit.; R. Higgins, op. cit., and R. Falk, op. cit. See also: S. Tiewul, "The United Nations Charter of Economic Rights and Duties of States," Journal of International Law and Economics (1975), p. 645; J. Dubitzky, "The General Assembly's International Economics," Harvard International Law Journal (1975), p. 670; J. Castañeda, "La Charte des Droits et Devoirs Economique des 'Etats,'" Annuaire Francais de Droit International, XX (1974), p. 31; "The UN Charter of Economic Rights and Duties of States Toward a New International Law of Welfare?" The Record (Association of The Bar of the City of New York, May/June 1975), p. 409.

(379) Falk, op. cit., p. 785.

(380) UN Document, TD/B/AC.12/p. 4 at 2.

(381) UN Document, TD/B/AC.12/2, note 25 at p. 3.

(382) J. Castañeda, "La Charte des Droits et Devoir Economique des Etats," op. cit., p. 35.

(383) UN Document, A/9946, p. 20, paragraph 8(a).

(384) Ibid., p. 19, paragraph 7(a).

(385) Ibid., p. 20, paragraph 8(a).

(386) UN Document, TD/B/AC., 12/3, Annex II, shows the early proposals to include a Chapter IV on implementation and dispute settlement and a Chapter V on final provisions, including a provision on adherence. Both of these provisions were dropped by the Fourth session of the Working Group, and the remaining provisions were merged in a new Chapter IV.

(387) C.N. Brower and J.B. Tepe, Jr., "The Charter of Economic Rights and Duties of States: A Reflection or Rejection of International Law?" International Lawyer, (1973), p. 295.

(388) G. Feuer, "Reflexions Sur La Charte des Droits et Devoirs Economique des Etats," Revue Generale de Droit International Public (April/June 1975), p. 274.

(389) J. Castañeda, "La Charte des Droits et Devoirs Economique des Etats," op. cit.

(390) J. Castañeda, Legal Effects of United Nations Resolutions, op. cit.

(391) J. Castañeda, "La Chart des Droits et Devoirs Economique des Etats," op. cit., at p. 39.

(392) Ibid.

(393) Ibid.

(394) J. Dubitzky, "The General Assembly's International Economics," op. cit.

(395) Ibid., p. 675, footnote 31, where he cites Judge Tanaka's opinion in the South-West Africa Cases, (Ethiopia v. S. Africa, Liberia v. S. Africa), second phase (1966), I.C.J.,6,292. He states that Tanaka "does not maintain that UN resolutions are legislation but only that they evidence which norms are customary in international practice, and Tanaka's opinion stresses that resolutions must be repeated to have such significance."

(396) Ibid.

(397) S. Tiewul, "The United Nations Charter of Economic Rights and Duties of States," op. cit.

(398) Subsequent to the time period covered by this book an important arbitration award was made which included a discussion on the legal effect of United Nations resolutions.

In the Libyan Award (Award on the Merits in Dispute between Texaco Overseas Petroleum Company/California Asiatic Oil Company and the Government of the Libyan Arab Republic (compensation for Nationalized Property). International Legal Materials (January 1978), p. 9. See in particular pp. 27-31), following the nationalization of various foreign assets, Professor Dupuy (the arbitrator) discusses and compares the legal effect of various United Nations resolutions concerned with nationalization and compensation of foreign owned assets. Utilizing the dual standard of the basis of circumstances under which they were adopted and by analysis of the principles which they state he concludes that Resolution 1803 (XVII) of 1962 reflects the state of existing customary law. He bases this decision on "consensus by a majority of states belonging to the various representative groups" which differentiates the 1962 resolution from the Charter where most of the market economy states opposed Article 2. Thus Professor Dupuy has opened a "back door" entry for the principle of consensus provided a majority of states belonging to the various representative groups concur.

This important opinion deserves more extensive treatment than is possible here. The author intends to prepare a comment on this ruling in the near future.

Chapter 4

(1) The principal forums were the United Nations Conference on Trade and Development, the General Assembly of the United Nations, the United Nations Industrial Development Organization, the UN Specialized Agencies, the UN Regional Economic Commissions and Regional Development Banks, the meetings of the Non-Aligned States, Commonwealth meetings, and ad hoc meetings such as the Conference of Developing Countries on Raw Materials (February 3-8, 1975), the Third World Forum, and meeting of Third World economists.

(2) The Seventh Special Session met at the United Nations in New York from September 1 - 16, 1975. The Conference on International Economic Cooperation (CIEC) began in Paris on December 16, 1975 and ended on June 2, 1977. UNCTAD IV took place in Nairobi, Kenya, May 5-31, 1976.

(3) New York Times, October 25, 1974, p. 1.

(4) Ibid.

(5) E/AC.62/6, April 15, 1975, p. 31.

(6) OPEC Annual Review and Record 1975, p. 61.

(7) Ibid., p. 65.

(8) New York Times, April 8, 1975, p. 49.

(9) Ibid., p. 51.

(10) Ibid.

(11) New York Times, April 17, 1975, p. 57.

(12) Ibid.; and B. Gosovic and J. Ruggie, "On the Creation of a New International Economic order: Issue Linkage and the Seventh Special Session of the UN General Assembly," International Organization, (Spring 1976), p. 318.

(13) See p. 3.

(14) For example, see Report by Congressional Advisors to UNCTAD IV, 94th Congress, 2nd Session, July 21, 1976, pp. 1, 2. See also letter dated May 23, 1975, to Secretary of State Kissinger, signed by 12 U.S. Senators on the Senate Foreign Relations Committee, expressing "deep concern over the current stage of U.S. preparations for the United Nations Seventh Special Session."

(15) Ibid.

(16) Ibid.

(17) Ibid.

(18) Ibid.

(19) Issues at the Special Session of the 1975 U.N. General Assembly Hearings before the Subcommittee on International Organizations of the

Committee on International Relations, House of Representatives, 94th Congress, 1st Session, May 19, 21, and July 8, 1975.

(20) Ibid., pp. 53, 98.

(21) Ibid., p. 53, 61.

(22) Ibid., p. 100.

(23) Ibid., p. 98.

(24) Ibid., p. 86-120.

(25) Ibid., p. 231. The speech is an Appendix to the Hearings.

(26) Report by Congressional Advisors to the Seventh Special Session of The United Nations' Committee on International Relations, U.S. House of Representatives and Committee on Foreign Relations, U.S. Senate, October 13, 1975. The Speech is included in an Appendix to the Report.

(27) Mimeograph speech of Mr. Mariano Rumor, Minister of Foreign Affairs of Italy, President of the Council of the European Communities, September 1, 1975.

(28) Ibid., p. IX. (Those parts of the speech paginated by Roman numerals were on behalf of the EEC.)

(29) Ibid., p. XIII.

(30) Ibid.

(31) Statement by Y. A. Malik, Chairman of the Delegation of the USSR, at the Plenary meeting of the Seventh Special Session of the United Nations General Assembly Devoted to Development and International Economic Cooperation, September 3, 1975. (mimeographed copy) p. 6.

(32) Report of the Preparatory Committee on its Third Session, E/5749, August 29, 1975, p. 3 and Annex I. See also working paper No. 1, September 4, 1975, and Add. 1, September 11, 1975, of the Ad Hoc Committee of the Seventh Special Session.

(33) See B. Gosovic and J. Ruggie, op. cit., p. 322, and footnote 30.

(34) B. Gosovic and J. Ruggie, op. cit., p. 322.

(35) Ibid., p. 321-324, and footnotes 26, 34. See Also E/AC.62/L15, August 28, 1975,   Annex V, a paper presented by the United States on "The World Food Problem," pp. 25-28. The issues and background are summarized in the U.N. publication, The Seventh Special Session of the General Assembly: issues and background, 1975.

(36) A New United Nations Structure for Global Economic Cooperation, E/AC.62/9 (1975).

(37) B. Gosovic and J. Ruggie, op. cit., p. 327.

(38) Ibid., p. 325.

(39) UNGA Resolution 3362 (S-VII). See also Report by Congressional Advisors to the Seventh Special Session of The United Nations, op. cit.; New York Times, September 17, 1975, p. 1; and September 19, 1975, p. 1.

(40) B. Gosovic and J. Ruggie, op. cit., p. 327.

(41) Ibid., p. 342.

(42) Ibid., p. 343.

(43) North - South Dialogue, report of a Staff Study Mission to The Conference on International Economic Cooperation held in Paris, December 16-19, 1975. (February 9, 1976). The Memorandum is printed as Annex I.

(44) Ibid., p. 7.

(45) Ibid., pp. 7 - 9.

(46) Ibid., p. 6.

(47) Ibid., p. 6. See also New York Times, October 17, 1975, p. 6.

(48) Ibid., p. 9.

(49) Ibid., p. 8.

(50) Ibid., p. 9.

(51) New York Times, November 27, 1975, p. 55.

(52) New York Times, December 14, 1975, p. 20.

(53) The United States, United Kingdom, Federal Republic of Germany, France, Japan, Italy, Netherlands, Belgium, Luxembourg, Ireland, Denmark, Canada, Sweden, Switzerland, Australia, and Spain.

(54) See Appendix B, p. 417.

(55) See Appendix B, p. 420.

(56) Conference on International Economic Cooperation - Ministerial Conference, (Paris, December 16-19, 1975), Final Communique, CCEI-CM4, December 19, 1975, p. 2, para. 3.

(57) Ibid., p. 3, para. 7.

(58) Report on the First Session of The Commission (Paris, February 11-20, 1975) unofficial document prepared by the U.N. Secretariat Representation office in Paris, p. 1.

(59) Ibid., pp. 2, 3.

(60) Ibid., pp. 3, 4.

(61) Ibid., pp. 4, 5.

(62) Ibid., pp. 5, 6.

(63) Proceedings of the United Nations Conference on Trade and Development IV TD/218 (1977).

(64) Evaluation of the Fourth Session of the United Nations Conference on Trade and Development, TD/216, September 14, 1976, p. 2, paragraph 7.

(65) Proceedings, UNCTAD II op. cit., p. 13.

(66) Proceedings, UNCTAD IV op. cit., p. 3, para. 4.

(67) Manila Declaration and Programme of Action, February 12, 1976, TD/195.

(68) Ibid., p. 1. The nine areas were: commodities; manufactures and semi-manufactures; multilateral trade negotiations; money and finance and the transfer of real resources for development; transfer of technology; least developed among the developing countries, developing island countries, and developing land-locked countries; economic cooperation among developing countries; trade relations among countries having different economic and social systems; review of the institutional arrangements in UNCTAD.

(69) Proceedings, op. cit., p. 3, paragraphs 5, 6.

(70) Report by Congressional Advisers to UNCTAD IV, 94th Congress, 2nd Session, July 21, 1976, p. 4.

(71) Ibid., p. 5.

(72) Evaluation of the Fourth Session, op. cit., p. 3.

(73) For its history see, An Integrated Programme for Commodities, TD/B/C.1/166, December 9, 1974.

(74) See footnote 26.

(75) Proceedings, op. cit., Resolution Vol. I, 93 (IV), May 30, 1976. See also An Integrated Programme for Commodities, TD/B/C.1/193, October 28, 1975, and Report of the Ad Hoc Intergovernmental Committee for the Integrated Programme for Commodities on its Third Session, TD/B/IPC/AC/11, July 29, 1977.

(76) Proceedings, op cit., Vol. I, Resolution 93 (IV), p. 7, II, Commodity Coverage includes: bananas, bauxite, cocoa, coffee, copper, cotton, and cotton yarns, hard fibres and products, iron ore, jute products, manganese, meat, phosphates, rubber, sugar, tea, Tropical timber, tin, and vegetable oils, including olive oil and oil seeds. The number of products has varied considerably: in TD/B/C.1/166, it was 19; and TD/B/C.1/194, it was 17 commoditites; and TD/B/C.1/184, speaks of 10 "core" commodities, see Table 1 in TD/B/C.1/194, for a listing of the 17, and the 10.

(77) The Role of International Commodity stocks, TD/B/C.1/166 Supplement 1, December 12, 1974; and International Arrangements for Individual Commodities within an Integrated Programme, TD/B/C.1/188, July 8, 1975.

(78) The Role of Multilateral Commitments in International Commodity Trade, C.A. Blyth, TD/B/C/186, June 20, 1975. For an earlier report on the same subject see TD/B/C.1/166 Supplement 3, December 13, 1974.

(79) Elements of an Agreement on a Common Fund, TD/IBC/CF/con-
ference/3, February 22, 1977; A Common Fund for the Financing of
Commodity stocks: Amounts, Terms and Prospective Source of Finance,
TD/B/C.1/184, June 24, 1975; Consideration of Issues Relating to The
Establishment and Operation of a Common Fund, TD/B/IPC/CF 2,
November 10, 1976; and A Common Fund for the Financing of Commodity
Stocks; Suitability for Stocking of Individual Commodities, Country
Contributions and Burden Sharing, and Some Operating Principles,
TD/B/C.1/196, October 6, 1975.

(80) Ibid.

(81) Compensatory Financing of Export Fluctuations, TD/B/C.1/195, October
16, 1975; see also TD/B/C.1/199, November 10, 1975; TD/B/C.1/166/
Supplement 4, December 13, 1974; R.F. Meagher, "The Expansion and
Modification of the IMF's Compensatory Finance Facility," International
Lawyer (1977) p. 277; and Guy Erb, North-South Negotiations, and
Compensatory Financing, Overseas Development Council, Washington,
D.C., June 9, 1977.

(82) See p. 126.

(83) See items cited in footnote 80.

(84) TD/B/IPC/CF/2, November 10, 1976, p. 6.

(85) The Times (London), May 28, 1976.

(86) Proceedings, UNCTAD IV, op. cit., Vol. I, p. 7.

(87) Proceedings, UNCTAD IV, op. cit., Vol. I, p. 7.

(88) Ibid.

(89) Ibid., Under International Measures of the Programme, 2.

(90) Ibid., p. 8, 2. (a)-(j).

(91) Ibid., p. 8, para. 3 of III.

(92) Ibid., p. 8, IV, Procedures and Timetable.

(93) Ibid.

(94) TD/B/C.1/166, December 9, 1974.

(95) Proceedings, UNCTAD IV, Vol. I, p. 7, III 1.

(96) Ibid., p. 8 IV, 4.

(97) Report by Congressional Advisors to UNCTAD, op. cit., p. 6.

(98) Manila Declaration, op. cit., p. 22.

(99) World Debt Tables, Vol. I, (World Bank EC - 167/77, September 2, 1977),
p. 40. For a sophisticated statement of the debt problem see A. Fishlow,
"Debt Remains a Problem," Foreign Policy No. 28, p. 133 (1977).

(100) Ibid., p. 22, para. 3.

(101) Ibid.

(102) Ibid.

(103) Ibid., p. 22, paragraph 4.

(104) The Regional Development Banks also have differentiated funds for "hard" and "soft" lending. See Annual Reports of the Inter-American Bank, The Asian Development Bank, and The Africa Development Bank.

(105) Manila Declaration, op. cit., p. 23, para. 6.

(106) Proceedings, UNCTAD IV, op. cit., Vol. I, p. 60, para. 116.

(107) Ibid., p. 16, resolution 94 (IV).

(108) Proceedings, UNCTAD I, Vol. I, (U.N. publication, Sales No. 64-II-B-11, 1964), Annex A.-IV-26, para. 3.

(109) The Possibility and Feasibility of an International Code of Conduct on Transfer of Technology, TD/B/AC/11/22, June 6, 1974, p. 26.

(110) Proceedings, UNCTAD III, Vol. I, TD/180, p. 108, (1972).

(111) Ibid., p. 110.

(112) Ibid., p. 111.

(113) Report of the Committee on Transfer of Technology on its first session, TD/B/593, (1976), p. 1.

(114) Ibid., p. 12, para. 84.

(115) Manila Declaration, op. cit., pp 31-35.

(116) Ibid., pp. 31, 32.

(117) Ibid., pp. 32, 33.

(118) Ibid., p. 33.

(119) See An International Code of Conduct on Transfer of Technology, TD/B/C.6/AC. 1/2/ Supplement 1/Rev. 1, p. 1, (1975), for a listing of previous resolutions and actions relating to a Code of Conduct. See also footnote 112.

(120) Manila Declaration, op. cit., p. 34, para. 12.

(121) Ibid.

(122) Ibid., p. 34.

(123) Ibid., p. 34.

(124) Ibid., p. 34.

(125) Proceedings, UNCTAD IV, op. cit., Vol. I, pp. 17, 21, 22.

(126) Ibid., p. 17, Resolution 87 (IV), strengthening the Technological Capacity of Developing Countries.

(127) Report by Congressional Advisors to UNCTAD IV, op. cit., p. 197.

(128) Proceedings, UNCTAD IV, op. cit., Vol. I, Resolution 88 (IV).

(129) Ibid., p. 22, Resolution 89 (IV).

(130) Ibid., p. 13, Resolution 97 (IV).

(131) Ibid., p. 56, para. 77.

(132) Ibid., p. 55, paragraphs 73, 75.

(133) Ibid., p. 57, para. 86.

(134) Ibid., p. 58, para. 90.

(135) Ibid., p. 53-54.

(136) Report by Congressional Advisor to UNCTAD IV, p. 84 at 90-91.

(137) Proceedings, UNCTAD IV, op. cit., Vol. I, p. 54, para. 55.

(138) Minerals and Energy in The Developing Countries, (World Bank, Report No. 1588, May 4, 1977), Annex B contains a Summary and Analysis of the Proposal. See also Business Week, April 26, 1976, p. 32 for a Summary of the Proposal.

(139) Proceedings, UNCTAD IV, Vol. I, op. cit., p. 53, paragraphs 46-54.

(140) Report by Congressional Advisors to UNCTAD IV, pp. 6, 7.

(141) Ibid., p. 7.

(142) New York Times, July 19, 1976, p. 1.

(143) Congressional Advisors Report of The Conference on International Economic Cooperation 95th Congress, 1st Session, Document No. 95-61, August 1977, pp. 30-32, where Richard Cooper, Under Secretary of State, points out the friction with U.S. participants at the July meeting.

(144) New York Times, September 11, 1976, p. 34.

(145) Congressional Advisors Report of The Conference on International Economic Cooperation, op. cit., p.3.

(146) Ibid., p. 22, reproduced as an Appendix.

(146a) Final Communique of the Conference on International Economic Cooperation, Paris, June 3, 1977.

(146b) Ibid.

(147) Report of The Second General Conference of the United Nations Industrial Development Organization. ID/Conference 3/31, May 9, 1975, p. 44. Reprinted by The United Nations A/10112, June 13, 1975. (Hereinafter referred to as Lima Declaration.)

(148) Distributed to The Preparatory Committee for the Seventh Special Session of the U.N. General Assembly as E/AC. 62/4, April 15, 1975.

(149) Lima Declaration, op. cit., para. 28.

(150) Ibid., p. 1, para. 69.

(151) Ibid., para. 29-57.

(152) Ibid., p. 52, The Plan of Action.

(153) Ibid., para. 47.

(154) Ibid., para. 68.

(155) Draft Constitution of a Specialized Agency for Industrial Development, A/10202, August 20, 1975, p. 9, para. 3.

(156) Economic and Social Council, 59th Session, E/5711.

(157) Ibid. Resolution, 1953 (LIX), July 25, 1975.

(158) Lima Declaration, op. cit., paragraphs 72, 73.

(159) Annual Report of The World Bank, 1976, p. 150.

(160) Annual Report of The Executive Director, 1974 (UNIDO).

(161) Annual Report of The Executive Director, 1973 (UNIDO), pp. 190, 191.

(162) "Lomé Dossier," The Courier (European Community) No. 31, March 1975, reprints the Lomé Convention, explanation, summaries and background to the negotiations.

(163) Belgium, Denmark, France, Federal Republic of Germany, Ireland, Italy, Luxembourg, Netherlands, United Kingdom.

(164) See Appendix B for a list of the ACP States.

(165) See Treaty of Rome, signed on March 25, 1957, and entered into force on January 1, 1958, establishing The European Economic Community.

(166) See Treaty of Accession in Command, 4862 I and II, signed in Brussels on January 22, 1972, and subsequently ratified.

(167) The following Commonwealth Countries became ACP States: Bahamas, Barbados, Botswana, Fiji, Gambia, Ghana, Grenada, Guyana, Jamaica, Kenya, Lesotho, Malawi, Nigeria, Sierra Leone, Swaziland, Tanzania, Tonga, Trinidad and Tobago, Uganda, Western Samoa, Zambia.

(168) Liberia, Sudan, Ethiopia, Guinea, Equitorian Guinea, and Guinea-Bissau.

(169) Lomé Dossier, op. cit., Title II of The Convention entitled: Export Earnings from Commodities, see also p. 24-28, for an explanation of STABEX.

(170) I. Gruhn, The Lomé Convention Inching Towards Independence," International Organization , (Spring 1976) p. 249. See also I.W. Zartman "Europe and Africa: Decolonisation or Dependency," Foreign Affairs, (January 1976), p. 325.

(171) "Help for the Raw Materials Producers," Dun's Review, April 1976.

(172) David Wall, The European Community's Lomé Convention: "STABEX" and The Third World's Aspirations, (Trade Policy Research Centre, London, Guest Paper No. 4, 1975).

(173) European Development Aid, (EEC), p. 8.

(174) W. Friedmann, G. Kalmanoff, and R. Meagher, International Financial Aid (New York: Columbia University Press, 1966), p. 125-31.

(175) Information Memo, p. 13, (Commission of The European Communities, February 1975).

(176) See Footnote 165.

(177) First Yaoundé Convention, op. cit., Title I, Article 3.2.

(178) See for example: R.F. Meagher, Public International Development Financing in Senegal (Columbia University Law School Monograph, 1963).

(179) Ibid.

(180) Yaoundé I, Title III, Article 17.

(181) Ibid, Articles 20 and 17 (4).

(182) Ibid., Article 16(a).

(183) Ibid., Article 16(b), and Protocol 5.

(184) Ibid., Title III.

(185) Yaoundé II, Title II, Article 18(a).

(186) Ibid., Article 18(b).

(187) David Wall, op.cit., p. 4.

(188) Ibid.

(189) For example, the author lived in Senegal from 1962 to mid-1963 when virtually all foreign products were French. In subsequent years he found the stores had many products from EEC countries other than France.

(190) Treaty of Accession, Volume I, op. cit.,, Annex VI, p. 69.

(191) European Development Aid, op. cit., p. 12.

(192) Treaty of Accession, op. cit., Protocol No. 22, p. 98. See also Gruhn, op. cit., pp. 244-245.

(193) Treaty of Accession, op. cit., Protocol No. 22, p. 99.

(194) These countries were not seen as being on the same footing as other ACP states.

(195) Treaty of Accession, op. cit., p. 117.

(196) Burundi, Cameroon, Central African Empire, Chad, Congo, Dahomey, Gabon, Ivory Coast, Madagascar, Mali, Mauritania, Mauritius, Niger, Rwanda, Senegal, Somalia, Togo, Upper Volta, and Zaire.

(197) See footnote 166.

(198) Gruhn, op. cit., p. 251.

(199) Ibid., p. 252.

(200) Ibid.

(201) Ibid., p. 253.

(202) Ibid.

(203) Ibid.

(204) Ibid., p. 259.

(205) Ibid., p. 260.

(206) Ibid.

(207) Ibid.

(208) Ibid., p. 248.

(209) "Lomé Dossier," op. cit., Chapter 1, Article 2, para. 1 of Title 1. See also Wall, op. cit., pp. 8-9.

(210) See Chapter 5, pp. 303 et. seq., for a discussion of STABEX and a comparison of it with the IMF's Compensatory Financing Scheme.

(211) "Lomé Dossier," op. cit., Title IV, Article 42, p. 13 of The Lomé Convention.

(212) ODI Briefing Paper - The Lomé Convention, (Overseas Development Institution, London, October 1975), p. 6.

(213) Gruhn, p. 257.

(214) "Lomé Dossier," op. cit., Title IV, Article 42.1(a) and (b).

(215) Ibid., Article 42.2.

(216) Ibid., Article 48.

(217) Ibid., Article 47.2.

(218) Ibid., Article 50-55.

Chapter 5

(1) "Lomé Dossier," op. cit., p. 23. The principle of non-reciprocity.

(2) Lomé Convention, Title II, Chapter 2 and Protocol No. 3.

(3) Export Earnings, Fluctuations and Economic Development: An Analysis of Compensating Financing Schemes (A.I.D. Discussion Paper No. 32, Bureau for Program and Policy Coordination, 1975), p. 6.

(4) Compensating Financing of Export Fluctuations, a second report by the International Monetary Fund (no date).

(5) Decision No. 1477 - (6318) of the IMF Executive Directors, adopted February 27, 1963.

(6) The Fund does not use the words loans or repayments in relation to the facility because when a member uses the fund's resources the member pays an equivalent amount of its own currency for the currency it receives. See Gold, J. The Stand-By Agreements of the International Monetary Fund, (IMF, 1970), p. 8.

(7) Compensatory Financing of Export Fluctuations, op. cit., p. 3.

(8) Proceedings of the United Nations Conference on Trade and Development, E/Conf. 46/141, Vol. I (1964). Resolution A.IV.17 (herein cited as Proceedings).

(9) Proceedings, Resolution A.IV.18, op. cit.

(10) Compensatory Financing of Export Fluctuations, op. cit., p. 2.

(11) Decision No. 2192 - (66/81) of the IMF Executive Directors, adopted September 20, 1966.

(12) Compensatory Financing of Export Fluctuations, op. cit., pp. 12, 13.

(13) TD/97, Vol. 1 (1968), p. 431 et seq.

(14) Ibid., pp. 43, 290.

(15) Ibid., p. 290.

(16) Compensatory Financing of Export Fluctuations, op. cit., pp. 8-12, 27.

(17) Proceedings of the United Nations Conference on Trade and Development, third session TD/180, Vol. 1 (1972), Resolution 54(III), p. 79.

(18) A/Res/3201 (S-VI), May 9, 1974.

(19) A/Res/3202(S-VI), May 16, 1974.

(20) TD/B/C.1/166 and Supps. 1, 2, 3, 4, 5.

(21) TD/B/C.1/166.

(22) Ibid.

(23) Ibid.

(24) The Courier-No. 31, Special Issue March 1975. This issue contains the text of the Convention as well as articles on the negotiations. For a critical view of STABEX see Wall, David, The European Community's Lomé Convention: STABEX and the Third World's Aspirations (London: Trade Policy Research Center, 1976).

(25) For a listing of the 32 least developed, landlocked or island ACP states see Ibid., Article 24.

(26) The unit of account of the European Communities was converted to U.S. dollars at the rate of E.U.A. 1.00 = $1.10188, the exchange rate applied on the date STABEX announced transfers for 1976.

(27) A/Res/3362 (S-VII), September 19, 1975.

(28) United States Proposals for Stabilizing Export Earnings of Developing Countries, September 12, 1975.

(29) IMF Survey, Vol. 21, No. 27, July 11, 1969, p. 213 and Vol. 22, No. 48, December 4, 1970, p. 393.

(30) Press Release No. 75/65 of the IMF dated December 29, 1975 and the attachment which is the 1975 decision.

(31) G. Erb, North-South Negotiations and Compensatory Financing (Washington, D.C.: Overseas Development Council, mimeographed, June 8, 1977), p. 16.

(32) L. Goreux, Compensatory Financing of Export Fluctuations: Application of the 1975 Decision, Appendix II, p. 10, IMF, 1976.

(33) See Press Release No. 76/1 of the IMF dated January 8, 1976.

(34) The text of the decision and instrument to establish the Trust Fund has been reproduced in IMF Survey, Vol. 5, No. 10, May 17, 1976, p. 147 et seq. See also "The Trust Fund" by Ernest Sturc in Finance and Development, Vol. 13, No. 4, December 1976, p. 30 et seq.

(35) IMF Survey, Vol. 7, No. 2, January 23, 1978, p. 25.

(36) IMF Survey, Vol. 5, No. 15, August 1, 1977, p. 251.

(37) IMF Survey, Vol. 6, No. 5, March 7, 1977, p. 66.

(38) Ibid.

(39) Ibid.

(40) Ibid.

(41) Guy Erb, North-South Negotiations and Compensatory Financing, op. cit., p. 25.

(42) Ibid.

(43) G. Erb, North-South Negotiations and Compensatory Financing, op. cit., J.D.A. Cuddy, "STABEX: How Good a Model for International Relations." (Geneva: unpublished, 1976). David Wall, The European Community's Lomé Convention, Guest Paper No. 4 (London: Trade Policy Research Centre, 1976).

(44) G. Erb, North-South Negotiations and Compensatory Financing, op. cit., p. 16.

(45) An interest subsidy account was established to administer contributions by a number of members to reduce the effective cost of the 1975 oil facility of the IMF for those developing member countries designated by the United Nations "most seriously affected." Finance and Development, Vol. 13, No. 2, June 1976, pp. 6, 7.

(46) See Chapter III.

(47) Report of the World Food Conference (E/Conf.65/20, 1974).

(48) Ibid., Resolution XIII.

(49) Ibid.

(50) The three developed countries were Australia, Netherlands and New Zealand.

(51) See Footnote 48.

(52) See Chapter I supra for a discussion of the confrontation between the developing countries and the developed countries.

(53) UNGA Resolution 3348(XXIX), December 17, 1974.

(54) Report of the Preparatory Commission to the Governing Council and the Executive Board, IFAD/PC/13, October 28, 1977, p. 1.

(55) "Global Consensus and Economic Development," address by Hon. Henry Kissinger, Secretary of State of the United States, before the Seventh Special Session of the United Nations General Assembly, New York City, September 1, 1975.

(56) UNGA Resolution 3503(XXX), December 15, 1975.

(57) Report of the Preparatory Commission, op. cit., p. 1.

(58) IFAD - Draft Cooperation Agreement (International Bank for Recon- struction and Development - Sec M77-538, June 29, 1977), p. 1.

(59) R. Michael Gadbaw, "Report on the International Fund for Agricultural Development." Unpublished report prepared for the American Bar Association's Committee on International Economic Organizations. Mr. Gadbaw attended the meetings on the establishment of IFAD on behalf of the United States Treasury Department.

(60) Report of the Preparatory Commission, op. cit., pp. 6, 8. On page 8, paragraph 45, reference is made to "arrangements with other agencies to carry out operations on behalf of the Fund."

(61) Agreement Establishing the International Fund for Agricultural Develop- ment (herein referred to as "Agreement"), A/Conf.73/15, August 4, 1976. The Pledges are found in an Addendum A/Conf.73/15/Add.1/Rev.2, January 14, 1977. The actual amount is SDRs 884853780 (Equivalent of U.S. $1,011,776,023 valued as of June 10, 1976).

(62) Agreement, op. cit., Article 3, Section 3 and Schedule I.

(63) Agreement, op. cit., Article 7, Section 2.

(64) Agreement, op. cit., Article 4.

(65) Agreement, op. cit., Article 6.

(66) Ibid.

(67) Ibid.

(68) Ibid., Sections 3 (Governing Council) and 6 (Executive Board).

(69) Agreement, op. cit., Schedule I, Part I: Category IA.

(70) Ibid. See also Report of the Meeting of Interested Countries to the Secretary-General on its Third Session (Rome, January 28-February 6, 1976), (IFAD/CRP.21) at 10.

(71) Agreement, op. cit., Article 6, Section 3.

(72) Agreement, op. cit., Article 6, Section 6.

(73) Agreement, op. cit., Article 7, Section 2(e) and (g).

(74) Ibid.

(75) Gadbow, op. cit., pp. 19, 20.

(76) Governing Committee of the OPEC Special Fund, Resolution No. 4, May 11, 1976.

(77) Gadbow, op. cit., p. 23.

(78) Ibid.

(79) Both Venezuela and Norway requested that contributions made by them ($10 million and $9.98 million respectively) be returned to them so that they could transfer them to IFAD. The General Assembly approved the request at its 101st Plenary Meeting on December 16, 1976. (A/31/443).

(80) Final Act, A/Conf./73/18, June 21, 1976. See the resolution attached to the Final Act.

(81) IFAD - Draft Cooperation Agreement, op. cit., p. 2.

Chapter 6

(1) W. Friedmann and G. Kalmanoff (eds.), Joint International Business Ventures, (New York: Columbia University Press, 1961) and W. Friedmann and J.P. Beguin (eds.), Joint International Business Ventures in Developing Countries, (New York: Columbia University Press, 1971).

(2) For a discussion of this article see p. 101 et seq supra.

(3) W. Friedmann and R.C. Pugh, Legal Aspects of Foreign Investment, (New York: Columbia University Press, 1959); E.I. Nwogugu, The Legal Problems of Foreign Investment in Developing Countries, (Manchester, Eng.: Manchester University Press, 1965, Chapter II.

(4) The most comprehensive regional scheme is that of the Andean Pact Countries. Many of the underlying agreements have been reproduced in International Legal Materials (ILM): "Agreement on Andean Subregional Integration," 8 ILM 910 1969; "Aggreement Establishing the Andean Development Corporation," 8 ILM 940 1969; "Andean Commission: Decision Concerning Treatment of Foreign Capital," 10 ILM 152 1971; "Codified Text of the Andean Foreign Code," 16 ILM 138 1977. See also A. Zamora, "Andean Common Market-Regulation of Foreign Investments: Blueprint for the Future?" International Lawyer (1976) p. 153; Darrel Dudley, The Andean Integration Movement: An Appraisal, (U.S. Department of State, External Research Program, September 1, 1975); Andean Pact: Definition, Design and Analysis (Council of the Americas, November 1973); Covey Oliver "The Andean Foreign Investment Code: A New Phase in the Quest for Normative Order as to Direct Foreign Investment" American Journal of International Law (1972) p. 763; S. Holland and E. Ferrer (eds.), Changing Legal Environment in Latin America: Management Implications, Vol. II, (Council of the Americas, May 1975).

(5) Aspects of International Investment, U.S. Department of Commerce (a selection of articles from the Survey of Current Business of February, August, and October 1977), pp. 33, 34.

(6) Ibid., p. 33.

(7) UNGA Resolution 626(VII), December 21, 1952.

(8) See above.

(9) United Nations General Assembly, Document A/9716, 20 September 1974, Annex, p. 2, Table 1.

(10) Permanent Sovereignty over Natural Resources, A/9716, 20 September 1974, Annex, p. 6, Table 2.

(11) Ibid.

(12) Ibid.

(13) Ibid., Annex, p. 5.

(14) Ibid., Annex, p. 13.

(15) Ibid.

(16) Ibid., Annex, p. 9.

(17) Ibid., p. 4 of seq.

(18) Theodore Moran, "The Evolution of Concession Agreements in Under-developed Countries and the United States National Interest," Vanderbilt Journal of Transnational Law, No. 2 (Spring 1974); and Louis Wells, Jr., "Evolution of Concession Agreements," Economic Development Report No. 117 (Center for International Affairs, Harvard University, September 1968).

(19) Reprinted in J.C. Hurewitz (ed.) Diplomacy in the Near and Middle East, Vol. I. Document No. 102 (New York: D. Van Nostrand, 1956).

(20) Louis Wells, op. cit.

(21) See for example "The Group (Red Line) Agreement of the Turkish (Iraq) Petroleum Company," 31 July 1928 reprinted in J.C. Hurewitz, op. cit. Vol. II, Document 54, and the Achnacarry Agreement, September 17, 1928 discussed in detail in John Blair, The Control of Oil, (New York: Pantheon: 1976). Blair also discusses other collusive efforts in Chapters 2 and 3. The Achnacarry Agreement is also discussed in The International Petroleum Cartel, a staff report to the Federal Trade Commission submitted to the Subcommittee on Monopoly of the Select Committee of Small Business, U.S. Senate, 82nd Congress, 2nd Session, August 22, 1952, p. 199 et seq.

(22) Compare for example the D'Arcy Concession (Footnote 19 supra) with the Turkish Petroleum Concession in Iraq, March 14, 1925, reprinted in J.C. Hurewitz, op. cit., Vol. II, Document No. 44.

(23) Luis Vallenilla, Oil: The Making of a New Economic Order - Venezuelan Oil and OPEC, (New York: McGraw-Hill, 1975), p. 67 et seq.

(24) The Iran-Consortium Agreement: September 19-20, 1954, reprinted in J.C. Hurewitz, op. cit., Vol. II, Document No. 104.

(25) James Hyde, "Economic Development Agreements," Recueil des Cours (Leyden: Sijthoff 1962). See also D. Smith and L. Wells, Negotiating Third World Mineral Agreements (Cambridge, Mass.: Ballinger 1975), Chapter 2, where it is argued that change in structure is not necessarily advantageous to host countries.

(26) The most recent book on OPEC is D. Rustow and J. Mugno, OPEC: Success and Prospects, (New York: New York University Press, 1976), Chapter 1.

(27) Ibid., p. 7.

(28) Ibid., Appendix C, p. 166 et seq.

(29) Seijiro Matsumura, "'Participation Policy' of the Producing Countries in the International Oil Industry," The Developing Economies (March 1972), p. 36 et seq.

(30) Ibid., p. 34.

(31) All of the data in this paragraph is from Permanent Sovereignty over Natural Resources, A/9716, 20 September 1974, pp. 4-7.

(32) Ibid., p. 4, para. 9.

(33) Ibid., p. 6. See Footnote 6.

(34) Z. Mikdashi, The International Politics of Natural Resources, (Ithaca, NY: Cornell University Press, 1976), pp. 110 et seq., gives a brief discussion of the origins and activities of the IBA. On page 113 he points out that Jamaica's taxes on bauxite production and alumina processing rose from $25 million to $200 million in 1974.

(35) E/C.7/53, p. 11, Table 1.

(36) A/9716, op. cit., p. 8.

(37) E/C.7/53, 31 January 1975. These events are summarized in paragraph 16 at pp. 6, 7.

(38) A/9716, op. cit., p. 10, para. 20.

(39) E/C.7/53, op. cit., p. 6, ftn. 6.

(40) Ibid., p. 10, para. 26.

(41) Conversation with Henri Guda, Secretary General of the International Bauxite Association.

(42) A/9716, op. cit., p. 10.

(43) Ibid. All of the data in the paragraph comes from this document.

(44) Ibid., Annex, p. 20, Table 12.

(45) "New Developments in Third World Mining Agreements," Natural Resources Forum (April 1977), p. 239.

(46) Ibid., p. 240.

(47) Ibid., p. 242.

(48) Ibid., p. 249.

(49) Both the introduction and abandonment of quotas is discussed in Permanent Sovereignty over Natural Resources, E/C.7/66, 17 March 1977, pp. 32, 33.

(50) A/9716, op. cit., p. 11, para. 11.

(51) E/C.7/53, op. cit., p. 13, para. 34.

(52) Ibid., p. 14.

(53) Ibid., p. 15.

(54) E/C.7/66, op. cit., p. 8, para. 11.

(55) See Footnote 3 of this chapter supra.

(56) R. Bosson and B. Varon, The Mining Industry and Developing Countries, (London: Oxford University Press, 1977), p. 17.

(57) E/C.7/66, op. cit.

(58) Ibid., p. 9, para. 16.

(59) Ibid., p. 9, para. 17.

(60) Ibid., p. 9, para. 18.

(61) Ibid., p. 10, para. 19.

(62) Ibid.

(63) Ibid., p. 11.

(64) Ibid., p. 12.

(65) Ibid., p. 13, para. 30.

(66) Ibid., p. 13.

(67) The Impact of Multinational Corporations on Development and on International Relations, E/5500/Rev.1, 1974.

(68) UNGA Resolution 1913(LVII), November 1974.

(69) K. Takeuchi, G. Thiebach and J. Hilmy, "Investment Requirements in the Non-Fuel Mineral Sector in the Developing Countries," Natural Resources Forum (April 1977), p. 267.

(70) Ibid., p. 268.

(71) Ibid.

(72) J. Shaw, "Investment in the Copper Industry: Needs and Policies," Natural Resource Forum (January 1978), p. 115.   See also S. Zorn, "The United Nations Panel on International Mining Finance," Natural Resources Forum (April 1978), p. 294.

(73) S. Zorn, "New Developments in Third World Mining Agreements," Natural Resources Forum (April 1977), pp. 248, 249.

(74) The Economist, September 16-22, 1978, p. 82.

(75) E/C.7/68, op. cit., p. 34, paragraph 99. Z. Mikdashi, The International Politics of Natural Resources (Ithaca, NY: Cornell University Press, 1976) discusses these schemes at p. 142 et seq. See also A.A. Fatouros, Government Guarantees to Foreign Investors (New York: Columbia University Press, 1962); and M.N. Whitman, Government Risk-Sharing in Foreign Investment (Princeton, N.J.: Princeton University Press, 1965). T. Meron, Investment Insurance in International Law (Dobbs Ferry, N.Y.: Oceana 1976).

(76) T. Meron op. cit.

(77) E/C.7/68, Annex II, p. 1. See also Joseph Shaw, op. sit. at 117 et seq.

(78) R. Bosson and B. Varon, op. cit., p. 187.

(79) Ibid., Appendix D; and Annual Reports of the World Bank and International Finance Corporation.

(80) E/C.7/68, op. cit., p. 33, paragraph 95 and p. 35, paragraph 100. See also "Investment in the Copper Industry: Needs and Policies," op. cit., p. 116. Just prior to publication of this book the World Bank, in a major shift of policy, was readying plans to lend $450 million in risk capital to less developed countries to explore for oil and natural gas over the next five years. Boston Globe December 24, 1978.

(81) April 8, 1974 (DP/53). See also Basic Facts About...The United Nations Revolving Fund for Natural Resources Exploration (United Nations Development Program, March 1976).

(82) See p. 251 et seq supra. See also J. Shaw, op. cit., pp. 116, 117.

(83) See Bruce Aitken, "Multinational Enterprises and International Law: A Selected Bibliography," International Lawyer (Winter 1977), p. 69, for an extensive list of recent books and articles. See also L.R. Primoff, "International Regulation of Multinational Corporations and Business - The United Nations Takes Aim," Journal of International Law and Economics (1977), p. 287; and O. Schachter, Sharing the World's Resources (New York: Columbia University Press, 1977), pp. 124-134.

(84) R. Barnet and R. Muller, Global Reach (New York: Simon and Schuster, 1974) is probably the widest read of recent critical publications. There are extensive references in the notes. See also Yanqui Dollar (North American Congress on Latin America, 1971) and a supplement published in April 1972; H. Magdoff, The Age of Imperialism (New York: Monthly Review Press, 1969); and a critique of this thesis, B.J. Cohen, The Question of Imperialism (New York: Basic Books, 1973).

(85) (New York: Basic Books, 1971). See also R. Vernon, Storm Over the Multinationals (Cambridge, Mass.: Harvard University Press, 1977). His conclusions are summarized in an article of the same name in Foreign Affairs (January 1977), p. 243. An interesting supplement to this book is B. Vernon and L. Wells Economic Environment of International Business, (Englewood Cliffs, N.J.: Prentice-Hall, Second Edition, 1976).

(86) See for example, Aitken, op. cit., pp. 83, 84.

(87) See Footnote 67.

(88) See Footnote 83. In February 1976, Columbia University Law School held a Conference on the Regulation of Transnational Corporations. A summary of the Conference proceedings may be found in Columbia Journal of Transnational Law (1976) p. 370. See also R. Barovick, "Congress Looks at the Multinational Corporation," Columbia Journal of World Business, (November-December 1970), p. 75.

(89) S. Rubin, "Multinational Enterprise and National Sovereignty: A Skeptic's Analysis," Law and Policy in International Business (1971).

(90) P. Goldberg and C. Kindelberger, "Toward a GATT for Investment: A Proposal for Supervision of the International Corporation," Law and Policy in International Business (1970), p. 295.

(91) G. Ball, "Cosmocorp: The Importance of Being Stateless," Columbia Journal of World Business (November-December 1967).

(92) Goldberg and Kindleberger, op. cit.

(93) S. Rubin, op. cit.

(94) C. Lichtenstein, "Current Proposals for Marshalling Data on and Disclosure by Multinationals," International Lawyer (Winter 1977), p. 61. See also Aitken op. cit. at 82, 83.

(95) The Role of Accounting in Economic Development (Society for International Development, 1977).

(96) J. Forry and P. Lerner, "Taxing Multinational Enterprises: Basic Issues of International Income Tax Harmonization," International Lawyer (Fall 1976), p. 623. Aitken op. cit.

(97) R. Beard, "International Securities Regulation-Absorption of the Shock," International Lawyer (Fall 1976), p.635.

(98) "International Antitrust Law Symposium," Journal of International Law and Economics, Nos. 1 and 2 (June and December 1973). See also Aitken op. cit. at pp. 74-77.

(99) A. Skol and C. Peterson, "Export Controls and Multinational Enterprises," International Lawyer (Winter 1977), p. 29.

(100) The Dusseldorf Conference. See D. Wallace (ed.), International Control of Investment, (New York: Praeger, 1973).

(101) G. Ball, op. cit.

(102) Goldberg and Kinderlberger, op. cit., p. 298.

(103) Ibid.

(104) Ibid., p. 317, citing S. Rubin, "The International Firm and the National Jurisdiction," in The International Corporation, Kindelberger (ed.), (Cambridge, Mass.: MIT Press, 1970).

(105) Ibid., p. 318, citing George Ball's article in Footnote 91 supra.

(106) Ibid., p. 320.

(107) Ibid.

(108) Ibid.

(109) Ibid., p. 322.

(110) Ibid.

(111) Ibid., p. 323.

(112) Ibid.

(113) Ibid., pp. 322, 323.

(114) Ibid.

(115) Ibid.

(116) Ibid.

(117) S. Rubin, op. cit.

(118) Ibid., p. 30.

(119) Ibid.

(120) Ibid., p. 31.

(121) Ibid., p. 30.

(122) Ibid., pp. 33, 34. "On the too little side, it is merely a uniform corporation law, providing for minimum capital, specifying the kinds of shares which may be issued and their voting rights, etc., it would be useful but hardly essential. If, on the other hand, it went into substantive regulatory matters, it is very likely to run into difficulties, of which the worker representation issue in the EEC Company Law projects is a minor example."

(123) Ibid., p. 34.

(124) Ibid., p. 35.

(125) Ibid., p. 36.

(126) Ibid.

(127) Ibid., p. 37.

(128) Ibid., p. 36.

(129) Ibid., pp. 37, 38.

(130) D. Wallace, op. cit., p. 8.

(131) Ibid., p. 9.

(132) Ibid., p. 175.

(133) Ibid.

(134) Ibid., p. 9.

(135) Ibid., p. 11.

(136) S. Rubin, "Developments in the Law and Institutions of International
Economic Relations," American Journal of International Law, (1974), p.
475. See also Hearings on the Multinational Corporation and International
Investment before the Subcommittee on Foreign Economic Policy of the
Joint Economic Committee, 91st Congress, 2nd Session 1970.

(137) Ibid., Rubin p. 480.

(138) Ibid.

(139) Ibid., p. 484.

(140) See Footnote 67 supra.

(141) UNGA Resolution 1913 (LVII) of 1974.

(142) The activities of the Commission and the Centre are summarized in
The CTC Reporter published periodically by the Centre on Transnational
Corporations.

(143) The CTC Reporter, No. 2 (June 1977), p. 7.

(144) Ibid., p. 16.   See also Development of an Information System,
C/C.10/28, March 31, 1977; Feasibility Study of Availability of Information, E/C.10/27, March 28, 1977; and Establishment of a Comprehensive Information System on Transnational Corporations: Government
Replies, ST/CTC/1, 1977.

(145) CTC Reporter, No. 2 (June 1977), p. 23.   See also Research on
Transational Corporations. ST/CTC/3 (in preparation).

(146) CTC Reporter, No. 2 (June 1977) 14 et seq. See also Programme of
Technical Cooperation on Matters Related to Transnational Corporations,
E/C.10/29, 24 March 1977.

(147) The CTC Reporter, No. 2 (June 1977), pp. 3, 13. Technical Papers:
International Standards of Accounting and Reporting for Transnational
Corporations, ST/CTC/5 (in preparation) and Major Issues to Be
Considered in the Examination of the Problem of Corrupt Practices, in
Particular Bribery, in International Commercial Transactions by Trans-
national and Other Corporations, Their Intermediaries and Others
Involved. E/AC.64/7 (1977).

(148) The CTC Reporter (June 1977), pp. 9-12. See also: Transnational
Corporations: Material Relevant to the Formulation of a Code of
Conduct, E/C.10/18, December 10, 1976; Transnational Corporations:
Views and Proposals of States on a Code of Conduct, E/C.10/19, December
30, 1976; Work Related to the Formulation of a Code of Conduct,
E/C.10/31, May 4, 1977.

(149) The CTC Reporter, Vol. 2 (June 1977), pp. 26-30.

(150) For a brief description of OECD see J. McLin, The Rich Man's Club, XI Field Staff Reports No. 1 (Europe), (American Universities Field Staff, January 1976).

(151) ILM (July 1976), p. 867.

(152) Ibid., Annex, p. 969.

(153) Ibid., p. 967.

(154) Ibid., p. 969.

(155) Ibid., p. 978.

(156) Ibid., p. 980.

(157) Ibid.

(158) Ibid., p. 970, para. 6.

(159) Ibid., p. 970, para. 3.

(160) Ibid., p. 970, para. 6.

(161) Ibid., p. 970, para. 7.

(162) Ibid.

(163) Ibid., p. 972.

(164) Ibid., p. 975, para. 2 under Taxation.

(165) Ibid., p. 975, para. 1 under Employment and Industrial Relations.

(166) Ibid., p. 976, para. 8 under Employment and Industrial Relations.

(167) Ibid., p. 977, para. 1 of the Decision of the Council on Inter-Governmental Consultation Procedures on the Guidelines for Multinational Enterprises.

(168) M. Joelson and J. Griffin, "International Regulation of Restrictive Business Practices Engaged in by Transnational Enterprises. A Prognosis," International Lawyer (Winter 1977), pp. 18-20.

(169) Ibid., p. 20.

(170) D. Plaine, "The OECD Guidelines for Multinational Enterprise," International Lawyer (Winter 1977), p. 339.

(171) R.B. Lillich (ed.), The Valuation of Nationalized Property in International Law, three volumes (Charlottesville, Virginia: University Press of Virginia, 1975). See in particular R.B. Lillich, "The Valuation of Nationalized Property in International Law: Towards a Consensus or More 'Rich Chaos'" in Volume III, p. 183.

(172) See Hearings, "United States Policy Toward Asia," Report of the Subcommittee on the Far East and the Pacific of the Committee on Foreign Affairs, House of Representatives, 89th Congress, 2nd Session, House Document 488, May 19, 1966, p. 188 et seq.

Chapter 7

(1) See note 372 in Chapter 3.

(2) Subsequent to the time period covered by this manuscript the United Nations passed an important resolution on Restructuring of the Economic and Social Sectors of the United Nations System (A/Res/32/197, 9 January 1978). Under its provisions the General Assembly invited the Secretary-General "to appoint in full consultation with Member States, a Director-General for Development and International Economic Cooperation".... On March 14, 1978 Mr. Kenneth Dadzie of Ghana was selected as the first occupant of the post. It is too early to comment on the significance of this new office.

Appendix A

(1) See Proceedings of the United Nations Conference on Trade and Development, Third Session, Vol. I, Report and Annexes (United Nations publication, Sales No.: E.73.II.E.4), annex I.A.

(2) TD/B/AC.12/4 and Corr.1.

Appendix B

(1) Branislav Gosovic, UNCTAD: Conflict and Compromise, (Leiden, The Netherlands: A.W. Sijthoff, 1972), pp. 3-27.

(2) Alfred Sauvy (ed.), Le "Tiers Monde": Sous-developpement et developpement, Travaux et Documents de l'Institut Nationale de'Etudes Demographiques, Vol. 39, 2nd ed. of Vol. 27, (Paris: Presses Universitaires de France, 1961). Sauvy agreed in 1960 to let his phrase be used as the title of a French journal on developing countries, Le Tiers Monde, (Paris, Presses Universitaires de France) January 1960 to date.

(3) Ibid., Alfred Sauvy, "Evolution Recente du Tiers Monde," p. vii.

(4) In addition to the sponsoring countries, the following 24 countries participated in the Conference: Afghanistan, Cambodia, China, Egypt, Ethiopia, Gold Coast, Iran, Iraq, Japan, Jordan, Laos, Lebanon, Liberia, Libya, Nepal, Philippines, Saudi Arabia, Sudan, Syria, Thailand, Turkey, Democratic Republic of North Vietnam, State of Vietnam, and Yemen. The list of conference participants and the full text of the Final Communique appear in Carlos P. Romulo, The Meaning of Bandung, (Chapel Hill, N.C.: University of North Carolina Press, 1956), pp. 92-102.

The origins of this conference may be traced back eight years to the earliest meetings of developing states: the unofficial Asian Relations

Conference (New Delhi, March 1947) and the Asian Conference on Indonesia (New Delhi), January 1949). At the Asian Relations Conference, seventeen Asian states, either independent or soon to become so, came together for the first time in history and tried to form a permanent organization, but rivalry between India and China rendered it ineffectual from the outset. This first conference also considered a proposal for a Neutrality Bloc to prevent foreign assistance from reaching colonialist powers which were suppressing local independence movements.

Twenty months later, at the Asian Conference on Indonesia, Egypt and Ethiopia joined Asian countries to discuss in indecisive fashion the need for a permanent regional organization. The main accomplishment of this conference was to assert the right of Asians to be heard on Asian questions. It presented to the United Nations Security Council a forceful recommendation that Indonesian independence should be restored and that sanctions should be imposed against the Netherlands. (See G.H. Jansen, Non-Alignment and the Afro-Asian States, (New York: Praeger, 1966), p. 26ff.)

(5) Final Communique of the Bandung Conference, Section A, points 3 and 4. G.M. Kahin, The Asian-African Conference (Ithaca, New York.: Cornell University Press, 1956), pp. 76, 77.

(6) J.D.B. Miller, The Politics of the Third World, (London: Oxford University Press, 1966), p. 33. See also Ernest Lefever, "Nehru, Nasser, and Nkrumah on Neutralism," in Lawrence Martin (ed.), Neutralism and Non-alignment, (New York: Praeger, 1962).

(7) For the organization of the Coordinating Bureau, see NAC/Conf. 5/S/4, pp. 19-20, "Documents of the Fifth Conference of Heads of State or Government of Non-Aligned Countries. This and other institutional developments are discussed by Jayantanuju Bandyopadhyaya in "The Non-Aligned Movement and International Relations," India Quarterly, Vol. XXXIII, April-June 1977.

(8) The Fifth Conference of Heads of State or Government of Non-Aligned Countries reports that the following countries (and organizations) participated as Members in the Conference (NAC/CONF. 5/S.2, 21 August 1976): Afghanistan, Algeria, Angola, Argentine Republic, Bahrain, Bangladesh, Benin, Bhutan, Botswana, Burma, Burundi, Cameroon (United Republic of), Cape Verde, Central African Republic, Chad, Comoros, Congo, Cuba, Cyprus, Democratic Kampuchea, Egypt (Arab Republic of), Equatorial Guinea, Ethiopia, Gabon, Gambia, Ghana, Guinea, Guinea-Bissau, Guyana, India, Indonesia, Iraq, Ivory Coast, Jamaica, Jordan, Kenya, Democratic People's Republic of Korea, Kuwait, Lao People's Democratic Republic, Lebanon, Lesotho, Liberia, Libyan Arab Republic, Madagascar, Malaysia, Mali, Malta, Mauritania, Mauritius, Morocco, Mozambique, Nepal, Niger, Nigeria, Oman, Palestine Liberation Organization, Panama, Peru, Qatar, Republic of Maldives, Rwanda, Democratic Republic of Sao Tome and Principe, Saudi Arabia, Senegal, Seychelles, Sierra Leone, Singapore, Somalia, Sri Lanka, Sudan, Swaziland, Syrian Arab Republic, United Republic of Tanzania, Togo, Trinidad and Tobago, Tunisia, Uganda, United

Arab Emirates, Upper Volta, Socialist Republic of Viet-Nam, Yemen Arab Republic, Yemen People's Democratic Republic, Yugoslavia, Zaire, Zambia.

The Conference granted a special status to Belize including the right to address the Summit.

(9) Conferences of Non-Aligned States: Documents, Ministry of External Affairs, (New Delhi, 1973), "Declaration of the Non-Alignment and Economic Progress," made in 1972 in Lusaka, Zambia.

(10) "Economic Development and the Action Programme for Economic Cooperation of the Fourth Conference of Heads of State and Governments of Non-Aligned Countries," A/9330.

(11) Proceedings of the United Nations Conference for Trade and Development, 1964 op. cit. "Joint Declaration of the 77 Developing Countries," pp. 67-68.

(12) Richard N. Gardner, "The United Nations Conference on Trade and Development" in The Global Partnership, editors: R. Gardner and M. Millikan (New York: Praeger, 1968). This is a reprint of the Winter 1968 issue of International Organization.

(13) The list of states which are members of UNCTAD is given in the Proceedings of the United Nations Conference on Trade and Development, Fourth Session, (Nairobi, 5-31 May 1976), Vol. I, pp. 41-42. In accordance with paragraph 1 of General Assembly Resolution 1995 (XIX), these members are states which are members of the United Nations, or members of the specialized agencies, or of the International Atomic Energy Agency.

A

Afghanistan	Madagascar
Algeria	Malawi
Angola	Malaysia
Bahrain	Maldives
Bangladesh	Mali
Benin	Mauritania
Bhutan	Mauritius
Botswana	Mongolia
Burma	Morocco
Burundi	Mozambique
Cape Verde	Nepal
Central African Republic	Niger
Chad	Nigeria
China	Oman
Comoros	Pakistan
Congo	Papua New Guinea
Democratic Kampuchea	Philippines

Note 13 - Continued

Democratic People's Republic
    of Korea
Democratic Yemen
Egypt
Equatorial Guinea
Ethiopia
Fiji
Gabon
Ghana
Gambia
Guinea
Guinea-Bissau
India
Indonesia
Iran
Iraq
Israel
Ivory Coast
Jordan
Kenya
Kuwait
Lao People's Democratic
    Republic
Lebanon
Lesotho
Liberia
Libyan Arab Republic

Qatar
Republic of Korea
Republic of South Viet Nam*
Rwanda
Sao Tome and Principe
Saudi Arabia
Senegal
Sierra Leone
Singapore
Somalia
South Africa
Sri Lanka
Sudan
Swaziland
Syrian Arab Republic
Thailand
Togo
Tunisia
Uganda
United Arab Emirates
United Republic of Cameroon
United Republic of Tanzania
Upper Volta
Western Samoa
Yemen
Yugoslavia
Zaire
Zambia

*Now Socialist Republic of Viet Nam.

B

Australia
Austria
Belgium
Canada
Cyprus
Denmark
Finland
France
Germany, Federal Rep. of
Greece
Holy See
Iceland
Ireland
Italy
Japan

Liechtenstein
Luxembourg
Malta
Monaco
Netherlands
New Zealand
Norway
Portugal
San Marino
Spain
Sweden
Switzerland
Turkey
United Kingdom of Great Britain
    and Northern Ireland
United States of America

Note 13 - Continued

C

Argentina	Guatemala
Bahamas	Guyana
Barbados	Haiti
Bolivia	Honduras
Brazil	Jamaica
Chile	Mexico
Colombia	Nicaragua
Costa Rica	Panama
Cuba	Paraguay
Dominican Republic	Peru
Ecuador	Surinam
El Salvador	Trinidad and Tobago
Grenada	Uruguay
	Venezuela

D

Albania	Hungary
Bulgaria	Poland
Byelorussian Soviet Socialist	Romania
Republic	Ukrainian Soviet Socialist
Czechoslovakia	Republic
German Democratic Republic	Union of Soviet Socialist
	Republics

(14) TD/195. The Manila Declaration and Programme of Action, 12 February 1976, Annex I, p. 9.

(15) Gosovic, Ch. 9, "Relations between GATT and UNCTAD."

(16) Ibid., p. 203. As of 1976, the complete list of contracting parties to GATT and countries applying the General Agreement on a de facto basis was the following:

APPLICATION OF THE GENERAL AGREEMENT

(December 1976)

A. Contracting Parties to the General Agreement

Argentina	Guyana	Peru
Australia	Haiti	Poland
Austria	Hungary	Portugal
Bangladesh	Iceland	Rhodesia
Barbados	India	Romania
Belgium	Indonesia	Rwanda
Benin	Ireland	Senegal
Brazil	Israel	Sierra Leone

Note 16 - Continued

Burma
Burundi
Cameroon
Canada
Central African
    Empire
Chad
Chile
Congo
Cuba
Cyprus
Czechoslovakia
Denmark
Dominican Republic
Egypt
Finland
France
Gabon
Gambia
Germany, Fed. Rep. of
Ghana
Greece

Italy
Ivory Coast
Jamaica
Japan
Kenya
Korea, Rep. of
Kuwait
Luxembourg
Madagascar
Malawi
Malaysia
Malta
Mauritania
Mauritius
Netherlands,
    Kingdom of the
New Zealand
Nicaragua
Niger
Nigeria
Norway
Pakistan

Singapore
South Africa
Spain
Sri Lanka
Sweden
Switzerland
Tanzania
Togo
Trinidad and Tobago
Turkey
Uganda
United Kingdom of
    Great Britain and
    Northern Ireland
United States of
    America
Upper Volta
Uruguay
Yugoslavia
Zaire

B. Acceded Provisionally

Colombia
Philippines
Tunisia

C. Countries applying the General Agreement on a de facto basis

Algeria
Angola
Bahamas
Bahrain
Botswana
Cape Verde
Equatorial Guinea
Fiji
Grenada

Guinea-Bissau
Kampuchea, Democratic
Lesotho
Maldives
Mali
Mozambique
Papua New Guinea
Qatar
Sao Tome and Principe

Surinam
Swaziland
Tonga
United Arab Emirates
Yemen, People's Dem
    Rep. of
Zambia

Source: General Agreement on Tariffs and Trade; Basic Instruments and Selected Documents, 23rd Supplement, (Geneva, January 1977), p. vii.

(17) Resolution 1995 (XIX), December 30, 1964.

(18) Resolution 2089 (XX), December 20, 1965. UNIDO grew out of the ECOSOC Committee for Industrial Development.

(19) Resolution 2152 (XXI), November 17, 1966.

(20) "Lima Declaration on Industrial Development and Cooperation," in Joseph T. Vambery (ed.) Annual Review of United Nations Affairs, 1975, (Dobbs Ferry, New York: Oceana Publications, Inc., 1976), pp. 168-189.

(21) The United Nations makes the following breakdown for the purposes of computing the flows of resources to the developing countries from the developed market economies and from centrally planned economies: Developed countries comprise the seventeen members of the Development Assistance Committee (Australia, Austria, Belgium, Canada, Denmark, Finland, Federal Republic of Germany, France, Italy, Japan, the Netherlands, New Zealand, Norway, Sweden, Switzerland, United Kingdom, and the United States) plus Iceland, Ireland, Luxembourg, Portugal and South Africa. Developing countries comprise all the countries and territories in Africa except South Africa; in America, except Canada, Greenland, Puerto Rico, the United States, and the Virgin Islands; in Asia, except China, the Democratic People's Republic of Korea, the Socialist Republic of Viet Nam, Japan, Mongolia, and Turkey; in Oceania, except Australia, New Zealand, and the U.S. possessions and territories. (However, the trust territory of the Pacific Islands is included in the list of developing countries.)

Less developed countries in Europe comprise Cyprus, Gibraltar, Greece, Malta, Spain, Turkey, and Yugoslavia.

Centrally planned economies comprise Bulgaria, China, Czechoslovakia, The German Democratic Republic, Hungary, Poland, Romania, and the Soviet Union. (Source: Statistical Yearbook, 1976, (New York, United Nations, 1977), pp. 816-817.)

(22) The Development Assistance Committee considers developed countries to comprise OECD members except Greece, Turkey, Spain, and Portugal, plus two non-OECD members - Australia and New Zealand. Developing countries comprise market economies which are not developed countries, plus the centrally planned economies of Yugoslavia and Cuba. (Source: OECD Flow of Resources to Developing Countries, (Paris: OECD, 1973).)

(23) Industrial countries comprise Austria, Belgium, Canada, Denmark, Federal Republic of Germany, France, Italy, Japan, Luxembourg, Netherlands, Norway, Sweden, United Kingdom, United States, and Switzerland (a nonmember). More developed primary producing countries comprise Australia, Finland, Greece, Iceland, Ireland, Malta, New Zealand, Portugal, Romania, South Africa, Spain, Turkey, and Yugoslavia. Less developed primary producing countries comprise all other Fund member countries. (Source: IMF Annual Report, 1976, Table 1, p. 5.)

(24) Ibid., p. 23.

(25) IMF Annual Report, 1972, Memorandum to Table 5, p. 18.

(26) Algeria, Ecuador, Gabon, Indonesia, Iran, Iraq, Kuwait, the Libyan Arab Republic, Nigeria, Qatar, Saudi Arabia, United Arab Emirates, and

Venezuela. (Source: IMF Annual Report, 1976, p. 4 and OPEC Annual Report 1976.)

(27) Zuhayr Mikdashi, The International Politics of Natural Resources, (Ithaca, New York: Cornell University Press, 1976), Ch. 3.

(28) Members of CIPEC are Chile, Peru, Zaire, and Zambia. (Ibid., p. 83.)

(29) Members of IBA are Australia, Dominican Republic, Ghana, Guinea, Guyana, Haiti, Jamaica, Sierra Leone, Surinam, Yugoslavia. In addition, Greece, India, and Trinidad and Tobago are official observer nations. (Ibid., p. 112.)

(30) Membership in AIOEC is Algeria, Australia, Brazil, Chile, India, Mauritania, Peru, Sierra Leone, Sweden, Tunisia, and Venezuela.

(31) UNCTAD Secretariat, International Action on Commodities in the Light of Recent Developments: Problems of the World Market for Iron Ore, Geneva, May 26, 1971, pp. 31-32 (TB/C.1/104). Cited in Mikdashi, p. 104.

(32) Membership of the Fourth Tin Agreement comprised the tin consuming countries of Austria, Belgium-Luxembourg, Bulgaria, Canada, Czechoslovakia, Denmark, Federal Republic of Germany, France, Hungary, India, Ireland, Italy, Japan, the Netherlands, Poland, Republic of Korea, Romania, Spain, Turkey, the United Kingdom, the USSR, and Yugoslavia; and the tin producing and exporting countries of Australia, Bolivia, Indonesia, Malaysia, Nigeria, Thailand, and Zaire.

(33) As of 1976, the International Coffee Organization had 63 members comprising 42 exporting countries which account for some 99 percent of the world's production of coffee, and 21 importing countries which account for close to 90 percent of the world's consumption of coffee. (Source: Tea and Coffee Trade Journal, July 1976.)

(34) Escott Reid, The Future of the World Bank, (Washington, D.C., International Bank for Reconstruction and Development, September 1965), pp. 36-37.

(35) World Bank, "International Development Association: Resources and Operations," May 1977, p. 1.

(36) Ibid., p. 3.

(37) Ibid.

(38) World Bank memo, "Per Capita Income Guidelines for Operational Purposes," June 24, 1977.

(39) World Bank, "International Development Association: Resources and Operations," p. 4.

(40) Some countries which would appear to be eligible for IDA lending on poverty grounds have export prospects which make them creditworthy for IBRD loans as well as loans from private sources. The list of IDA eligible countries, ranked by 1976 GNP per capita, was the following as of 1977:

Income Group and Country	1976 GNP per Capita
Morocco	540
Congo	520
El Salvador	490
Papua New Guinea	490
Swaziland	470
Liberia	450
Zambia	440
Botswana	410
Philippines	410
Bolivia	390
Honduras	390
Senegal	390
Nigeria	380
Thailand	380
Grenada	370
Western Samoa	350
Mauritania	340
Equatorial Guinea	330
Cameroon	310
Sudan	290
Egypt	280
Yemen, People's Dem. Rep. of	280
Togo	260
Sri Lanka	250
Yemen, Arab Rep.	250
Indonesia	240
Kenya	240
Central African Empire	230
Haiti	200
Madagascar	200
Sierra Leone	200
Comoros	180
Cambia, The	180
Tanzania	180
Guinea	170
Lesotho	170
Pakistan	170
Afghanistan	160
Nigeria	160
India	150
Guinea-Bissau	140
Malawi	140
Zaire	140
Benin	130
Burma	120
Burundi	120
Chad	120

Note 40 - Continued

Income Group and Country	1976 GNP per Capita
Nepal	120
Bangladesh	110
Somalia	110
Upper Volta	110
Ethiopia	100
Mali	100
Rwanda	100
Lao P.D.R.	n.a.
Viet Nam	n.a.

Source: World Bank Memo, "Per Capita Income Guidelines for Operational Purposes," June 24, 1977, Attachment 1.

(41) World Bank, "International Development Association: Resources and Operations," p. 5. See also "The Allocation of Aid by the World Bank Group," Finance and Development, September 1972, p. 22.

(42) UNGA Resolution 1710 (XVI),December 19, 1961.

(43) UNGA Resolution 2626 (XXV), October 24, 1970.

(44) Ibid., para. 56-59.

(45) Proceedings of the United Nations Conference on Trade and Development, Annex AI-1.

(46) "Charter of Algiers," TD/38.

(47) Proceedings, UNCTAD II, Vol. I, p. 54.

(48) Official Records of the Economic and Social Council, Fifty-first Session, Supplement No. 7, (E/4990), Ch. 2. The 25 hard-core least developed countries are listed in paragraph 66, as follows: In Africa: Botswana, Burundi, Chad, Dahomey, Ethiopia, Guinea, Lesotho, Mali, Malawi, Niger, Rwanda, Somalia, Sudan, Uganda, United Republic of Tanzania, Upper Volta. In Asia and Oceania: Afghanistan, Bhutan, Laos, Maldives, Nepal, Sikkim, Western Samoa, Yemen. In Latin America: Haiti. The UN General Assembly approved this list in Resolution 2768 (XXVI).

(49) The additional countries are Bangladesh, Central African Empire, Gambia, and Democratic Yemen.

(50) TD/B 515, p. 7.

(51) Landlocked states which are classified as hard-core least developed countries are: Afghanistan, Bhutan, Botswana, Burundi, Central African Empire, Chad, Laos, Lesotho, Malawi, Mali, Nepal, Niger, Rwanda, Sikkim, Uganda, and Upper Volta. Other landlocked developing countries are Bolivia, Paraguay, Swaziland, and Zambia. For the report of the Expert Group on the Transport Infrastructure for Landlocked Developing

Countries, see TD/B/4531/Add 1 Rev. 1, "A Transport Strategy for Landlocked Developing Countries," 1974.

(52) See Proceedings, UNCTAD I, Vol. I, p. 25.

(53) Resolution 3504 (XXX), December 15, 1975. In its Thirty-first Session, the United Nations General Assembly called upon the United Nations Development Program to manage the Fund during the interim period and requested the Secretary-General to convene a pledging conference. (A/Res/177, "Statute of the United Nations Special Fund for Landlocked Developing Countries.")

(54) Proceedings, UNCTAD III, Vol. I, p. 74.

(55) The island developing countries and territories are: Bahamas, Bahrain, Barbados, Bermuda, Brunei, British Solomon Islands, Cape Verde, Comoros, Cuba, Cyprus, Dominican Republic, Fiji, French Polynesia, Gilbert and Ellice Islands, Grenada, Guadeloupe, Haiti, Hong Kong, Indonesia, Jamaica, Macao, Madagascar, Maldives, Martinique, Mauritius, Netherlands Antilles, New Caledonia, New Hebrides, Papua New Guinea, Philippines, Portuguese Timor, Reunion, Ryukyu Islands, Sao Tome and Principe, Seychelles, Singapore, Sri Lanka, Tonga, Trinidad and Tobago, Trust Territory of the Pacific Islands, Western Samoa, and West Indies. (TD/B/443/Rev. 1, "Developing Island Countries," 1974.)

(56) UNGA Resolution 3202 (S-VI) Section X, May 1, 1974.

(57) UNGA Official Records, Sixth Special Session, Supplement No. 1, A/9559, pp. 10-12. See also "Economic Problems Worsening for 'Most Seriously Affected'" IMF Survey, April 28, 1975, p. 113.

(58) Afghanistan, Bangladesh, Benin, Burma, Burundi, Cameroon, Cape Verde, Central African Empire, Chad, Egypt, El Salvador, Ethiopia, Gambia, Ghana, Guatemala, Guinea, Guinea-Bissau, Guyana, Haiti, Honduras, India, Ivory Coast, Kampuchea Democratic Republic, Kenya, Laos, Lesotho, Malagasy Republic, Mali, Mauritania, Mozambique, Nepal, Niger, Pakistan, Rwanda, Senegal, Sierra Leone, Somalia, Sri Lanka, Sudan, Tanzania, Uganda, Upper Volta, Western Samoa, Yemen Arab Republic, and Yemen People's Democratic Republic.

(59) IMF Annual Report, 1976, pp. 98-100. For the decision to create the oil facility, see Annual Report, 1975, p. 94.

(60) UNGA Resolution 3348 (XXIX).

(61) WFC/10, May 8, 1975, "Review of the World Food Situation and the Critical Issues with which the Council Should be Concerned."

(62) UN Chronicle, July 1976, p. 38.

(63) UN General Assembly Resolution 3503 (XXX) (15 December 1975), "Establishment of the International Fund for Agricultural Development."

(64) UN Chronicle, July 1976, p. 38.

(65) Helen C. Low and James W. Howe, "Focus on the Fourth World," in James W. Howe (ed.), The U.S. and World Development: Agenda for Action, 1975, The Overseas Development Council (New York: Praeger, 1975), p. 36.

(66) Dudley Seers argues that the basis for unity among the countries of the Third World is not that they are developing, but that they are "dependent." Both OPEC and non-OPEC developing countries depend on the industrial countries for imports of technology, equipment, and arms. In addition, non-OPEC developing countries depend on imported cereals and oil. To buy these, they rely largely on export revenues from less essential commodities, such as coffee, tea, bananas, cocoa, sugar, and cotton. (Dudley Seers, "A New Look at the Three World Classification.")

(67) International Development Association, Resources and Operations, May 1977, pp. 7-8.

(68) Ibid., p. 8.

(69) Ibid.

(70) Department of State, Agency for International Development, "Information Memorandum for the Administrator" from John H. Sullivan, 18 May 1977.

(71) The members of the Group of Ten are Belgium, Canada, Federal Republic of Germany, France, Italy, Japan, Netherlands, Sweden, United Kingdom, United States. Switzerland also participates in the work of the Group. The General Agreements to Borrow (GAB) was created in 1961 in response to the need felt by these ten states for protection against possible financial difficulties resulting from the liberalization at that time of controls over capital movements. IMF Annual Report, 1962, pp. 234-245.) In 1964, the Group of Ten extended its discussions to issues relating to global liquidity needs and the international monetary system.

(72) See UNGA Resolution 2208 (XXI), December 1966, and TD/140/Rev. 1, "The International Monetary Situation: Impact on World Trade and Development," 1972, pp. 38-40.

(73) Proceedings, UNCTAD II, "Lima Declaration," pp. 377-378.

(74) The Group of 24 was established by decision of the Group of 77 at their April 1972 meeting in Caracas. (IMF Survey, January 6, 1975). Members are equally divided between Latin America, Africa, and Asia. Latin America: Argentina, Brazil, Colombia, Guatemala, Mexico, Peru, Trinidad and Tobago and Venezuela. Africa: Algeria, Egypt, Ethiopia, Gabon, Ghana, Ivory Coast, Nigeria, and Zaire. Asia: India, Iran, Lebanon, Pakistan, Philippines, Sri Lanka, Syria, and Yugoslavia. India and International Monetary Reform (New Delhi: Ministry of Finance 1975), p. 142.

(75) India and International Monetary Reform, op. cit., p. 139.

(76) IMF Annual Report, 1972, p. 92. See also John V. Surr, "The Committee of the 20: Its Origins, Evolution, and Procedures," Finance and Development, (June 1974), pp. 24-33.

(77) Members of the Committee of 20 were the Group of Ten industrial countries plus Argentina, Australia, Brazil, Ethiopia, India, Indonesia, Iraq, Morocco, Venezuela, and Zaire. See International Monetary Reform: Documents of the Committee of Twenty (Washington, 1974).

(78) Benjamin Cohen, Organizing the World's Money, (New York: Basic Books, 1977), p. 111.

(79) IMF Annual Report, 1974, pp. 49-50, 110-112.

(80) Members of the Interim Committee are Argentina, Australia, Belgium, Brazil, France, Federal Republic of Germany, India, Indonesia, Iraq, Italy, Jamaica, Japan, Morocco, Netherlands, Nicaragua, Nigeria, Norway, United Kingdom, United States, and Zaire. (IMF Survey, January 20, 1975, p. 22.)

(81) Cohen, op. cit., pp. 114-116.

(82) IMP Survey, May 12, 1975, and IMF Annual Report, 1975, p. 41. See also "Composite Resolution on the Work of the Ad Hoc Committee on Reform of the International Monetary System and Related Issues and on a Program of Immediate Action," Resolutions Nos. 29-7, 29-8, 29-9, and 29-10, adopted on October 2, 1974, in Selected Decisions of the International Monetary Fund and Selected Documents (Seventh Issues, 1975), pp. 178-93.

(83) Members of the Development Committee are appointed for a term of two years by members of the Bank and members of the Fund, alternately. As of 1975, members were Australia, Belgium, Canada, Chile, France, Germany, India, Italy, Ivory Coast, Japan, Kuwait, Malaysia, Mexico, Netherlands, Philippines, Sweden, Trinidad and Tobago, Tunisia, United Kingdom, and United States. (IMF Survey, January 20, 1975, p. 24.)

(84) IMF Survey, June 23, 1975.

(85) IMF Survey, August 11, 1975.

(86) IMF Annual Report, 1976, pp. 43, 125-126.

(87) The Group of 19 consisted of Algeria, Argentina, Brazil, Cameroon, Egypt, India, Indonesia, Iran, Iraq, Jamaica, Mexico, Nigeria, Pakistan, Peru, Saudi Arabia, Venezuela, Yugoslavia, Zaire, and Zambia.

(88) The Group of Eight included Australia, Canada, EEC (as one unit), Japan, Spain, Sweden, Switzerland, and the United States.

(89) Jahangir Amuzegar, "A Requiem for the North-South Conference," Foreign Affairs, July 1973, pp. 150-151. See also Communique of Meeting of Senior Officials (CCEI-CP7), CIEC, Paris, July 10, 1976.

(90) The ACP states are: Bahamas, Barbados, Botswana, Burundi, Cameroon, Central African Rep., Chad, Congo, Dahomey, Equatorial Guinea, Ethiopia, Fiji, Gabon, Gambia, Ghana, Guinea, Guinea-Bissau, Grenada,

Guyana, Ivory Coast, Jamaica, Kenya, Lesotho, Liberia, Madagascar, Malawi, Mali, Mauritania, Mauritius, Niger, Nigeria, Rwanda, Senegal, Sierre Leone, Somalia, Sudan, Swaziland, Tanzania, Togo, Tonga, Trinidad and Tobago, Uganda, Upper Volta, Western Samoa, Zaire and Zambia. (Source: The Courier, No. 31, Special Issue, March 1975).

(91) "Lomé Convention Seen as Model for Trade and Economic Ties with All Developing Countries," IMF Survey, (March 10, 1975), pp. 76-77.

(92) The indexes to International Organization and The American Journal of International Law provide an illustration of this change in terminology. Prior to 1966, they had listings for "underdeveloped countries"; from that year on, they have listings for "developing countries." The change in terminology has not, however, been adopted by many major indexes, nor by all Western writers. As of December 1976, The New York Times Index, The Humanities Index, and The Social Sciences Index continued to list references to African, Asian, and Latin American countries under "underdeveloped areas" or "underdeveloped countries."

Selected
Bibliography

This is a selective list of books, articles, and documents directly related to the subject matter of the text. It does not include all of the material cited in the footnotes. For purposes of brevity, I have excluded references to the bibliographical data underlying Chapter 2 on the background to the New International Economic Order. Key documents are referred to in the notes to that chapter. The bibliography is organized as follows:

I. The New International Economic Order (including the Sixth Special Session and the Twenty-ninth Session of the General Assembly.

II. The Oil Crisis of 1973-74.

III. The Charter of Economic Rights and Duties of States.

IV. Seventh Special Session of the General Assembly.

V. Conference on International Economic Cooperation.

VI. United Nations Conference on Trade and Development, 4th Session.

VII. Compensatory Finance Schemes.

VIII. Foreign Private Investment.

IX. Miscellaneous.

I. THE NEW INTERNATIONAL ORDER (INCLUDING THE SIXTH SPECIAL SESSION AND THE TWENTY-NINTH SESSION OF THE GENERAL ASSEMBLY).

A. Books

Bergsten, C.F., The Future of the International Economic Order: An Agenda for Research (Lexington, Mass.: Lexington Books, 1973).

Bergsten, C.F., and Krause, L.B., (eds.), World Politics and International Economics (Washington, D.C.: The Brookings Institution, 1975).

Bhagwati, J.N., (ed.), The New International Economic Order: The North-South Debate (Cambridge, Mass.: M.I.T. Press, 1977).

Camps, M., The Management of Interdependence: A Preliminary View (New York: Council on Foreign Relations, 1974).

Cohen, B.J., The Question of Imperialism (New York: Basic Books, 1973).

Corbert, H., and Jackson, R., (eds.), In Search of a New World Economic Order (London: Broom Helm, 1974).

Fishlow, A., et. al., Rich and Poor Nations in the World Economy (New York: McGraw-Hill, 1978).

Haq, M., The Poverty Curtain: Choices for the Third World (New York: Columbia University Press, 1976).

Helleiner, G.K., (ed)., A World Divided: The Less Developed Countries in the International Economy (Cambridge, Eng.: Cambridge University Press, 1976).

International Labour Office, Employment, Growth and Basic Needs: A One-World Problem (Geneva: International Labour Office, 1976).

Magdoff, H., The Age of Imperialism (New York: Modern Reader, 1969).

Meadows, P.H., et. al., The Limits of Growth (New York: Universe Books, 1972).

Sauvant, K.P., and Hasenpflug, H., (eds.), The New International Economic Order (Boulder, Colo.: Westview Press, 1977).

Schachter, O., Sharing the World's Resources (New York: Columbia University Press, 1977).

Sewell, J.W., et. al., The United States and World Development: Agenda 1977 (New York: Praeger, 1977). An annual publication of the Overseas Development Council.

Tinbergen, J., Reshaping the International Order: A Report to the Club of Rome (New York: E. P. Dutton, 1976).

Singh, J.S., A New International Economic Order (New York: Praeger, 1977).

B. Articles

Chenery, H.B., "Restructuring the World Economy," Foreign Affairs (1975), p. 242.

Diaz-Alejandro, C.F., "North-South Relations: The Economic Component," International Organization (1975), p. 213.

Hansen, R.D., A "New International Economic Order"? An Outline for a Constructive U.S. Response (Overseas Development Council Development Paper 19, July 1975).

Hansen, R.D., "The Political Economy of North-South Relations: How Much Change?" International Organization (1975), p. 921.

Haq, M., The Third World and the International Economic Order (Overseas Development Council Development Paper 22, September 1976).

McCulloch, R., "Economic Policy in the United Nations: A New International Economic Order?" (Harvard Institute of Economic Research: Discussion Paper Number 490, 1976).

Smith, T., "Changing Configurations of Power in North-South Relations Since 1945?" International Organization (1977), p. 1.

United States Council of the International Chamber of Commerce Inc., A Realistic U.S. Policy on North-South Issues (March 1977).

C. Documents

1. United Nations

   a. Official Records of the United Nations General Assembly

      - Sixth Special Session

        i. Plenary Meetings A/PV. 2207-2231.

        ii. General Committee and Ad Hoc Committee of the Sixth Special Session A/AC. 166/SR. 1-21.

        iii. Annexes

      - Twenty-ninth Session

        i. Plenary Meetings A/PV. 2233-2325.

        ii. Second Committee A/C. 2/SR. 1586-1653.

        iii. Annexes

2. United States Government:

Hearings before the Sub-Committee on International Organizations of the Committee on Foreign Affairs, House of Representatives, February 4 and 5, 1975, "Review of the 1974 General Assembly and the United States Position in the United Nations."

Hearings before the Sub-Committee on International Organizations of the Committee on International Relations, House of Representatives, May 19 and 21, and July 8, 1975, "Issues at the Special Session of the 1975 U.N. General Assembly." The Annex to this document contains many basic documents including the Resolutions on the New International Economic Order, the Charter of Economic Rights and Duties of States, the UNIDO Lima Declaration, the UNCTAD Integrated Programme for Commodities of 1974, a number of Henry Kissinger's speeches, and R. Hansen's "A 'New International Economic Order.'"

Kissinger, H.A., "Challenges of Interdependence," Bureau of Public Affairs, Department of State, April 15, 1974.

II. THE OIL CRISIS OF 1973-74

"The Oil Crisis: In Perspective," Daedalus (Fall 1975) [A collection of scholarly articles on the crisis].

Mikdashi, Z., The International Politics of Natural Resources (Ithaca, N.Y.: Cornell University Press: 1976).

Rustow, D., and Mugno, J., OPEC: Success and Prospects (New York: University Press, 1976).

III. THE CHARTER OF ECONOMIC RIGHTS AND DUTIES OF STATES

A. Book

Castañeda, J., Justice Economique Internationale (Paris: Gallimard, 1976).

B. Articles

Association of the Bar of the City of New York, "The U.N. Charter of Economic Rights and Duties of States - Toward a New International Law of Welfare?" The Record (1975), p. 409.

Brower, C.N., and Tepe, J.B., Jr., "The Charter of Economic Rights and Duties of States: A Reflection or Rejection of International Law?" International Lawyer (1975), p. 295.

Brower, C.N., "The Charter of Economic Rights and Duties of States and the American Constitutional Tradition: A Bicentennial Perspective on the 'New International Economic Order,'" International Lawyer (1976), p. 201.

Castañeda, J., "La Charte des Droits et Devoirs Economiques des Etats," Annuaire Francais de Droit International (1974), p. 31.

Colard, D., "La Charte des Droits et Devoirs Economiques des Etats," Etudes Internationales (1975), p. 439.

Dubitzky, J., "The General Assembly's International Economics," Harvard International Law Journal (1975), p. 670.

Feuer, G., "Reflexions sur la Charte des Droit et Devoirs Economiques des Etats," Revue Generale de Droit International Public (1975), p. 274.

Haight, G.W., "The New International Economic Order and the Charter of Economic Rights and Duties of States," International Lawyer (1975), p. 591.

Rozental, A., "The Charter of Economic Rights and Duties of States and the New International Economic Order," Virginia Journal of International Law (1976), p. 309.

Tiewul, S.A., "The United Nations Charter of Economic Rights and Duties of States," Journal of International Law and Economics (1975), p. 645.

Vanzant, J.C., "Charter on Economic Rights and Duties of States: A Solution to the Development Aid Problem?" Georgia Journal of International and Comparative Law (1974), p. 441.

Virally, M., "La Charte des Droits et Devoirs Economiques des Etats" Annuaire Francais de Droit International (1974), p. 57.

Yiannopoulos, D., "Premiers Efforts Pour Une Charte des Droits et Devoirs Economiques des Etats," Revue Belge de Droit International (1974), p. 508.

C. Documents

1. United Nations:

    a. Official Records of the United Nations General Assembly

      - Twenty Ninth Session

      i. Plenary A/PV. 2315, 2316.

      ii. Second Committee A/C.2/SR. 1638-1640, 1642, 1644, 1647, 1651.

      iii. Annexes: Agenda Item 48, Document A/9946.

b. Reports of the Working Group on the Charter of Economic Rights
   and Duties of States:

First Session:	TD/B/AC.12/1	6 March 1973.
Second Session:	TD/B/AC.12/2	8 August 1973.
	TD/B/AC.12/2/Add.1	9 August 1973.
Third Session	TD/B/AC.12/3	8 March 1974.
Fourth Session	TD/B/AC.12/4	1 August 1974.

IV. SEVENTH SPECIAL SESSION OF THE UNITED NATIONS
GENERAL ASSEMBLY

A. Articles

Gosovic, B., and Ruggie, G., Jr., "On the Creation of a New International
Economic Order: Issue Linkage and the Seventh Special Session of the
General Assembly," International Organization (1976), p. 309.

Mervis, C.D., "The United Nations Seventh Special Session: Proposals for a
New World Economic Order," Vanderbilt Journal of Transnational Law (1976),
p. 601.

Primoff, L.R., "Global Consensus and Economic Development: The Kissinger
Proposals," International Lawyer (1976), p. 711.

B. Documents

1. United Nations

   a. Official Records of the United Nations General Assembly

   - Seventh Special Session

   i. Plenary A/PV. 2326-2349.

   ii. Ad Hoc Committee of the Seventh Special Session A/AC. 176/SR.
   103.

   iii. Annexes 1-16 September 1975.

2. United States Government

   Committee on International Relations and Committee on Foreign Rela-
   tions, Report by Congressional Advisors to the Seventh Session of the
   United Nations 94th/1st October 13, 1975. This Report includes the
   Resolution of the Seventh Special Session, as well as the text of Henry
   Kissinger's address to the Seventh Special Session.

V. CONFERENCE ON INTERNATIONAL ECONOMIC COOPERATION

The documentation on CIEC was kept very private. However, the United States Government published a number of reports giving background data and some of the documentation. The relevant reports are:

Committee on International Relations (94/2nd) North South Dialogue (February 9, 1976).

U.S. Senate (95th/1st) Congressional Advisors Report of the Conference on International Economic Cooperation (Document No. 95-61, August 1977).

The Annex to the Final Report of the Conference contained the detailed decisions of the Conference. In its preliminary form the reference was Annex to the Report of the Conference (CCE I-CM-6, 2 June 1977).

VI. UNITED NATIONS CONFERENCE ON TRADE AND DEVELOPMENT, 4TH SESSION

A. Documents

1. United Nations:

Proceedings UNCTAD, 14 Session TD/218, 2 volumes.

Evaluation of the Fourth Session of the United Nations Conference on Trade and Development, TD/216, 14 September 1976.

Manila Declaration and Programme of Action, TD/195, 12 February 1976.

2. United States Government

Report by Congressional Advisers to UNCTAD IV (2nd Congress 94th/2nd, July 21, 1976).

VII. COMPENSATORY FINANCE SCHEMES

A. Articles

Cuddy, J.D.A., "STABEX: How Good a Model for International Relations?" (Unpublished 1976).

Gruhn, I.V., "The Lomé Convention Inching Towards Interdependence," International Organization (1976), p. 241.

Erb, G.F., North-South Negotiations and Compensatory Financing (Overseas Development Council, 8 June 1977).

Meagher, R.F., "The Expansion and Modification of the IMF's Compensatory Finance Facility," International Lawyer (1977), p. 277.

Wall, D., "The European Community's Lomé Convention: 'STABEX' and the Third World's Aspirations," (Trade Policy Research Centre 1976).

VIII. FOREIGN PRIVATE INVESTMENT

A. Books

Aharoni, Y., The Foreign Investment Decision Process (Boston, Mass.: Harvard Business School, 1966).

Barnet, R.J., Müller, R.E., Global Reach: The Power of the Multinational Corporations (New York: Simon and Schuster, 1974).

Bosson, R., and Varon, B., The Mining Industry and the Developing Countries (London: Oxford University Press, 1977).

Carroll, M.B., U.N. Proposals for the Regulation of Transnational Corporations (New York: American Management Associations, 1975).

Fatouros, A.A., Government Guarantees to Foreign Investors (New York: Columbia University Press, 1962).

Friedmann, W., and Beguin, J.P., Joint International Business Ventures in Developing Countries (New York: Columbia University Press, 1971).

Friedmann, W., and Kalmanoff, G., Joint International Business Ventures (New York: Columbia University Press, 1961).

Kapoor, A., and Grub, P.D., (eds.), The Multinational Enterprise in Transition (Princeton, N.J.: Darwin Press, 1972).

Kindleberger, C.P., (ed.), The International Corporation: A Symposium (Cambridge, Mass.: M.I.T. Press, 1970).

Lall, S., and Streeten, P., Foreign Investment, Transnationals and Developing Countries (Boulder, Colo.: Westview Press, 1977).

Lea, S., and Webley, S., Multinational Corporations in Developed Countries: A Review of Recent Research and Policy Thinking (Washington, D.C.: British-North American Committee, 1973).

Madden, C., (ed.), The Case for the Multinational Corporation: Six Scholarly Views (New York: Praeger, 1977).

Mughraby, M.A., Permanent Sovereignty Over Oil Resources (Beirut: The Middle East Research and Publishing Center, 1966).

Nwogugu, E.I., The Legal Problems of Foreign Investment in Developing Countries (Manchester, Eng.: Manchester University Press, 1965).

Smith, D.N., and Wells, L.T., Negotiating Third World Mineral Agreements (New York: Ballinger, 1975).

Vernon, R., Sovereignty at Bay: The Multinational Spread of U.S. Enterprises (New York: Basic Books, 1971).

Vernon, R., Storm Over the Multinationals (Cambridge, Mass.: Harvard University Press, 1977).

B. Articles

Aitken, B., "Multinational Enterprises and International Law: A Selected Bibliography," International Lawyer (1977), p. 69.

Ball, G., "Cosmocorp: The Importance of Being Stateless," Columbia Journal of World Business (1967), p. 25.

"The Conference on the Regulation of Transnational Corporations," Columbia Journal of Transnational Law (1976), p. 269.

Gess, K.N., "Permanent Sovereignty Over Natural Resources," International and Comparative Law Quarterly (1964), p. 398.

Goldberg, P.M., and Kindleberger, C.P., "Toward a GATT for Investment: A Proposal for Supervision of the International Corporation," Law and Policy in International Business (1970), p. 295.

Hyde, J.N., "Permanent Sovereignty Over Natural Wealth and Resources," The American Journal of International Law (1956), p. 854.

North American Congress on Latin America, Yanquai Dollars: The Contribution of U.S. Private Investment to Underdevelopment in Latin America (1971).

North American Congress on Latin America, Yanqui Dollar, Project Mailing #1 (April, 1972).

Oliver, C.T., "The Andean Foreign Investment Code," The American Journal of International Law (1972), p. 763.

Rubin, S.J., "Developments in the Law and Institutions of International Economic Relations," The American Journal of International Law (1974), p. 475.

Rubin, S.J., "Multinational Enterprise and National Sovereignty: A Skeptic's Analysis," Law and Policy in International Business (1971), p. 1.

Schwebel, S.M., "The Story of the U.N.'s Declaration on Permanent Sovereignty Over Natural Resources," American Bar Association Journal (1963), p. 463.

Zamora, A.R., "Andean Common Market - Regulation of Foreign Investments: Blueprint for the Future?" International Lawyer (1976), p. 153.

C. Documents

1. United Nations:

Transnational Corporations: Material Relevant to the Formulation of a Code of Conduct E/C.10/18 December 30, 1976.

Transnational Corporations: Views and Proposals of States on a Code of Conduct E/C.10/19 December 30, 1976.

Work Related to the Formulation of a Code of Conduct E/C.10/31 4 May 1977.

Multinational Corporations in World Development ST/ECA/190 1973.

The Impact of Multinational Corporations on Development and on International Relations E/5500/Rev. 1 1974.

Summary of the Hearings Before the Group of Eminent Persons to Study the Impact of Multinational Corporations on Development and on International Relations ST/ESA/15 1974.

Basic Facts About...the U.N. Revolving Fund for Natural Resources Exploration, The U.N.D.P., March 1976.

The C.T.C. Reporter, Centre on Transnational Corporations, an occasional publication by the U.N.

2. United States Government Documents:

Aspects of International Investment, U.S. Department of Commerce (Reprints from various issues of the Survey of Current Business) 1977.

3. Andean Pact Documents:

Agreement on Andean Subregional Integration, International Legal Materials (May 26, 1969), p. 910.

Agreement Establishing the Andean Development Corporation, International Legal Materials (February 7, 1968), p. 940.

Andean Commission: Decision Concerning Treatment of Foreign Capital, International Legal Materials (December 31, 1970), p. 152.

Andean Commission: Codified Text of the Andean Foreign Investment Code, International Legal Materials (November 30, 1976), p. 136.

IX. MISCELLANEOUS

A. Books

Cutajar, M.Z., and Franks, A., The Less Developed Countries in World Trade (London: Overseas Development Institute, 1967).

Friedmann, W., Kalmanoff, G., and Meagher, R.F., International Financial Aid (New York: Columbia University Press, 1966).

Gosovic, B., UNCTAD: Conflict and Compromise (Leyden, Netherlands: Sijthoff, 1971).

Goulet, D., The Uncertain Promise: Value Conflicts in Technology Transfer (New York: IDOC/North America, 1977).

Lauard, E., International Agencies: The Emerging Framework of Interdependence (Dobbs Ferry, New York: Oceana Publications, 1977).

Morton, K., and Tulloch, P., Trade and Developing Countries (London: Croom Helm, 1977).

B. Articles

Bergsten, C.F., "The Interdependence and the Reform of International Institutions," International Organization (1976), p. 361.

Gadbaw, R.M., "Report on the International Fund for Agricultural Development." Prepared for the American Bar Association's Committee on International Economic Organizations (unpublished) 1976.

C. Documents

1. United Nations:

   Agreement Establishing the International Fund for Agricultural Development A/Conf. 73/15 4 August 1976.

   Report of the Second General Conference of the United Nations Industrial Development Organization A/10112 13 June 1975. (This document contains the Lima Declaration and Plan of Action on Industrial Development and Cooperation.)

   A New United Nations Structure for Global Economic Cooperation E/AC.62/9 28 May 1975.

   The Future of the World Economy (Leontief Report) ST/ESA/44 1976.

2. European Community:

"Lomé Dossier" The Courier No. 31 Special Issue (European Community March 1975). The entire Lomé Convention, including annexes and protocols, is included in this publication along with commentary on the negotiations and other aspects of the Convention.

3. Nonaligned Countries:

It is extremely difficult to find the documents of the nonaligned states. Some have been reprinted by the United Nations and issued as U.N. Documents. Through June of 1977 there have been five Conferences of Heads of State or Government of nonaligned Countries. Those most relevant to this book are the Fourth and Fifth Conferences. In addition, the Dakar Conference on Raw Materials is extremely relevant.

Fundamental Texts IV Conference of Heads of State or Government of Nonaligned Countries, Algiers, 5-9 September 1973.

Documents of the Fifth Conference of Heads of State or Government of Nonaligned Countries, Colombo, Sri Lanka 16 to 19 August 1976. Circulated by the United Nations as A/31/197 8 September 1976.

The Dakar Declaration (Conference of Developing Counties on Raw Materials, Dakar, 3-8 February 1975). Circulated by the United Nations as E/AC.62/6 15 April 1975.

Lima Programme for Mutual Assistance and Solidarity, Conference of Ministers for Foreign Affairs of Nonaligned Countries NAC/FM/Conf.5/15 30 August 1975.

Index

299

About the Author

ROBERT F. MEAGHER is Professor of International Law at The Fletcher School of Law and Diplomacy, Tufts University, specializing in Law and Development. In addition, he is a private consultant to various governments, international organizations, and private business groups. Just recently (1975-1976, he was Visiting Fellow at the Overseas Development Council. Educated at the City College of New York, Yale Law School, and the Bombay School of Economics (Fulbright Scholar), Robert Meagher has lived in Asia, the Middle East, Africa, and Europe. He is co-author of International Financial Aid, and has published a number of monographs, articles, and book reviews.

Pergamon Policy Studies